MW01278072

Recommendations

(1) *The Long Safari* is a treasure-trip as you read. Revelations appear and are received and obeyed on most every page. You will be challenged and changed as you make your way on Safari with the Jones family. You will be enriched.

I found that I identified with the reality of the life journey. The setting was mine. The wonderful African people, I knew them, were familiar to me, and so like the many who accepted me, patiently loved and forgave me. And, most of all, received my Lord Jesus as their own.

The Jones story endears our Lord and His servants to you. He is faithful to His own, keeps and provides for them, and empowers and works through them for His Glory.

Start your read with an expecting excited heart. You won't be disappointed. But you will see how our Lord can use all of us for His glory as He reaches a needy world and builds His Church. Let heaven happen.

And, yes, you will laugh at times so rejoice and have fun.

A blessed Co-worker on Safari
Dr. Bud Fray, Missionary in Southern Africa,
Missions Professor, Southwestern Baptist Theological Seminary
Author, *It is Enough and Both Feet In*

(2) A Long Safari is an incredible chronicle of life and fruitful ministry. The development of Southern Baptist missionary work in East Africa, the challenges of living, demanding roles of responsibilities, a challenging environment, dangerous situations and sometimes government upheavals tell an amazing story. In Georgia, USA or East Africa, as an engineer or a missionary, ways to use God given talents to serve the Lord were found.

The days we were in Tanzania with Tom and Nancy are a highlight to us. Curtis loved his time with the students and hearing them sing each day at Mt. Meru University. When we watched the 1962 John Wayne movie, Hatari, we recognized places filmed in Arusha, which looked the same 40 years later.

We appreciate the transparency and subtle humor about shared concern to develop language fluency. When we were in Tanzania, several Africans told us that Tom spoke better Swahili than they did.

A Long Safari is a beautiful love story and partnership between Tom and Nancy and the passion and compassion that both shared for serving the Lord and their family.

Dr. Curtis &Linnie Porter, First Pastor of Grace Baptist Church, Parkersburg, West Virginia

(3) In *A Long Safari* Tom Jones reminds us how Biblical faith and simple obedience bring extraordinary experiences into ordinary everyday lives. Relatable personal stories from business, friendships, local church, and international missions are certain to inspire readers of all ages. Page after page we are challenged to join in the adventure God has for our life beginning right where we are and perhaps taking us to the other side of the world.

Andy Childs, Pastor, Ebenezer Baptist Church - Toccoa, GA

(4) This delightful book chronicles the life of a man who sought first the Kingdom of God and His righteousness in every era. There is history, humor, and an honest look at how the Lord uses us in spite of our insecurities and short-comings. All this is woven into a description of world travels and interaction with a variety of cultures. A great read!

Deanna Brown, Missionary Kid, Christian Blogger
www.strokemanswoman.wordpress.com

(5) It was my privilege to be Tom and Nancy Jones's pastor during their time in Duluth, Georgia. After years of service as missionaries in Africa, the Joneses retired in our area and continued to serve the Lord with Kingdom purpose. Now, my good friend Tom tells his life story with a missionary's flare in his new book, *A Long Safari.* I highly recommend this inspirational read. Tom recognizes the sovereignty of God in every aspect of his life. He sees the thread of God's purpose weaving the tapestry of his family life, and ministry. You will be blessed to read his story, hear the heart of his faith, and see the power of his God.

Mark Hearn
Senior Pastor, First Baptist Church of Duluth Georgia and author of *Technicolor: Inspiring Your Church to Embrace Multicultural Ministry*

(6) Joining Tom and Nancy on *A Long Safari* became my Independence weekend inspiration. Getting a glimpse of so many places, cruise ships across the Atlantic, and more was undertaken with three small children who became responsible adults. As a nurse, I was interested in Nancy's health care ministries. I feel honored to endorse their story.

Peggy J. Beckett, President/CEO, Baptist Retirement Communities of GA

A Long Safari

A Journey
of
Faith and Ministry

Thomas A. Jones, Sr.

Printed in the United States of America

ISBN: 978-1719504430

Dedication

This labor of love is dedicated to my wife, Nancy Barbara Kirk Jones. From the first day I met her at First Baptist Church in Atlanta in 1953 until the day in 2015 when she drew her last breath on earth, I cherished our loving relationship. She was known for her smile, hospitality, and love of nursing. She was beloved by her mission family and people of other cultures. She was a prayer warrior and most mornings after we retired, she sat in the chair she called her nest surrounded by her morning coffee, Bible, and prayer list. Her encouragement and love kept me focused on the important things of life. She was happiest when she was serving others, whether treating their sickness, teaching her knowledge of God's Word, or entertaining the hundreds of people who stayed in our home in Kenya.

She loved our children unconditionally and made uncounted trips to Rift Valley Academy to visit them in boarding school. She always welcomed the friends they brought to our house to get a good, home cooked meal. Often missing the point of the joke, Nancy had a unique sense of humor. This tendency led her to tell our children they would never know when she got dementia because she would be just the same. God blessed me by bringing this beautiful woman into my life and I always thank Him for letting me share fifty-seven years of my life with her.

Table of Contents

Acknowledgements

Where there is no guidance, a people falls, but in an abundance of counselors there is safety. Proverbs 11:14 (ESV)

Many friends offered encouragement about writing a book someday by saying they would like to read it. The attention-capturing books and blogs written by two missionary kid friends, Catherine Palmer and Deanna Brown, were an inspiration. Books written by fellow missionaries and thoughts about my experiences made me wonder if I could write something interesting and meaningful? Language has always been a problem for me, whether verbal or written. Remembering the writing class at Hiawassee Park, the Baptist Retirement Community, and the teacher, Irma Flanagan, who had guided our storytelling development and the quality of the stories other students wrote challenged me to develop this skill where I still feel inadequate.

After Nancy died in 2015, I moved to Hartwell Lake. While I was unpacking boxes labeled "historic papers," a treasure trove of research material emerged. It included hundreds of letters Nancy had written to our mothers and many from others we had known in East Africa. Nancy had also kept letters I had written to her before and during our engagement period. Armed with this information and the history books of our team's mission work written by Laura Lee Stewart and Jo Scales, I began to organize a book strategy. In addition, numerous correspondences and reports were on my computer from our missionary service. A multitude of people had provided information through letters, newspaper clippings, notes of encouragement and invitations which opened opportunities for me to find my way in ministry during the past sixty-five years.

I reminisced about periods in my life when the spiritual environment enhanced my spiritual growth like the two summers on the Ridgecrest staff during college and our early married years when Nancy and I worked at developing a devotional and prayer partnership. We felt called as lay people to seek an opportunity to help plant a new church and our years at Grace Baptist in Parkersburg, West Virginia, became the laboratory to learn church leadership. Working with John Snedden, who was the first home missionary in West Virginia, and a committee to develop the groundwork for the West Virginia Convention was valuable training.

Eucled Moore's counsel led to accepting God's call to become a missionary in Africa. Morris Wanje, Arthur Kinyanjui, and Eliud Mungai became my African culture teachers. Watching Samson Kisia lead many successful church planting efforts in Kenya became true inspiration. Relationships with fellow missionaries were always helpful but Clay Coursey, Jack Conley, Al Cummins, and Roy Brent became the brothers I never had. The transformation of First Baptist Duluth to reach the new people groups in the community began while I was a Deacon Officer and Pastor Mark Hearn became a close friend. In my life, an abundance of mentors provided growth and challenges.

This encouragement became the perseverance to the final stages. While reviewing and tweaking the text, I began seeking an editor. The first contact was a Baptist publishing entity who said the subject did not meet their current publishing strategy. Kim Davis, an African missionary who had edited some books written by other missionaries, offered significant advice about the book's structure and self-publishing. Then, one day an email from Irma Flanagan shared about a devotional book she had edited, written by one of her friends. We met and discussed the book. She agreed to guide the process through self-publishing. The rest is history.

My greatest appreciation is to my Savior, Jesus Christ, whose grace and forgiveness has blessed me all these years. He has opened doors of ministry opportunity I never dreamed were possible and given spiritual gifts I never deserved. To Him, I give all Glory.

Prologue

The college student had just had a deep religious experience. What did it mean, he wondered? Did God have some special plan for his life? As he pondered these questions, he thought about where he was and what had just happened. After an immensely challenging freshman year at a prestigious engineering school, he had gone with a group of fellow students to a religious conference center seeking a respite. On Sunday morning, the preacher's message was powerful. At the end, the nearly three thousand students sang "Wherever He leads, I'll go" and in his heart, he said, "I will go anywhere God leads me, at whatever the cost." He did not know where his path of life would lead, but he was confident that God would show him one step at a time. Suddenly, his mind was peaceful because he had no doubt about his future. I was that student and, as Paul Harvey always said, "Now for the rest of the story."

Chapter One
Early Years

In the wee hours of a December morning during the 1930's when the Great Depression lay heavily across the United States, a baby boy was born at his grandfather's house in Martin, Georgia. The new parents, John Dexter Jones and Sarah Elizabeth Dean Jones, had no idea what the future held for their baby destined to be their only child. I, Thomas Arthur Jones, was that child.

My father was a dedicated high school teacher and coach with about twelve years' experience in South Carolina, Florida, and Georgia. He was certainly not aware of the difficulties of supporting his family nor that his coaching girls' basketball and teaching math and physics would end that year in 1935 at Smyrna High School.

When I was born in Mom's childhood bed, my parents lived in a duplex on Banks Street, very near the Smyrna town center. The other side of the duplex was occupied by Reed and Mary McCollum and my family became lifelong friends with them. My parents never told me how they chose my name, but I assumed Arthur was for granddaddy Dean and I suspect that Thomas came from Thomas Reed McCollum.

Dad's degree from Clemson University was in agriculture with a specialty in dairying, He began working for the U.S. Department of Agriculture in Gainesville, Florida, and Montgomery, Alabama. He left those jobs to return to Atlanta where he worked for the U.S. Postal Service. We rented an apartment near the big Sears Roebuck complex on Ponce de Leon Avenue. After a brief period, we moved to a duplex near Grant Park.

The earliest memory of my life was in the duplex kitchen near Grant Park. We were packing for our move in 1937 to a house they bought on Bellevue Drive in the Virginia Highlands section of Atlanta where I lived until graduation from Georgia Tech. While they were focused on gathering and packing boxes, I, a two-year-old, picked up a curtain rod, put the rod end into my mouth, and cut my palate. Mom held me over the sink where I was spitting a lot of blood. Memory is a strange thing and I am not sure why this incident is still so vivid in my mind.

As soon as we moved to Atlanta, my parents joined First Baptist Church and enrolled me in the Cradle Roll. The pastor was Dr. Ellis Fuller who led the church for fourteen years until he was elected the President of the Southern Baptist Theological Seminary in October of 1942. During his time at First Baptist, he served as President of the Home Mission Board and the Georgia Baptist Convention. He was a stately man with an encouraging personality. I have one snapshot memory of visiting his house on Peachtree Road near Buckhead. His daughter who was about my age at six years, played in the basement with me.

Bellevue Drive was a short, very hilly street, beginning at Highland Avenue and ending at the bottom of a steep hill. Playing ball was an adventure because when you didn't catch it, you had to chase the ball to the bottom of the hill where invariably it rolled into the storm drain.

It was a clear Tuesday, the day after Labor Day in 1939, when my mom walked with me to my first day of Kindergarten. The streetcar tracks ended about halfway to the school, making walking the rest of the way necessary. Dad rode the streetcar to work, but because he did not work every day and we could not afford the gasoline for the Model-A Ford, soon I was walking by myself up the hill to Highland Avenue, north along Highland to the traffic light at East Rocks Springs, and left to the school.

The one very vivid, life changing event of the year occurred during the Christmas Program. All the kindergarten kids were on stage to sing Christmas songs. I had been chosen to sing a solo part and when my time came, I began to sing. Suddenly, my voice broke. I was very embarrassed and lost my self-confidence. I became extremely shy and tried to avoid groups who were not friends.

During the war, we regularly had collection days. Students brought newspapers tied into bundles and stacked them along the sidewalk. These huge piles were arranged by our classes. In those days, chewing gum was wrapped in wax paper which had a thin coat of aluminum foil. We peeled the foil off the paper and rolled it into balls. We competed to see which student could bring the biggest ball on collection day.

Dad was the Warden on Bellevue Drive during World War II and spent many evenings patrolling the street to make sure light was not peeping out of windows. He also had to make sure every house had sand buckets in the attic in case incendiary bombs fell on the houses.

When I was in the second grade, I got my first job. A neighbor boy asked me to help him deliver the Atlanta Journal on his paper route. I made the first major decision of my life when I stayed after school to watch an all-star baseball game. When I did not show up to help him, he called the school and told me to come immediately or he would not pay me to help deliver papers. I decided to stay and watch the game and was "fired" for the first time in my life.

Dad was an ardent supporter for me, helping me assume responsibilities. When I was in the fourth grade, I got a paper route delivering the Atlanta Journal to about one hundred customers beginning at Moe's and Joe's, a bar in Virginia Highlands. I was the only person under eighteen years old permitted to enter the bar. My next customer was Fire Station No. 19 and I really enjoyed visiting with the firemen and seeing the two trucks. I was intrigued by the polished pole in the middle of the room. The paper route ended at Briarcliff Road about 1.5 miles from the beginning, but I had to walk along each side of the streets.

I observed the delivery of papers daily and the collection of fees weekly was very time consuming. Thus, I asked my one hundred customers if they would consider paying monthly. About half of the customers agreed and this consolidation was a significant savings of time.

The route was about 2.5 miles long and I lived a half mile from the beginning; therefore, I had plenty of exercise. Very quickly, I learned to fold and tuck the paper together and developed good throwing skills where almost always I could make the paper land by the front door from the sidewalk. Since this time was before plastic bags had been invented, on rainy days I had to place papers behind screens or storm doors, and my delivery time was extended at least an hour each day. In those days, the largest paper except for Sunday's was forty pages on Thursday, the day when all the grocery ads and other sales were advertised. I could carry all in my shoulder bag except for Sunday when my Dad helped by keeping papers in the car until I needed them.

I had a frightening event one Saturday when I was collecting on Stillwood Drive. It was a pleasant morning and only the screen door of a customer's house was closed. Suddenly with no bark or noise, a huge male Boxer about my size burst through the screen.

A neighborhood boy on my street two years older than I had the route which included the street where we lived. He and I made an agreement to deliver each other's route when we needed to be away.

Climbing the Bellevue Drive hill on a gearless bicycle was a serious challenge, requiring a switchback route. One Christmas, my parents gave me a wheeled sled called a Flexy. It was great fun riding down the sidewalk and turning into the driveway ending at the bottom of a walkway behind the house. What was not fun was missing the turn into the driveway and hitting the front of the house.

Because of the lingering effects of the Depression, my parents rented rooms in our house on Bellevue Drive before and during World War II. The first renters I remember were Mildred and Tipp Mosely who were with us in 1940. Most memorable about this young couple in their mid-twenties was Tipp's height at about six and a half feet while Mildred might have been five feet. They were like Mutt and Jeff. They were followed by three single sisters also in their twenties. My cousin Marcille and her new husband Claude Sorrells lived with us in 1944 while he studied pharmacy in Atlanta.

We had a coal fired furnace for central heat in the house. One of my jobs was to keep the feed hopper full of coal. One corner of the basement was a huge coal bin and coal was delivered by the ton and unloaded through a basement window into the bin. I would fill buckets of coal and empty them into the hopper.

When I was nine, my mother was the Superintendent for the church's Junior Department. I asked my parents to make an appointment with our pastor, Dr. James Middleton, so I could discuss salvation. He guided me through this decision and I was baptized in June 1944.

I was a member of Royal Ambassadors (RA's), finishing my Knight rank. The Rep Landers had a house at Jackson Lake and a screened bunk house. A few times, RAs were invited to spend a couple of days there. He had a small boat with an older version of a wake board. It was a flat wooden piece about three by five feet with a rope handle attached. You stood up on it like you would use water skis. One day, I was on the board when the boat driver took a sharp turn and I sped outside the boat's wake going at least thirty miles per hour. Suddenly, the rope broke, and I went flying across the lake. Fortunately, I was not knocked out as in those days, we did not wear life jackets.

We went to RA camp at Lake Louise near Toccoa, a conference center built by R.G. LeTourneau. During World War II, he built a huge factory there to build earth moving equipment for the war effort. One of my uncles worked in this plant a few years. My wife, Nancy, worked at the conference center when she was in high school. In 1947, Georgia Baptist Women's Missionary Union (WMU) started Camp Pinnacle near Clayton and I went to RA camp there one week. I rode back in a car driven by Reece Landers with a few RAs. She was instructing her son Bobby about driving around curves. As I listened, she told him to keep some acceleration through the curves rather than braking.

After RA meeting one school afternoon, I was supposed to ride home with a family who lived close to my house. I was very upset when we went to the husband's shop and I did not get home until after 8:00 pm. I had a lot of homework to finish that night.

My mother told me stories about school being suspended during the fall for two-to-three weeks, so that the kids could pick cotton. Many farmers in the area raised cotton in the early part of the twentieth century. Mom attended Martin School, finishing the eleventh grade in 1922 and receiving her diploma. For twelfth grade, she lived with her sister Winnie Mary and attended Science Hill High School in Johnson City, Tennessee, receiving her diploma in 1923. She attended Georgia State College for Women in Milledgeville for two years, getting a diploma in 1925. She became a school teacher and taught at Martin School, in Bowersville, and at the Toccoa City Elementary School before she married my Dad in June 1932. Dad and Mom never talked with me about their courtship and engagement. The only story I ever heard was that after their wedding at granddaddy's house in Martin, my Jones grandparents had to ride in the rumble seat of Uncle Jim Jones's car back to Liberty.

The Jones Family

Memories are reinforced by my family's oral history and my genealogy research. Dad was born in Union County, South Carolina in 1898, and by 1910, he and his five siblings lived with their parents in Varennees Township, Anderson County. Sometime before he graduated from Liberty High School in May 1916, they bought the farm on the Pickens Highway. He entered Clemson Agricultural College and was drafted in September 1918 to be trained at Camp Gordon for service in World War I. November found him in New York City, scheduled to sail for Europe on the 11th. With the Armistice, he returned to Clemson and graduated in June 1920 with a BS degree in Agriculture with an emphasis in Dairying. His Clemson Yearbook depicts a side of him I have never recognized like the reference to dancing. He also received Diplomas from the Palmetto Literary Society and the Agricultural Society.

Going shopping before and during World War II required riding the streetcar to downtown Atlanta, about five miles. I always felt safe while walking the mile to Morningside Elementary School alone, a practice beginning in kindergarten. Today, parents get arrested for abusing their children by permitting them to walk alone at such an early age.

My first memory of my Jones Grandparents was at their farm house when we attended Aunt Louise's wedding in 1939. The farm house was built with white boards, a porch across the front of the house, and several front steps since it was located on the side of a hill. Granddaddy had a wood shop in a small red building and I was intrigued by the belts he used to operate the machines. Beyond the shop was a peach orchard and sheep grazed on the hillside. For many years, I slept under a red blanket made from the wool of these sheep.

One of the challenging events for me when we visited was eating breakfast. My grandmother made what was called "liver mush." It was ground liver mixed with something and fried in a patty like a salmon croquet or hamburger. To this day, I will not eat liver of any kind which frustrated Nancy since she loved chicken livers.

My grandmother seemed to be a somber woman when we would visit. The Jones family relationships were never warm like the Dean family. Since three of my aunts also lived in Greenville, we visited them when we traveled to see my grandparents.

My mother always said Grandmother Jones did not hear from us very often. My grandmother wanted my Dad to write letters to her, not Mom or me. So, since Dad's letter writing was infrequent like mine, she did not hear often. I found a letter from her to my parents written in October 1933, just after a visit with them in Smyrna. I finally understood where I got my penmanship skills since I could not read every word. After World War II, they sold the farm and moved to Greenville to a house next door to Aunt Irene and Uncle Tom Wrenn. Aunt Ruby, who never married, lived with them.

My memories of my father are very skimpy during the early years of my life. It is like looking at the snapshots in a photo album. A glimpse of one was riding in the backseat of our car going to see my grandparents in Martin. The pre-World War II paved road leaving Toccoa suddenly became a rutty, muddy road at Confidence Methodist Church.

A proud day in 1940 for my dad was bringing home a new model Chevrolet from the John Smith dealership in Atlanta. Later the windshield had several stickers during the war to indicate how much gasoline could be purchased because of rationing. We received an extra allotment because of the farm my mother inherited from Granddaddy.

The Deans

I have very few memories of my grandmother since she died in October 1941 before my eighth birthday. She was a very thin lady who had developed a heart condition and died before her sixty-fifth birthday. My mind's eye sees myself watching her roll around the Martin house sitting on a high-back straight chair. My grandfather had put caster wheels on the four legs. She seemed to be a sweet, loving lady who was called Memama by her grandchildren. I was the third oldest of eight grandchildren. Only five of us had been born when she died two months before Pearl Harbor.

Granddaddy was a few months more than twenty years older than she was. I heard the story from their children many times about their courtship and marriage. Granddaddy said: "She was a cute little girl, so I waited for her to grow up when I could marry her." They were married in 1895.

When Memama died, I stayed with my Aunt Joan and her baby Melinda in the "little house" next door. Very soon, my Aunt Winnie Mary left her job with the Clinchfield Railroad in Erwin, Tennessee to move back to Martin to care for Granddaddy. During most summers while he lived, I spent a couple of weeks with them. As most farm kids did in those days, I did not wear shoes. I learned to milk cows, watched Aunt May wring chicken necks, and occasionally found myself not watching where I was stepping and felt the warmth of a recently dropped cow patty. Mom's family were delightful story tellers and I was always intrigued by their stories.

It was a bright sunny day as Granddaddy hid behind the picket fence in 1865. He was very nervous, peeking out between the pickets as he watched long lines of Union soldiers walking along the dusty road leading by the side of his house near the Tugalo River. As a watching eight-year-old boy, he knew Sherman's troops were pilfering food and they might kill him even though the war was over. He began to think about his house and wondered how he could have been so foolish by not climbing the stairs and entering the secret place where the family hid. The "hidey hole" had been built by his father, Russell, before he went off to fight in the war. It was a small, dark cubicle and was also a place of fear. How was he to compare the fear of seeing the troops with the fear of being found in the secret place?

A story about granddaddy during the depression goes as follows: His sister, Lucinda Sally Dean Thompson, lived in Atlanta. Granddaddy walked the hundred miles from Martin with a cow because her family needed milk. During my childhood, on many Sunday afternoons my parents visited Aunt Lou; her son, Von, and his wife, Pearl. They lived on Flat Shoals Avenue SE and we drove through Little Five Points going there. Von owned and operated a florist business and had several greenhouses. When I would get bored with the discussions, I would go into those greenhouses and wander around looking at all the plants and flowers. Their son, Richard, was a pastor and for many years pastored Indian Creek Baptist Church in DeKalb County. Granddaddy was an active member of the Martin community. He was one of the residents who contributed $1,000 to build the Martin School, the first brick school building in Franklin County. My mother attended this school and later was a teacher there. I visited one day when there were two classes in the same room.

Uncle Yow told the story several times about racing granddaddy on foot when he was about twenty years old and granddaddy was over sixty. Granddaddy always won. I only knew my grandfather as an old man since he was seventy-eight when I was born at his house in Martin. Dressed in overalls, he kept his one-acre garden behind the house properly hoed and weeded. He was a bee keeper and one day he covered me in the garb to keep bees from stinging me as we approached the bee hives just behind the washhouse, a place where the women boiled the clothes in huge, iron pots set in a brick framework to permit a roaring fire just beneath the pots. Granddaddy smoked the bees and opened the hives. Then we collected the honeycombs full of delicious honey.

One-day granddaddy took cotton to the gin to have it baled. We rode the wagon and waited for the cotton to be processed into a bale. It was very interesting as the cotton seeds were removed and the cotton pressed into the five-hundred-pound bale.

Another vivid memory is the day I rode with him in the wagon pullled by two mules from the Martin house to the farmhouse where he was born in 1856. Sitting beside him on the wooden bench in the springless wagon, I was jolted with every bump in the dirt road as we made the nine-mile trip each way that day. He introduced me to Henry Arthur, a legend to me. Henry was the child of one of my great-grandfather's slaves in South Carolina. He had gotten into some trouble there prompting Granddaddy to bring him to the Georgia farm and give him one of the share-cropper houses where he could live. He was a remarkable story teller and this young lad was enthralled as I sat with him on his porch listening to the tales. I only wish I could remember the stories. My cousin, Marcille, kept in touch with his daughters for years. One day when I was about ten, Uncle Richard let me plow the corn following a mule on the tract along the railroad in Martin. The plow handles were above my shoulders and the furrows were very crooked.

We made several trips from Atlanta to Smyrna during the war to visit the McCollums. We rode the streetcar to downtown Atlanta and transferred to one which went to Marietta, but we got off in Smyrna. They had built a stone house just down Banks Street from the duplex which had a creek at the rear of the property. Reed built a fish pond and stocked it with goldfish. Often, we had cookouts by the pond and Mary made the best potato salad I have ever eaten.

There was a family gathering on the back porch in Martin and I saw Granddaddy hold his hat with five slips of paper inside. He had sub-divided the farm into six tracts, about 200 acres each. Aunt Mae got the tract where the home-place house was located. It was originally built as a two-story log cabin about 1787, and the other children drew a slip in birth order for the remaining ones. My Mom got the tract along the road adjacent to the Mullins Ford Baptist Church. Granddaddy had a ruptured appendix, caught pneumonia in the hospital, and died in 1947. I sat in the living room with the family during the wake until I fell asleep.

Chapter Two
Middle School Years

My six-grade school year started after VE Day. Military fathers had come home from the war and one day, we had "show and tell" day from students who had souvenirs. One boy brought a steel German helmet and, without paying attention, he swung it, colliding with my face and chipping two front teeth. I am thankful that all that was required from the dentist was polishing the surfaces. Dental visits as a child were interesting. The dentist kept my attention because he attached a small piece of cotton to the belts for the drill and told me to watch the rabbit run.

A skating party was planned for one Saturday. I asked one of the girls in my class to go with me and she agreed. I was looking forward to the event but was devastated when she called on the morning of the party to tell me she could not go with me. This rejection was another major blow to my self-esteem and I carried this burden for many years.

My favorite sport was baseball. At home, I practiced alone by throwing the baseball against the garage door, trying to hit the padlock. I had dreams of becoming a pitcher, but I was not very good. I had a first baseman's mitt and during recess, we would play baseball. I was nearly always chosen last and put in right field, probably because I had dropped an easy fly ball early in the school year.

In sixth grade, our teacher had the class pair off for some review studies before our tests. I always tried to get paired with one of two girls, Shirley Harris or Ivy Wallace. They were very smart and very pretty. I never dated either one because Ivy's father became a professor at the University of Mississippi after sixth Grade and I never saw her again. Shirley was in my high school class, but I was very shy. She was very popular, and I felt she would not be interested in me and I was afraid of the rejection.

Entering seventh grade at O'Keefe Junior High began a huge transition. I had to ride public transportation to get to school, several miles away near the Georgia Tech campus. It was the first time I had different teachers for the various subjects. Students came from a few elementary schools making several homerooms in each grade level necessary.

My Mom had started me with a piano teacher when I was about nine years and now she wanted me to play an instrument. We talked to the music teacher and she introduced me to the bassoon. Learning to play it was a challenge because it was almost as tall as I was, and I had to learn how to protect the double reed. But, I fell in love with the bassoon which was vastly different from the piano. I never wanted to practice my piano lessons, an attitude that resulted in poor playing skills.

Home rooms played softball competitively during the spring. Our home-room team played well during the season and made the playoffs at the end of the school year. During the championship game, I played catcher and remember one play when I made two outs in a triple play, tagging a runner out at home plate. I was ecstatic because this play won the game. This victory really boosted my ego.

It was generally an uneventful year for me and my only year in junior high because the school board changed the entire structure from a 6-3-3 system to a 7-5 system.

I was active in choirs at First Baptist beginning when Don Winters started a graded program for children beginning at 2.5 years through adults. Don Winters was inducted into the US Army in 1943 and Ray Smathers became our minister of music. I sang in three choirs until I moved from Atlanta in 1956. After high school, I sang in the adult choir with my dad. At thirteen when I was in youth choir, my voice had not changed. One day I was sitting on a piano bench before practice and a few older teenage girls gathered around and paid a lot of attention to me. Their doing so boosted my self-esteem.

On Wednesday evenings I went to prayer meeting and church conferences. I was very interested in how the church made decisions after I was baptized and became a member. I do not know why I was so interested but remember the decorum shown by the elderly gentlemen as they discussed issues the congregation was considering. These stately leaders shared different viewpoints very graciously and there was always acceptance of the will of the majority. In my adult life, I have been very disappointed to observe strife in many discussions leading to church splits. Many Baptist churches today never have conferences which make me wonder why so many churches have lost this Baptist distinctive.

First Baptist had Baptist Training Union on Sunday evenings and it was a part of my family's church activities. It was a challenging time for me because I still carried the fear of standing and speaking in front of people. I could barely read my part. During one party when I was fourteen, our leaders allowed us to play "spin the bottle," and I had my first kiss with a girl I had known since kindergarten. This kiss stimulated me so much I did not sleep much that night, remembering that kiss.

Mom got a job as cashier in The Grill at Georgia Baptist Hospital when I was in high school. We had a huge freezer which was full of food. In the summers, we went to the farmer's market and bought bushels of several vegetables. We spent hours shelling peas, stringing and snapping beans, and preparing other foods for the freezer. The freezer also had pints of sherbet and ice cream, and many afternoons when I got home from school, I ate one. Once at the farmers' market, we bought six watermelons for a dollar.

I very rarely saw Uncle Jim Jones and his family, but we visited Aunt Louise often in "Little" Washington, North Carolina. They had a second home on the Pamlico Sound and we always went during the summer. I enjoyed taking shrimp to the end of the pier and catching crabs which Aunt Louise used to made excellent stuffed crab. Since I only ate it when we visited her and Wiliam, I stuffed myself every visit.

Dad and Me

Dad was never a hunter even though there were deer on the farm Mom inherited from her father in Stephens County, Georgia. He did like fishing and on a few occasions, he carried me with him. We fished a few times in a local river and we once went with his friend, Ben Lindsey, a teacher at Grady High School, to their cabin on the Suwannee River in Florida. We also fished the Gulf of Mexico. I did not catch the joy of fishing until our sons and I fished for bass in Kenya at Lake Naivasha and went deep sea fishing along the coast of the Indian Ocean.

Dad was a school teacher at heart. In 1923, he taught at Easley High School in South Carolina and was the first football coach there. Following this experience, he taught and coached at Toccoa High in Georgia and in Lake City, Florida before he married my Mom, Sarah Dean, in 1932. After they married, he taught at Walhalla, South Carolina and he taught physics and coached girls' basketball in Smyrna, Georgia from 1933 to 1935.

My favorite story from his teaching days was from his physics class at Smyrna High. He had gone into a lot of detail explaining the technical aspects of the internal combustion engine when a young man raised his hand and with a very serious expression on his face asked, "Mr. Jones, how big do elephants grow in Africa?" Every time I heard him tell the story, I had a vision of the exasperation on his face in the classroom that day.

Teachers were not well paid during the depression. In fact, sometimes they were paid in "script" and could only get a portion of its value to buy food or for other expenses. In 1935, Dad left teaching and was employed by the U.S. Forest Service. During the next year and a half, we lived in Gainesville, Florida and in Montgomery, Alabama. My parents never explained the reason he left this job and began working for the Post Office in Atlanta. In the beginning, he rode the mail car on Southern Railroad trains to and from Savannah. One of my memorabilia is his Post Office Badge NO. 45325.

He used his love for teaching by mentoring math students, one of them being me. I remember many times sitting at the breakfast room table with him as he tried to help me understand word problems. His favorite statement was "Read the problem" and deciphering them was often very frustrating. His point was to always break down the clues in each word, so I could understand the logical steps. His persistence paid off for me since in 12th grade, I got a medal for being the best math student at Grady High School.

Most students gifted in the arts like music and poetry are not also gifted in math and science. After seeing his patience mentoring the daughter of our minister of music at First Baptist Church in Atlanta, I secretly asked myself why I did not feel the same patience when he was helping me.

Chapter Three
Secondary School Years

Grady High School was located on the old campus of Tech High and Boys High schools near Piedmont Park. The school was just over one mile from my house and I walked to school the five years I studied at Grady High. The campus had several wooden temporary buildings left over from World War II. During my first year there, a football stadium was built. Boys in the younger classes spent recess time trying to jump across the foundation and column pits.

In eighth grade, I was very clumsy. I was a thin lad, about four feet ten inches but my shoe size was eleven. I was constantly tripping over those huge feet. Fortunately, I grew very quickly and by graduation, I was five feet ten inches and 170 pounds. This size sounds very small today because many football linemen weigh 300 pounds and are over six and one-half feet tall. In my era, the tackles on our football team weighed almost 200 pounds.

In eighth grade, new subjects were introduced to me. The first one was wood shop. We only used hand tools and I learned the use of saws and a wood plane. I made a small hexagonal plant stand about four inches tall. It survived nearly seventy years at Mom's house and more recently mine. It finally rotted from water damage in 2015. One semester the course was drafting where I made crisp drawings of the blocks and cylinders, but my lettering was horrid. My favorite course was print shop where we learned to hand set lead type and use a printing press. Civics was interesting where we learned about the US government, voting, and the importance of the freedom we enjoy as Americans. Some of the boys really tried to tease and embarrass the girls in this class.

English was required every year and I continued to make poor grades in these courses. I enjoyed the reading assignments but did not like book reports because I had a tough time expressing ideas with good grammar. In tenth grade, we had to take a "foreign language" and three were offered: French, Spanish, and Latin. I chose Latin and made poorer grades than in English. I failed Latin and went to summer school. The placement officer, Mr. Baxter who had been my seventh-grade math teacher, remembered me as an A student. He could not believe I was the same student since I had failed Latin. This experience taught me that impressions we make are important. In eleventh grade, I took Latin 3 and did not take Latin 4.

Math was always easy for me and I excelled because of my dad's tutoring. Algebra, geometry, and trigonometry were a snap and I was always about the first student to finish tests. In eleventh grade, I chose chemistry and physics as my subjects in science. My chemistry teacher, a German named Mr. Hitechew, was notorious for difficult tests. I discovered this truth when the results of the first test were posted and I made the fourth highest grade in the class, 26 out of 100. I studied hard to make better grades and ended the semester with an average score of 56. I was one of a very few students to pass the course first semester, and very few took Chemistry II. In biology during my senior year, I chose a project to observe scurvy in a guinea pig. It was interesting but as I watched the little animal begin to show the effects of scurvy, I was very disturbed.

I had always thought I wanted to be a doctor. During the summer after my junior year, I visited a popular swimming lake in Atlanta. The lake had a cable stretched across it where people could hold onto a pulley for the zip line crossing the lake. A good friend and I went together to enjoy the early evening. As he rode the pulley, it stuck, and he dropped into the shallow water. He asked me to shake the cable to see if we could dislodge the pulley. I was successful, but the pulley fell onto his head, cutting it. Since he was bleeding, I carried him to the doctor's office. The doctor told us he needed stitches, but he could not deaden this location and I needed to secure my friend's head while he sutured it. I did not enjoy this minor surgery. During my senior year at Grady, as I studied the requirements of college and medical school, I remembered the event at the lake and my poor study habits. I concluded medicine was not a good career choice for me and applied to study chemical engineering at Georgia Tech.

Like most high schools, there were various dance events. I never had dancing lessons and between my shyness and feeling clumsy, I was a very poor dancer. I did go to the prom but did not really enjoy it.

I was a member of the band and orchestra at Grady all five years. Since the bassoon was not a football game instrument, I carried a piccolo for four years. During my senior year, I auditioned for the Drum Major position but was beaten by my good friend, John Bauer, the first chair in the clarinet section. I carried the bass drum that year.

During my junior year, I was chosen to be a member of the all-state orchestra. I traveled with another Jones boy, an oboe player, to Milledgeville for practice. A cute little blond girl was sitting behind me. I learned she was from Toccoa and we talked some about her home town. Years later, I saw her again and discovered she was the sister of Nancy's best friend in Toccoa.

At this event in Milledgeville, a couple of us went out after practice one evening. My friend convinced me to drink a couple of beers. I did not really like the taste and when I woke up the next morning, I had the worst headache of my life. Immediately, I decided I had had my last alcoholic drink.

When I turned sixteen, the district circulation manager asked me to become his assistant. I inventoried papers each day that had been taken off the delivery truck, put them inside the store front building we had on Virginia Avenue, and counted them out for each route carrier. I collected payments for all the papers each carrier received and gave the total to my manager. One of the responsibilities was to deliver individual papers to customers in the district when their paperboy failed to deliver their paper. I have a vivid memory of one very rainy night when I drove out Briarcliff Road to deliver a paper. My mother wanted to ride with me since I was a "new driver." Another car was tailgating me with bright lights while I was searching for the correct address. In my frustration, I blurted out, "Come on by, damn it." It got very quiet and I realized what I had said. Fortunately for me, nothing else was said. I knew my mother was shocked and hurt.

This process enhanced my understanding of responsibility. I kept this job until I graduated from high school and entered Georgia Tech a month later. For a few months during my senior year at Grady, I also delivered the morning Constitution to about 200 customers, but I soon quit because this job was too much to handle with all my school responsibilities.

The Jones family celebrated the 55th wedding anniversary of my grandparents in February 1952. My mother made the wedding cake (three layers) and we drove to Greenville in our 1940 Chevrolet saloon. As we approached Greenville on US-123 highway, we crossed a railroad track. It was a very bumpy crossing and the cake rose from the plate Mom was holding in the back seat. She repaired it when we arrived. Over 100 guests came, and it was a memorable day. On Sunday, Aunt Thelma treated the family to a dinner in her home across town. I saw Granddaddy for the last time at this meal because he had a stroke and died June 13th. I could not attend his funeral since I had already started my studies at Georgia Tech for the summer term.

Graduation in May. 1952 was held in the Atlanta Auditorium downtown where the circus and many other events were held. My class was large, and the 226 students took a long time to walk across the stage to get our diplomas. It was a great night because this chapter in my life was complete.

Chapter Four
College Years

I matriculated to Georgia Tech in June of 1952, three weeks after graduating from high school. Because it was a summer term, all the classes normally taken in the first quarter were not available, but my aptitude for math gave me the opportunity to take the first two math courses simultaneously. Chemistry and chemical engineering majors had special chemistry courses during the freshman year. My 8:00 a.m. class was chemistry taught by Dr. Monroe Spicer, the head of the department who became my favorite chemistry teacher. He required close attention in class because of his teaching method. He would stand at the blackboard, chalk and eraser in hand. As he lectured, he would write chemical equations on the board with his right hand and erase them with his left. Fast copying was a necessity. Years later I was sent to a National Society of Chemists meeting by my company and saw him there. I was very surprised that he remembered me.

When I arrived on campus, I was invited to join two very different activities. Three fraternities invited me to rush week and Glen Swicegood invited me to Baptist Student Union. I visited one fraternity and one meeting at the BSU. I recognized this choice was a fork in my road to the future. At the fraternity, there was a lot of alcohol, so God was clearly leading me to become active in the BSU, a decision I never regretted.

During the summer term of 1952, BSU meetings were held in the YMCA building on North Avenue but in the fall, First Baptist Church Atlanta purchased a house on Techwood Drive, a half block from the football stadium. With very few modifications, it made a good place for students to meet, visit, or study. The most interesting room was in the basement where the ping pong table was located. This table almost filled the entire room, but we had about two to three feet between the table and walls on all four sides. The room's smallness cramped our playing style, but we did not let it interfere with our fun.

German was a required freshman course for Chemical Engineering students since many technical papers were published only in this language. You already know my issues with languages. On top of this limitation, my teacher was apparently an alcoholic and missed many classes. I promptly failed the course my first quarter. I did finally pass the three German courses in my fifth quarter at Tech.

My Dad worked in the distribution center at the downtown Atlanta Post Office, diagonally across the street from Rich's Department Store. He got me a temporary job during the Christmas season after my second quarter at Tech when I turned eighteen in December of 1952. I was assigned a section of racks for rural post offices. The second floor of the building was a huge room filled with banks of racks containing mail bags for packages. There was a short conveyor belt where incoming packages were dumped and sorted by a few employees into rolling bins. These bins were taken to a group of racks and the packages were put into an individual post office bag, labeled when full, and sent to the transport area. I worked all the Christmas seasons during college and this income plus my savings from my paper route paid my tuition and book costs for all my studies at Georgia Tech.

Dr. Roy O. McClain became pastor at First Baptist Atlanta in 1953 and the church began to grow significantly. There was a very active student department, primarily students from Georgia Tech and Georgia Baptist School of Nursing. Many romances, including mine, between Tech students and the student nurses began at First Baptist Church. Chester Henry was a couple of years ahead of me and lived in a campus dorm. Every Sunday morning, he would go through the dorms, knocking on doors and then walking to the church with a large crowd of students following him like the Pied Piper. He was a one-man dynamo mobilizing Tech students to be involved in the church. The college department was very active, and we certainly enjoyed the nursing students from Georgia Baptist Hospital. In fact, many of us married one of those students.

Academics

Tech required six quarters of physical education. In the freshman year, swimming, gymnastics, and track were the required courses. Students could choose their courses during the sophomore year. The swimming course was known as "drown proofing." It was taught by Freddie Lanoue, known for developing programs during World War II to train sailors and marines how to survive if their ships were sunk. There were ten tests, each counting 10% of our grade. Three tests required having limbs tied so they were useless: hands and feet tied, feet tied with them tucked near the waist, and hands tied. We had to survive in the pool of water seven feet deep for forty-five minutes for each test. Because of a fear of drowning,

I only tried the tests where my hands were free. Another test required swimming underwater two lengths of the Olympic size pool without surfacing. I got eight points out of ten on that test. Collecting a brick from the bottom at a ten-foot depth was another test. I was proud of my "C" in the course.

Gymnastics was fun and challenging. There were flying and travelling rings, parallel bars, a pommel horse, and a rope climb. I did well on everything except the rope climb. The top of the rope was about 20 feet above the gym floor and we climbed against the clock. I made it to the top but when I reached to touch the ring, my left hand slipped, and I started falling. I grabbed the rope with both bare hands and took a large amount of flesh off my palms during my descent.

Many Sundays while I was at Tech, my family invited some of my Tech friends who attended First Baptist to our house for a southern Sunday dinner. Mom was a good cook; all enjoyed filling their stomachs, sometimes to the extreme.

At the end of the spring quarter in 1953, several BSU members from Georgia Tech planned to attend student week at Ridgecrest. The spiritual atmosphere was exceptional and during the week, I made one of the most significant decisions of my life. I offered my life in Christian service.

Two of the three international students from Tech decided to accept Christ. Curtis Martin and I had a long discussion with Frank Liu, a Chinese student from Taiwan, about his decision. The next morning, Frank and I spent a long time at Lake Dew reading our Bibles and praying. I tried to explain many of the things he did not understand. Later at Tech, Frank and I were lab partners in one of our chemical engineering courses.

Summer at Ridgecrest

Don Hammonds, one of the key leaders in our BSU at Tech, was on the staff at Ridgecrest. Since I had no plans for the summer, knew Don well, and more summer staff were needed, I pled with Willard "Daddy" Weeks to give me an opportunity to spend the summer working at Ridgecrest. To quote my life history written for the Foreign Mission Board selection process: "That summer was a highlight of my life. Many rich Christian experiences occurred, and I made a multitude of good friends."

I called my parents to tell them I was staying and later wrote a letter to them about experiences and my work. A part of the letter said: "I haven't had a chance to tell you yet, but last Sunday in the service I felt God's call for my life. I don't know what I am to do and where He will lead me, but I am ready to go wherever and whenever, no matter what the cost is."

My work assignment was to be a busboy in the dining hall. I was teamed with two waitresses, Betty Butler and Gladys Arakawa, both students at Blue Mountain College in Mississippi. We had four tables of ten diners for the three meals every day. My responsibility was to bring all the clean dishes from the kitchen for the girls to set the tables. We served "family style" so after the blessing, I brought the food from the kitchen to be placed on the tables. There could be as many as thirty bowls or platters of food. After people finished eating and left the table, I collected the stacked dirty dishes and carried them to the dish washer in the kitchen. The girls cleaned the tables and swept the floors.

We had free time between the meals and often a group would hike to one of the nearby mountains or the waterfalls on the Catawba River. God saved my life one day that summer. Several of us had gone to the falls for a picnic on July 15th. A few of us had climbed the trail beside the falls to get a beautiful view of the mountains. As I was climbing down the slick trail, my foot slipped. I tripped forward hitting my chin on a rock making a deep gash. I somersaulted down the trail. Just as I regained my feet and began running, I grabbed a small tree trunk which kept me from falling over a sheer 75 foot drop to rocks. My roommate and I made a forced march including passing through the railroad tunnel to Ridgecrest, about six miles in forty minutes. I went to the clinic and the nurse put a bandage on the gash. After supper, I went back and saw Valda Long, the lead nurse who sent me to the hospital in Ashville where I got 13 sutures in my chin, a tetanus shot, and antibiotic ointment with the dressing. I still thank God when I remember His protection that day and many others. Valda became a missionary and served in Nigeria before she transferred to the Baptist Hospital at Mbeya Tanzania in 1968.

Weekly conferences began with supper on Thursday and finished the following Wednesday. Every Wednesday evening, we had staff chapel services since work schedules did not permit all staff to attend a worship service. Twice, Dr. Billy Graham was our speaker and brought inspiring messages.

The ratio of girls to boys on staff was about 3:1. I became just like the little boy in a candy store who wanted to sample every flavor. I made many friends, dated a lot of girls, and was completely enthralled with the Christian atmosphere.

Nancy

Nancy and I first met in the fall of 1953 when she was a nursing student at Georgia Baptist Hospital and I was an engineering student at Georgia Tech. I discovered she was from Toccoa, Georgia, where I had relatives and that she was born in Toccoa. As we talked, I learned she and I were both delivered by Dr. John Terrell, a brother to my Aunt Ruth's husband, Fred. We talked about what our parents did before we were born. As we merged their stories, it became obvious there was a common thread. Our mothers both taught in the elementary school in the Toccoa City School System and my dad was the Toccoa High football coach and math teacher. With this common heritage, we became friends.

The nursing school was a three-year program leading to a RN license. Her tuition for the entire three years was $300.00, but she always said the hospital got her education expenses through physical labor. Student nurses were required to work many hours on the hospital floors assisting patients. This clinical experience was invaluable at the beginning of nursing careers.

In those days, nurses wore white uniforms, white stockings, white shoes, and a cap unique to the nursing school. I was among many Georgia Tech students who attended the capping ceremony for Nancy's class held at First Baptist Church. This ceremony occurred at the end of the first year of studies and the nurses were excited and pleased to achieve this step in their studies. Nancy was close to many of her classmates. Jackie and Trish were bridesmaids in our wedding and Peggy was on the Ridgecrest staff with me in 1953.

Warren Woolf was the BSU campus minister for many years before he joined the staff of the North American Mission Board. He and Sue loved us and were outstanding mentors. Their influence resulted in a substantial number leaving engineering after completing our studies and answering God's call to vocational Christian ministry. Glen Swicegood and I served with the Foreign Mission Board. Another became a church planter in Alaska and several pastored churches in many parts of the U.S. Henry Fields ultimately became pastor at Nancy's home church, First Baptist in Toccoa, and Chester Henry became a minister of education in several churches. Many did volunteer work in churches and in mission projects. Stan Markum and his wife spent time with us in Kenya where he drew architectural plans for church buildings. I stayed active in BSU and in my junior year was chosen to be the secretary. I felt that I did not do a very respectable job since my writing skills were poor at that time and I procrastinated.

Tech Again

I had several chemistry courses: general, physical, analytical, and organic. Every course had a three-hour lab except organic which was six hours. The day I had organic chemistry lab, my class schedule began at 8:00 a.m. and finished at 6:00 p.m. with no break. We had morning classes six days a week. Our average class load was over twenty credit hours per quarter totaling 243 hours for graduation. Very few students completed their course work in twelve quarters. I was thankful to "get out," the Tech saying for graduation, in thirteen quarters. Professors told us they expected that two hours of study per class hour would be required to succeed. With 18 class hours and 9 to 12 lab hours per week most quarters, time spent amounted to almost 70 hours per week. On most afternoons during the first three years, I had labs four to five days a week. So, there were many nights with only a few hours to sleep.

We had several other required courses: English, engineering drafting, strength of materials, physics, math with a year of calculus, some twenty chemical engineering classes, and a few electives. The dumbest decision I made at Tech was to choose differential equations as a substitute for a required course not offered during my final quarter before graduation.

Often, I studied with friends in my chemical engineering courses. Frequently, I was asked to help them solve the assigned problems and usually successfully explained the procedure to get the correct answer. I was frustrated many times when they received a higher grade in the course.

Another dumb decision as some would say was to write an English paper about the Resurrection of Jesus for one English course. God protected me because after I gave it to the professor, I realized he was Jewish. I was surprised when I got an A on the paper with his comment, "This is a good paper, but I am not convinced."

Ridgecrest, Summer 1954

During the summer of 1954, I returned to Ridgecrest and my work assignment was in the bakery. "Mr. Sam," a very jolly large black man from Morganton, North Carolina, was the baker. He was a great teacher and an enjoyable work partner. I learned how to make little balls of yeast dough for the dinner rolls, various kinds of cake or pie, and many other types of desserts. Most mornings, we toasted hundreds of pieces of bread since often there were more than 2,000 people attending a conference.

One morning Mr. Sam was late; thus, after breakfast, I began to prepare the dessert for lunch. The food services manager was not pleased, and I am sure if there was a performance review, it would have been very bad. When Mr. Sam arrived and we discussed what I did, I had done all the correct procedures. I just did not have authority to make this decision. Many people would probably say I did this same thing in other stages of my life. Now, I believe this behavior was the result of overcompensating for my low self-esteem.

One of my highlights in 1954 came during music week. Warren Angell conducted Mendelssohn's Oratorio, Elijah. I joined the chorus singing bass and the music really spoke to me about the awesomeness and power of God and how God gave extraordinary gifts to His servants. I still remember the thrill of singing "Take all the prophets of Baal."

In 1954, Katie Blackerby and I were both back on the staff at Ridgecrest. We dated a few times in 1953 and I had visited her in Alabama twice during the school year. Our relationship began to blossom and before we returned to school, we had talked about the idea of one day getting married. In the fall, I began to feel Katie's pressure to get married before graduation. I recognized I was not mature enough for marriage and it would interfere with the completion of my college work.

The only time I lived on campus at Georgia Tech was the fall quarter of 1954. I vividly remember borrowing Henry Field's car to take Nancy back to her dorm at the hospital after a church skating party for the college group in December. I parked Henry's car on the street near her dorm and we talked for a while. Suddenly, without thinking, I leaned over and kissed her. It was the sweetest experience I had ever had. We said goodnight at the door of the dorm. I headed back to Henry's car and was instantly overwhelmed with guilt.

I had been going "steady" with Katie since 1953. I had been worried about that relationship because Katie was a year older than I was and was pushing for us to get married. I was not very mature but wise enough to know that while facing two more years of engineering school, marriage was not a wise decision. My family had an emergency the week after Christmas and I had been working at the main Atlanta post office with my dad. When I called Katie to tell her I could not come see her before school started in January, she insisted if I really loved her I would come. During this very stressful conversation, I began to recognize that if she really loved me, she would not demand I come. By the end of this conversation, I had broken off the relationship. I know we were both hurt by the experience.

Chasing Nancy

In the spring of 1955, Nancy and I began to date regularly. Before long, I thought I was falling in love. During the dating process. I learned a lot about Nancy's life before nursing school. Nancy was nine years old when her brother, Frank Brooks, was born in 1944. She loved him but also had some minor resentment for having to miss school to care for him when he was sick while her mother taught her class. In January of 1948, her father died unexpectedly and tragically. Sitting on the front porch, he shot himself early one morning with his Post Office pistol. They had a tough time dealing with the grief. Nancy's mother told her he had an infection which attacked his brain and I believe my mother-in-law never reconciled her feelings about the incident. In her life history for the International Mission Board application in 2000, Nancy wrote: "When I was 12 years old, my father committed suicide. He loved to gamble and had gotten so deeply in debt that, he said in the note he left, he could think of no other way out. This was a very difficult time in our lives. Mother went back to college, taking courses and going to summer school until she graduated, teaching all the time. She took good care of Frank and me."

The four Brooks women were always close. Nancy's favorite was Aunt Frances who paid close attention to all the nieces and nephews since she never had any children. Nancy enjoyed going to Royston because Aunt Charlotte's children lived there. Nancy talked about riding the mail truck from Toccoa to Royston with her daddy. Jerry, Frank, and Arlene Mason were not much younger than she was and the adventure of riding the mail truck to see them was always exciting to her.

Nancy's best friend was Claire Simpson and they spent a lot of time together. They would meet on the street and walk to elementary school together, invariably close to being tardy. They made friends with the black janitor and if he saw them coming while he was ringing the tardy bell, he always kept ringing it until they were safely in class. They became lifelong friends, just like sisters. Claire told Nancy she wanted to be a nurse, so Nancy said, "I do, too." Claire found out she hated the sight of blood and became a math teacher, but Nancy kept nursing as her ambition.

She spent many summer days at the Toccoa swimming pool with friends. Her high school days were before sun screen was invented, but old fashioned remedies existed. She always said her skin was very dark by the end of the summer. She described the memories of going with her family and friends to one of the Georgia Power lakes in Northeast Georgia. They rented lake houses and had a happy time fishing and playing in the lake.

She made friends easily and they commented about her smile and her friendliness. In high school, she was in the band and a basketball cheer leader. Like most teenage girls, she had secret crushes on some of the boys and I am sure many were attracted to her just like I was as a college student.

She was always interested in nursing, confident it was her calling. When she was fifteen, she got a job at Stephens County Hospital. The staff told her she was too young for many of the jobs and assigned her to be a lab tech. She typed and cross-matched patients' blood and did other tests.

Many times, Nancy would talk about trips with Trish to her parent's home in Red Rock near Albany. Trish's father was a peanut farmer and Nancy loved the peanuts but hated the gnats. Georgians often describe living above or below the "gnat line."

About May of 1955, Nancy told me she believed she still had feelings for her high school boyfriend, Bobby Mitchell, and thought we should "just be friends." She went to the Spring Military Ball at North Georgia College with him. I was very disappointed but what could I say or do?

All the classes and clinical studies were taught at the hospital except for the psychiatric clinical work at the mental hospital in Milledgeville. One weekend while doing her clinical studies at Milledgeville, she was travelling to Atlanta to see her family and friends. As she was riding in the front seat of a pickup truck with a classmate and her boyfriend that night, a loaded log truck pulled out into the road and they crashed into the side. Nancy was thrown forward, breaking the windshield with her head. The black log truck driver looked at her and said; "Lordie, I done killed a white girl." He immediately fled the scene, abandoning the truck.

Nancy was taken to Georgia Baptist Hospital where she had several surgeries during the next few weeks. Her jaw was wired shut and she had to take her food through a straw. She said: "The only good thing about a broken jaw was I got to drink a lot of milkshakes." She had several plastic surgeries to repair the cuts in her face and jaw. Several years after we were married, a small, rectangular piece of glass about a half inch long worked its way out of her jaw.

I went to visit Nancy in her room at Georgia Baptist Hospital after her wreck in the fall of 1955. When I saw her broken jaw, multiple facial cuts, and serious bruises, I kept quiet because she looked awful with black eyes and deep purple bruises all over her face plus a wired jaw.

In the fall, I dated Barbara, a Baptist girl from Tift College. One Saturday, I asked to use my parent's car to go to see Barbara at Tift, but they refused me, so I rode the Greyhound bus to Forsyth. I caught the last bus back to Atlanta which arrived at the downtown bus station just after midnight. Public transportation was not operating at that late hour and I could not pay for a taxi. I walked home, six miles away. My Mom was waiting at the door when I arrived about 3:00 am. The next time I asked to use the car, it was okay. My relationship with Barbara ended at Christmas time.

Looking back, I learned many things about relationship development and the importance of a consistent lifestyle of faith through my experiences at Ridgecrest.

Last Years at Tech

I, along with many of my friends, experienced a growing faith and the importance of using our God given gifts wherever God places us in life. I stand amazed at God's use of some like Sam Cannata, a medical student while at Ridgecrest and missionary doctor in Africa whose ministry was truly blessed. Or the high school kid, Jimmy Henry, who we called the "pot boy" in 1954 because his work assignment was scrubbing all the cooking pots used in the kitchen. He became a key pastor and Baptist leader, retiring from the God-blessed church in Orlando, Florida. God created in many of our hearts a special commitment to live out "Wherever He leads, I'll go."

During my junior year, the physics class was in a large room with over 100 students. It was an inside room with no windows. One day, a student dropped off to sleep during the class. When the professor finished his lecture, all of us crept quietly out of the room and turned off the lights. I heard later he slept five hours and missed all his other classes that day.

I enlisted in Air Force ROTC when I enrolled at Georgia Tech. We had classes and drills regularly for three years. During my junior year, I held the rank of Sargeant and was drum major of the Air Force band. In my Air Force ROTC class one day, the lecturer was explaining about the technical aspects of making a plane fly. He described lift, the aerodynamics of the vacuum created by the wing design, and talked about gravity as the force to overcome so that the plane stays in the air. He said, "What goes up always comes down" and proceeded to toss his chalk eraser into the air. Imagine our amusement when the eraser did not come down but got stuck in the light fixture. At the end of my junior year, the Korean War had been concluded. We were told the Air Force did not need all the ROTC students; thus, we could opt out. We might be drafted later but I chose the option to leave ROTC and was never drafted.

My neighbor, John Mattison, was two years older and played trumpet in the Tech band. I joined the band and participated all four years wearing our gold and white uniforms when we performed. I thought the band looked very sharp in our marching formation which was eight members wide and twelve deep with two drum majors and several majorettes who were not students. My class at Tech had the first two female students in the school's history. We marched in several parades in down town Atlanta and had some performances where I could play the bassoon. During football season and parades, I played cymbals. It was great fun making loud noises.

During my last two football seasons, I was music librarian which also required designing all the band formations for halftime shows. John Mattison was librarian my first two years in the band and taught me the tasks as I helped him. This role was very enjoyable, and I got a small scholarship for this work.

The band made four train trips to bowl games while I was a student: three to the Sugar Bowl and one to the Cotton Bowl. The trip to the Sugar Bowl in 1954 was uncertain for a period. Tech was scheduled to play West Virginia and the Governor of Georgia declared we could not play them because they had a black player. There were many demonstrations and the Governor relented to a very upset student body and alumni. Of course, we won the game.

I spent three New Year's Eves in New Orleans. One year, we explored Bourbon Street and had a great meal at Arnauds, a famous restaurant. On the return trip from Dallas, four of us spent the entire trip in the baggage car playing bridge. These events occurred during a very successful football period when Bobby Dodd was coach. His two main assistant coaches became outstanding head coaches.

One of the leading trombone players was also in the Air Force band and when he graduated, he became a fighter pilot in the Air Force. Wayne Waddell was shot down in Vietnam and spent more than five years as a prisoner of war. Many days, I prayed for his release

Our engineering courses started during our junior year after we got a foundation in other subjects. I enjoyed them very much. I especially liked my professor who was the head of the department, Dr. Grubb. One Chemical Engineering professor who had the reputation of giving only one A in each of his classes and never more than one A to any student in a quarter. He liked my design project and I received two A grades and one B grade in the courses he taught my final quarter. I was very thankful.

During the winter quarter of 1956, my last at Tech, many professional recruiters came to campus representing the companies who employed them. I had the opportunity to interview with 30-40 of them. I still have my file of response letters to remind me of the vast number of rejections I received.

I did receive three offers of a job. I rejected one immediately and gave careful study to the other two: Phillips Petroleum and United States Rubber Company. The Phillips offer was interesting but required a three-year training program where I would move every six months to a new job site at a different refinery in the western states. The offer with Naugatuck Chemical Division was different and the location was in a southern state at Baton Rouge, Louisiana. I was invited for an onsite interview and made my first airplane trip on a Delta plane filled with only two passengers where I received a lot of attention from the flight crew. After the interview, I accepted an assignment as a supervisor in the quality control lab. I began work on April 1, 1956; however, I kept the rejection letters as a reminder of how God opens the right door if we listen to the Holy Spirit.

Chapter Five
First Engineering Job, A New Culture

When I finished my course work at Tech in March of 1956, Mom and Dad drove me to my first job in Baton Rouge since I did not have a car. I rented a room in a house near the state capital building. They carried me to the entrance for Naugatuck Chemicals where I got out of the car and walked toward the security gate for my first day of work. My parents told me later they cried because I never looked back or waved goodbye. I guess my behavior was a collision of my excitement for my first workday as an engineer and their realization that they were then empty nesters since I was an only child.

I visited First Baptist on Wednesday evening when I went to Baton Rouge for my job interview. As soon as I moved, I joined the church and became active in the young people's department in Sunday School where there were a lot of LSU students. I began to make friends quickly. One Sunday morning, a new member came into the class, looked at me and said, "I know you, you went to Georgia Tech." Bill McCurry had been in my class and graduated in June. He had studied civil engineering and been a member of Tabernacle Baptist Church; therefore, we had no contact at college. We became life-long friends.

Another chemical engineer, Nelson Stuckey, also joined the church after graduating from the University of Alabama. Bill worked for Plantation Pipeline Company and Nelson Esso. We all became friends with Bill Stracener, a few years older but still single. In June 1957, Wayne Wingate joined the church staff as minister of youth and became one of the "gang."

In the summer of 1956, I bought a new car, a 1956 Chevrolet convertible with a stick shift and four-barrel carburetor. It was a "hot" car and was black and gold with a white top, reminding me of the Tech colors. A couple of weeks after I bought it, the dealer asked me if I would drive it in the Baton Rouge parade, so that Miss Baton Rouge could ride in it sitting on top of the back seat. Since I had a car, I began visiting the LSU BSU center and got acquainted with several students. I began to date some of the girls.

My first assignment was as a shift supervisor of the quality control lab and doing technical service work in the manufacturing unit. My college work did not prepare me for the technical aspects of the assignment, and the people I was supposed to supervise were very experienced. Not only did they not think they should be supervised by a young college jerk, but most were Cajuns and I had never met one of them before. I tended to agree with them but thankfully, after several months, I began to gain their confidence and the tension became less. They played tricks on my ignorance of Cajun culture, and I made lots of mistakes, bringing light hearted teasing. I made embarrassing errors with names like my pronunciation of the engineering department secretary's name upon first meeting her. Her name was Sophie Braud (pronounced Breaux) and I said: "Good morning, Mrs. Broad." I had to listen carefully when they talked because the dialect was new to my ears. It took a while to begin to understand their humor in the stories they told, many designed to shock me. The company had a banquet for employees and Justin Wilson was the speaker. Later, he was on television as the Cajun Chef. He told story after story about the escapades of Boudreaux and Thibodeaux. By this time, I had developed some understanding of the Cajun culture.

There were two Cajun ladies who were lab techs on day shift. They were very accomplished in performing the necessary tests and their work quality was outstanding. They called one of the guys "Foots" because he wore a size fifteen shoe.

Christmas of 1956 was a new experience. It was the first time I had not been with my family at this special time of the year. I was also scheduled to work day shift on Christmas Day. Everyone brought food and it was my first Christmas meal where the main course was spaghetti, not turkey and dressing. One of guys brought a jar of peppers he had cooked and asked me to try one. I did, and doing so was a huge mistake. My entire digestive system burned for three days. Later, they told me the hot peppers were fresh and which meant they were extremely hot. Tabasco sauce was mild in comparison. Of course, all laughed at my discomfort, but this example is one that illustrates progress in our relationships.

There were many very nice, pretty girls in the church and each of us dated several. I dated Margaret Ann Stacey a few times but by December 1957, Bill McCurry had chosen Margaret Ann and they were married. I dated several other girls and when my Dad had his stroke, I was dating JoAnn. Nelson and Wayne married a few years later but Bill Stracener never married although he dated the same girl for over thirty years.

First Baptist had a newspaper for youth titled Youth Speaks. Bill McCurry was the editor until June 1957, when Uncle Sam beckoned him to service and I was chosen as editor. I wrote an editorial for every bi-weekly issue until I married. As I researched the boxes of old papers we had collected, I found copies of all my editorials. I have read them and have been surprised by what I wrote at that youthful age. There was a special issue for the period when new students were coming to LSU for college in 1957. The following is my editorial for that issue:

> Editorial ethics usually demands that the newspaper policy be indicated but no personal feelings be revealed. Forgive me if I break this code but I want to speak from my heart.
>
> Many of you are leaving parents and your homes for the first time. This is a trite phrase which you have probably heard many times during the last few days, but it is certainly applicable. Now, you are a big person, a high school graduate, and leaving home. You can make all the decisions, go when and where you desire, and do what you wish all the time.
>
> Before your head swells too big, stop and consider a few things. Now you are making the choices. Right and wrong are still the same as when you left home. It is still right to associate with the nice crowd. It is still right to be a nice guy or girl. It is still right to study and educate yourself. After all, that should be the reason you are coming to college. It is still right to go to church and participate in its activities.
>
> Do not be as many students like myself. When I left for college, I was a big shot, a high school graduate, and sitting on the top of the world, going to have a good time.
>
> When I arrived at college, the first person I met was a BSU council member who invited me to BSU and the church. I thanked him, but I was a big shot; I had more important things to do. Then, I met the boys who beckoned for a good time.
>
> I spent many sleepless nights that first week. I was young, but I recognized I had to choose between church and the good times I thought I wanted. I made my choice and jumped into the full swing of church activities. I found good times I never knew existed.
>
> Parental influence, church and the Master won in my game of life. The battle was hard, but the win was decisive. You do not need to fight. Anyone who has fought the battle will tell you, you will never be happy unless you live the Master's way.
>
> We have a good group of young people here and the church staff is the greatest. Try us and see if we can make you the happiest individual alive. Join us—the Master is on our side."

I was active at church and spent a lot of time at the LSU BSU Center. I made a lot of friends and was enjoying life. I attended the church conferences because I was interested to see if they were like First Baptist Atlanta where I was impressed with the gentlemanly discussions. Thus, being "very wise young men of twenty-one," Nelson and I endeared ourselves with the pastor, Dr. Norris Palmer, by our questions as we sat on the front pew. As I became more mature, I realized I wanted answers to questions, but it would have been wiser to ask them in a different venue.

After graduation and passing her nursing board exams in the fall of 1956, Nancy and Peggy Hammond moved to Winston-Salem North Carolina to work at the Baptist Hospital there. Peggy was a Pembroke Indian and this location was not far from her North Carolina home. Since this was the farthest distance Nancy had lived from Toccoa, it took three months for her to decide home in Toccoa was a desirable place and she moved back to work at Stephens County hospital as an RN.

A little while later, she moved back to Georgia Baptist to be a clinical instructor in the nursing school and to pursue her class work for a degree in nursing at Georgia State University. Little did she know what her future entailed.

By 1957, I was more competent in my work and was gaining some maturity. My work assignment was changed to process engineering and my office was with the other engineers in the middle of the plant. Our plant was tucked into the edge of the Esso refinery along Scenic Highway because it was originally built in World War II to manufacture specialty oil resistant rubber used for gaskets in military vehicles. U.S. Rubber had bought the plant and the Paracril product line from Esso. They had also started production on a plastics product line composed of three chemicals called ABS plastics.

Bill Calloway was the chief process engineer and a good mentor. He was about 25 years older than me and his experience was an inspiration. He kept a coffee pot going in the office and I gradually learned to drink the dark roast Community coffee he brewed. I accused Bill and Cajuns of making coffee so the spoon would dissolve when adding sugar and cream.

Management asked me to serve as the chief advisor for the Junior Achievement chapter we sponsored. I had been a member of Junior Achievement in Atlanta during high school. The Atlanta chapter was sponsored by the company where my mother's first cousin, Clarence Palmer, worked. As we discussed a business plan with the Baton Rouge kids, it was decided we would make plastic cases for fishing rods. It was successful, and many people bought our product. It was also a good learning experience because I absorbed a lot of principles used in the business world. I know this was helpful for future work assignments.

There was a company softball team and I enjoyed playing with them. We were very competitive, even with several "old" guys on the team. I also joined a fast pitch team which played in the Municipal Stadium where the Class D professional baseball team played. I was not a very good hitter, but I was fast on my feet as I played center field.

Many will probably call me prudish when I relate this story. A girl I was dating wanted to go to a high school football game in her home town, several miles from Baton Rouge. We went and after the game, since it was late, a young married couple invited us to spend the night at their house. I had very conservative attitudes at the time and did not think it would be "proper" for us to stay. The girl did not understand, and we never dated again.

In 1957, construction began for a new plastics production plant at Scotts Bluff in the northern suburbs of the city. I was assigned responsibility to assist in bringing this facility online and beginning production there. It was an intensive work experience because I was commuting from the original plant to the new plant at Scotts Bluff. Much of the time I was still working various shifts as process engineers were required to cover production 24/7. I and other engineers rotated shifts. There was an economic downturn during this period and for a few months, we worked a schedule where we operated production ten days with one long weekend of four days. Another engineer and I rotated between twelve hour shifts and I really struggled when I had to work ten days from 7:00 pm to 7:00 am. I never slept well in the daytime and the summer of 1957 was very hot when my bedroom did not have air conditioning.

I had lived in two different houses where I rented a room. Nelson Stucky, one of my engineering friends from church in Baton Rouge, and I had lived in rented rooms in the house owned by a little old Cajun lady. She made the strongest coffee I ever drank. Even a demitasse cup was too much to enjoy. After I bought a little house from Atlanta friends who moved to Mississippi, Nelson lived with me in this house until Esso sent him on assignment to Aruba.

During the startup period at Scotts Bluff, many days I spent sixteen or more hours a day in the plant. Often, I got called in when there was some issue needing resolution.

Home

After I bought my first car in 1956, there were a few visits home for holidays. The trips were long since there were no interstate highways then. I talked to my Dad on the phone when his mother died in February of 1958, and he encouraged me not to come to the funeral because of the distance. It was the last time I spoke to Dad. On an evening in late February of 1958, Mom called me when I got home from work about midnight to tell me Dad was very sick. After packing, I was on the road about 1:00 am for the long trip, over 500 miles. As I was driving very fast on a rural road in eastern Lousiana, I rounded a curve and there was a herd of cows all over the road. Somehow, God guided my car and I did not hit one. After an 8.5-hour trip, I met a neighbor who told me Dad was in Georgia Baptist Hospital. I went directly there and found Dad completely comatose from a massive stroke.

I Capture Nancy

When I learned that Nancy was a clinical instructor in the nursing school, I asked one of the floor nurses who knew her to take word about my Dad. Nancy came to his room after she finished her teaching. My Mom and I asked her if she could do some private duty nursing for us on the 3-11 shift. She was living with her Aunt Frances in Decatur; I promised to take her home every night.

About the fourth night, we were sitting in my car in Aunt Frances's driveway talking. I know I said something stupid, not a loving proposal. I probably said, "Do you want to get married?" instead of "I love you. Will you marry me?" God performed a miracle for me because she said, "Yes"!!! This engagement began a loving, adventure of life for us, culminating fifty-seven years later when God called her to her heavenly reward on April 22, 2015.

Dr. Roy McClain led the memorial service for my Dad and shared a message I will never forget: "What did he leave?" It was a message about his life being empty of possessions but filled with the investments he had made in people. God has given me the grace to share this message with some people whose memorial services I have led as recently as 2014.

I had been dating JoAnn in Baton Rouge and when my Dad died, she called me and wanted to come to the memorial service. I told her it was not wise, and I would explain when I got back home in Baton Rouge. When I was back in Baton Rouge, we had a long, stressful phone conversation as

I explained I was engaged.

I found a letter I wrote to Nancy about two weeks after my Dad's Memorial Service which said I was called into the plant at 4:30 a.m. Sunday morning and worked until about 3:00 p.m. I rushed home, cleaned up, sang a concert with the Esso Men's Chorus, went to church that evening and went back to work until 2:00 a.m. Monday morning. My memory is that there were many days like that during late 1957 and early 1958.

Small town newspapers wrote a lot of local interest stories during the 1950's. Imagine my surprise as I was going through boxes of memorabilia collected by our mothers and us when I found a "human interest story" about Nancy and me, published in the Toccoa Record a few days before our wedding. The title was "How Boy Meets Girl." It is copied here.

> The easiest way to meet the best friends is at church – and that's what Nancy Kirk and Tom Jones will tell you.
>
> Nancy and Tom will soon be wed at a church ceremony at the First Baptist Church in Toccoa, the culmination of a friendly meeting at the Young People's Training Union at First Baptist Church in Atlanta.
>
> Nancy was born in Toccoa, the daughter of Juddie Brooks Kirk and the late Frank Kirk, who was the son of the late Frank and Nancy Hathcock Kirk, natives of Franklin County. Her mother is the daughter of Mrs. Frank Brooks and the late Mr. Brooks of Royston. Mrs. Frances Brooks Stephens is an aunt.
>
> Tom's mother is Sarah Dean Jones, who taught in the city schools of Toccoa many years ago, and the late Mr. Jones. Mrs. Fred Terrell is his aunt.
>
> After graduating from Toccoa High School, Nancy was graduated from the Georgia Baptist Hospital School of Nursing, later attending Georgia State College. She is presently employed as a clinical instructor in the Education Department at Georgia Baptist Hospital. For her wedding, she will wear the wedding gown of a close friend, the former Clair Simpson, and the veil of Kathryn.
>
> Jarrard Herndon, symbolizing her something borrowed. Her something "old" will be the charming medal which was won by her maternal grandmother when she was a girl. Her "blue" will be a good luck coin encased in blue satin – and she will carry a "new"white Bible.
>
> The bridegroom-elect is a graduate of Georgia Institute of Technology, being employed as a chemical engineer for the U.S.

Rubber Company in Baton Rouge, LA, where the couple will reside.

Nancy and I set the date of our wedding for July 12, 1958 after considering waiting until September. This date was a very appropriate since it was the first anniversary of Claire and Page Godwin. Claire had offered her wedding dress for Nancy to wear which she gladly accepted. We knew the distance would be an emotional crisis because we wanted to be together as soon as possible. We were so excited and so much in love we decided we could not wait that long.

My aunt and uncle, Ruth and Fred Terrell, gave us our rehearsal dinner at their restaurant as a wedding gift. It was a beautiful occasion and we have cherished the dessert dishes and glasses they gave us from those used at the dinner.

Saturday morning began as a very rainy day. Soon, it turned very muggy and warm. My groomsmen friends from Baton Rouge had planned to fly to Toccoa in a private plane since Bill Stracener was a pilot. But, with all the weather problems they had to drive the 600 miles and stayed on the road all night arriving an hour before the wedding began. To say I was nervous is a gross understatement. I truly believed I might have to escort guests to their seats. The remaining groomsmen stepped up and all went well.

The ceremony was beautiful at the First Baptist Church. The stained-glass windows glistened with the sun shining through the remaining raindrops on them. Nancy's longtime pastor, Dr. Cline, was inspiring. I did not drop her ring and at the end, we almost ran down the aisle. The reception was beautiful with large punch bowls and all the wedding food. We went to Nancy's house to change clothes and hopefully make our escape for our honeymoon in an undecorated car. My 1956 Chevrolet convertible was hidden in the garage of her neighbor, Col. Clyde McClure, whose first wife was one of Nancy's paternal aunts. We had packed all our wedding gifts and other things the day before. We escaped with only loud blowing of car horns and made our way to a hotel in Clemson, South Carolina, where we had a reservation.

As we walked into the dining room for our dinner, we saw a couple who had attended our wedding, friends of my parents. We said, "Hello" and ate our dinner. When I asked for the check, the waiter told me those friends had paid the bill.

Sunday morning, we began our circuitous route to Baton Rouge. Our first stop was at Ridgecrest, a favorite place of mine. We attended the staff worship, greeted Mom and Dad Weeks, managers of the conference center when I was on staff. After lunch, we made our way east in North Carolina and the rest of our trip included Charleston, SC. down the Atlantic Coast and along the Gulf Coast to Baton Rouge.

Life Continues

After our honeymoon, we settled in the house I had bought in 1957. It was located on the southside of the city, very near LSU. It was an easy commute to my work and church. It was a small, two-bedroom house with a window air conditioning unit in one bedroom and an attic fan. We made probably the dumbest decision of our married life before the summer was over. Hoping to keep the house cool, we had extra insulation blown into the attic. Imagine our dismay when we turned on the attic fan and discovered insulation blowing everywhere. It was a huge one month's salary mistake.

Nancy joined the church in July of 1958 when we arrived in Baton Rouge after our honeymoon. We were asked to be the leaders of the fifteen-year-old Sunday School Department, about fifty teenagers. We agreed but it was very stressful. As I began to recruit teachers and could not find enough, discouragement began to set in. Supply teachers were impossible to find and when a teacher neglected his or her duties, Nancy and I had to teach their class. This irresponsibility led me to place a high value on dependability. We resigned at the end of the church year.

The church had a Sunday School class for young married couples as well as a Training Union group. We thoroughly enjoyed the fellowship and friendship in BTU which developed. The BTU group decided to do a "mission project" in the bayous of southern Louisiana. We collected personal items like tooth brushes, tooth paste, soap, wash cloths, hair brushes and combs. We put all these things in a bag along with a New Testament. We planned a trip to an area south on the west bank on the Mississippi River. When we got there, we found a group of Cajun children and discovered none spoke any English, only Creole. It was a challenge, but we did communicate some with sign language. We played games with them, told Bible stories, and tried to show our love for them. We made two trips before Nancy's pregnancy kept her from going again. This first exposure to missions inspired our hearts and laid the foundation for our beginning to consider moving to a "pioneer area" for Southern Baptist work.

I thought it would be nice one day to take Nancy and introduce her to the lady in whose house I had rented a room. We were welcomed into her living room and after a few minutes of conversation, she excused herself. When she returned, she handed Nancy several letters Nancy had written to me in 1957. She kept them hoping I would visit her.

Neither Nancy nor I were good cooks at the time, a fact which made our meals interesting. Nancy packed a lunch for me to take to work since there was no cafeteria at the plant. After a few weeks of having the same kind of sandwich every day, I politely asked if I could have another kind some of the time. We have always laughed at this simple learning experience of the marriage relationship.

Schedules were somewhat easier after production problems at Scotts Bluff were solved. After Nancy and I married in July of 1958, usually the work schedule was a normal forty-hour week except when we put a new product into production.

Nancy applied and got a nursing job at Baton Rouge General Hospital a few weeks after arrival. She was assigned as a scrub nurse in surgery and enjoyed it. It was not long until she discovered she was pregnant with our daughter. She learned a few other scrub nurses were also pregnant. Every evening she described the emotions displayed by the surgeons when 2-3 nurses had to break scrub because of nausea, and we laughed together. The surgeons were not a happy group most days.

During the depression of 1958, Naugatuck Chemical needed to downsize some of the engineers. While I was deeply appreciative of being kept as an employee and getting a draft exemption requested by the company, I was not sure the strategy to keep me was sound since it was based on who was married or single. As Nancy and I discussed my dissatisfaction with my job, we began to talk about Southern Baptists promoting church planting in what was called the "pioneer areas." We considered what I believed was my call from God, "to be the best layman I can be in my church." Surely God would give me a job in an area where there was a new church start we could join and pour our lives into helping it grow.

As the months passed, I became more and more dissatisfied with my employer. Company management was reluctant to make changes and made many poor decisions. It appeared they made indiscriminate cutbacks in personnel causing some of us to be unable to adequately cover our responsibilities. I began to investigate other job possibilities.

Because I had taken one course for Master's Degree work in Chemical Engineering at LSU in the spring, I got two season tickets for LSU football in the fall of 1958 for $30.00. It was a great season because it was the year Billy Cannon was an All-American. Nancy often commented about missing a lot of the game because she would drop off to sleep at the game because she was pregnant.

While I was taking this course, Nelson was also in the class. I had a paper to present and since I had to work, I asked Nelson to turn my paper into the professor. When I failed the course, I asked the professor why and he told me he never received my paper. Later, I found my paper under the seat of Nelson's car. I was very hurt but never told Nelson.

Sally Is Born

Nancy worked until two months before Sarah Sue Jones was born on April 25, 1959. Sarah Sue was named for her two grandmothers. We knew there would be jealousy if we called her either name. We began calling her Sally. Today, we always know when people became acquainted with her. If before college, she is "Sally." After college, she is "Sarah."

Nancy's Aunt Charlotte came to Baton Rouge to help with the new baby since both grandmothers were teaching school and could not get away. She was a huge help and we were deeply appreciative. After school was out, the grandmothers came to help.

In early 1959, we began to talk about our future and prayed about a new location where we could make a Christian impact on others. Since I was feeling the need to seek a new job, Nancy and I began discussing the issue as we awaited the birth of our daughter in April. As we discussed location, we considered the emphasis the Home Mission Board of Southern Baptist had on church planting in "pioneer areas." This became a major factor in our future location.

The week our daughter was born in April 1959, I was responsible for monitoring the polymerization progress of a new rubber product we were manufacturing for the first time. The quality control lab called me every hour I was not in the plant. Between these phone calls and our baby waking up during the night to be fed, we were exhausted. The next week, I broke my thumb playing softball and upset Nancy because I could not change diapers.

We sang in the adult choir and enjoyed it very much. Our first anniversary was on a Sunday, July 12, 1959. When Dr. Palmer finished his sermon and the invitation, the organist began playing the wedding march and J.O. Terry and Mabelee walked down the aisle and were married. They served with the International Mission Board for many years.

In my job search, I discovered Marbon Chemicals, a Division of Borg Warner Corp., located just south of Parkersburg, West Virginia. As we prayed, a job offer came, and we decided to accept the job and move north to either start or help strengthen a new church start. When we contacted the Home Mission Board and asked about churches in West Virginia, we learned John

Snedden had just been sent to the state as the first SBC home missionary there. I also learned a new church plant had started in Parkersburg the last week in July. So, I accepted the job and we made plans to move. Nancy visited with me and we found a house and community we truly liked in Belpre, Ohio, just across the Ohio River.

I resigned from Naugatuck effective September 1, 1959.

Chapter Six
A New Job, Another Culture

As we made plans to move to Belpre, Ohio, in late September of 1959, I helped Nancy with the chores in the house and taking care of our new baby. My dad usually washed all the dishes and I followed his example in our marriage relationship. Dad would help washing dishes when we went to the large family gatherings for holidays. He would comment on our way home that certain cooks found a way to use every dish, pot and pan in the kitchen preparing the meals. This comment is an example of his teasing.

We drove from Baton Rouge to Parkersburg at the end of August, spending a night in Atlanta and another in Toccoa. The three of us left for Parkersburg, West Virginia, early the next morning. Interstate highways had not been built between Atlanta and Parkersburg yet. The two-lane highway from Toccoa through Greenville, South Carolina, was very familiar since I had travelled it many times with my parents when we went to visit my Dad's family. US-25 to Ashville, a beautiful drive, was easy but as we began the route through the North Carolina and East Tennessee mountains, it became very crooked. I remembered a story my Aunt Mae had told about a bus trip to Martin from Erwin, Tennessee, where she lived. It was during the winter and there was snow on the road. The Greyhound Bus was slipping and sliding as it descended the mountain road toward Ashville and she was very nervous. She said to the bus driver, "Mister, if you will stop this bus, I will get off and walk." He replied: "Lady, if I could stop it, I would get off with you."

When we reached Bristol, Tennessee, we followed US-19 through the Virginia valley between two mountain ranges. After all the curves on the mountain road in East Tennessee, this reasonably straight road was a welcome sight. But then, we arrived at Bluefield, West Virginia, to turn onto the West Virginia Turnpike, a serious misnomer. The "turnpike" was two or three lanes, but the curves were not as extremely sharp as those previously traveled that day. When we arrived at the last of three "rest stops" between Bluefield and Charleston, dark was nearing. We made a brief rest stop, getting gasoline and food and continued to the end of the "turnpike" south of Charleston. The highway we joined passed between the West Virginia Capital Building and the Kanawa River. The building was brightly lit and a beautiful sight. Soon, the very dark twisty West Virginia Highway #21 began taking us through Ripley to Parkersburg. We finally found the Holiday Inn on US-50 highway east of Parkersburg and promptly collapsed in the welcomed bed at midnight, an almost twenty-hour trip. I was destined to live in this room for the entire month of September.

The realtor, a Mormon, was very nice and showed us several houses in Parkersburg, Vienna, and Belpre. We chose one in a new sub-division on a corner lot in Belpre. It had three bedrooms, one and a half bathrooms, a living/dining room with a mural on one wall, a great room with a fireplace, and a full basement. A covered breezeway connected it to a two-car garage which we had screened later. It seemed huge after our tiny two-bedroom house in Baton Rouge, but its 1,350 square feet was also small by today's American house standards. Nancy and Sally flew back to Baton Rouge and finalized moving arrangements. Marbon covered all our moving costs and Nancy and Sally flew to Parkersburg after the packers left Baton Rouge. The Straceners kept the two of them and carried them to the airport for their journey.

I had accepted the research chemist position at Marbon to begin my new job September 1, 1959. John Snedden, the new missionary in West Virginia, told me a new church plant had started in Parkersburg on July 26th. First Baptist Church in Athens, Ohio, had agreed to be the sponsoring church.

I learned the location of this new "chapel" in the Labor Union Hall in Parkersburg and attended the first Sunday in September. I found three families and a lay bi-vocational pastor sweeping beer cans and cigarette butts out of the meeting room. This environment was a serious transition for me since I had previously been a member of two churches: First Baptist Atlanta and First Baptist Baton Rouge, each with more than 3,000 members. The small group had decided to give 10% of the Sunday's offerings to the Cooperative Program. After worship, one of the families invited me to their home for dinner. Sargeant Jack Donaho was the local Air Force recruiter and I joined Alma, their teen age daughter Karen, and Jack at their table. As soon as Jack finished the blessing for the food, he raised his head and said, "Do not eat too much, I cannot afford it." This visit began a close friendship which lasted many years. The next Sunday, I was told they had bought a play pen for our infant daughter. I am sure God told them my family was there to stay.

Marbon also made ABS plastics so there was a concern by Naugatuck management about my working for a competitor. They were assured I would work on products for different applications. Marbon's research director talked with the management in Baton Rouge and assured them my activities would be with blending resins for PVC which did not compete with any of their products. I soon discovered that the manufacturing processes had no similarity.

When I joined the company, we had two chemists doing applied product research on polymerization products and a blending lab where studies were made converting resins into final plastic products. The key researcher in the blending lab was a Polish engineer who was brilliant, having over a dozen patents. His desk was always piled high with papers and technical journals, and I was amazed every day at how he could reach into a pile and select exactly what he was seeking.

As we began to get settled from our move in October, we met some of the Belpre neighbors and Nancy met people who were attending the new church start in Parkersburg. The church folks planned a Thanksgiving celebration at a restaurant in Belpre on US-50 highway. It was a nice event but when we left after dinner, six inches of snow covered the ground which demanded that I learn how to drive in it. This valuable lesson prepared me for the muddy roads in Kenya. Growing up in Atlanta I only remember one snowfall which was in 1940 and about eight inches. One night, I went outside in the Baton Rouge plant to see a very few tiny flurries. We had lots of snow during our time in Belpre. Our driveway was concrete to the asphalt road except for about eight feet which was gravel. Invariably, when the snow plow came on our road, snow was piled in this area and I often got stuck in my driveway.

As we became acquainted with the Appalachian people, we knew the language was different from the deep south. I discovered a "clothes press" was not an iron, but a closet. A fellow church member who had moved from Texas went to the grocery store one day and wanted to buy some turnip greens. She found turnips which still had the greens attached so she asked a store employee for some. When he cut the greens from the turnips, he began throwing them in the trash. She told him she wanted the greens, so he gave her all she wanted at no charge. The population of Parkersburg was 98% white and I discovered quickly there was more prejudice against black people there than in Georgia. I was surprised.

When Nancy met the research director, he had recently moved from Massachusetts. She commented about moving north and he responded, "I thought this was the South." We had a good laugh about this event. I settled into the job and enjoyed my work. I had a lab assistant who was very sharp, and the work was going well. Our product development efforts began to mature into saleable products in 1961 eliminating much frustration and we became optimistic. Our sales were growing exponenlly.

In the winter of 1960, our small congregation believed that with financial assistance available from the Home Mission Board for a fulltime pastor, we could accelerate our growth. A pulpit committee of five was chosen and I was elected chairman. We found a commercial building to rent with an accessible area on the ground floor and an apartment upstairs. We signed a twenty-six-month lease agreement and began meeting there on April 3, 1960. No more sweeping out beer cans and cigarette butts but one Sunday we did have to mop up the meeting area when the sewer backed up, a comparison that made beer cans seem desirable.

After reviewing several resumes, our pulpit committee invited Curtis Porter, who was graduating from Southwestern Baptist Theological Seminary, to visit Parkersburg in June and preach in view of a call to become pastor of Grace Baptist Chapel. God confirmed all our hearts and Curtis and Linnie moved to the upstairs apartment in the rented commercial building so that Curtis could preach his first sermon as pastor on July 2nd. On July 26, 1960, Grace Baptist Church was constituted with 26 charter members. Charles Magruder, pastor of our mother church; John Snedden, West Virginia Baptist missionary, and Ray Roberts, Executive Director of the Baptist Convention in Ohio led this service. The charter members voted to affiliate with the Pioneer Baptist Association and the Baptist Convention in Ohio. In November, a new association, Upper Ohio Valley, was organized and we voted to join this wide-spread association. Grace Baptist was the most southern church and the most northern was in Pittsburg, Pennsylvania. Churches on both sides of the Ohio River were members.

On October 3, 1960, Grace Baptist had a scheduled deacon meeting in the evening for the three deacons with the pastor. About 6:00 pm, Nancy went into labor with our second child, Tom Jr. I called Pastor Curtis and told him I would miss the meeting. He replied he would get Garry Biggers and Jack Donaho, and they would come to the hospital and where we could meet while I waited for Nancy to deliver. The four of us gathered on a stairwell landing and held deacons meeting in St. Josephs Catholic Hospital. To my knowledge, it has been the only Baptist deacons meeting ever held at a Catholic Hospital. Tom Jr. arrived just before midnight.

When Tommy was about three months old, Nancy left both kids with me one evening to go somewhere with other women. I had the playpen near the fireplace in the family room to keep him warm. Sally was not quite two years old and wanted to see her baby brother up close. She stood on the base of the playpen and leaned over the rail to get a closer view. Suddenly, she leaned too far and fell into the playpen on top of her baby brother. I was scared to death and my first thought was that Nancy would never let me take care of the kids alone again. Thankfully, he was not injured.

In April 1961, Grace Baptist voted to purchase a piece of property on Rosemar Road near the Route 2 intersection. It would become a very strategic location. Ten men in the congregation agreed to co-sign a $30,000 loan. This amount was a real step of faith for me because my commitment was about 40% of my annual income. I struggled with the decision because my dad had counseled me to never cosign a loan. A family member of his had defaulted on a loan he cosigned, and he had to make the settlement. When the purchase was finalized, the Porters moved into the house. Sunday School classes no longer had to meet in their home upstairs at the storefront building.

In the fall, Nancy and I visited my Tech BSU mentor, Glen Swicegood, in Nashville. Glen was working in the architecture department of the Sunday School Board. Glen designed a first unit plan for our church and in December the church approved this plan.

When we learned there would be a third child, we decided a convertible might not be the best vehicle for our family. We had enjoyed it very much, even going to the drive-in theater during the winter and using two car heaters. We bought a 1962 Chevrolet station wagon. Since seat belts were not a requirement in 1962, we could let the back seat down and spread blankets for the kids to sleep when taking the long trips to visit family in Georgia. That model had a luggage compartment under the floor behind the rear seat. With it and a roof rack, we could carry everything we needed.

The church held a groundbreaking ceremony on March 25, 1962, and construction began in earnest. The men of the church volunteered to do construction after our workday and we generally worked from before 6:00 pm to about 10:00 pm five days a week. Once the footers and walls were finished to floor level, we began hauling fill dirt in wheel barrows. This feat took several days because the rear of the building required about five feet of fill dirt.

For the first seven months, Nancy's third pregnancy was normal. In the eighth month, she spent three days in the hospital spotting blood. During the ninth month, she spent over half of her time in bed and did not do much except attend Sunday church services.

May 18, 1962, was like any other morning when I woke up. After rushing around bathing, shaving, and getting dressed, I was ready for the breakfast Nancy had prepared. She was nine months pregnant with our third child. Our lives were somewhat chaotic since we had been married less than four years. Sally was three years old and Tommy was seventeen months.

I vividly remember standing by the back-door kissing Nancy good-bye when suddenly she began gushing blood all over the great room floor. Panicking, we got a neighbor to care for the children and I rushed her across the Ohio River to one of the hospitals in Parkersburg, West Virginia. They carried Nancy to the ob-gyn delivery area and I began walking in circles in front of the elevator watching for Dr. Cruikshank to arrive. I had been told he was at the other hospital delivering a baby. I was more than a nervous father as I paced in circles. I was afraid both Nancy and our new baby, Andy, would not survive. As I walked and prayed, I saw her doctor rush to the elevator. When I saw Andy's birth time, it was three minutes after the doctor got on the elevator. We were later told Nancy's condition was an enlarged placenta which partially tore causing massive bleeding and requiring an emergency c-section. The bleeding required several pints of blood and later in life, it was determined one pint did not completely match so she had "funny blood." I cannot remember how many times I have thanked God for sparing both their lives. Nancy's recovery from the emergency c-section was rapid, assisted by our mothers sharing time with us for the first two months, helping take care of her.

Our church lease was due to expire on May 31st; therefore, we asked the owner for a three-month extension. He refused. We worked hard and by the end of May, we had the walls up and the roof completed. There were no windows or doors, and nothing finished inside except the slab floor. We moved into the building on May 30th and celebrated our new facility. The owner had an experience reminding me of Jonah and the gigantic fish. He was very anxious to lease the building when he refused an extension for us, but God prevented him from leasing the building for nearly three years.

We continued working on the building. One stressful day, we were trying to nail the metal lathe to the trusses for the ceiling. It was arduous work standing on the scaffold and trying to hammer vertically. The most difficult part was trying to hammer a nail through the overlap of four pieces of sheet metal lathe. Pastor Curtis was working at this task and he missed the nail and hit his fingers. When he looked at them, he had cross marks bleeding where the lathe had cut his fingers. He said what was the closest to an expletive he ever said, "Lord, Thou knowest."

In July, we voted to sponsor a new church plant in Marietta, Ohio. The pastor would go preach early Sunday evenings and return for the worship time at Grace. One Sunday, I was asked to preach there. It was my first sermon and I knew it would be short. I arrived and met the piano player, a "little old lady" who was probably in her late 50's. No one else came. Remember, I was still young in my mid-20s. She heard all my 10-minute sermon and we both went home.

Nancy was committed to the WMU organization in our church and the local association. Each month, Nancy collected Linnie Porter, Sylvia Keown, and five or more kids, depending on the year, in our 1962 Chevrolet station wagon and drove to several associational WMU meetings. Grace Baptist was the southernmost church in the association; thus, every trip went north. I am so thankful I did not have to be included in this vehicle for these trips with the noisy, little kids.

Vacation

In late August 1962, there was a Chemical Engineering Society Conference in Denver, Colorado, and Marbon wanted to send me. Since it lasted a week, Nancy and I decided to take my two-week vacation after this meeting and tour the west in our "covered wagon." We drove all night crossing Ohio, Indiana, and Illinois on US-50 to St. Louis. Following what has become I-70, we drove into Kansas and stopped at a roadside park to spend the night. Rather than pitching our tent because we were very tired, we opened the tailgate of the wagon, tucked the kids in, and Nancy and I crawled into our sleeping bags with our feet under the rear axle and our heads under the tailgate. The next day, we drove into Denver and checked into the motel where we would stay.

When the meeting was over Friday, we left Denver, drove to Estes Park and pitched our tent. It was beginning to feel cold. We dressed our kids in their snow suits, and Nancy and I crawled into our sleeping bags. The next morning, I crawled out of my bag and unzipped the tent flap. When I looked out, I was greeted with a beautiful view of three inches of snow around our tent.

When we left Estes Park, we drove to the Dinosaur National Monument Park, arriving at the camp ground in the late afternoon. When I was pitching our tent in the sandy soil, I noticed the picnic tables had a huge log chain from the bottom of the table to a large round concrete slab. After supper, we went to a meeting where the park ranger talked about the history of the area. It was very interesting and when he was finished, I asked him about the reason for the log chain, "Do people steal the tables?"

"No," he replied. "They are to keep the tables from blowing away. We get a lot of wind here." I had visions of being blown across the Colorado-Utah line during the night.

The next day, we drove to Salt Lake City, visited the Mormon Tabernacle and took a route toward eastern Oregon, following the Columbia River to

Portland. When we left Portland, we drove to Seaside, put our toes in the Pacific Ocean and froze them off. Then, we continued to Seattle and stayed in a motel. Nancy had told me before we left Belpre, it was ok to tent camp if we stayed in a motel every third or fourth night to take a hot bath. The next day, we went to visit the brand-new Space Needle. After a full day of walking around with the three kids, we were exhausted even with Andy in a stroller. We started back to where we had parked our car and could not find it. I wandered around nearly an hour before we could get in the car and collapse.

We left Seattle, drove to Spokane, and stopped at a campground. It was very cold when we arrived after dark. We decided to bundle up and sleep in the car rather than pitch our tent. The next morning as we left we discovered the temperature was ten degrees when we headed to Yellowstone.

In West Yellowstone, we found a beautiful log cabin with three bedrooms and a fireplace. We were amazed that the cost was only $7.00 per night since it was the end of the season. We spent two nights there driving through the park during the day. Old Faithful was an amazing sight. We saw many animals including bears and elk.

We left Yellowstone, drove across Wyoming into South Dakota, stopping by Mount Rushmore. As we were approaching the mountain on a narrow two-lane road, we saw a sign saying, "Divided Highway Ahead" and came to a separation of the two narrow lanes where a huge tree was located between them. We laughed a lot about this "major divided highway." We spent the next night at Mitchell, South Dakota. We did not sleep much in Mitchell because there were millions and millions of mosquitos. After this stop, we travelled to the south side of Chicago, through Fort Wayne, Columbus and on home in Belpre. It was a wonderful twenty-four-day trip of over 8,000 miles and a very memorable vacation. It was not easy traveling with three children between three years and four months, but it was well worth it.

Life Continues

The following year was very hard when a co-lead was promoted to be my supervisor. We had the same level of experience, but I considered him to have a closed mind and a negative controlling personality. I believe these characteristics make research work very difficult.

Because one of Nancy's spiritual gifts was hospitality, we had many prayer meetings, socials, and even a Loyalty Banquet in our home when the congregation was small. We also kept most of the visiting pastors and church guests in our home. We considered it a privileged ministry. She became close with church members, most of who were transplanted Southern Baptists in the early days. People in our neighborhood represented a different culture than our heritage. In time, she made friends with neighbors but never as close as our church friends.

During the period of 1963-64, Nancy was active in church and the social life of our community. She was in a community bridge club and we often had bridge parties in our home. She was committed to taking care of our three kids but longed to also have an opportunity to keep up her nursing skills. Dr. Nichols, a local doctor in Belpre, hired her to work two evenings a week and I kept the kids. He closed his office in June of 1964 and moved. The gossip was that he had an affair with a day nurse and got a divorce.

Our technical department was reorganized, and I was promoted to Senior Research Chemist and then to Group Leader within three months. We designed and built a new research lab. I was given responsibility for two chemists and a few lab techs. Soon, we hired a Ph.D. chemist for my group and added another technician. When one of the chemist's work performance did not improve in two years, I had to terminate her. Her episode of crying when given this news was difficult for me. Marbon had a policy with which I wholeheartedly agreed. The terminated employee was escorted out of the building and paid her notice without working. This protects the morale of other employees.

The real beginning of maturity growth came in 1963. Marbon sent all our professional employees who were managers to Pittsburg for psychological evaluations. This process created a better understanding of my life, strengths, and weaknesses. I had minimal self-confidence and did not know how to balance it with humility, initiative, and tolerance. The counselor told me he believed I could accomplish anything I thought God wanted me to do. I began to work on fairly assessing each situation and to improving my listening skills. I became much more optimistic and less inclined to worry.

Marbon had a bowling league and I participated. As my skills improved, I moved to the company "scratch league" which was not handicapped. I was quite excited the night I bowled the high score of my life, 257. At the end of the season, I received a trophy for the highest score and my average was a respectable 185. Nancy and I also bowled in a mixed church league. One night, I noticed the pins were fuzzy, so I had my eyes checked and began to wear glasses for distance. I could still read well without glasses.

Marbon had an annual sales meeting where all the sales staff and many people representing management attended. I was asked to make a presentation at the meeting in the early 1960's to introduce two new products being developed by my research group. My fear of public speaking reared its ugly head again as I worked on the presentation. All the visual tools we use today like Power Point or videos did not exist. Somehow, with a lot of prayer and God's help, I squeaked through this presentation. It was well received and gave me a boost of confidence for future speaking opportunities.

I knew Nancy was struggling with life and trying to carry a lot of the family burden. I did not realize completely how she felt until I recently read her life history for the mission board. She wrote, "Being a dutiful wife and owning a house were the only things that kept me from begging Tom to leave Marbon and let us go back south. . . The lack of a close friend to share problems with and being far away from family and home drew Tom and me closer together, and I had to depend on him for counsel and help."

Church Changes

In May, 1964, Curtis Porter resigned as pastor to accept a call from a church in the Buffalo, New York area. I was the current chairman of deacons and was chosen again as chairman of the pastor search committee. Our committee found supply preachers, usually Ray Roberts from Ohio, John Snedden from West Virginia, or an associational missionary. Ray Roberts was scheduled to preach in October and when the time for him to preach arrived, he was not there and had not been seen. I prayed, "God, he is not here so help me share something." I opened my Bible to Isaiah 6 and read about Isaiah's call and prayed. As I finished praying, Ray walked down the aisle and preached a wonderful sermon using this text. God does answer prayers made in a panic. Dr. Roberts had forgotten it was the day to change from daylight savings time.

Before Curtis left for New York, he talked with John Snedden about his position on the West Virginia Missions Committee. This group was formed because churches physically in West Virginia were members of four different state conventions: Virginia, Maryland, Ohio, and Kentucky. This strategy group was to draw all West Virginia churches into a fellowship, so that a West Virginia convention could be organized at some future date. John asked me to serve and I think I was the only lay-person on the committee. I made a lot of friends with the pastors and, looking back, I believe this experience was bonus training for developing relationships with seminary trained missionaries.

The church authorized me to lead baptisms until we had a new pastor.

I remember my first people to baptize were a young couple, Alvie and Ann Edwards. After a few years, God called him to preach and he was a pastor in West Virginia for many years.

The church was without a pastor for thirteen months. I believe God prevented us from having a new pastor until members gave up an attitude of being pastor oriented rather than focusing on God. Membership had left ministry details to the pastor and Curtis had become burdened with tasks which should have been done by members. During this period, we had issued a call to a man we thought God was calling to become our pastor. When he did not give an answer for three months, we withdrew the call and later found out he was also called by another church at the same time and was using both churches. I considered his behavior highly unethical.

In 1964, other professionals and I interviewed a potential new boss and he was hired. He was very theoretical and did not understand product development processes. He was an autocratic leader and since my belief was that decisions should be made at the lowest competent level, we had many disagreements.

The skill of assessing the capabilities of professional people developed in 1965 when other organization leaders and I interviewed nearly one hundred potential employees, including a number with a Ph.D. in chemistry. We had four or more managers interview each candidate during a one-day visit.

In 1965, Nancy recognized for the first time that she enjoyed living in Belpre and did not want to leave. She was active in church and living a good Christian life, but she did not believe her Lord was satisfied with her. She prayed, however, and God answered her prayer through Keith Oliphint. We saw Keith at associational meetings and knew he was pastoring in Ohio to get the two-year church staff experience required by the Foreign Mission Board for appointment. He came to Grace Baptist to preach a week's revival and stayed in our home. Nancy talked a lot with Keith while I was working, and he perceived she "needed to get right with God." He asked her if she thought she was called to be a missionary. She admitted feeling a call in her youth but now felt her mission field was in Parkersburg and "she had not really done that." I did not know about this spiritual struggle until much later.

In June 1965, Grace Baptist called Jerry Brock to be our new pastor. He and Margaret were socially compatible with members and Jerry was very evangelistic. One year while he was pastor, Grace baptized 104 people, almost doubling the size of the congregation.

For several months, Nancy openly dreaded turning thirty in September.

I called the bakery to order a birthday cake. When they started to take the order, I asked if they could decorate it with black roses and write "In sympathy for thirty years." The lady reluctantly said they could and asked my name. When I said Tom Jones, she almost hung up the phone, but I convinced her I was a legitimate person. On her birthday, I collected the cake and took it to Bob Stemple's house. The Stemples were our neighbors across the street. I asked them to bring it over later. At the appointed time, Nancy opened the kitchen door and looked through the storm door glass. All she could see was the cake on an extended arm. When Bob and Mert Stemple entered, Bob said he was afraid Nancy would hit him. She said she never lived down this response and all of us were waiting to see her reaction when she became forty. I was not disappointed when she turned forty with grace.

We did a lot of door to door visitation. During one visit. I knocked on the door and when the lady answered, I explained who I was and invited her family to visit Grace Baptist. She thanked me, and I started walking to the house next door. Before I could get to the sidewalk, she ran after me and asked for more information. She said, "No one has visited me before to invite me to church." She and her husband started coming to our church. She worked at the local TV station and the next Christmas in 1966, she asked me as Choir Director to bring the choir to the TV studio to record our Christmas choir presentation for broadcast.

Because the church was growing so rapidly, a Young Adult Women's Sunday School class was formed, and Nancy was elected the teacher. She studied hard and I know she was an excellent teacher because the young ladies showed signs of a maturing faith.

Andy was always an adventurous child. He always "pushed the envelope" and tried a lot of new things. A major challenge occurred when he was about three years old. He wanted to see if he could climb on our swing set in the backyard and transverse from one end to the other, about seven feet above the ground. One Saturday, he was making satisfactory progress when the chain supporting one swing got in his way and he fell, hitting his arm against the swing seat. He cried for a while but settled down and seemed ok. Nurse Nancy noticed a little dent in his arm and decided she would ask our pediatrician when Sally had an appointment on Monday. We learned that he had a greenstick fracture of his arm and the doctor put a cast on it.

Marbon had a Christmas party for all the employees' children every year. Nancy and I always laughingly asked, "How long do you think the boy's toys will survive this year before they are broken?" On more than one year, the boy's toys were broken in less than a week. Ladders which could be raised on fire trucks were broken off the truck. One year, Andy was standing on the basement stairs and looked up to see a small toy car thrown at him by his brother. The impact cut his lip. Sally tells the story about how she and her brothers would make up plays and Nancy and I would watch her brothers perform with her. Some really made us laugh but they also presented Bible stories.

We lived in a middle-class neighborhood in Belpre where most of the 100 lots had occupied houses on them. It was secluded since there were only two streets entering the sub-division. It was safe for the kids to play outside in several different yards. One Wednesday afternoon, Andy was playing with neighbor kids and Nancy was busy inside our house. We did not worry because the area was very safe for kids and there were many families with small children. When it was time to get the kids ready for church, Nancy called Andy. When he came to get his bath, she noticed he was clutching something in his hand. As she pried his hand open, she found the item was a small toy like we used to get from bubblegum machines. Nancy knew the only machine available was at the grocery store, a round trip well over 2.5 miles. Andy had walked down the street, gone the way we traveled to Sally's school, and from there, crossed the B&O railroad mainline. He walked to US-50 and along it about a quarter of a mile to the store. She asked Andy if he was tired and he said "Yes." After this adventure, we paid more attention to where the kids were playing, even in a safe neighborhood.

I was transferred to the production department in January 1966, partly at my own initiative. Our research group had grown dramatically and most of the group leaders had Ph.D. degrees. Since I had production experience, I was made Group Engineer in the resin section. It was a very positive change for me. The Group Manager, Mel Hoover, had worked in the pilot plant for several years. We lived in the same neighborhood in Belpre and carpooled many days. He was a Chemical Engineer from Ohio State. We made a good leadership team and had an elevated level of trust in each other. My responsibilities included supervising the process engineers, keeping and reporting production records and raw material usage, evaluating new equipment, and supervising relief unit supervisors and chemical operators.

In 1966, a technical book was published titled Macromolecular Synthesis Volume 2 published by John Wiley & Sons, Inc. This book included instructions for the preparation of thirty copolymers. Detailed instructions for the preparation of cellulose, rubber or plastics were given. Various researchers were asked to duplicate the reactions to validate duplicate results. I was the testing chemist of two processes on pages 57 to 66. I was also the coauthor of an article published in the May 1967 issue of Modern Plastics titled ABS reinforcing modifiers for PVC.

In 1966, Sally accepted Jesus as her Savior and her childlike faith encouraged us. Then, in 1967, her brother, Tom, Jr., made his decision. We prayed for Andy to recognize his need for salvation at the right time. Our family had devotions and prayed together. We had a practice of reading the Open Windows devotions every morning and prayed at the breakfast table with our children. In the evenings, we asked each child to read from their Bible as they learned to read and had a prayer time before the kids went to bed.

My job responsibilities at Marbon increased when I transferred to the production department and I had always given several hours a week to church ministry. In early 1967, management developed a cross training plan. I was temporarily assigned as Group Manager of the resin department. Mel Hoover became the acting Group Manager of the latex department. This assignment gave me responsibility for five million dollars of assets, a large operating budget, and supervision of more than 150 employees in nine resin production units. I learned there is a major difference between a staff assignment and management where total responsibility for decisions rests on your shoulders. This new assignment occurred during a hesitation in the national economy and I had many challenges. The plant manager was complementary when I finished it. During my nine years at Marbon, our annual production volume went from twenty-five million pounds of product to over a quarter of a billion, a 700% annual growth. It was the best of times.

We Are Called

Nancy and I enjoyed having guests and many people who came to Grace Baptist to preach or teach stayed in our home. During one special revival week, Keith Oliphint, pastor from St. Clairsville, Ohio, was our house guest. After services, we would sit in our family room and visit. Keith explained how God had called Peggy and him to become international missionaries. He was pastoring in Ohio because the mission board required every missionary working with churches to have at least two years of pastoral experience. When this requirement was met, Keith expected to be commissioned to become a missionary in Tanzania. I tucked this information into my memory, but God had not called me to become a foreign missionary. My calling was to be the best layman God could make out of me.

On most trips to Charleston for West Virginia Mission Committee meetings, Eucled Moore, Pastor in Moundsville, met me in Parkersburg and we travelled together to the meeting. One trip, he began to tell me about hearing from Keith Oliphint about his experiences in Tanzania and God had used this to confirm a call to Eucled and Janelle to also seek missionary service in Tanzania. Over the years, I had felt a prompting from God's Spirit that I should be a missionary. I had resisted for years because I knew I was not qualified. My call was to be the best layman I could be in a church. I was not called to preach. I decided against medical school because of my grades. I had heard the "horrow stories" from my parents about school teaching as a profession and I did not want any part of it. Missionaries were preachers, school teachers, or doctors. "Lord, I am none of these. What am I to do?" This time, I began to ask God what He was trying to tell me. Now was not the time to leave West Virginia. The blessings of God were enormous. Our church's evangelism had never been better. The state work was beginning to coalesce. As Ken Medema wrote is his song Moses; "Not me Lord."

I did not say anything to Nancy, but we made plans to attend the mission conference at Ridgecrest in the summer of 1967. During the Sunday morning service, the President of the Home Mission Board, Arthur Rutledge, was preaching. When he gave the invitation for people called to be missionaries, I told Nancy I was not trained to be a missionary but felt God was asking me to surrender. She said, "God called me when I was a teenager to become a missionary nurse," something she had never told me. After we walked the aisle together, we found Jess Fletcher of the Foreign Mission Board. Jess told us after we explained our background that the board had just started sending missionaries to carry the business responsibilities to free other missionaries from this task and allowing them to concentrate on the use of their skills and training. Nancy and I made our decision to give our lives to international mission service. We began the process of seeking approval to be missionaries.

When we began our discussions with the Foreign Mission Board at Ridgecrest, Jess Fletcher advised that my assignment would be in business management. After we returned home to Belpre, Nancy and I began to discuss actions we would need to take in preparation for missionary service. As we talked, it became obvious I should have some training in accounting. I suspected this skill would be invaluable for handling any business affairs for missionaries. I had been told the assignment was a support ministry designed to free missionary time from these routine tasks.

As I investigated opportunities for study, I learned Marietta College, about 20 miles from our home, offered accounting in evening classes. I registered, began night classes in September and finished two courses the following May.

During one of the trips home from class, I came face to face with God's protective grace. The Ohio River begins in Pittsburg where the confluence of the Allegheny and Monongahela rivers occurs. It flows southwestward to merge with the Mississippi River at Cairo, Illinois. As the transportation system developed in the United States, a large volume of river traffic emerged. Because of the need to transport coal via large barges from mines in West Virginia and Kentucky and because of two major floods, the federal government built a system of river locks in 1937.

Highways parallel the river between Marietta and Belpre on the Ohio side and Williamson and Parkersburg on the West Virginia side. During some spring thaw periods, these highways can be submerged by flood waters. Parkersburg has a flood wall around its perimeter and large gates are closed when the river reaches a certain flood stage. The normal pool level near the lock close to Belpre is sixteen feet.

While we lived in Belpre, there were two floods which submerged downtown Belpre, closing the bridge across the river into downtown Parkersburg. During these floods, I had to cross the toll bridge north of Belpre on higher ground. The highest flood we saw was fifty-three feet, a few feet short of breaching the flood wall for Parkersburg In Marietta, a downtown hotel had dinner and a movie many Friday nights. On special occasions, Nancy and I would get a babysitter and go there for a nice dinner. The hotel entrance was about ten steps above the sidewalk and in the dining room, there was a mark on the wall about fifteen feet above the floor. This mark identified the water level for the 1937 flood.

One spring school night, I had driven to Marietta along the river highway. As I was returning home, I suddenly drove into flood waters. By the time I was completely stopped, the water level was almost entering the car. God protected me because I backed out of the water before it plugged the exhaust pipe and drowned the engine. I went back to Marietta and took a country road into Ohio, safely making my way home. I never told Nancy about this stupid thing I had done.

As the strategy emerged in the West Virginia Missions Committee, I was elected as the Vice Chairman, responsible for the budget. We developed a unified budget of both internal gifts and external support. During the year, the committee did a lot of soul searching. We desperately wanted a state convention to unify our churches physically located in West Virginia but did not meet the criteria of fifty churches required by the Home Mission Board. After many hours of prayer and discussions, we made plans to organize a general association. This strategy was implemented, and I was elected to the Executive Committee. In early 1967 when the association's President and Vice President resigned, one to a new pastorate outside West Virginia and Eucled Moore to international missions, I was elected as President to complete the term and was re-elected during the October, 1967, annual meeting at Grace Baptist Church. This office required meeting on a more frequent basis and some travel.

After we went to the Missions Week at Ridgecrest in June of 1967, the paperwork for our applications for the Foreign Mission Board consumed hours of discussion and typing where I still used a hunt and peck system of four fingers. After meeting Jess Fletcher at Ridgecrest, we sent a letter asking for more information. He passed us to Bill Marshall, the regional personnel consultant, beginning a personal relationship which we cherished. I was intrigued that our first letter from him was written on our ninth anniversary. After Bill left the FMB and became the Executive for the Kentucky Baptist Convention, he came to Kenya during our partnership.

From July, 1967, to March, 1968, many evenings were spent on this process until we had completed the paperwork necessary for approval. The process began with a preliminary information form and continued through frequent correspondence and additional information requests. The next form was a seven-page application requiring paragraphs of explanations about our aim for our missionary service, our Christian message, a sketch of our life histories, any relationships with people of other cultures, religions, or national backgrounds, and acceptance of conditions of missionary life. A twenty-five-page life history was required from each of us. As I wrote Bill Marshall, this rewarding six-week process "helped me understand my self-better. I also came to realize that anyone who completed the task was called to be a missionary or he would quit."

We always felt God calling us to somewhere in Africa. When we started the process, requests for business managers were available for three countries in Asia, two in South America, and one in West Africa. It turned out the Ghana one was for a missionary associate, not a career position. Bill Marshall had written that this temporary status should not be a concern since the missionary confirmation process would take two years and since new job requests arrived from the field frequently.

In mid-November, we wrote long letters to our mothers telling them we were working through the process to become missionaries. I am sure their first thought when they read their letter was "You are taking our grandchildren where?"

The next step for us was to supply references in certain categories of our relationships totaling twenty-five each. Two additional personal information forms quickly followed, each covering distinct categories of questions. Between these two forms, we made a trip to Richmond just before Christmas of 1967. While we were there, we had the opportunity to meet with several people including Dr. Goerner who was Leader for Africa, Jess Fletcher, and Bill Marshall.

During our discussion with Dr. Goerner, he shared that there were two requests in Africa: a Hospital Administrator in Ogbomosho, Nigeria and Business Manager for East Africa based in Nairobi. The Nigeria position had the highest priority, but East Africa was more attractive to us.

We had driven to Atlanta during the Christmas Holiday and flew to Richmond while our mothers cared for our kids. On the return flight, we could not discuss anything. The Piedmont Airline plane was small, there was severe weather, and we fought air-sickness. There was a stop in Ashville, NC, where I took a Dramamine. When we arrived in Atlanta, I was very "loopy" and staggered through the airport. In the terminal, we looked at the schedule message board and it said the flight from Ashville had been cancelled. Of the countless flights I have taken, this one was the worst.

Nancy and I began an intense time of talking and praying about the choice before us. It was obvious Nigeria had the highest priority and gave Nancy a long-term opportunity to use her nursing skills. We recognized it would be a 24/7 job and very stressful. East Africa was the place we had missionary friends. "Lord, how do we choose?"

As we struggled about this important, lifetime decision, I wrote Bill Marshall the following about East Africa:

1. The Nairobi assignment would not be so confining and would give opportunity to work with churches much more.
2. The work is much newer and would give many chances to minister by using unique approaches.
3. The language would be easier to learn. For some reason, I have felt from the beginning that Swahili would be the language I would learn.
4. The long-range contributions are probably greater.

We still were not sure. Did we fill the greatest need or are our friendships with the Oliphints and Moores clouding our minds? After many hours of seeking God's answer, we chose East Africa and had peace.

As we discussed the position of business manager with Dr. Goerner, he said, "Tom, it may just be that after you have been on the field a couple of years, the mission may ask you to be the treasurer." Little did he know that it would take three weeks!

We made another trip to Richmond in February for medical exams including psychiatric and physical exams. Our pediatrician in Parkersburg had done exams on the children. After we had finished all the paper work including medical, we were notified in mid-March that we had been approved by the Trustee Committee for appointment, subject to acquiring the required seminary studies. In April, Grace Baptist recommended us for seminary studies at Southern Seminary and on May 22nd, I was ordained to the ministry at Grace Baptist. Dr. Ray Roberts preached my ordination sermon from (you guessed it) Isaiah 6.

When we received approval for appointment in March, 1968, I approached Bob Hoye, the plant manager, about a leave of absence. He was gracious to approve it. During our conversation, he reached into his desk drawer and took out an organization chart. He said, "Well, I need to tear this up and start over." I assumed he had plans for a promotion for me, but I never learned what it was. I also never looked back because I knew God had called Nancy and me to Africa. All three kids attended Stone Elementary School beginning with kindergarten. It was a short walk, just over one-half mile. They seemed to enjoy it and attended until we moved to Louisville in June, 1968.

Chapter Seven
Training and Transition

When we received tentative approval from the Foreign Mission Board for appointment, we made application to Southern Baptist Theological Seminary to complete the required study for appointment. In our case, since we would not be appointed as church workers, a Masters' Degree was not required. Only twenty-four hours were necessary for me, and Nancy needed a few. I was required to take the Graduate Record Exam and I made 70% on verbal skills and 95% on math skills.

We made plans to move to Louisville on Memorial Day weekend and were assigned an apartment in Seminary Village. The only size available was M-1, a one-bedroom apartment with a sleeper sofa in the living room. We were told we could get a two bedroom one in September. The Mission Board gave a scholarship of $375.00 per month for our studies. If we were not appointed, it would become a loan and would have to be repaid. It was a financial stretch since the total of our mortgage payment for the Belpre house, our car loan, and seminary apartment rent exceeded this amount. Fortunately, we had accumulated savings which would tide us over for a while.

We loaded our Volkswagen bus and a trailer and began our trip from Belpre to Louisville during the Memorial Day weekend. Nancy had two of the kids with her in our Volkswagen Bug and I had one with me in the bus. When we arrived in Huntington, the rear bumper was broken off by the trailer I was towing. After repairs, we continued and arrived at the seminary housing office at dark. I stopped to get the key to our apartment and when I tried to crank the bus, it would not start. Nancy in the bus and I in the Bug pushed the bus and trailer up the hill with the Bug. Did you think a Bug has no power? We unloaded enough for the night and finished the next day.

Our mothers came to visit a few days after we arrived and the seven of us crowded into this one-bedroom unit. All I remember is that we survived the crowding.

We met several missionaries during the summer. Jim and Jenny Musen left in August to attend missionary orientation at Ridgecrest before going to Kenya for their first term. The Paul Millers, music missionaries from

Nigeria, were there for graduate studies, and we moved into the M-10 apartment vacated by Dr. Osadolor Imasogie who became the first African President of the seminary in Nigeria. The summer schedule had two "J" terms. Classes were two hours every day for four weeks, so I earned credit for eight hours during the summer. My first class at 8:00 a.m. in June was taught by Dr. Dale Moody. He wanted to teach this course on Romans because he was preparing to write the commentary for this NT book in The Broadman Bible Commentary published in 1970.

Dr. Moody entered the class the first day and the only notes he used the entire term were from the Greek New Testament. He proceeded to lose me since a major part of his vocabulary was theological words I had never heard as a layman in the churches I attended. This was the most challenging course I had of the 26 hours I completed. I did manage to get a C+ grade. Other courses during the summer were History of Baptists, Hosea, Amos, and Leadership Recruitment and Training. We joined St. Matthews Baptist Church because the pastor, Al MacEachern, had been a pastor in Huntington, West Virginia, and I knew him quite well.

During August, we agreed to a sales contract on our house; therefore, we went to Ohio and moved our furniture to Georgia. I am sure we looked like the Beverly Hillbillies as we traveled those mountain roads. There were few Interstate highways and the West Virginia Turnpike was mostly two lanes. While we were in Belpre, we sold our VW Bug to Frank Arnold, a friend and fellow deacon in Grace Baptist. I felt very bad when the engine froze a few weeks later, but Frank was kind and did not let me help pay for the repairs.

In the fall, we returned from seminary to attend the General Association meeting to complete my term as President. I recognized the challenges of pastors in West Virginia. Most of the churches were new church plants and were very small. Even with some support from the Home Mission Board, most pastors were struggling financially with a small income. Since many were discouraged, I prepared a message of encouragement focusing on God's provision of their needs since He had called them to this location to serve. When I completed my President's message, God led me to give an invitation, a call which is very unusual at association meetings. God's Holy Spirit penetrated hearts of many pastors and nearly fifty people attending this service made renewal commitments to God. They had been discouraged about difficulties for their families, living conditions, financial support, or poor response. God did a miracle in their hearts that day.

Since there was no set curriculum for missionary candidates who required 24 hours, I opted to choose a wide variety of courses during the fall term. I took survey of the Old and New Testaments, Religious Education, Missions, and bassoon playing in the Seminary Orchestra.

Dr. Bryan Hicks was our mission professor for the two mission courses Nancy and I took. He had taught at a theological school in the Philippines and was very interesting. We heard current mission strategy concepts as well as entertaining stories. His description of one delicacy in the Philippines, a half-grown chick embryo with forming feathers which was swallowed whole, made me wonder what kind of food I would face in Africa. He was a big, very bald man and an avid baseball player lovingly called "Mr. Clean." He told one story about a game where the score was tied in a late inning when he came to bat. He said he was determined to "hit it out of the park." He took mighty swings on the first two pitches and missed. As the third pitch was coming, he heard a kid behind him yell, "Hit it, God." Of course, he struck out.

Nancy and I bought bicycles, so that we could ride to class to save on automobile expenses as well as get some exercise. We rode to class every day from our M-10 apartment in seminary village in the campus. There was a railroad nearby where one train blew its whistle as it passed. Usually we did not hear this noise in the night. One Saturday morning, I was lying on our sofa bed watching television. The sofa began to vibrate, and I commented to Nancy that I did not remember the train shaking the apartment like this. Later, we learned there had been a small earthquake. During the Christmas holiday, we travelled to Georgia to spend time with our families: our mothers, uncles and aunts, and several cousins. It was a good, relaxing period. We headed back to Louisville on a cold wintry night before New Year's Day. About fifty miles from Louisville, the engine on the bus stopped a mile from an exit on I-75. I walked to a service station at the next exit and called Bill Lawman, a seminary student in Church Music. Bill and Glenda had been members at Grace Baptist and started seminary studies in the fall. Bill and Glenda's father came and towed the bus to Louisville. As we said goodbye and I shook the hand of Glenda's father, I felt something in my hand. When I got inside our apartment and looked, it was a $100.00 bill, a real blessing from God, a fact that was confirmed when I got the repair bill for the bus. The bill totaled $99.00.

We completed all the required studies except final exams and went to Richmond the first week of December, culminating with our appointment on December 5, 1968, at the Foreign Mission Board building. We gave testimonies and I shared about my discussion with God about His call since I was not a preacher, teacher, or doctor. Then I said, "I got over that." Apparently, this struck a chord with one lady. As she came through the receiving line during the meet and greet refreshment time, she shook my hand and said, "I am so glad they finally appointed a funny missionary."

After final exams in January, we moved to Ridgecrest Baptist Conference Center in Ridgecrest, North Carolina, for 15 weeks of missionary orientation. We were given adjoining bedrooms on the third floor in Rhododendron Hall for the two boys, Nancy, and me. Sally shared a room with another missionary kid (mk) down the hall.

For many years, the Foreign Mission Board had provided limited training before sending new missionaries to the field to learn language and begin their ministry. In the fall of 1967, new missionaries were given a new plan for training to begin cultural learning and skills to live in community. A contract agreement was made with the Ridgecrest Baptist Assembly to house and feed new missionary families for up to four months while they received this training. Children attended public school at Black Mountain Primary since missionaries were not appointed who had children over twelve years of age. Nancy and I were in the fourth and last group to attend this program at Ridgecrest. Our kids were in the first, second, and fourth grades at Black Mountain Primary from mid-January until early May. Beginning with the next session, training was done at Callaway Gardens in Pine Mountain, Georgia, and later a new training center was built near Richmond, Virginia, donated by individual Baptists who loved missions and missionaries.

Over one hundred missionaries with lots of children arrived to begin our training. Nancy and I had met a few who were appointed in the same service with us. As we began to get acquainted with others, we awoke the first Saturday morning to an eighteen-inch snowfall. The interstate highway in front of the property, I-40, was filled with eighteen-wheel trucks who could not make the climb to the top of the hill before the highway descended over twelve hundred feet to Old Fort, North Carolina. During the next two months, there were several snowfalls and missionaries and kids alike enjoyed sledding and playing in the snow. There were a few "near misses" with the sleds. One night I was sledding down the hill from Nibble Nook and missed the turn, hitting the side of the auditorium. Tom Jr. tried a different route and missed the bridge across the creek running under the dining hall and plowed into the stone bank of the creek. On many snow days, the kids had no school and there was no plan for activiities for them.

There were many aspects of our program of study. David and Susie Lockhard were the directors of the program and led some of the training sessions. They arranged for many other teachers to assist in our training. We were given several study assignments, participated in some group dynamic activities, prepared a paper about our target country, introduced to language learning, and given many other opportunities for learning.

One of the exercises in group relationships involved wives and husbands being put in separate groups. Small groups of about eight were established and we had various scenarios to do role play. During one session a man in our group became very aggressive and spoke very loudly. As stress increased in this session, one of the wives, Pat Herndon, also from Georgia, slid her chair so that she could be closer to me. She felt very threatened. It was a good learning experience.

One of the measuring tools was a language learning aptitude evaluation. As I have written, language learning was not a God-given gift for me. A lot of terms used in linguistics were just as strange as the theological vocabulary Dr. Moody used in my seminary class on Romans. I had problems making the sounds expected. I knew there would be a challenge when I did the language learning evaluation, but I tried my best and submitted my results. A few days later, David Lockhard called me in to give me the results. He said, "Tom, you made the lowest score I have ever seen for this evaluation." This observation was not a shock to me. I was just surprised that I held this record. We had learned a little about the Swahili language which we needed to speak, and I thanked God it has an organized structure and uses only pure vowel sounds with very few exceptions. Perhaps I could eventually learn to communicate reasonably well. I had learned enough about cross-culture communication and relationships to be aware my ministry effectiveness would depend on developing a reasonable level of fluency. I told God I would work hard but He had to insure any success.

Andy had a couple of adventures where God was his protector. One snow day, Pat Coursey looked out the window to see Andy walking on the flat roof of Holly Hall, a three-story building without any guard rails. On another day he was trapped in one of the elevators when it got stuck between floors.

Four couples assigned to Africa decided we would attend and join an African-American Baptist church in Black Mountain. The Middletons and Swaffords were going to Malawi and the Courseys and Joneses were going to Kenya. We found ourselves being welcomed with open arms into the fellowship of the loving congregation at Mills Chapel Baptist Church. Pastor Lytle was a dynamic preacher and an outstanding vocalist who led the congregational singing. The congregation always sang with gusto accompanied by an outstanding pianist. Of all the music, my favorite was "We've come this far by faith, leaning on the Lord." They even let four missionaries sing a quartet number one Sunday morning; I sang bass.

While we were in training, we were told there was no housing currently available for us in Kenya until July. When our fifteen weeks were completed, we moved to Toccoa to live with Nancy's mother. During the school year, our kids attended school at three different schools in three states. I still marvel at their resilience.

The Journey

During our training, we learned that we could travel either by air or ship, but it was not recommended to travel all the way to Kenya via ship. We decided we would like to have the adventure of sailing part way; therefore, we made bookings to travel from New York City to South Hampton, England, on the SS United States. We took my mother's car and the five of us plus our mothers drove to New York City where we said good-bye to board the ship. The ship was 900 feet long and over 100 feet wide. There were 2,000 beds for passengers and a crew of one thousand including fourteen officers. Our cabin was on the main deck which had an enclosed promenade. We had access to almost the entire ship during our five-day voyage. The kids enjoyed the movie theater and their playroom. Food service was very good for the three meals and we ate more than enough. The crossing, beginning July 7th, was calm and very enjoyable. It was warm enough to sit in lounge chairs on the open promenade deck. When we disembarked at South Hampton, there was a "boat train" to take us to London.

During the next two days, we toured London and saw the changing of the guard at Windsor Castle, saw Big Ben and Westminister Abby, rode a boat on the Thames including passing a lock, and had wonderful adventures. It was uncomfortable one day because the temperature in London was the highest in twenty-five years.

The next day we flew to Amsterdam where we stayed with the Ron Smith family. Ron had been production manager at Marbon and was transferred to start a new plant in the Netherlands. They carried us to see windmills and a miniature city, and to take a boat ride on the canals in Amsterdam. When we entered the boat, the captain said, "Congratulations" because Apollo 11 was on its way to the moon. In the evening, we flew to Rome and checked into our hotel. When I inquired about transportation to the airport the next day, the concierge told me he could arrange a driver and car to tour for the day that would drop us at the airport for the same price as the bus fare. The next day we rode in a Mercedes Benz, visited the Vatican, took pictures of the Swiss Guards, saw some catacombs, had an Italian lunch, and spent most of the day fearing the traffic.

That night we boarded a plane for Nairobi with a stop in Addis Abba for fuel. As the plane was nearing the airport during descent in Nairobi, we looked out the window and saw a lot of wildlife on the plains in Nairobi National Park. In those days, there was a platform where people could stand and look for their friends who were arriving. We walked down the moveable steps brought to the plane and as we neared the terminal, we saw a crowd of people standing with a sign and waving to welcome us. Seeing the entire crowd made us feel very welcome. After we cleared immigrations and customs, we loaded our luggage in a Ford bus and Roger Swann, a journeyman, drove us to Shauri Moyo for a welcome tea. A crowd meant we met a lot of people, but I have no idea who was there. I have always had a challenging time remembering the names of people. After an all-night flight, my mind did not focus on anything. After the tea, Roger drove us to Brackenhurst Baptist Assembly in Tigoni where we would live. On the way, after we passed Banana Hill, the bus ran out of gas. We got enough fuel to get to Tigoni from the boys' center and made it to our house where we would live for the next year.

The Brackenhurst Baptist Assembly was formerly a hotel whose original buildings were constructed in 1917. "The Three Tree Farm" got its name from the three Muna trees on it. One remained near the Bateman's house. The property encompassed 169 acres located across a ridge where the peak was about 7,500 feet above sea level. On the Tigoni town side, the property line was a creek. The property entrance led to a dam which created a pond in the valley. When the property was purchased in 1964 for $42,000, it included all the buildings, furnishings, and equipment including kitchen utensils and linens for the cottages. A golf course had been developed for the guests. When the hotel was built, it was a popular stopping place for the colonialist farmers living in the white highlands because it was a one-day oxcart journey from Tigoni to Nairobi where they went to get supplies. Later, it was known for the motorcycle hill climb races from the pond to the hotel complex. As air travel developed, BOAC and other airlines contracted with the hotel as a layover rest stop for flight crews. At independence, these contracts were cancelled, and the property went into receivership.

Our house was an interesting place. It had four rooms, with three closed in verandas and two bathrooms. One of the veranda rooms had been converted into a kitchen and one was made into a closet. Each room had a fire place and during the cold damp season in July and August I stayed very busy trying to keep fires going in every room. The firewood was Australian wattle which was very green. We always joked that we had to boil the firewood before it would burn. We used lots of ashes soaked with kerosene to light a fire, make the wood boil, and then burn.

The mission assigned Ralph and Rosalind Harrell to be directors of this new ministry and to get it ready for operation as a conference center. Several of the veteran missionaries told me one of the first things Ralph did was to empty the vast array of wine bottles found in the wine cellar into the sewer. Also, Dr. Gorner gave instructions to dismantle the golf course since its maintenance was not important to the conference-center's purpose. Later, the irrevelance of the swimming pool at the missionaries' guest house in Nairobi prompted him to apply the same principle of utility.

Our neighbor, Mrs. Howard, whose father had built the original buildings, gave us a lot of local history as the years progressed. An auto mechanic in Tigoni told me stories about the motorcycle hill-climb races since he had raced in them when he was a kid. Over the years, I learned a lot of local history from the British who stayed in the community after independence. Dallas and Margie Bateman were assigned as agricultural missionaries. When we arrived in 1969, they had a dairy herd and chickens which provided milk, eggs and meat for the conference center.

We learned our Swahili studies would not begin until September when we would drive to Nairobi for classes at the Anglican Cathedral. The annual meeting of all the missionaries would be held in August. We began to get settled and acquainted with our neighbors at Brackenhurst, with missionaries and with African staff. We quickly learned our bodies needed to adjust to the elevation of nearly 7,500 feet. The grounds at Brackenhurst were beautiful with their gorgeous flowers and trees.

During 1966-67, Paramount Pictures filmed part of the movie, *The Last Safari,* at Brackenhurst. When we saw the movie, we were surprised to see the dining hall prominently displayed. We later learned some of the beautification added for the movie was still visible.

When we arrived, the East African Mission consisted of 107 missionaries in two countries, Kenya and Tanzania. When they all arrived for the annual mission meeting, they and their children made a large crowd. New missionaries did not have voting privileges during the business sessions so those of us in language school taught vacation Bible school to MKs in 1969. Nancy and I were assigned to teach the kids in second grade. This was Andy's class and there were seventeen boys and Deanna Moore (poor girl). The kids were very active, and it was a challenge for me.

At the April 1969 meeting, the Executive Committee gave work assignments to the five couples in our MLC group: The Courseys, to teach at Mombasa Baptist High School; the Dolifkas, to evangelism at Kigoma;

the Walkers, to evangelism in Tanga; the Hills, to Baptist Publications, and the Joneses as Business Managers based at Tigoni. Before the mission meeting, Harold Cummins had told me the personnel committee wanted to recommend me to become mission treasurer after language study. I was elected treasurer to begin after completion of language study, not after a wait of a few years like Dr. Goerner had told me.

A lot of activities took place during our break times. One afternoon, several missionaries and some older MKs decided to play football. Of course, I joined the game. On one play, I went out for a pass but stumbled and fell with Stacy Houser, my chin crashing into his knee. My chin split and began to bleed, and Dr. Lorne Brown told me it needed to be sewn up. He could not find any sutures, so he sewed my chin with orange thread.

Language study began in early September in Nairobi at the All Saints Cathedral. There were about forty students from many different mission groups and countries. Most in my class were not from the U.S. and several read and spoke more than four languages; one from Sweden spoke ten languages. With my "aptitude" I was linguistically challenged. Nine class sessions convened each day. Canon Bakewell, an Anglican Bishop, taught one class. Another was taught by Fred Ainsworth, his assistant, who was involved in writing the music for the national anthem, "Eh Mungu Nguvu Yetu" ("Oh God of all Creation"). Others were taught by Africans. Conversation classes were usually one on one to emphasize the need to become fluent in speaking. I was determined to succeed in learning Swahili; therefore, in the afternoons when I got home, I sought a staff member with whom to practice. This strategy usually worked but more than a few times, the African answered in English because he wanted to become fluent in my language.

The eight of us commuted to Nairobi in two vehicles because the Dolifkas and Walkers had very small children. The Hills were associates and were not required to study Swahili. The four women returned to Brackenhurst at lunchtime while the men stayed for the afternoon classes. On the first day of class, the other women climbed in the back of the Ford bus telling Nancy she had to drive because it was her birthday and all the Baptists in America would be praying for her that day. Language study in Nairobi was completed before Christmas and plans had been made for us to continue Swahili study at Brackenhurst in the new Baptist Language School with Carlos Owens as the director.

In the fall, we were given a mission owned vehicle to drive, a new 1969 Toyota Corolla station wagon. It was quite small, but our three kids managed to sit together in the rear seat. Since I sit tall in my seat because of short legs, my head rubbed the fabric over my head, resulting in a very stained spot over the years. I was already bald, so I did not lose much hair in this vehicle. After the hundred thousand miles I drove it during my first term, the journey girls who had it assigned to them named it takataka (trash).

The Eucled Moore family invited us to spend Christmas with them in Tukuyu Tanzania, one thousand miles south of Nairobi. One morning, with plans to drive to the seminary in Arusha spending our first night on the road, we packed the car. We drove through Nairobi to Athi River where the route left the Mombasa highway and became a dirt road to the Kenya border at Namanga. A heavy rain of over six inches during the night had made the road very muddy. There were places we had to leave the road and drive on the grass plains to go around major deep mud sections. The road from Namanga to Arusha was paved but the two-hundred-mile trip took all day. Thankfully, we arrived before dark at 7:00 pm. We stayed with the Bedenbaughs who introduced us to their pet, a bushbaby in a cage in the dining room. As we got acquainted, we discovered we were distantly related by marriage. Charles's mother was the sister of my Aunt Irene's husband. Thus, we began to call each other "cuz."

The next day we left early with a plan to drive to Iringa, stopping for lunch at Dodoma with a couple who had been in our Swahili class in Nairobi. The road was paved from the seminary north of Arusha to about thirty miles south of Arusha. The rest of the trip this day was dirt and the first fifty miles were also muddy. After lunch, I was driving and suddenly realized the rear door enclosing the luggage area had popped open. I stopped to close it and found the guitar we were taking for the Moore's oldest son was missing. We back tracked several miles looking to find it and after a couple of failed tries continued our way. Nightfall came before we reached the White Horse Hotel in Iringa. Before we arrived, we began climbing a steep twisty narrow road up a mountain. We were suddenly behind a large herd of cattle walking on the road. One of the herders said in Swahili, "Zima taa" which means "turn off the lights." I was not very fluent in Swahili yet, but I responded, "Taa ni nzima" which means "the lights are bright." We had quite a time getting past those cows and the exasperated herder to continue to Iringa where we arrived after 10:00 pm without supper.

The next morning, we left early to drive to Tukuyu on a very dry dusty road. We were making satisfactory progress when we caught up with a convoy of huge trailer trucks. It took over an hour eating dust before we could pass all ten of them. When we got to Mbeya to turn on the Tukuyu road, we found that it was paved up the mountain. We arrived just before dark and found the Moore's house. Three days of hard driving had been very exhausting.

The view from the Moore's house was awesome. We looked across the tea fields down into the valley maybe fifty miles where we could see Lake Nyasa (Malawi). One day we drove to the lake and had an enjoyable time swimming. It was a perfect day for all seven kids. While we were in Tukuyu, I attended my first African funeral. I was interested in the way the Nyakusa people buried their dead. After the eulogy, we stood by a rectangular pit about six feet deep. At the bottom, an area about two feet deep was cut into the side wall. The body was wrapped in a blanket and carefully placed in this indentation. The grave site was then filled with dirt as the people sang. As the dirt was piled into the grave, a couple of men walked on the dirt to pack it. Other funerals I attended had diverse cultural practices.

Christmas Day started well, and I looked forward to a great celebration of the birth of my Savior. I was still learning details about living in Africa and its culture. After breakfast, I went to brush my teeth. Without thinking, I used tap water which was a huge mistake. Very soon, I became nauseous and spent the rest of the day in the bathroom. I had forgotten that not every water source is clean like American water systems and my digestive system still had not gained immunity to many different things. Our return trip to Limuru was uneventful and in January we began our Swahili studies at Brackenhurst.

All the MKs at Tigoni attended Rosslyn Academy off Limuru Road near Nairobi. It was a small school, less than one hundred students in grades 1-9, owned and operated by the Mennonites. There were four classes: Grades 1-2, 3-4, 5-6, and 7-9. There was a large group of school age MKs living at Brackenhurst while we were in Language School. The three familes with work assignments (Harrells, Batemans, and Owens) had eight, and the Joneses and Courseys had three each. Parents alternated driving the school bus to Rosslyn, about fifteen miles. Sally, Tommy, and Andy were in different classes and seemed to enjoy getting acquainted with MK's from other mission groups. My kids laughingly commented that their Mom had to stand up, so she could push the clutch in when she drove because she was so short she could not reach the pedals of the Ford bus.

Later in the school year, Rosslyn had a field day and our boys signed up for five events each. Andy won second place in one race, but I especially remember my frustration and anger at the principal about Tom's five events. He won four races and finished second in the fifth. When the three medals were presented, and he did not get one, I went to the principal to complain and ask why. He told me they patterned the scoring after the Olympic plan of giving a weighted score. I told him as pleasantly as I could that they did not know how to do their job of weighting and needed to change the system. They refused to change the plan that year but eliminated weighted scoring the next year. That answer did not really soothe my feelings.

During teacher conferences the first year, we were pleased with the reports about Sally and Tommy's progress. When we met with Andy's teacher who was brand new and inexperienced, we got really upset with her. She told us Andy worked very slowly prompting her not to require the same level of performance expected of the other kids. To this day, I believe Andy's interest and performance in school was damaged by this teacher because she did not challenge him.

Because of my commitment to work with churches, I began to work with John Kihogo to begin a new church in Banana Hill. I went with him on Sunday evenings to meet in a home there for the small group who attended. In late January, he asked me if I could preach in Swahili. Because our studies were giving us the vocabulary and some skills in sharing the Gospel, I agreed. There was a new language class which began in January. I asked Vestal Blakely if he would like to go with me to visit this small group. He agreed, and we went to worship. When it was my time to preach, I stood up to share my ten-minute message and expected to stumble through it. Imagine my dismay when my preaching attempt was translated into English for Vestal.

God began to bless this outreach effort and several people made decisions for salvation. The leader and I planned a baptism service in a pond located in a coffee plantation near the meeting place. The day arrived, and the congregation and I walked to the pond. I baptized those who had accepted Jesus into their heart. Sometime later, I was approached by a very conservative missionary evangelist and asked if I had baptized some people. He asked, "Who gave you permission to baptize those people?"

Not knowing how to answer, I simply said "God."

The next question was "Are you ordained?"

I replied, "Yes, twice." Nothing more was ever said.

The language program expected students to continue working on building vocabulary and fluency. There were four levels of fluency and we were evaluated at the end of each term before travelling to the U.S. for our stateside assignments. Job assignments dictated the level needed for their ministry. Missionary wives whose assignments were home and church had the lowest level required. School teachers and support people like me needed the second level while evangelists/church planters were required to achieve the third level. Teachers of theology had to achieve the highest level. I continued to converse with Swahili speakers regularly to enhance the rate of my improvement. If a fluency level was not achieved, missionaries had to take a refresher course when they returned from stateside assignments. I began to learn about the great differences between the fluency, vocabulary, and speed of speaking between the various people groups. Coastal Kenyans and Tanzanians have a purer form of Swahili. Many upcountry Kenyans, especially the Kikuyu, use a dialect lovingly referred to as "kitchen Swahili." A large group of colonialists had huge farms in the highlands where most Kenyans are Kikuyu people and did not make much effort to learn quality Swahili, especially the wives.

When I first went to southern Tanzania and heard Nyakusa speakers, they spoke at least twice as fast as most Kenyans I had heard. I began to recognize I needed to use different vocabularies depending on the people group. I was challenged because my work assignment required me to travel to most areas of both countries. At first, I did not feel very successful, but as my fluency level increased after a few years, I became more comfortable.

Chapter Eight
Implementing Our Call

When I finished the formal language study, I turned my attention to the learning curve for my business manager position and for when I assumed the office of treasurer on June 1st. The many components in the business position included freight and travel arrangements for missionaries, negotiating leases for rental property, immigrations, purchase of vehicles and property, and a variety of other tasks in cooperation with various committees of the mission.

When I became mission treasurer, I was responsible for mission bank accounts, paying the mission's bills, being the legal SBC representative in the country and holding a power of attorney, paying the support missionaries received from USA Baptist churches through the FMB, and auditing the records missionaries kept for their budget funds and those of the local Baptist institutions like high schools, community centers, hospitals, and clinics. Budget preparation was needed to present to the annual mission meeting for approval and forwarded to the FMB for funds appropriation. At the time I began, there were two assistants: a journeyman Roger Swann and a Kenyan Elisha Chagusia. Roger's two-year journeyman term finished soon and a new Journeyman assistant, Sam Devore, arrived before the mission meeting in August. Ralph Harrell turned the responsibilities over to me on June 1st and I immediately began working on the 1971 budget plan to be presented in about ten weeks along with the other daily responsibilities.

When the date for the meeting arrived, I thought I was prepared. I had consulted with the committees, evangelists, and institutions, received their recommendations, and assembled a proposed operating budget for 1971. I had also prepared a list of capital funds to be requested. At the appointed time, I presented the plans to be recommended and asked for discussion. I was surprised when several missionaries stood and said, "I need funds to be added (some being several thousand dollars) because I forgot this need when I submitted my request." These oversights caused me to reflect on many budgets I had prepared in my engineering career where, if I had forgotten something, I would have been held accountable and severely reprimanded. I was further astounded when the missionaries approved everyone to be added. Before I sat down, I made a statement in my frustration that damaged my hope of good relationships with my fellow missionaries. I said, "Friends, this is the poorest run million-dollar organization I have ever seen."

Our family began to expand as we added a horse, a dog, a cat, and a hamster. Sally wanted a horse and had for a few years. Her desire was increased because Beverly Harrell and the Owens girls had horses. We found a mature thoroughbred, a gentle horse named Ambiona. Our dog named Snoopy was a mixed breed of Rhodesian Ridgeback and Alsatian (German Shepherd). She was very sweet and had thirteen puppies once. Sally always wanted a cat, but she woke one morning to find four kittens had been delivered on her pillow during the night. There was a small stable just behind our house where a Kenyan cared for the horses. During many afternoons, Andy would go there to visit Reuben, the Kenyan who was roasting corn on charcoal. Almost every day, Andy ate an ear of roasted corn which his body never digested. When we left for furlough, we gave the cat and Snoopy, our first dog, away.

Mary Saunders asked Nancy to go with her to volunteer at the African Inland Mission Hospital in Kijabe. They went many times and worked in surgery when their nursing staff was smaller than needed. Nancy enjoyed it very much and Mary became a close friend as well as a mentor.

Since both of our mothers wanted to see us, they flew to Nairobi as soon as school was out for the summer. We planned a lot of activities for them to see the work plus a nice safari. We drove to Kisumu for a night and then to Jinja Uganda and stayed at the Web Carroll's house. When we stopped at the border, Nancy's mother took a picture of the immigrations building and the Uganda flag. I thought she was going to be arrested or have her camera confiscated. I talked very nicely to the policeman and he finally agreed for me to remove the film and give it to him, so that we could keep the camera. The next day, we drove across Uganda to the National Park at Murchison Falls. The lodge was very nice, and we had rooms on the ground floor near the Nile River. During the night, I heard a crunching sound which woke me. I peeped out the window and saw a hippo grazing about five feet from me. I was thankful for the building's stone wall.

The next day we rode a boat up the Nile River and saw the falls which were massive and beautiful. On the way were hundreds of crocodiles sunning on the shore, some probably nearly twenty feet long. Elephants were also playing in the river. After this adventure, we drove into Tanzania and stayed in a lodge in the Serengeti National Park. The next day we drove through the park looking at wildlife on our way to Ngorogoro Crater. We stopped to see a large pride of Lions, maybe twenty-five, and I parked the Land Rover very close. They were lying in tall grass on the other side of the vehicle from me. My window was open, and I grabbed a long piece of grass. When it snapped, several lions quickly stood up and stared at us.

At the crater, we stayed in a hostel that was very rough -- no showers or other amenities. We had a fantastic game drive inside the crater and saw many different animals. We drove to Maasai Mara and spent the night at Keekorok Lodge. After a restful night with a very nice buffet dinner, we made our way back to Brackenhurst and home. It was a long trip but very enjoyable, and it gave our mothers many memories.

On another safari, we took our mothers to Treetops Lodge in the Aberdare Mountains. It was famous because Princess Elizabeth learned her father, the King of England, had died while she was there and became the Queen. In the afternoon, a high tea was served on the open deck at the top floor of the lodge, about fifty feet above ground. It was a pleasant day with gorgeous sunshine. I was standing near the rail when I saw a huge male baboon walking down the rail. I backed away and after he passed me, there was a blond woman standing near the rail who had not seen him. He reached over to touch her blond hair and when she felt his hand, she screamed very loudly. The baboon was frightened and reacted by flinging his hand toward the sky. As he did, her blond wig flew about thirty feet straight up. Many tourists cleared the deck.

At mission meeting in 1970, the Owens were transferred to Moshi Tanzania and the Marshall Duncans were assigned to evangelism based at Tigoni. Our kids and the two Duncan boys became very good friends. After I got my hunting license, we planned a hunting trip with them during a school holiday to a hunting block south of Narok toward Maasai Mara National Park. When we were inside the assigned block, we began looking for a good place to pitch our tents. We saw a nice grove of trees and stopped beside them. Marshall and I began walking along the edge of the trees to find the best place to pitch our tents. We had walked more than a hundred yards. It had been a long ride and there were no bathroom facilities. Nancy and Margie decided they would go into the woods and find a place which met their need. Suddenly we heard screams and saw our wives run out of the woods. We raced to the Land Rover. When we got there, Nancy was inside with the door locked and Margie could not get inside. They told us as they prepared their place in the woods, an elephant made noises and scared them to death. We pitched our tents, had supper, and went to bed. No one slept well that night because we heard the elephants playing in the nearby river all night long.

Because I had shown interest in working with churches, I was asked to cover the furlough of Bill Holloway who was assigned to evangelism in the Nakuru area. That year from the middle of 1970 till the middle of 1971 was a difficult but rewarding time. I visited a church in the work area almost every Sunday, and usually Nancy and the kids went with me. The closest church to Tigoni was in Naivasha, about fifty miles, on mostly paved roads. The most distant churches were near Kericho or Thompson's Falls (Nyahururu). On many Sundays we drove five or more hours. The language of worship in these churches was Kikuyu, not Swahili. I understood very little, but worship was joyful as the women and children sang and danced in celebration of God's love. When we began going there, there were sixteen churches, all started since 1967. Often, the African kids would come to sit by Andy who was very blond and lightly rub his arm. I think they wanted to know if the white would rub off because they probably had never seen a white child.

In the fall of 1970, there was an African Evangelistic Crusade. In several countries, several hundred missionaries and local pastors worked to share the Gospel message. I worked with the pastors in the Nakuru area. Jack Green from the U.S. preached in the open-air meetings. I remember our time with him in Nakuru town in an undeveloped area near one of the schools. One afternoon, Arthur Kinyanjui and I went to the top of a mountain near the place where the road to Kericho branches off from the Nakuru-Eldoret highway. We visited hut to hut in the afternoon and I went home for the night. When I arrived early the next morning, Arthur was praising God. After I had left the night before, he witnessed to a witch doctor who got saved. They gathered all his paraphernalia in front of his hut and set a huge bonfire. I saw the smoldering ashes and said a prayer of thanksgiving, praising God for the action of the Holy Spirit.

During these October meetings, over 700 people were baptized in the Nakuru area. The most exciting thing to me was the response of the Kipsigi people group. Over one hundred decided to follow Jesus, the first from this group reached through witnessing by Baptists from Nakuru. During my year working in Nakuru, Arthur Kinyanjui and Eliud Mungai became mentors to me, teaching me how to visit with Kikuyu people. They taught me about Kenya history and the culture of the Kikuyu. Eliud had been imprisoned during the Mau Mau era in Arusha and I absorbed all I could as they shared their lives with me. Each of them later became Moderator of the Baptist Convention of Kenya.

At Christmas time in 1970, we wrote a letter to Nancy's home church, First Baptist in Toccoa. We planned to live in Toccoa during our first time in the U.S. since moving to Kenya and expected to arrive the following July. The following is an excerpt of what we wrote which describes things we had learned.

> This year has been a busy, fruitful, rewarding, frustrating, and maturing year. We were very happy when we finished language school in February, anticipating a day yet to arrive when we will be fluent in Swahili. We quickly learned to laugh with the people and at ourselves about our Swahili MISTEAKS. We have learned to accept people for what they are, not what they have; to be equally at home in a mud hut and a carpeted living room; to eat food and enjoy it despite dirty silverware and swarming flies; to travel in dust and mud; and hundreds of other things which would frustrate or turn the stomach of middle class America. We have rubbed shoulders with people who have wisdom without book learning, simple people who understand the complexities of man, and people whose culture demonstrates brotherhood.

Kenya was an emerging democracy, having independence from the colonial period five years when we arrived. The British Government had granted major funding for Kenyan people to buy the huge colonial farms as the colonialists left Kenya to return to the United Kingdom. Many farms in the Nakuru area had been acquired by co-ops and Kikuyu people were moving to farm their personal small tract of land. One day I went with Arthur to a farm where we were trying to start a new church for the people who had just moved there. A couple of other pastors had joined us and after dark, we entered the farm house to spend the night. Late in the night, I awoke to the sound of the Land Rover door being slammed. I raced to the vehicle and found my camera bag which had been left inside was missing. I immediately shouted; "Mwizi" which means thief. All the pastors rushed out, caught the thief, returned my camera bag intact, and dispensed some African justice because he had embarrassed them by stealing from their mzungu (white man) friend.

I had one event which upset me very much. I was still learning Swahili and I knew that I often did not understand what was said. I always tried to minimize the number of times I asked people to repeat what they said. One night in Nyahururu, I was with Arthur, Eliud, and another pastor in a small room where we would spend the night. The pastor said something I thought I understood and I responded, "nzuri sana" meaning very good. Arthur said: "Bwana Tom, did you hear what he said?" I immediately knew

I had made an error, so I replied, "I guess I did not." Arthur replied; "He just told you his brother has died." I tried to apologize but knew in the future I would be sure I understood before responding.

God truly blessed me that year even though I drove thousands of miles. Because of the demanding work of the pastors and the Holy Spirit's action, eleven new churches or preaching points were started, and hundreds of people were baptized. The first Baptist church was started in Nakuru town because of Arthur's concern. When he could not preach on a Sunday because he went to another church, a Kenya army doctor or a primary school music teacher preached. Zacharia Kamau was in his fifties and a lay pastor. He led two strong churches where every Sunday people stood outside because the crowd was very large. He was a good example, giving me hope for the future.

In January 1971, Mary Saunders and Nancy began a clinic for small children in Mathari Valley, the largest slum in Nairobi. Like other slums in Africa, the people built shanties with whatever they could find: wooden and cardboard boxes, mud, tree limbs, tin cans, plastic, and other things we would call trash. When they started the clinic, the population along the Mathari River was about 65,000. Later, it grew to more than 250,000. Malnutrition and disease ran rampant. With teaching, medicines, and vitamins, babies weighing six pounds who were nine months old began to blossom and gain weight. But, some of the 1,400 they saw in 1971 died before the treatment was effective.

When the Dr. Gene Moores were in language school, he expressed an interest in the Maasai people. They had villages called bomas in the Rift Valley near Kijabe, so Nancy and I joined him on several occasions to hold a clinic and share the Gospel. We were very frustrated because we went to the same "bomas" but always found new people. Maasai were nomadic in those years and went where the water and grass could be found for their cattle and goats. We could never follow-up to see if any Maasai had responded to the Gospel.

The week before mission meeting in 1971, we went hunting with the Evans family to the same hunting block. I killed a zebra and a Grants gazelle which provided us with meat for a long time. Zebra steak became one of our favorite meats when we charcoaled it on our grill.

Baptists in Kenya and Tanzania each formed their own convention of churches during 1971. Representatives from Kenya churches met at Brackenhurst in March and approved a constitution. Morris Wanje from Malindi was elected Moderator. Five other men were chosen as officers including Will J Roberts as treasurer and I was asked to be the auditor. Kenya Baptists chose Nathan Koyi to be their first missionary at Bungoma in western Kenya. The Tanzanian people met in June and elected Ishmael Sibale as their first moderator. They also agreed to support a missionary in Dodoma, Ambokila Mwakatwila.

In 1971, I was asked to travel to Yemen to audit the books for the Baptist Hospital. Since I wanted Nancy to go with me and she agreed, we arranged for our kids to stay with other missionaries. We boarded an East African Airways plane and flew from Nairobi to Aden on the coast of the Indian Ocean. When we arrived, we were given a police escort to our hotel which we could not leave until the police escort took us to the airport the next morning. About 4:00 a.m., we left for the airport for a dawn flight. When it was time to board the Brothers Airways DC-3, we climbed aboard. It was still dark and there were no runway lights. During the pilot's pre-flight checks, he revved up the engine and it backfired. He had tried to get the engine going about three times when the huge Arab man across the aisle leaned over and said, "There is something wrong with the engines, we will not fly today." As he got these words out of his mouth, the pilot shoved the throttles to full and we began our way down a dark runway with only the plane's landing lights to guide us. After the short flight, we began our letdown at Taiz. I looked out the window and all I could see were rocky hills. When we landed, and exited the plane, my first view was a runway with rocks all over it and the plane had landed facing a mountain where the slope of the runway was maybe fifteen degrees up the slope. Suddenly, after taking this view in, I saw the terminal, a roofless stone building which might hold six people standing up. The hospital was in the southwest of what was then North Yemen. Our flight went to Taiz where hospital staff met us. We rode to the hospital at Jibla where we stayed with one of the missionary doctors.

The hospital stood on a hill above the residences and a row of maybe 150 steps led to its entrance. Jibla was a beautiful village with old traditional buildings. We walked there one afternoon along a narrow path parallel to the side of the steep hill. As we walked, I met a camel which forced me to the outside. I thought I would be bumped off the path and fall down the steep hill.

This audit was the first I did for the FMB. It was a real challenge because there were no banks in the area. Missionaries would take a FMB check in U.S. dollars to a local merchant and he would give them local currency. All the receipts were written in Arabic which I could not read, but I did my best to perform a reasonable audit.

On the return trip, we flew from Taiz to Asmara in present day Eritrea.

We had a charming hotel and good Italian food. The next day we flew to Addis Ababa and transferred to a plane flying to Nairobi. On another trip to Yemen, the plane had a hole in the floor where I could see the runway and a passenger had a live goat in the aisle as carry-on luggage. I flew from Addis to the coastal town of Assab on the Red Sea Coast. The terminal there was a warehouse with no roof. It was very hot, over one hundred degrees, and my plane left before the connecting flight arrived. Fortunately, it was only a few minutes late. African travel could be a real adventure.

With the organization of the two conventions, discussions began to find ways convention leadership could be consulted about mission decisions which might impact relationships. In the March 1972 Executive Committee meeting, Dale Hooper was chosen Treasurer as my furlough replacement.

In late July 1972, it was time for us to travel to the U.S. for our furlough year. Furlough was not a true definition because many requirements were given us. Churches and associations held mission conferences and we were expected to schedule several where we would share the mission story. We had to take a battery of medical evaluations to insure our health was not compromised by the health conditions in our field of service. If these tests showed health concerns, they had to be addressed before we had permission to return for our next term. Many churches wanted to hear the mission story and invited us to speak on Sundays or at meetings during the week.

We boarded the plane in Nairobi and flew to Frankfort, Germany, where David Biggers and his German wife met us. We stayed with them about three days and they showed us interesting sights in this country. David was in the U.S. Army posted in Germany and grew up in Grace Baptist Church in Parkersburg. After this wonderful visit, we flew to France and boarded the SS France to sail to New York.

The France was a beautiful luxurious ship, the flagship of the French Line from 1961 to 1974. The ship was 1,037 feet long, the longest passenger ship built before 2004. It accommodated over two thousand passengers and sailed at thirty knots making the crossing in five days and nights. We boarded at the home port, La Harve, and set sail. The ship called at the port of South Hampton, England, to board more passengers and then set sail to cross the Atlantic Ocean. The ship was famous for its French cuisine where three several course meals were served plus delicious snacks three times a day. Eating six times a day was a different lifestyle.

The ship's kitchen served the evening meal while we were crossing the English Channel. After leaving South Hampton, we decided it was time to retire to our cabin. Soon, we were asleep but were awakened when our cabin began to twist, turn, and go up and down as we passed south of Ireland. The rough swells and the corkscrew motion made all of us nauseated and we did not sleep well. The next morning, Andy had the fewest problems, a situation which surprised us since he always got car sick. We went to breakfast and found only about ten percent of the passengers eating.

The rest of the trip was very enjoyable with calm seas, beautiful sunshine, and a gorgeous starry sky at night. We stuffed ourselves every time food was available and enjoyed every tasty bite. I had dieted consistently before we left Kenya and was close to the weight I had when I was twenty-one. When we settled at Toccoa, I discovered I had gained seventeen pounds between Nairobi and Toccoa. My eating discipline had gone out the window.

We spoke at many churches. Sometimes Nancy and I spoke at different churches at the same time. The most interesting mission conference for me was the one in Noonday Association in Cobb County, Georgia. It was in October and thirty missionaries participated. I spoke at the breakfast meeting of the Marietta Chamber of Commerce. I have no idea why they chose me for this event, but the business people were very receptive to the things I shared. On December 8th, Nancy spoke for the morning service at Central Baptist Church in Newnan, Georgia, while I was speaking in another church in Atlanta. She told me later she really embarrassed herself. As she was walking to the pulpit, she stumbled, catching herself by grabbing the racks holding the hand bells. The bells discharged from the rack and clanged as they fell. I can imagine her feelings and the sounds. We had many other opportunities to tell our mission story. The kids went with us often and began to tell us we told the same stories and they would correct our mistakes on the way home.

In January 1973, Curtis Porter called to tell us about a spiritual renewal conference he and Linnie had attended for pastors at Peter Lord's church in Titusville, Florida. He said they were truly refreshed and wondered if we would like to go to another one in a few weeks. We said, "Yes" and made plans to drive there. The church was a loving congregation who had planned a few activities in the community in addition to the program. The one with special meaning for me was the visit to the space center at Cape Canaveral. We saw the launch pad and control room. Best of all, we rode the elevator to the capsule on top of the Saturn Rocket. The rocket was huge.

Nancy and I had had a difficult first term because of language learning, the frustration of not speaking Swahili quickly, learning culture, and a demanding work schedule. We never doubted our call to mission service and had confidence we would spend our lives in East Africa, but knew we needed a renewal of our spirits before we left the U.S. We went to Titusville expecting God to do something special for us in this meeting... and He did! Our hearts were cleansed during our individual prayer walks as God revealed sin and we confessed it. Nancy felt she was not truly saved when she was baptized as a child and needed to be baptized again. We left Florida rejoicing. Driving through the south side of Macon, we were suddenly in a snow storm which lasted until we got north of Athens, but we had none in Toccoa. We shared with Roger McDonald, our pastor in Toccoa, and he agreed to Nancy's request that I baptize her. It was a very special moment for both of us.

The boys attended Toccoa Elementary and Sally went to Stephens County Middle School in Eastanollee. Andy was in Miss Celeste Terrell's fifth grade class. Nancy had been in her class one year when she was at Toccoa Elementary. Celeste was Uncle Fred's niece and Dr. John Terrell's daughter. Dr. John had delivered Nancy and me. Nancy told the story many times about Miss Celeste's form of discipline. She would grab the hand of the offending student, hold it palm open and up, and proceed to slap the palm with her wooden ruler. Oh, how I wish this same discipline could be given in schools today.

Sally wanted to have a New Year's Eve party and we agreed. Just before we left Kenya, Arthur Kinyanjui had visited us in our home and given us a gift for the three kids. Each received a hand carved olive wood Maasai. Forgetting we had two boys, not two girls, Arthur sent carvings of two Maasai women and a Maasai Warrior. In those days, Maasai women and many people groups along the coast were bare breasted. We had placed the carvings on the mantle in the living room. Imagine our amusement when we saw the carvings the next morning. The women were facing the wall and had been adorned with green crepe paper bras by the eighth grade boys.

After school dismissed for the summer, the family went to Ridgecrest for Missions Week. I was on the program as the Bible teacher of Colossians for teen age kids. One day, I felt a little lump in my right side, so I asked Dr. Fowler from the FMB about it. When the week was over, he sent me to a doctor in Atlanta to get it checked. I had surgery at Georgia Baptist Hospital and the surgeon thought it was a cancer tumor when he saw it. When the pathology results were received, it was only a fatty tumor, a real praise. The surgery hampered my packing and crating for our return in a very few weeks.

Our family took us to the Atlanta airport and we had a very teary good-bye, one of many. We flew to New York to catch our El Al flight to Tel Aviv. We almost missed the flight because it took a very long time for security to pass me. They were very concerned about the Yemeni stamps in my passport and asked many questions about why I had been there more than once before they were satisfied. The flight was very long, over eleven hours. Even today, it has been my longest flight ever. We stayed in a Catholic hostel in Old Town Jerusalem which was quite adequate. One of our friends from MLC was serving in Israel and he drove us to see the sights. We went to Gaza to see the Baptist Hospital, to Bethlehem, and to Golgotha to see the tomb. One day, we went to Galilee and had supper by the lake. Of course, we ate fish. When the meal was served, we discovered the fish were baked whole with one eye staring up from the plate. Sally took one look at her fish and promptly placed a leaf of lettuce to cover the eye. The day we walked around Jerusalem was very hot. We found a little shop which sold icees and we stopped by it probably five times.

Another day, we went to the Dead Sea and saw the caves where the scrolls were found. I had to prove the stories; therefore, I got my newspaper and waded out into the sea and lay on my back. Yes, it is true. I simply floated while reading the paper. We could not get to the Jordon River because of the political tension. Six weeks later, the 1973 war began. Too soon, the week was over, and we went to the airport to fly on the weekly flight to Nairobi. When we arrived in Nairobi, cleared immigrations, and went to customs, we found one suitcase was missing. The suitcase would be delivered a week later by El Al's weekly flight and I learned an important lesson. I had packed our suitcases with each person having all their clothes in one bag. I went a week without a change of clothes and was thankful it was not one of the kids. After this event, I always packed some clothes for each person in more than one suitcase.

Chapter NIne
A Refreshed Return

Not long after we returned to Limuru, Baridi, who had been our groundskeeper and gardener, told us he would like for us to try him as our housekeeper, a job with more prestige to the Kenyan people. Because he had been a faithful, honest worker, Nancy started training him. It was a good decision and he was our housekeeper until we took our leave of absence in 1992. He became a very good friend to all our family. We had the opportunity to help his family with some school fees for his children. We hired Benjamin to be his replacement for the grounds.

While we were on furlough in 1972, the mission elected an ad-hoc committee to study ways to "streamline" the mission's organization because they had recognized the need to reduce time and energy spent on all the committees and to develop working relationships with the two new conventions. This committee was to study the issues and recommend a plan to the mission meeting in 1973.

They were considering several concepts regarding transferring some responsibilities to the national conventions. Consultation with conventions would be made concerning placement of missionaries and areas to begin new work. When feasible, subsidy funds would be channeled through local associations. Mission owned properties, especially church sites, would be transferred to the trustees of the conventions. This change was in keeping with local national laws which required a "society" to be registered with the national government and only registered societies could own property. Institutions would have boards composed of missionaries and nationals. Institutions serving both conventions such as the seminary, publications, and communications would have international members on their boards.

At the 1973 mission meeting, this committee of nine brought its recommendations. They proposed that a Missionary Support Council be established with two divisions: Missionary Staff and Finance, each having five members who would be elected to fill certain administrative responsibilities. Three positions would be Officers of the Mission and the Councils, Administrative Secretary, Administrative Assistant, and Budget Administrator. This council would handle all ministry related matters.

The committee made a second proposal which was to set up two joint committees later named Kenya Development Council and Tanzania Development Council. Each would be composed with ten members, five missionaries and five nationals from the country. Missionaries included Administrative Secretary, Personnel Coordinator, Budget Administrator, and two chosen missionaries. National representatives would be the Moderator of the convention and four other nationals chosen by the convention. These councils would jointly plan and carry out Baptist work and ministry. These proposals were approved, and a constitution committee was appointed to recommend revisions to the constitution and by-laws at the 1974 annual meeting. In 1974, proposed changes with amendments were approved which changed the structure of the mission and facilitated better operational management.

This restructure changed the way I spent my work time since I did not have to consult with as many committees about financial matters. I did gain additional work since audits were necessary for every association which received any subsidy from the mission and I had to develop training conferences for associational treasurers. Since I was on both development councils, I had a heavier travel schedule. Overall, the functioning of the mission became more cohesive as all of us became used to a new way of making things work.

When school started in September 1973, Andy and Tom returned to school at Rosslyn Academy for sixth and seventh grades. Sally moved to boarding school at Rift Valley Academy to begin ninth grade. This school, operated by the African Inland Mission, was a much larger school where all students lived in dorms except for the children of AIM missionaries who lived at Kijabe for their ministries. In addition to the school, there was a hospital, a publishing ministry, and other ministries. President Theodore Roosevelt laid the cornerstone for the main school building in 1909.

When it came time to make a personnel request for another assistant in the treasurer's office at mission meeting in 1974, I talked with the personnel coordinator about asking for a missionary associate rather than a journeyman. I thought it would be helpful to not have so many changes in personnel which required training and a learning curve every two years. This request was granted and Mildred Cagle, a lovely widow, arrived in May 1975. Nancy and I teased her because she was assigned the "Honeymoon Cottage," a gorgeous round bungalow cottage where she would live. She made herself endeared to all the missionaries and became a devoted friend.

We had tried to prepare our kids for the time they would go to boarding school. Nancy and I had decided when they asked to go to RVA, we would let them. We were pleased when the boys decided they wanted to start at RVA beginning in eighth grade. We believed they would adjust better if it was their decision rather than our requirement because there was no other option. Other than Andy's having a minor homesick week during his first term, all three-adjusted well, made lots of friends, and maintained lifelong friendships with classmates.

During this term, I had many opportunities to preach in churches in various parts of Kenya. After the Kenya Convention was organized, they wanted two missionaries to be members of their executive committee. Usually, the mission chairman and treasurer were given this responsibility. I thoroughly enjoyed developing relationships with the Kenyans on this committee. As relationships developed, many invitations to preach came. During one invitation to a Thompson's Falls Church in late 1974. Andy was still at home and Vance Kirkpatrick was starting to develop the non-residential theological education ministry. They both joined me. After worship and the discussions we had with pastors and members, we went to the lodge at the falls for lunch. Andy especially enjoyed the meal. The falls reminded me very much of Toccoa Falls.

Our playtime adventures in 1974 were also interesting as well as challenging. This duality was certainly true of two hunting trips we made with the Courseys. We had gone south of Narok to my favorite hunting block during the long weekend in June. Since we had all our kids and our house helper, Baridi, we took two vehicles. The first morning, Clay shot some zebra, but we never got close enough to kill any other animals that day. Since it was threating rain Sunday, we packed and, after an early lunch, we started back to Brackenhurst. We were moving along the road on the bottom of the Rift Valley between Narok and Mai Maihu when Clay's vehicle had two flat tires at the same time and he did not have enough spares. Clay, Mike, Tom Jr., and Baridi stayed with his vehicle while Nancy, Pat, and I with the other kids drove to Tigoni to get the tires fixed. While they were waiting, Tom and Mike wandered out on the plain looking at the wildlife while Clay and Baridi stayed with the vehicle. The evangelist, Clay, talked with Baridi about his relationship with Jesus and when I got back, Baridi had decided to follow Jesus. God turned a problem into a great blessing that day. Baridi was baptized at Tigoni Baptist Church and became a faithful member. Baridi was a Luhya and most of the congregation were Kikuyu. They respected him and he regularly received the offering at worship services during his early years as a believer.

On another hunting trip, Clay and I, along with our four boys and Daniel Nguku, went hunting east of Kajiado in Maasai territory. I had borrowed

Marshall Duncan's Toyota Landcruiser pickup and the boys rode in the pickup bed since it had a short wheelbase and only one bench seat. We planned for it to be an overnight trip. We left one morning and stopped by Shauri Moyo to collect Daniel Nguku who was the pastor of the church there. We had a successful hunt the first afternoon and the next morning. At midafternoon, Clay said he had licenses for zebra and wanted to look for one. We finally located a herd about an hour before night. Clay shot and killed three zebras, upsetting me very much. Zebra were the hardest animal to skin because the hide is so thick, and males are large. I normally needed an hour and a half or more to skin a zebra. In addition, the zebras were standing in a lava field when Clay killed them, making it impossible to drive the vehicle near where they lay. When we had skinned all three, cut off the hind quarters and steak along the backbone and carried the meat to the vehicle, it was after 10:00 p.m. As we started to leave the area, we could not find a way across the railroad track and wandered around looking for a way to cross. I suddenly realized we had a flat tire and when we inspected the vehicle, we had two flats and one spare. We installed the spare and started to remove the other flat.

The only thing we had to repair this puncture was a bicycle tire patch and band-aids. We jacked the car up and removed the other wheel. The tools we had would not separate the tire from the rim. Finally, we lowered the axle onto the tire near the rim and broke it free. We patched and filled it with air using the small foot-pump. After we had four tires with air, we finally found a way across the railroad and drove to Nairobi, dropped Daniel off, and continued to Brackerhurst arriving about 4:00 a.m. The boys were lying on top of the meat with the camping gear very near the canvas cover over the pickup bed as we traveled. We unloaded the meat into the large walk-in refrigerator at Brackenhurst and went home, tired and dirty. I climbed into the bathtub to wash all the dirt and blood off my body and while bathing, I discovered I had about twenty-five ticks attached to me. This adventure made a delightful story to tell and the meat was delicious. The next morning, Marshall needed his vehicle for a meeting. When he came to get the Landcruiser, we went to the vehicle and discovered all four tires had punctures, some caused by the long thorns from Acacia trees. What a trip!

When the new school year began in September 1974, Andy went back to Rosslyn for seventh grade and we took Sally and Tom, Jr. to RVA for tenth and eighth grades. Sally was glad to be back with her friends. Tom began adjusting to boarding school and making friends with kids he did not know. Nancy and I made a trip to Moshi for me to sign the papers for the deed to the Greek Orthodox Church building we were buying. Their congregation had dwindled after independence and they could no longer maintain the building due to finances. This purchase helped the Owens to have a visible presence in the area since it was located on the main Arusha highway to Dar es Salaam.

Nancy and I made a trip to Kitale to visit with the Evans and I had two memorable experiences. Chuck owned a small private airplane and he took me for a ride one afternoon. It was a nice flight in a very small plane, but when we began to land on the grass runway at the very small Kitale airport, Chuck's descent was very rapid. We hit the runway very hard and the plane bounced at least thirty feet into the air before it settled on the runway. The next day, Chuck and I left Kitale in his Landrover to go to the Turkana area to show a Biblical movie and share the Gospel. We had to ford a river and Chuck told me on another trip, he had to wait three days before he could cross the river to return home because the river was flooded. I was interested in seeing the Turkana people for the first time. I knew they were a Nilotic people with a culture like Maasai. The Turkana live in the very northwest region of Kenya which is very arid and hot.

When we arrived, we began to set up the movie projector and hung a bed sheet to provide a projection screen. Many people began to arrive in their traditional dress and the Morans (young warriors) were carrying their spears. The Wazee (old men) were bringing their chairs carved from a tree trunk. These chair/stools were less than a foot tall, had three legs, and a seat which was about eight inches in diameter. Chuck found a Swahili speaker to translate and he explained why we had come and about the movie. When he started the movie, the projector bulb was burned out and he did not have a spare bulb. The Turkana began to be very agitated and I became afraid I would get speared. We packed the Land Rover very quickly and fled the scene. Later, I became acquainted with several young Turkana as they became the security guards for many people in Nairobi.

We had a nice Christmas celebration because my Mom came for the holiday since she had retired that year in June. The kids went back to school in January 1975, and we went to RVA one Saturday to visit the kids and watch a basketball game. After we left, Tom and David Marrow tried to walk down on the handrail for some steps. David was on the steps teasing Tom. Tom jumped off, stepped on David's foot, and broke three bones in his foot. Tom spent three weeks with a cast and had to use crutches. We were thrilled to get a very positive report from the principal at Rosslyn about Andy's school performance. We had noticed an improvement in his study habits at home but when we were told the principal and Andy's teachers were pleased with the change, we were very thankful.

In February, we had a huge crusade in Nairobi, Mombasa, and Nakuru. Skeeter Davis was the vocalist which was a big hit with the Kenyans since her music was very popular in Kenya during those years. I drove her and part of the team around during the crusade. Over three thousand people made decisions to accept Jesus as their Savior, but I am not sure how many were added to the churches. During this period, we began to recognize that crusades and mass preaching events do not grow the church like door to door evangelism where church leaders can easily follow up on decisions. I had the opportunity to take one of the visiting pastors hunting and he was thrilled.

March was a busy travel month since I visited several towns in both Kenya and Tanzania doing the paper work for plots for the local churches. There was also a one-week conference in Rhodesia for treasurers from all the countries in eastern and southern Africa. This trip gave me the opportunity to visit Victoria Falls for the first time. It was rainy season and a heavy mist covered the falls. I got soaked since I did not have a raincoat. I acted like a tourist and rode in a small plane to view the falls and the Zambezi River. It was a beautiful sight. On the way back to Nairobi, I stopped by Malawi to audit the mission's books.

In early 1975, Nancy began a three-month course studying the Kikuyu language in Nairobi because she felt it would be helpful since most of her clinic patients were Kikuyu and most churches we attended worshipped in Kikuyu. Sam Turner was in her class. I had thought about studying Kikuyu but knew how difficult the language was and did not really have time with my work load. They went to town for lunch one day and ordered their sodas along with lunch. When the sodas were brought to their table, Sam took a sip of his and discovered it had been "spiked" with an alcoholic beverage. I really gave Sam grief about his drinking habit. When the study was over, Nancy invited two Catholic priests from their class to our house for dinner with the Turners and us. As they came in the door, they handed her a bottle of wine as a gift. She graciously told them we did not drink wine ourselves but would be happy for them to open the bottle and drink it themselves.

For Mother's Day, I took Nancy to two very nice game lodges, The Ark and the Mt. Kenya Safari Club, to celebrate her "graduation" and her special day. The Hoopers went with us and we enjoyed both locations. Dale and I played golf at the Safari Club.

There was a period of tension in Kenya due to the murder of J. M. Kariuki in March 1975. Many believed he was assassinated because of his vocal opposition to the corruption taking place in Kenya. He and

President Kenyatta had an ongoing feud about the corruption. Kariuki and Kenyatta were detained from 1953 to 1960 because the colonialists believed they were a Mau Mau. His murder has never been solved.

Tom Jr., Andy and I went hunting during the April school break and Tom Jr. killed his first animal, a wildebeest, with one shot. His skill made me very proud because he has always been a better shot than I have. He also shot a Thompson's gazelle and I killed two impalas, giving us plenty of meat in the freezer again. I did not let Andy shoot my rifle, a 300 Magnum, because I thought he was too small to hold it safely.

In May, the Whitsons invited us to visit them to teach some of their pastors. We flew to Mtwara instead of Lindi because the fire truck at the Lindi airport was broken. We rode a bus to Lindi and drove over to Masasi for the meetings. I taught the church leaders about church finances and Nancy taught the women good health practices. Nancy and Betty Ann stayed where the women slept, and David and I put our sleeping bags in a room inside a building in town. There was an area behind the building which had a corrugated iron sheet fence surrounding it. It was very hot in this southern Tanzanian area near the Mozambique border. We decided to take our sleeping bags outside where it was cooler. Suddenly, I was awakened by a loud crash when a hyena ran full speed into the fence. While we were there, we bought several wooden carvings the Makonde people carved out of ebony. One piece which cost $10.00, an Ujamaa (family tree), was over three feet tall and weighed about forty pounds. I could carry it on the DC-3 flight to Dar es Salaam and on to Nairobi as carry-on luggage. When it stood by my seat, I was crowded. Today, it is still on display at my house. We also bought a couple of chess sets made of pieces carved from ebony and ivory. This was before the ban on ivory imports to the United States.

In June 1975, the mission had a management skills seminar that I coordinated. Dr. Olin Hendriz led the meeting and this event was well received by the missionaries. At the mission meeting in August, we discussed the concept of separating the work in the two countries because several issues confronted our future. The number of missionaries had significantly increased, and the conventions had been organized. The planning to officially divide the East Africa Mission into missions in Kenya and Tanzania effective September 1, 1977 began when the mission passed a motion to this effect. Financial division would occur on January 1, 1978.

One-day Patrick, a Brackenhurst staff member, knocked on our door. When we opened it, he was holding a limp Andy in his arms. Andy had been riding one of the horses on the grounds and tried to ride under a clothesline. He ducked but the clothesline caught his forehead and peeled him right off the horse. We were very thankful he was not seriously hurt. The mission asked me to oversee the Brackenhurst Conference Center ministry while the Batemans went on furlough for six months after the RVA term was over.

One day in mid-July, Nancy drove to Nairobi to get the ice cream order while I was in a MSC meeting. She interrupted the meeting when she entered, and I saw her knee was bleeding profusely. I left to take care of her. On her way back from town, the road had been very foggy. As she drove on the long straight road past the windmill hill, there was a lorry moving very slowly. She looked carefully and decided to pass. Suddenly, a Peugeot matatu (local taxi) appeared out of the fog and she took evasive action by going off the road. Unfortunately, the matatu driver left the road and they hit head-on in the ditch. A British lady stopped and brought her to Brackenhurst. We knew we had to get police; we went to the police station at Tigoni and were told we had to go to Limuru to find the two policemen walking in town and take them to the scene to investigate. Another missionary had gone to see about our car, allowing us to go to Nairobi to have the cut on her knee stitched at the SDA clinic after leaving the policemen at the accident site.

She was charged with reckless driving and had to go to court in Kiambu. When we arrived at the court house for her hearing, she was held in the back. When her case was called, she was brought to the courtroom where I was sitting and appeared before the judge. The policeman gave his report and the judge began to ask Nancy questions. One question was, "Are there any mitigating circumstances?" She said, "Sorry." The irritated judge said: "Did you hear the question?" Nancy replied, "Yes sir, I do not know the meaning of the word." Pacified, the judge explained, and Nancy responded. She was fined Ksh 100 which I paid, and we went home, very relieved.

In 1975, Tom McMillan began learning about some unreached people groups and took special interest in the Giriama people north of Mombasa. The Giriama are one of the nine tribes referred to as the Mijikenda. The traditional religion of the Giriama was animistic and included ancestor worship and shrines for prayer and sacrifices. Families had "god huts" represented by a pole where ancestors communicated with the family through dreams and visions. Tom discussed ideas with Clay Coursey and Louis Scales, the church planters in Malindi and Mombasa. They developed a plan of evangelism during these discussions and made a proposal to the mission that two-man teams composed of an Arusha Seminary graduate and a Giriama Baptist would move through Giriama villages for one year, spending two weeks in each village. God blessed the plan and about one hundred congregations were established during the first year. The plan became a model to be used later with other people groups.

Earlier in the year, the Mennonite leaders had approached our mission leaders about needing assistance with the management of Rosslyn Academy. They had very few Mennonite students and many more Baptists and I was involved in the discussions. At the end of our discussions, we had agreed to recommend that Baptists partner with the Mennonites to operate Rosslyn Academy. There would be a new school board composed of three Mennonite representatives and three Baptists plus one person selected by the board from another mission group having children in the student body. Baptists would provide up to three journeymen teachers in lieu of an influx of cash. The support cost of the journeyman teachers would be the Baptist way of "buying our share of the partnership." The mission approved this plan in the August 1975 mission meeting.

At the mission meeting, one of the new couples who had just finished language school and moved to their assigned ministry location did not arrive. After this meeting, James Hampton who was the Mission Chairman and I met with the husband who told us his wife and son had gone to the U.S. and that he was selling their things and would leave soon. We were very disappointed they did not give us a chance to work with them on ways we might salvage their ministry because we saw a lot of potential in them. We were never told the reasons they left.

During our first term, a group of WMU women from Alabama came to learn about our ministry. One of the ladies was Eloise Townsend from Dothan. Her church invited Nancy and me to speak at their church during our first furlough. We bonded with Eloise and Clyde and have maintained contact. Clyde owned the Honda motorcycle dealership in Dothan and had visited some countries in South America by riding one of his motorcycles from Alabama. He asked if I would ship a Honda motorcycle with my crates in 1973 and he would visit later. When he arrived in 1975, it turned out the motorcycle did not have a Kenya license because the freight agent had failed to report it when he cleared my shipment in 1974.

The Missions Board appointed Rollie and Eva Ennis in 1974 as agricultural missionaries to Tanzania and we wanted to place them at Kasulu, east of Kigoma. Dallas Bateman and I were to evaluate a potential farm to purchase in the area which was recommended by the missionaries living in Kigoma. I planned a training session for Tanzanian associational treasurers in Dodoma at a Christian conference center. I drove a borrowed Land Rover to Dodoma and planned to drive to Kigoma. I awoke about 3:00 the morning after the meeting and decided to start my safari since I had to drive halfway across Tanzania. The entire route was over dirt roads and in most places, there were no road signs. After daylight, I had passed Singida and knew I needed to take a left fork off the road. I came to a small road which I thought was the one to take but there were no signs or people to ask. On faith, I decided to make the turn and drive until I saw someone I could ask. Consider my relief when after driving about fifty miles, I finally saw someone. He told me I was on the correct road. I finally arrived well after dark, very tired and dusty. While I was there, I stayed with the Chester Todds, a doctor doing church based clinics. The Todds and Marrows took loving care of me including taking me on a visit to see the monument where Livingston and Stanley met at Ujiji.

Chuck Todd had a clinic scheduled on the shores of Lake Tanganyika about fifty miles south of Kigoma. Since Dallas and Clyde Townsend would not arrive for a few days on the Mission Aviation Fellowship plane, I agreed to go with Chuck in the boat for the clinic. An American nurse, the wife of an American under contract for some project, went with us. The morning we left, there was a heavy rain storm on the lake. The boat, donated by a Tennessee Baptist group and named Wajumbe, was loaded with our supplies, medicine, gasoline, and camping equipment. As we left the dock, the swells were severe and with the heavy load, water spilled over the bow of the boat. Thankfully, the windshield kept the water from swamping the boat. In a little while, we cleared the squall and the lake became smooth in the sunshine. Chuck asked me if I would drive the boat allowing him to water ski. He got on his skis and skied the entire trip to the church. I was exhausted just watching him ski for more than an hour without resting.

People in the community heard the boat and began arriving for the clinic. It went well, and he treated a huge crowd. The church leaders prepared our evening meal serving dried dagaa, a local fish. Since they were dried by laying them on the sandy beach, a few bites included grains of sand. Later, we spread our sleeping bags on the dirt floor in the church. The church walls were made of bamboo with sizeable gaps to allow good light and the breeze inside. The fishermen went out on the lake at night and we could see many lanterns on the boats. I was awakened about 3:00 a.m. by people shouting "siafu (safari ants)." These ants have huge hives underground and hundreds can be seen marching in wide bands. Many times, animals had been killed when covered with hundreds of these ants. I quickly rose, grabbed my flashlight, and looked around my sleeping bag. I saw a wide band of siafu marching down the side of my sleeping bag and turning to march along the foot. I was thankful they did not get on me. I remembered Andy running into our house at Brackenhurst yelling, "These mosquitos are bad," and stripping off his clothes. He was covered in safari ants and jumped into the tub to get them off him. He said: "These mosquito bites really hurt."

The next morning, we held another clinic and boated back to Kigoma, arriving after dark. I got my bar of soap and went into the lake to bathe because the water storage tanks at the house were nearly empty. The next morning, Dallas and I went to Kasulu to evaluate the farm, decided it was worthy to purchase, and developed a contract for purchase.

We left Kigoma the next morning to drive to Mwanza where we would stay with the Dolifkas before continuing to Nairobi. Dallas was driving, and Clyde was sitting between him and me. The edge of the dirt road was very sandy and when we met a big truck, the wheels of our short-wheel base Land Rover got caught by the sand. We skidded, turning the vehicle over and ending with my side on the ground. My head slammed against the door frame, knocked me out, broke my sunglasses, and cut my eyebrow. When I regained consciousness, Clyde was crushed between Dallas and me. Clyde is a very short, small man and I was afraid he was really hurt. Thankfully, I had the only injury. Some people in a Land Rover passed, stopped, and helped us lift our Land Rover back on its wheels. We checked the oil, added some, and found two of our gas can lids had popped open. Relieved these two were empty, we continued our safari and I drove. We had a long wait at the ferry but arrived at the Dolifkas about 10:00 p.m. Don carried me to the ER at the local hospital where a female Russian doctor stitched the cut on my eyebrow. Dallas flew home because he had some digestive problems, and Clyde and I made our road trip back to Nairobi without incident.

All three kids went to RVA at the beginning of September. It was Andy's first term and after a couple of weeks, he got homesick. Instead of going with me to an Arusha meeting, Nancy stayed home so she could go to see Andy after school every day at RVA while I was gone. After a couple of days, he was happy and never had homesickness again. We always tried to visit our kids when there were ball games or other activities and many Saturdays they came home for the day when an off-campus permit was approved. They always brought lots of their friends with them. God blessed us because we lived so close to the school (25 miles) and tried to be surrogate parents to many of the students. In late October, Andy was "campused" which meant he could only leave the dorm area for classes and meals for a week. His chores were to chop wood for the wood-fired, hot water heater, dig a big stump out of the ground, and write the nineteen dorm rules ten times that week. Additionally, he had a date for the Halloween party Saturday and his dorm parent, "Sarge" Hause, said he might be able to go if he finished his chores. When we got there Saturday, he had not finished the stump, so I gave him some advice about how to accomplish the task. The tree was about a foot in diameter and had several roots. After Tom's soccer match was over, he and Sally, in addition to some of Andy's classmates, and even Mr. Hause helped us work on the stump. Before sundown, Mr. Hause was satisfied and told Andy he could go to the party. Andy had sore muscles, but we were thankful for the learning experience he had about discipline.

Nancy flew with me to Zambia in September, so that I could audit the books and teach Norman Wood more skills for treasurer's work. It was one of the many audit trips I made that year. In many missions, missionaries who had been pastors had to be treasurer and needed training. We had wonderful fellowship with the Woods and found Lusaka to be a very nice city. We bought several Malachite jewelry pieces. We visited Victoria Falls and since it was the dry season, we saw a beautiful view of the Zambezi River. It was a good celebration for Nancy's birthday.

James Tidenburg was holding stewardship conferences in Kenya and helped organize a group of eight MK singers at RVA which included his son, Tim, and our daughter, Sally. This group had several opportunities to sing in many places in Kenya.

Tom, Jr. had the same dorm parent, Warren Day, for the second year. At the end of first term, he was asked to become a prefect for the dorm, a situation which pleased us. The boys were active in sports. Sally was a cheerleader and sang in the choir during her junior year.

In December 1975, a World Council of Churches met in Nairobi and the Kenya convention leaders invited the Baptists to have Sunday lunch at Brackenhurst. Our staff planned a nice meal and we had all of them to our house for appetizers; nearly fifty came. It was interesting and enjoyable to meet Baptists from Russia, Hungary, Poland, England, and Nigeria.

Before Christmas, we had had some problems with staff thievery, and I had worked on ways to better supervise employees and manage inventory. One incident resulted in the need to let go of a staff member. His job was to look after the chickens, to collect and count eggs every day for our records. One Monday morning when I reviewed his weekly report, I saw there were no eggs collected on the weekend while we usually got three to four dozen. I asked him what had happened to the eggs and he said that the hens did not lay any for two days because they were on vacation. Since egg production had been consistent, I knew he was not telling me the truth and was suspicious because his mother had a reputation of stealing. I had profound respect for his father on our staff. I told him I knew he was not telling me the truth, and I had to fire him for stealing. He immediately dropped to his knees and began begging me to let him keep his job. I told him to stand up, act like a man, and keep his dignity. We went to the office where I gave him the wages he had earned and told him goodbye.

While the Batemans were on furlough, Patrick, an assistant, quit his job at Brackenhurst. As I thought about whom to seek for his position, Samson Kisia, a Kenyan Luhya, who was on staff at the seminary in Tanzania and wanted to return to Kenya, came to mind. I talked with Tom McMillan, the seminary principal, and he agreed to let me hire Samson. He proved to be a major blessing over the years.

The women in Tigoni Baptist Church presented the Bible story of the birth of Jesus at Christmas. They asked Nancy to be Joseph and borrowed Cara Kirkpatrick's blond, white doll to be Jesus. It all went well but I was surprised and amused when the ending was a scene killing all the babies after Mary, Joseph, and Jesus fled to Egypt.

Before Nancy's mother arrived to spend Christmas with us, we had a "family council" about furlough plans. The mission board had changed policy from a full year furlough for East African missionaries to a graduated plan with furlough length options between a twenty-two month and a forty-eight-month term. Tom, Jr. was a good athlete in soccer and rugby and felt if he missed eleventh grade, he probably would not make the varsity teams. We told the kids we could take a furlough any time since we were already eligible for a short one with the changes in policy. We said any plan where the three of them could agree would be acceptable to us. They discussed the issues and decided for us to leave Kenya in time to spend July 4th in the U.S. to celebrate the two hundredth celebration of our independence and stay six months. We would return for the January term at RVA. After the kids went back to RVA in January 1976, we had an opportunity to visit two game parks and Malindi on the coast with Nancy's mother. Meetings and audit trips required a lot of time in February, making me very glad the Batemans had arrived and I could be relieved from the conference center management.

Weather patterns in Kenya were a lot different than in the U.S. In a normal year, there are long rains for about ten weeks from mid-March to June and short rains for about six weeks in October and November. Serious droughts can occur if rains fail and flash flooding takes place when they are very heavy. Temperature varied from the mid-thirties to mid-eighties at Brackenhurst while in Nairobi it was mid-fifties to high eighties during the year. Some people said the temperature in Nairobi was stuck on perfect. We developed a producing vegetable garden with flowers growing in the yard the entire year. One year I harvested a cabbage which weighed twenty-five pounds. Sometimes we had heavy thunderstorms. One night I had worked late in the office. After nightfall, a heavy thunderstorm started, and I knew I needed to go home. I locked the building and started running to my car which was parked by the squash court. Three steps led up to the driveway and a few inches of water was cascading down them. As I stepped into this water, lightning struck, and all the lights went out. I thought I had had a heart attack for a few seconds. I got home safely, very drenched.

When RVA's term was over at the end of March, the Baptist juniors and seniors had a retreat in Mombasa and Sally went with them. My family and Scott Coursey drove to Malindi, but Sally and Laura came later from Mombasa. We drove through Tsavo East National Park since this dirt road was about fifty miles shorter. We were making satisfactory progress and were more than halfway from Voi to Malindi when we came to an area where a heavy rain had occurred earlier that day. Suddenly, we came to a place where about thirty feet of the road had been washed out by a flash flood. There was no way to pass because both sides of the road were flooded, and water was flowing through the break rapidly. We had to backtrack to Voi and go via Mombasa to Malindi. A normal eight-hour trip took nearly twelve hours that day. On our return to Voi, we had a flat tire and as I got out to change it, I saw a rhino about twenty-five yards away. Andy and Scott kept watch while Tom Jr. helped me change the tire very quietly. Rhinos have poor eyesight but charge any sound.

Daniel Kinuthia became the pastor of Tigoni Baptist. He and his wife had a traditional Kikuyu wedding before they were saved, but decided they needed to have a Christian ceremony. Marshall Duncan performed the wedding after the worship service where I preached. Their seven children were involved, and everyone was pleased. Margie Duncan and Nancy worked together preparing the wedding cake. Daniel was very evangelistic, and the church blossomed during his leadership.

After the convention meeting was over in April, Vance Kirkpatrick, Tom Jr. and I went to Lake Naivasha to work on our boat motor. The lake level was down, and many boats were out of the water at the shore line. We failed to get the motor to crank but noticed some crayfish. We began to tip boats over and collect this beloved food from my Louisiana days. The Kirkpatricks were from Louisiana and crayfish were a favorite food of theirs. We literally filled the rear floor area of the Landrover with the crayfish, maybe ten gallons. We had a huge dinner party! Cherry prepared the crayfish since she is a good Cajun cook, while Nancy and Margie Bateman prepared the rest of the banquet for our families who totaled thirteen.

I had a teachable moment with Andy in May. He and three other boys in his RVA class went to Nairobi one Saturday on the school bus. They decided they would shoplift some small items. Andy got caught and was suspended from school for a month. Andy was caught in Woolworths and held in the office until I could get there. He was very honest with me and showed me the things he had taken there and from another store. I told Andy he did not act like a Christian should and he needed to apologize to the store manager and return the items. He did, and the manager was gracious and forgave him. We went to the other store and I told the manager, an Indian, what he had done. He said, "That's impossible; we have three security people in the store." I replied, "Andy, show him what you took." Andy removed three items from his pocket and gave them to him. He said thank you and proceeded to browbeat his guards. We slipped out quietly. Andy was very repentant and cooperative the month he was at home. He returned to RVA in June and promised to stay out of trouble.

A major crisis developed in southern Tanzania in May 1976. For many years, Doug Knapp had paid the farm workers with used clothes donated by Baptists in the U.S. The Tanzania government imposed a total ban on the use of clothes in lieu of paying cash for work and instructed the farm to pay the minimum wage specified by the government. Because cash sales for the produce grown at the farm were insufficient to pay all the workers, staff was reduced, and the farm operation disbanded when the Knapps retired.

One of Nancy's favorite hobbies was decorating cakes. She made birthday cakes and tiered wedding cakes. She had lots of cake pans and tools from Wilton. She asked Andy what cake he wanted for his fourteenth birthday in May and he said, "Angel food." He wanted it decorated with red, white, and blue icing with a thirteen-star American flag and the inscription 1776-1976. Since 1976 was Sally's junior year at RVA, she volunteered her Mom to bake twenty-five angel food cakes for the junior-senior banquet. It was a challenge using up all those egg yolks!

We spent much of June preparing for our six-month furlough. We had shipped a small crate earlier and spent the last two weeks in June storing our furniture in Sally's bedroom since the Betheas were to live in the house while we were gone. Ralph Harrell was going to cover for me as Treasurer and I needed to spend a lot of time with him since many changes had been made in procedures since I replaced him as Treasurer in 1970.

We sold Ambiona, Sally's horse, since she would finish RVA in six months after returning. During our preparations, we booked our flight plans to leave Nairobi, fly to Cyprus, visit Bill Marshall's family, and spend three days in Zurich, Switzerland. When we checked in at the Nairobi airport, we were told the flight to Entebbe was delayed and we would miss our connection. They rerouted us to Cyprus via Athens, but we had to go to a travel agent in Athens to resolve our ticket issue. Our visit in Cyprus was enlightening as we observed the division within the country because of the two cultures.

We had a delightful hotel in Zurich which included breakfast. For our other meals, we went to the grocery store and bought food for sandwiches and snacks. Since we spoke neither French nor German, I held out my hand with money in it, allowing the cashier to choose enough for the payment. We rented a car and drove to Lake Geneva and then up into the Alps. When we crossed a high mountain pass in the Alps, we stopped to play in the snow. It was our first time to see snow in late June. Then we flew to New York and on to Atlanta, arriving July 2nd in time to celebrate the two hundredth anniversary of the U.S. independence. When we arrived in New York and got our boarding passes for Atlanta, we were delighted to see they had upgraded us to first class. This one and only time we flew this class was not significant to us since we all promptly went to sleep for the entire flight.

First Baptist in Toccoa rented a small three-bedroom house for us and the week after our arrival, we moved in and tried to get settled before Mission Week at Glorietta. We drove to Oklahoma City and visited the Glenn Boyds. They carried us to Falls Creek one night and the huge crowd of teenagers sang with a lot of spirit. Then, we drove on to Farmington, New Mexico, and stayed with Nancy's high school classmates, Jack and Carolyn Wilson. Jack was pastor of First Baptist Church there. After a good visit and seeing the four corners, we drove to the Grand Canyon, saw the Petrified Forest and the Painted Desert. Our week at Glorietta was very inspiring and the kids made lots of friends with the other MKs they met. When we left, we spent one night at Erene's house in west Texas, one of the journeymen assistants I had in the Treasurer's office. From there, we visited Houston and Baton Rouge on our way back to Georgia. We really enjoyed this very long trip.

Toccoa First Baptist Church had a new pastor, David Turner, and we enjoyed his fellowship and ministry when we could attend. We had enrolled the kids in Stephens County High School in ninth, tenth, and twelfth grades. Tom Jr. went out for football and made the B team playing cornerback, wearing number forty-five. He had played rugby two years at RVA and was using the rugby style of tackling which was not acceptable to the coach who kept yelling at him to change his style. Frustrated, Tom, Jr. decided to quit. Years later, I believe he decided it was a decision he regretted.

We had a lot of invitations to speak at mission conferences and in churches. Most of my speaking was in West Virginia. John Snedden invited me to promote the Cooperative Program at West Virginia churches and in the six months, I spoke in almost every church in the state convention, about fifty. On one trip, Nancy and the kids had gone with me to visit our friends in Parkersburg. One evening, Sally rode with me to Clarksburg where I was supposed to speak. On our return trip to Parkersburg about 10:00 pm, a female deer jumped in front of the Oldsmobile I was driving and hit the car's grill. After six years of driving around a lot of African wildlife, I killed my first animal with a vehicle in America.

Bill Marshal asked me to speak at a mission conference for Kentucky Convention churches located in southern Indiana. On this trip, I flew from Bluefield, West Virginia, where I had been speaking to Indiana. It required five flights and an entire day to get there.

In October, I made another trip to West Virginia and gave the missionary address at the Upper Ohio Valley Association meeting in Wierton. The following week, I delivered the Inspirational Message at the Mountain State Baptist Association of West Virginia's annual meeting in Princeton.

Dallas Bateman had back surgery at Nairobi Hospital. On the day he was to be discharged, October 29th, a blood clot caused his death. Nancy and I attended his memorial service in Franklinton, Louisiana, and drove from there to Parkersburg, West Virginia, where we were scheduled to speak at the annual meeting of the West Virginia Baptist Convention. I gave the report on behalf of the Foreign Mission Board and the missionary message.

Before Christmas, we began building and packing our crates for our shipment to Kenya. Since the mission needed several lawn mowers, I bought six and the boys helped me pack a short crate for them. We also added some of the heavy items in the empty space. When the shipper came to get them and began to pick up this crate, the bottom fell out because it was not banded. We had to rebuild it. I never had another one fall apart since I began using a distinctive style of construction.

Nancy was scheduled to have a hysterectomy in mid-December, but when she was admitted to the hospital, they could not cross match her blood in case a transfusion was needed. She had "funny blood" and they sent her home. Apparently when Andy was born, one of the pints of blood she was given did not match. The Red Cross had to check all over the Southeast before they found matching blood. We celebrated Christmas with her in her hospital room with a micro Christmas tree.

After Christmas with all the family, we had to wait for Nancy to be cleared by her doctor and the Foreign Mission Board before we could travel. Sally returned before the rest of us, so that she could go on RVA's interim which is a week the juniors and seniors take each January to do something special in Kenya. The rest of us left in mid-January.

Chapter 10
Facing New Challenges

When we arrived in Nairobi on January 17th, Sally and several missionaries were at the airport to meet us. Our plane from London had been overbooked, but the company sent another plane which was also very full. Sally had to be at RVA midday, but after we arrived at our house, the rest of us crashed on the borrowed beds but did not sleep well, a normal event with jet lag. The next day, the boys and I began to set up our furniture and get our house in shape. Nancy had to rest most afternoons until she got her strength back after her surgery. The boys went to RVA the first weekend and were in the same dorm as the prior year, Tom's third year with Warren Day as dorm parent.

After Dallas Bateman died, the mission asked me to be the interim director of Brackenhurst. Margie Bateman returned to Kenya with Tara and Lari, allowing Tara to graduate from RVA. Margie was a real asset for the Brackenhurst operation. When I returned from furlough, I found a lot of personnel problems with the Brackenhurst staff because of little supervision for three months. We caught two employees stealing and fired them. One of these had also stolen at the Limuru Country Club and was jailed. I also had to terminate two others because they were incompetent. In early February, I hired four young men, three very fine Christians. I knew the pastor fathers of two of them. We spent a lot of time reorganizing the staff and attitudes became better. One Saturday, a Kenyan knocked on my door at home. The Member of Parliament for Limuru had come to see me with two of his staff and wanted to know about the termination of one employee who had complained. Of course, I was nervous but explained the circumstances. He was gracious, and I think he just wanted to find out who this Mzungu (white missionary) was. We had a bowl of plastic fruit on the coffee table and when he picked up the banana to eat it, I had to quickly explain it was not edible. Later I learned there was some unhappiness with the Brackenhurst staff in mid-May. I called all the staff together one evening and we had very open and honest discussions to clear the air. It took about three hours but with the resolutions, it was worth it.

A major issue developed in the relationships between the Kenya and Tanzania governments. Tanzania had closed the Kenya border at the beginning of February to people wanting to enter Tanzania by ground transportation because East African Airways became defunct and Kenya had started its own airline, Kenya Airways. This development made it difficult for people to travel to the other country for meetings since a special visa was required to even fly and we could only fly on private aircraft, not commercial. Tanzania MKs could get permits to continue schooling at RVA.

Nancy started having conversations an hour every day to refresh her Kikuyu language skills. She also started teaching one of the Brackenhurst staff to read and write in Swahili. He worked hard but struggled learning these skills.

Samson Kisia and Elisha Chagusia came to me one day and asked if I would let them rent the Brackenhurst van so that they could go to Ruiru to visit and plant a church. I was very pleased with this commitment of staff. I told them Samson could drive the van for two trips a week when it was not in use and Brackenhurst would pay for the gasoline. It was exciting to see God bless their efforts and a strong church emerge there. Brackenhurst became a refugee center for missionaries when those ministering in Uganda fled because of continued armed conflicts. Regular news reports in March said Christians were being killed routinely. President Amin promised Americans safety if they wanted to stay but there was still a lot of conflict in the country. Those in Ethiopia began arriving in late May.

Pat Coursey wrote the following:

> Following an appendectomy in Mombasa Hospital, Clay Coursey was having trouble keeping his balance and walking straight and was sent to a neurologist in Nairobi. They thought he might have a brain tumor and put him to sleep for a carotid angiogram. He did not wake up and was on a respirator by the second day. He experienced Grand Mal seizures and his EEGs didn't show much activity. He was expected to die that night, or, if he lived, would be in a vegetative state. After consultation with an American and an Italian neurosurgeon, both of whom were teaching at the Nairobi University Medical Center, the Italian doctor ended up drilling a hole in his skull to relieve pressure on the brain and inject massive doses of antibiotics into the brain. No tumor or abcess was found, and cerebral malaria was also ruled out. After most of a week in a coma, he came out of that, and gradually got better. No cause was reported to Clay and Pat. Later that year while on furlough, he was discovered to have hypoglycemia. A few years later while undergoing a test for kidney stones, he almost became unconscious when

the dye was injected. Consequently, the doctor said he was allergic to the dye, with which conclusion the Courseys concurred. He was left with some of the side effects of a stroke but mostly recovered.

Missionaries were praising God for his healing. Nancy and I spent a lot of time with Pat at the hospital because we had been close friends since MLC. Nurse Nancy and Nurse Lynn Davis helped care for Clay. The Courseys stayed with us a week after he got out of the hospital until the doctor told him he could go back to Malindi.

Our crates arrived, and one had been opened and materials worth a thousand dollars had been stolen. We had insurance but were very disappointed because we lost many special things we had bought during our furlough. We had purchased a drum set for Andy that he wanted although we always closed the door when he practiced. Having not developed skills, he sold them to RVA. At the end of April, the kids returned to RVA for the third term of the year. It was Sally's last one because she graduated in July. Nancy had kept her sewing machine hot making Sally clothes that year.

We went to Nairobi to see Sally play volleyball with her RVA team. She told us Andy was running during a major rain storm and, when he got to the dorm's glass door, his arm poked through the glass cutting it severely, enough to get eighteen stitches. He seemed to function well, even with the bandage. That weekend was the junior senior banquet and we went to see Sally all dressed up in the dress Nancy made. Many of the kids went to unique events at RVA with good friends when they were not dating. Sally went to this banquet with Gary Allen, a good friend and Baptist MK from Zambia.

During that time, RVA had a flu epidemic and the nurse asked Nancy to help in the clinic for a weekend in June because one of the nurses was also sick. Andy came home with me Thursday because he had the flu and the infirmary was overcrowded. He was better Friday; therefore, I took him back to school and spent the weekend with Nancy at Kijabe.

Clark Whitson died in a tragic accident while they were on furlough in 1976. A chapel, styled like a log cabin, was built on the RVA campus in his memory with funds given at his memorial service in the U.S. We attended a dedication service for the chapel on May 26, 1977. It was very memorable with the RVA choir singing, a couple of missionaries speaking, and Tim Tidenburg sharing about Clark, representing their RVA class.

Dogs were important pets in our family and we had a variety of breeds during our time in Africa. Many times, we had other families adopt ours when we went on furlough and got new ones when we returned. For our six-month furlough in 1976, another family cared for our little red male Daschund named Kimbo (Kenya's answer for Crisco). Because we did not have a fence at our house, when we needed to keep him outside, we attached his leash to the clothesline. We discovered when cars passed on the driveway, he would run full tilt barking and racing the vehicle. When his leash reached the clothes pole, he would swing into the air a couple of feet and his body would rotate so that his nose was facing the clothes pole. Andy discovered this behavior and often ran with Kimbo to watch him swing.

In late May, we learned one of the teachers at RVA, Jack Wilson, was moving to another country and wanted to give their dog to a loving family. Malaika (angel) was a beautiful female Irish setter about three years old. Nancy said Malaika was my dog and Kimbo was hers. I think she made this decision because Malaika had two unpleasant habits. First, she knew how to open the front door and come in the house. She pushed down on the handle with her paw and the door opened unless we had locked it. Secondly, just after I bathed her and let her outside, she would race to find moist cow patties and roll in them. Repeat baths and keeping her inside were necessary after her baths.

We received a letter from Ethyl Jenkins, my Sunday School teacher when I was eight years old. She had "adopted" us and wrote regularly. In this letter, she said she wanted to pay the college tuition for Sally. What a great blessing for our family and another proof of God's care for us.

In June, the Baptist World Alliance Department of Evangelism held a conference at Brackenhurst for organizing a Baptist Union of Africa. Representatives from eleven national conventions attended and the program in the Clark Chapel was spoken in English and French. Because many of the the attendees did not understand either language, people could hear a multitude of vernacular languages being spoken simultaneously. Many discussions were held, and the final decision was to organize a fellowship group instead of a branch of the BWA.

LaBrone Harris, a professor at the University of South Florida, came as a short-term volunteer. He helped me for two weeks and wrote a short book for the associational treasurers to use as a training tool. He was an interesting guy because most summers he traveled with the circus based in Florida.

The American community held a July 4th celebration in Nairobi. The RVA choir sang and we enjoyed the U.S. hot dogs. All the missionaries at Tigoni celebrated the next day. The RVA choir gave a concert at the National Theater in Nairobi and Sally sang a solo. We thought she did very well and her friends said it was just the right song for her because it brought out her personality. Tom Jr. had rugby matches twice a week during the school term and we made as many as we could.

Nancy thought she was running a hotel most of the year. Our house, modified from the club house for the golf course, had four bedrooms, three bathrooms, and two dens. With the kids at school, we had plenty of room and many friends preferred to stay with us instead of Brackenhurst. When there was a conference, we ate many meals in the dining hall while I managed the conference center. I wanted to make sure the meal service and food were maintained with high quality.

Ethiopian missionaries were settling in as refugees in mid-July and Sam Cannata did the Bible study for an agricultural conference. He had been arrested in Addis Ababa and spent sixteen days in jail. We were so thankful he was discharged and safely arrived in Kenya. I was glad to renew my acquaintance with him after twenty-four years from our time on the Ridgecrest staff in 1953. He and Ginny were considering a transfer to Kenya and we asked God to guide them to serve with us.

Sally's graduation was a great celebration for sixty-one seniors, and she looked very nice in the dress Nancy made for her. After graduation, she and Laura Coursey rode the train to Mombasa where Clay and Pat met them. They enjoyed themselves on the twelve-hour overnight trip. The Courseys were getting ready to leave on furlough. Nancy, Tom, Andy, and I went to Mombasa and stayed in the guest house three nights, then drove to Malindi and enjoyed two more nights in the Eden Roc Hotel. It was a relaxing trip for us and we needed the rest after operating the "Jones Hotel" over a month.

During my furlough in 1972, I spoke at a mission banquet at Curtis Baptist Church in Augusta, Georgia. They sent a group to Mombasa later to start a new church in this coastal city, the second largest in Kenya. In late July 1977, the pastor, Dr. Bradley, and nearly thirty members came to be a part of the dedication service for the new building for Curtis Kongowea Baptist Church which they had funded. Nancy and I had a welcome tea at our house to greet them and meet other missionaries. We were glad it was a warm cloudless day since there were about seventy people. Some could visit outside. Dale Hooper, Sally, and I made the trip to Mombasa with them. On the return trip, the group spent a night at Voi Safari Lodge in Tsavo National Park. We were eating supper on the verandah overlooking the water hole when a buffalo, limping on three legs, came to get a drink. Somehow, his right front hoof had gotten caught in his horn. As we watched the buffalo, a pride of lions came, killed him, and proceeded to feast on his carcass. Many of the Americans were not happy with this dining part of their safari. Back in Nairobi, several went shopping as Nancy, Tom Jr., and Andy showed them where to shop. Several had clothes made with African style material.

Dina Bateman, Beverly Harrell, and Alan Duncan were in Kenya for the summer. This was the one trip the FMB paid for MKs to come home during college. It was nice to see each of them and Nancy planned a special meal for each family while the three were home. The Kirkpatricks returned from furlough and there was a huge welcome back dinner at our house. Sally and Kathleen Evans planned a multistop trip through Europe, but Kathleen learned her Board paid trip allowed only one stop. They flew to Vienna and spent five days there. Kathleen flew on to the U.S. while Sally flew to Portugal, spent a few days with the Harveys, and then flew to Atlanta.

With the division of the mission and with Mildred Cagle's help, the workload in the treasurer's office decreased. The workload of the two jobs would not be as stressful as when the Batemans were on furlough.

The Brackenhurst staff and I started preparing for the prayer retreat and mission meeting. Since this meeting was the last together as the East Africa Mission, everyone wanted it to be special. One hundred fifty would be coming to the prayer retreat, but we were expecting about three hundred twenty-five people to house and feed at mission meeting. Every nook and cranny would be filled with dining tables since the dining room only seated two hundred. We planned to keep two families at our house and other missionaries also kept some at their houses. The prayer retreat started very well, but on Wednesday, the well quit pumping water, a major crisis. The water pump was submerged in the water table more than three hundred feet below ground. We set up a hoist to raise the steel pipe, so that the water pump could be inspected. This job required each twenty-foot pipe section to be unscrewed and set aside. When the last section emerged from the ground, there was no pump. Having no safety chain, it had vibrated off the pipe and broken the electric cable.

Because I knew we had no time to fish the pump out of the well, I bought a new pump and had it installed. We had water again on Saturday. During the three days, our staff filled fifty-five-gallon drums with water from the pond on the entrance road and went room to room flushing toilets. We also hauled clean water from the Kirkpatrick and Boyd houses in Tigoni to wash dishes, cook, and drink. The well was fixed before all the huge crowd arrived for which I was very thankful. I truly appreciated the response from mission families who acted like they were in the bush instead of complaining. This week was one of the hardest in my life. When our volunteers,

Hal and Myrtle Blanchard, left Brackenhurst in 1976, they were replaced by Odell and Wilma Moore who left after mission meeting in 1977. Both couples were very important because of their ministry.

Tom and Andy went back to RVA and were in the same dorm again during Tom's fourth year and Andy's second. They were glad to be back. Tom Jr. was on the senior colts' soccer team since he had missed a season and the competition was strong. He was elected captain and played well in the games we saw. Since one of his courses during the first term was graphic arts, he started working on a newsletter for us to send. In August, I started teaching Andy to drive a car and his quickly developing skills pleased him. Andy took driver's education by correspondence, a method which has always amused me.

Tom and Andy both worked on a play about Helen Keller to be presented late in the term. Tom had a few lines and Andy worked with the stage crew. One of the boys got sick leaving a vacancy which allowed Tom to have a larger speaking role. Andy was on the high school social committee and enjoyed helping plan all their dedicated events. They both tried out for choir and Tom was chosen. He liked the music they were singing.

Sally started her college studies at Georgia Baptist Hospital School of Nursing in Atlanta. In the beginning, she wrote about enjoying this new venture in life. She went to Rock Eagle for a retreat and called us while she was there. She said she was enjoying her life in the U.S.

Two of my major tasks in October were auditing the financial records for Rosslyn Academy and training Jack Hull for the work of treasurer since he was chosen to be the first treasurer in Tanzania. I tried to relax and get exercise playing golf, mostly at the Limuru Country Club. I could go, play nine holes by myself, and be back in the office in about one hour. Nancy decided, after a lot of encouragement, she would try to play golf. Jack Conley had left his old left-handed clubs and told her she could use them. We played a few times together with Cherry Kirkpatrick or Tom Jr. and it was good exercise for both of us. The Limuru Country Club where we were members built a small swimming pool. We did not swim very many times because it was not heated, and the water was very cold. The first time I went, I dove in and swam to the other end before I could breathe. Being a member of the club was quite inexpensive. After the membership fee of about $200, the annual dues were about $50 with no green fees or any other fee. We did have to pay a caddy, but it was less than one dollar for eighteen holes.

I was listening to armed forces radio on my short-wave receiver about midnight during the first week in November when I heard about the dam breaking in Toccoa. The water rushed through the campus of Toccoa Falls College, a Christian college. The raging waters killed many people and did massive property damage. We heard later that Nancy's brother, Frank, had spent several days working in the hospital pharmacy near the college.

Nancy made her first trip to Malawi with me in November when I went to audit the mission books. Charles and Glenda Middleton carried us to Lake Malawi for a couple of days and we thoroughly enjoyed the visit because we needed a couple of rest days. Mildred Cagle left for a four-month furlough in late November and we missed her. Nancy added office work to her busy schedule to help me.

We were guardians for several RVA students from other countries. Occasionally, we had the opportunity to have them at our house when they got suspended for a brief period. We had one in late November from Angola who stayed until the end of the term and flew home with his brother.

Senior field day at RVA started during a heavy rain storm. Tom and Andy's classes played soccer against each other. Thankfully, both teams won one match and tied, saving some arguments. All the boys and girls played in big mud puddles that day making it necessary for our boys to bathe before lunch. The sun had shown itself the rest of the day, making it more enjoyable. The short rains were very heavy in 1977.

I tried to grow a beard before Christmas and Nancy wrote my mother that she was trying to like it. I am sure I did not keep it very long since I always tried to keep her happy: I ate a lot better when things were positive at home. On the Sunday before Christmas, Tigoni based missionaries had a community tea and carol sing for English speaking people in the area led by Glenn Boyd. About two hundred people attended this wonderful time of fellowship. Our hope was to develop relationships with more of the Brackenhurst neighbors. On the Friday before Christmas Nancy and I invited all the Brackenhurst staff and their families to our house for a "dinner on the grounds." We invited the staff children inside our house to see our Christmas tree which excited them. Most had never seen a decorated tree.

The week between Christmas and New Year's 1978 was extremely busy for Nancy and me. As we say in the Deep South, it "cleaned my plow." The work was not harder than normal; it just involved many more tasks at the same time. I had the normal end of the month's tasks. Jack Hull came to get help beginning the New Year, writing checks payable on the first of the month like payroll and ministry budget funds which I also had to do for Kenya. Additionally, we had two conferences at Brackenhurst and the Taylors were on vacation; therefore, Nancy had to take care of the meal service. We also were receiving six new language school families arriving in Kenya for the first time and had to get their cottages ready. It did not help when one family arrived three days earlier than scheduled. The Cannatas returned from furlough and needed a cottage after their transfer to Kenya. Andy cooked most of our meals that week because he enjoyed it and was on his way to becoming the gourmet chef he was in later years.

Each permanent family at Tigoni was asked to assist a new family with their business affairs which included opening a bank account, registering at the American Embassy, getting kids enrolled in school, getting a driver's license, and learning where to shop or eat in Nairobi. Grocery shopping was more difficult than in the U.S. Supermarkets did not exist there. We bought bread at the bakery, vegetables at the green grocery, meat at the butcher's shop, fish at the fish market, canned goods at the grocery store, and cosmetics at the chemists (pharmacy). Since it was a thirty-minute drive to Nairobi, shopping usually took all day.

Tom Jr. got a temporary driving license and I let him drive some for practice. He had taken drivers education at Stephen's County High. The second week of school at RVA was the interim week, and he chose to go with a group of six students who were riding motorcycles all over Kenya. He was riding along a dirt road and looked back to see another boy who was acting like a clown. The road turned but Tom did not. He took a spill in the bush, but was not hurt any of the three times he fell. He enjoyed the week's activities.

Sally wrote about her first term in nursing school. Her studies went well but her exciting news was buying a car. She learned how to negotiate prices in Kenya because she got it for 75% of the asking price and the owner also paid the taxes. She had heard about my beard, wanted to know if it was grey, and wanted me to shave it off before she came for the summer so that she could recognize me. Andy was chairman of the social committee and one of the MCs at the Valentine party. He was also in charge of the decorations. It was an exciting event and all the students were dressed nicely.

Early in the New Year, I started a Bible study and prayer time with several of the Brackenhurst staff. I also taught principles of witnessing and we practiced together. I was thrilled to see spiritual growth and commitment in many lives. The summer season from January to March was very cold and rainy in 1978 and we kept a fire going to try to keep warm. When we had our annual physicals, the doctor told both of us we were overweight. We tried to exercise. On the few warm days, we tried to swim at the country club pool. I am afraid it was not enough for us to successfully lose much weight.

Nancy was on the committee for the RVA junior-senior banquet and she made several trips to RVA to plan for the event. Nancy and Margie Duncan cooked a lot starting on the Thursday before the banquet when they made Jello salad and prepared stuffed potatoes. On Friday, I went with them and helped them make twenty-five recipes of bar-b-que sauce for 300 pork chops. A few other mothers worked on the rest of the menu. Tom Jr. helped with the decorations for the gay nineties theme. In the woodshop he made salt and pepper shakers which looked like street lamps. The globes were ping-pong balls and others helped make a surrey with fringe on top. He operated the spotlight during the program and had to climb through the ceiling to reach it. We enjoyed it very much, but we were very late getting home.

Becky Holloway planned to get married at Brackenhurst in March and Jane asked Nancy to make the tiered wedding cake. I think Nancy was nervous about it, but she practiced making roses and other decorations. It turned out beautifully. It was the first of many she made for weddings or special anniversaries. She taught Tom and Andy to make roses and they helped her make beautiful icing roses, also.

In mid-March, Jack and Ruth Partain along with Marilyn McMillan were in a serious car accident near Dar es Salaam. They left Dar early one morning before daylight to return to Arusha. As they were meeting a vehicle with bright lights, they ran into the back of a broken-down truck parked on the road. It had no lights or warning signs. Jack and Marilyn had broken bones, but Ruth had a serious head injury. When Ruth could travel after being transferred to Nairobi Hospital, the Partains and Nurse Lynn Davis travelled to Dallas for her treatment and ultimately took a medical retirement. The entire mission family spent many hours praying for all of them, especially Ruth.

Near the end of March, Sally called and told us she was changing the college she attended. We knew she loved her nursing and enjoyed her work in the hospital, but her dorm was a high-rise building where their classrooms occupied part of the building and there was a tunnel connecting the dorm building and the hospital. After all the outdoor freedom at Brackenhurst and RVA, she was having trouble making the adjustment of never being outside. Her good friend, Mena, was struggling with her scholastic work. Mena's family lived in Statesboro and agreed for the two girls to live in their home while they attended Georgia Southern College. Kathleen Evans was also a student there.

One of the things our family enjoyed was the annual Safari Rally. It lasted three days each year and the route was over five thousand kilometers. Over some dirt sections, the cars averaged over one hundred twenty miles per hour. We tried to find a good viewing spot every year and watch all the cars go racing by to the next check point. The 1978 race was very muddy because of major rains and, when the third stage started, only eighteen cars were left of the seventy that started. I enjoyed the rally more when it was filled with local drivers before it became an international event and top drivers in the world came to compete.

The Kenya Baptist Convention held their annual meeting in April. One evening, Jimmy Hooten was preaching and when he finished, an earthquake shook the chapel. We felt it at our house. I watched the pictures on the wall in our living room vibrate a few inches away from the wall. The Africans in the chapel stampeded out of the building, but the only injury seemed to be the hand of one pastor. Nancy was called to help the injured.

In May, the seminary asked me to come to Arusha and help them solve some problems with their bookkeeping. Since we could not drive because of the border closure, Nancy and I flew Missionary Aviation Fellowship in a four seat Cessna. We had to land at the Kilimanjaro Airport which was very near the mountain. As we approached, all we saw were clouds and the pilot began searching for a hole in the clouds. The pilot told us we might have to return to Nairobi if he could not find a break in the clouds. Nancy told him: “You have to find a way to land; I drank too much coffee this morning.” He found a small hole in the clouds and spun down very fast in a tight circle. He suddenly leveled out and went underneath the clouds about one hundred feet above the mountain slope. We were thankful to arrive safely.

All the lady missionaries in Nairobi plus Jane Holloway from Nakuru and Molly Houser from Thika were invited to join the Tigoni missionaries for a three day “sewing bee.” They made curtains and bedspreads for all the Brackenhurst rooms. They seemed to have a fun time and the rooms were very beautiful after their handiwork was installed.

Tom Jr. made the varsity rugby team during his junior year and we went to most of the matches. RVA’s team was very good and they played in the national finals against a club team made up of huge men. They played well for the championship but lost in a close match. Tom Jr. played wing and Nancy was worried he would get crushed in the rucks. He and Leonard Mpoke playing the other wing were the two fastest players on the team. Andy was in tenth grade and played with the senior colts. Sally came to Kenya on her board paid trip and arrived in early June. It was great to see her and get caught up on all her news about college. She went with us to RVA several times to see Tom and Andy play rugby. We were sorry she missed a match early in the season when Tom scored three tries. The varsity rugby team entered two teams in a seven's tournament and the first team won the tournament. Tom was on the second team and they played in the semi-finals. When we went to alumni day, Sally joined other alumni cheerleaders and cheered for the alumni team. One-day Bryan Houser, Rhea Snyder, and Sally were invited to RVA to be on a panel discussion for a class about "Problems of being a MK during the first year of college." Tom Jr. went to the sports banquet to receive two letters for volleyball and rugby. Tara Bateman was his date because he had to invite someone who played sports or was a cheerleader.

Brackenhurst seemed to be functioning well. We had a good leadership team composed of several missionaries helping part time and Samson Kisia. Members at the MSC meeting, passed a motion to ask me to assume the director's position full time. There were objections to this action from some missionaries and following the constitution, a write-in ballot was sent out. When ballots were received, the action was overturned with a vote of thirty-seven against and thirty-six in favor. I later heard that a bit of "politicking" had taken place. I was deeply hurt by the rejection and began seeking how to deal with my emotions. I received three notes of encouragement from fellow missionaries. I was especially touched by the one from Beulah Hooper. She had positive words for me but said I must not become bitter which would only hurt me. I took her advice and since then, when I face a disappointment of some kind, I ask this question, "Lord, what are you trying to teach me?" I believe this attitude has helped me to be more stable rather than ride an emotional roller coaster. I finished my work at Brackenhurst after mission meeting when Bill Curp became director.

During mission meeting lunch on August 22nd, Samson Kisia entered the dining hall to announce the news that President Jomo Kenyatta, a Kikuyu, had died in his sleep at Mombasa. He had been the first president for fourteen years, leading a strong central government. Kenya's first Vice President had been Jaramoji Odinga, a Luo. He broke with Kenyatta in 1966 and formed a left leaning political party. Joseph Murumbi served as the next vice president and Daniel arap Moi, a member of a smaller people group, the Kalenjin, replaced him in 1967. President Kenyatta's rallying cry was Harambee, a Swahili word meaning "Let's all work together." When we received the news of Kenyatta's death, we began to pray because of the uncertainty of a peaceful succession of the Vice President to the office of President per the nation's constitution. The next day we learned a security detail had protected Moi until he was sworn in as the interim president that day. The period of mourning lasted thirty days, and Mzee Kenyatta's body lay in state for ten days. An election date was set for October 6th and there was staunch support for Moi to become president. President Moi was elected and challenged the people to follow Nyayo meaning "footsteps." Moi served as President until the end of 2002.

Dr. Bryan Hicks, my mission professor at Southern Seminary, was the speaker for the mission meeting and would be in Kenya for four months during his sabbatical. He wanted to review our mission strategy as it related to the Bold Mission Thrust plan of the SBC. He visited many areas of Kenya, staying in our home during his research near Nairobi. During the pin awarding service at mission meeting, Davis Saunders presented Nancy and me with pins for ten years of service. It surely did not seem it had been that long.

In September, Sally returned to Georgia Southern College for her studies. Tom Jr. and Andy returned to RVA for their senior and junior years. Tom made the varsity soccer team and we were proud of him since he played on Senior Colts (third team) his junior year. He really enjoyed soccer and we thought he played very well. The coach placed Tom, one of the two fastest players, on the wings of the back line. We were excited when we saw Tom make a goal from mid-field in a match in early October which caught the upper left corner of the goal. Every varsity soccer team member made a goal that season. Tom also tried out for choir and made it again. Andy decided to skip tryouts for choir because he heard it was much more difficult that year. Sally wrote several letters during the fall quarter telling us about her school work. She seemed to enjoy many friendships at Georgia Southern and was very active in Baptist Student Union on campus. The BSU had a volleyball team and, when they played a match against the Physical Education majors, they won. She was very excited and wrote that one of the BSU guys told her she taught them everything they knew about volleyball. Her play at RVA really paid off. She had a tough time at Christmas because she really missed being with her brothers and parents, one of the problems MKs face at holiday times. She had spent a good bit of time with my mother, but Mom came to Kenya at the end of October to spend Christmas with us and see Tom Jr. play soccer. She stayed with us about three months.

Since we did not expect Sally to return for another visit before our furlough, Nancy and I decided to use the lower section of the house as the treasurer's office rather than keeping it at Brackenhurst. We moved our bedroom to the one where Sally had stayed, and we made the den and bedroom on the lower level as the office of the treasurer. It had an outside entrance and with the den fireplace was quite comfortable.

Tigoni Baptist Church planned a revival meeting at the end of September. Pastor Daniel Kinuthia asked me to preach the three services. Honored to be asked, I felt very comfortable preaching in Swahili because of the preaching and teaching I had done. I have thanked and praised the Lord every day for blessing me with fluency in Swahili after so many problems in earlier years with languages. Nancy wrote the following to my mother about the Sunday services:

> The morning service was full to overflowing, and Tom preached his best sermon ever. He said he felt very good about his command of Swahili, and he felt the Lord working in all of it. After the sermon, many people came to the front to say they had accepted Christ as their Savior—some had already made their first commitment in the preaching points during the week, but some had just made the decision.
>
> Then we had dinner on the grounds which mostly amounted to the tea, bread, and butter which the missionaries provided but some of the Kenya people brought boiled corn, arrow root, and their bean dish. After eating, we went back to the church for the ordination of our new pastor, John Muturi, and two deacons, John Gitau and Francis Koinyange, and for the good-bye presentation for Daniel. Vance preached this sermon and Samson presided. It was a momentous day.

The next week I helped Daniel move to the Subukia area where he planned to start a new church. Elisha Chagusia helped me take his possessions in a van, and Kefa, the mission driver, took a truck with the rest of his posessions. Since Daniel had seven children, a lot of things needed to be moved.

Parklands Baptist Church in Nairobi had been organized in 1976 and in early 1978, the mission gave them permission to use the mission property on Chiromo Lane. They made them responsible for maintaining the facilities. At the MSC meeting in November, they asked the mission to transfer the property to the trustees of the church and not the Convention. This action was tabled but a request was approved at mission meeting 1981 to ask the FMB to transfer title to the church. This action strained the relationships between the mission and the convention and it took several years to resolve the conflict with convention trustees.

We went to the lake at Naivasha on New Year's Eve to fish, but mostly for the boys to ski. Late in the afternoon, we were across the lake fishing when a wind arose blowing a floating island to where it blocked our exit from the cove. The boys and I struggled to push the boat through a very narrow opening between the floating island and the steep shore while my Mom and Nancy stayed in the boat. By this time, it was dark and, as we tried to pass through a sea of floating fauna, the boat motor overheated. We were stranded. We yelled until folks on the shore heard us and came in a boat to tow us to shore. They carried us to our car on the other side of the lake and we headed to Tigoni about midnight. As we were climbing a dirt road to the high road above RVA, we had a flat. I changed it and, before we reached the top, we had another puncture. I had to drive the twenty plus miles to Brackenhurst on the rim, but we finally arrived home about 4:00 am. What a way to celebrate the New Year!

In early 1979, I made several trips to seek land where houses for missionaries and churches could be built. Nancy spent several hours baking and decorating a cake for the 20th anniversary celebration for Baptist Women of Kenya.

In February, the Staff Division of MSC discussed a significant issue with missionary personnel. If a missionary was not functioning well in their ministry, no one in the mission had any authority to resolve inadequate performance or interpersonal relationship conflicts. There was limited support from the area office in Richmond because written communications were very slow between the U.S. and Kenya. A proposal was agreed and MSC authorized them to prepare a method of obtaining evaluations from peers, nationals, and a self-evaluation by the missionary. Within two months of beginning the development of a Kenya process, we were informed the FMB had instructed all missions in the world to develop such a process. Our process was refined over a period by streamlining and simplifying the forms. At mission meeting, we were commended for our progress and told we were more advanced than other missions in Eastern and Southern Africa. As expected, some missionaries strongly resisted, especially those whose self-evaluation was significantly different from their peers' or national partners'.

Daniel Kinuthia invited Nancy and me to come to his village in Subukia for the first weekend in March to teach and preach. We pitched our tent Friday afternoon in the school yard near his home and people began coming. They came from all five preaching points that he had started and by the time Sunday arrived, over two hundred were present. Each night they met all night in the school building, singing and praying. Thankfully, Nancy and I slept through most of the drums and singing. I taught Bible to the men Saturday and Sunday mornings plus preached three times Saturday and once Sunday. On Saturday afternoon, several of us went to a market and held an open-air service. Nancy taught Bible and good health to the women in the mornings. It was a great weekend, but Nancy and I soaked in a hot bath when we got home. She said as she lay in the tub, "Thank you, God, for making me an American."

A couple of weeks later we went with Samson Kisia to his home village close to Kakamega. His families including his mother made us feel very welcome. Samson was deeply interested in getting a church planted in his village. We went hut to hut visiting. I had the opportunity to share the plan of salvation using the bridge illustration. As we sat in front of huts, I took a stick and drew the picture in the dirt and described the way to receive Jesus as a personal savior. It was an exciting and rewarding experience, but I believe Nancy and I were blessed more than they were. It was the beginning of a church in Samson's home community.

In the March MSC meeting, Davis Saunders shared correspondence about a deficit of $75,000 in the budget account for missionary transportation. Davis instructed the mission to cover this deficit by the re-designation of other funds in our budget. This deficit could be covered but necessitated making major changes in the expense plans to operate within our budget. Action plans included eliminating any mission funds for the use of a personal vehicle, cutting individual vehicle budgets by 15%, doubling the monthly charge for a missionary's personal use of their assigned mission vehicle, and pre-approval of any maintenance on vehicles with most repairs being done at the mission garage located at Brackenhurst.

This crisis caused mission leadership to begin evaluating the entire operational plan of our work in Kenya. We had noticed our requests for church planter/developers were being filled at a much lower rate than specialists such as teachers, medical staff, social workers, and agriculturists. Since God called us to reach the lost, a reset in strategy was needed. Personnel requests had evangelists at the top of our priority list and we decided to only accept missionaries if financial support was allocated for them. Some of the missionaries assigned to non-church related ministries such as school teachers began to feel God was calling them to become church planters. The Foreign Missions Board (FMB) agreed for those missionaries to change their ministry assignments if they pursued a seminary degree during furlough. Our strategy position was not well received by the FMB leadership who wanted to send as many missionaries as possible.

The Convention made a request to mission leaders for the mission to begin reducing subsidy to associations. The Long-Range Committee called a meeting between mission and convention leaders plus all missionaries assigned to work directly with churches. It was a good meeting and a plan was developed to reduce subsidy over five years.

When I became treasurer, a monthly deduction was made for Kenya income taxes with regular payments to the government. Since this tax was based on income paid in Kenya, I worked with the office of finance in Richmond to pay all Kenya missionaries their support in the U.S. by a deposit into their bank account there. I mentioned this approach to a couple of finance officers in other mission groups and we decided to develop a consortium of missions to make a plea to exempt all missionaries from local income tax since we were making a prominent level of financial contributions to Kenya, especially with our educational institutions and relief efforts. About thirty-five mission groups joined the group and I was elected chairman. We made a petition through the office of the vice-president.

When the boys finished the RVA term at the end of March, we went to Malindi on a "working vacation," some work for me and vacation for the rest of the family. The landlord of the house the mission was renting for the Conleys raised the rent. It was financially and logistically viable to build a second house on the property of the mission house where the Courseys lived. Jack and I spent time at the city council offices to get plans approved and to start the process.

Malaika had three puppies but one was still born. The other two developed a fatal disease so I had to take them to the vet to get put down. It was sad for all of us, but we got a new puppy from the Courseys, putting us back to having three dogs. Tom Jr. named the puppy Acha (let go) and she was the grandchild of our dog named Tebby. We finally resigned ourselves to spending a fortune for a black and white TV because we would get to see the one U.S. program at night. With six hours of daily broadcast, mostly Swahili, we had delayed this step a long time.

Tom Jr. applied to both Clemson and Georgia Tech. We were getting worried when he did not hear from either school. He finally got accepted at Clemson in April but really wanted to attend Tech. My Mom got in touch with the Tech Registrar's office, and we learned he was accepted..

Sally had a challenging time at school because of some relationships, difficult course work, and loneliness for her family. She felt the need to talk to us and ask advice about life in general. She had planned to transfer to the Medical College at Augusta to return to nursing. She asked if we could help her travel to Kenya, so she could spend a few weeks before summer school at Georgia Southern for a course she needed before her transfer. We were very happy to see her and welcome her home the first week in June.

As we began to talk, she told us she had decided she would not move to Augusta because the school and dorms were not located in a safe area. She planned to change her major to Home Economics and continue at Georgia Southern. This change meant she could spend the whole summer in Kenya with us and probably travel to the U.S. with Tom Jr. after his graduation. We went to see Tom Jr. play rugby and then to the spring concert of the RVA choir. We were proud of Tom because he had a solo. His soccer team played a match against a U.S. all-star team and it was a very good match but RVA lost 5-4.

Gene Hampton told Nancy their daughter Connie was getting married in Kenya and asked her to prepare the wedding cake. It was a gift of love for Nancy, something she enjoyed doing. We learned that Andy needed a hernia repair at the end of July. Tom Jr. and Sally made their flight plans to arrive in Atlanta on August 23rd for Tom to be ready for new student orientation at Georgia Tech on August 26-28. Ruth Roberts, Lorrie Horton, and Doug Eaton planned to travel with them. We reserved a furlough house in Lithonia, Georgia, for our furlough beginning at the end of 1980. Chuck and Betty Evans had stayed in that house during a couple of furloughs.

Tom Jr's graduation ceremony was very nice. He sang with the choir and I was asked to lead the closing prayer. We went to the coast for a few days with other missionary parents of graduates, enjoyed the warm weather, and returned home in time for Andy's surgery. I was thankful he did not seem concerned about the surgery. Since Nancy had been sick with a cough and congestion, Sally and I had to do a lot of her work, especially preparing for the senior supper and packing for our coastal trip.

One neighbor to Baptist Publications and Baptist Communications on Likoni Road in Nairobi's industrial area approached Dale Hooper and Jay Stewart about the possibility of purchasing the mission property so that they could expand production facilities at Premium Drums.

As the concept developed, it was agreed Premium Drums would compensate the mission for the land at a value of $100,000 and rebuild our two buildings with an equivalent square footage using a design of our choosing. As Dale Hooper, Jay Stewart, Jimmy Maroney and I were driving along Thika Road one day, we passed a tall hedge with a dirt entrance road. We wondered aloud if five acres or more was behind the hedge since we had been looking for a tract about that size. Dale did research and learned the tract was nineteen acres and was an estate being prepared for sale. The price was much more than the $100,000 we had for land. Davis Saunders was consulted, and he agreed we could re-designate available capital funds with mission approval. While we waited for approval to re-designate the funds, I wrote an offer under $200,000 subject to the approval of the mission and FMB. The estate agent laughed at this offer, but we went to Thika Road, knelt on the land, and asked God to give this land for Baptist ministry. Dale, Jay, and I made a report at mission meeting and the mission members approved the purchase. The three of us were authorized to oversee the planning, construction, and transfer of the two properties with other missionaries as advisors. Dave Saunders dedicated the property on August 20, 1980.

After the East Africa mission divided in 1977, the Kenya mission continued to operate using the same structure of MSC and KDC. From the time I became treasurer, I had been the only full-time missionary doing administration, a situation which resulted in many non-financial items being sent to my office. Since council meetings were infrequent, the result was that I became the default point person for some urgent non-financial items.

As MSC reevaluated our structure, they decided to convert the MSC to members without portfolios like housing or transportation. Eight MSC members were to be chosen from at least six different areas of Kenya. A mission chairman and vice-chairman were to be chosen from MSC members and three administrators would be assigned; personnel, business, and finance. This plan was adopted at mission meeting. Since Nancy was chairman of the mission meeting planning committee, she had a lot of work getting everything ready. The guest speaker, Dr. Jack McEwen from Chattanooga, and his wife stayed with us for the meeting. It was a good meeting.

The Baptist Convention met at Brackenhurst in September and on Sunday afternoon, President Moi was the expected speaker. He sent word he would be in Arabia and would send Vice-President Mwai Kibaki in his place. This session was held in our front yard since it was the largest flat place at Brackenhurst. It was a cloudy, foggy afternoon. The government removed the fence between our yard and the pasture. The dignitaries had seats in our yard and the large crowd of about two thousand stood in the pasture behind them. Glenn Boyd organized a missionary choir to sing two songs (one English, one Swahili) and I also sang with the Tigoni Church choir. I tried to sway and move with this choir but was not completely successful with all the motions while singing. I had not achieved the proper combination of these skills.

The mission asked me to be the missionary assigned to churches in Muranga District beginning in August. I made plans to visit a church every Sunday if possible and have a meeting with all the pastors every month.

This planning began a ministry that continued for several years along with being treasurer.

In early October, Cliff Staton and I went to the new Thika Road property to do a boundary survey. Cliff had left Ethiopia and was staying in Kenya awaiting a new assignment. We worked long days and near the end of the second day, we were working on the long side nearest Thika. The grass was very high and as I drug the chain along the boundary, a bushbuck jumped out of the grass startling me. When I realized it was not attacking me and was not a dangerous animal, my heart rate returned to normal.

Joan Carter, Nancy, and I went to the Harold Cummins house on Joyce Farm at Ulu, so that the women could teach Maasai women and hold a clinic. I preached on Sunday while Nancy treated seventy-five Maasai on Sunday and one hundred on Monday. It was very encouraging for me to see all the Maasai who were interested in the Gospel after our failed attempts in the Rift Valley near RVA in 1971.

Nancy's mother and our ten-year-old nephew, Greg Kirk, came for a month's visit at the end of November. We sent them to Tree Tops with Andy one night and all of us went to Cottar's Camp for three days in Maasai Mara where we joined the Kirkpatricks, Vance's parents, the Yates, and Jack's parents. It was a very nice relaxing time for us. The most interesting trip while they were in Kenya was our safari to Lamu. We boarded the coastal bus with the Courseys in Malindi early one morning and made a side trip to discharge and load passengers. The day was very hot and the road quite dusty. Nancy's mother was sitting on the isle, allowing Greg to see out the window while Andy and Scott were on another seat. As I was watching the road through the front window, I noticed a huge Arab man stand in the aisle beside my mother-in-law. The bus hit a bump and I watched as the man's shuka fell to the floor leaving him naked below his waist.

The rest of the trip to the Tana River was uneventful until we stopped at the ferry. All the passengers were told to get off the bus and we watched as the driver eased the bus onto the old-time ferry. Then we walked onto the ferry and proceeded to pull it across the river by pulling on the rope which passed through a series of rings on the side of the ferry. We reloaded the bus and proceeded until we stopped at the shore of the channel surrounding Lamu Island. We boarded small boats, crossed to the island and walked to our hotel in the old town carrying our luggage. The only vehicle on the island was the District Commissioner's Land Rover. We had a couple of nice days on the island, but Nancy's mother made me tired because she was always anxious to go somewhere. Our trip back to Malindi and Tigoni was uneventful. A few years later, an article on the front page of the Daily Nation, a Nairobi English language paper, said in a bold headline: "Lamu District Commissioner orders all donkeys in Lamu must wear diapers."

When 1980 arrived, our visitors returned to the U.S. and Andy started the next term at RVA. He planned to go on the piki (motorcycle) safari the next week. The piki Clyde Townsend gave us was not working and was a street bike which was difficult to ride on the rough Kenya roads. John and Kathy Dillman agreed to let Andy ride their mission piki but it was at their house south of Narok near the Tanzanian border. One morning, Nancy and I drove to their house to get the piki and I rode it to Brackenhurst with Nancy following me in the car for about 150 miles to get home.

Andy and his friends left on their five-day safari with some faculty driving a Land Rover to carry supplies. We assumed everything was going well because it was the summer season and January was normally dry. When we saw Andy after their return, he told us he had taken a bad spill near Maralal the first day and broken his collarbone. He was riding about forty miles per hour and looked at the back tire to make sure it was not flat. The nurse on the trip with them strapped his shoulder with a figure eight Ace bandage and he rode in the Land Rover the rest of the trip to Lake Turkana and back to RVA. His shoulder was x-rayed at the hospital and the doctor strapped it again. Andy said it was quite uncomfortable. The next week, Andy had another x-ray and the doctor found his collarbone was broken in four places, not one. He put Andy in a sling instead of the figure eight strap and told Andy studies showed this method was more effective in healing the breaks, but Andy changed back to the figure eight because it was more comfortable.

Because Acha, our small mixed breed dog, caught tick fever when we went to Malindi for Nancy to teach health in the Bible School, we left her with our Nairobi vet because she was pregnant with Kimbo as the father. When we returned to get her, the vet said she was better and everything should be fine.

On our return trip from Malindi, we took the shorter route through Tsavo East National Park since it was the dry season. As I was driving in the park on a lonely road, we went over a little hill and there was a sharp drop in the road. When the car settled quickly and compressed the springs, the oil pan hit a huge rock in the middle of the road which punched a hole in the pan, leaking all the oil. Stranded, we waited for another vehicle to arrive to get help. After more than an hour, three tourist vans with American college students stopped to help us. We had an ice chest with sodas and they were very pleased to help us by giving us a ride to Voi, eighty kilometers away.

I found a wrecker to tow the car to Voi and went to get the vehicle while Nancy waited in Voi. When we reached the car, I was very hot and thirsty, but Nancy had kept the ice chest with her along with our other luggage. I opened a bottle of Sprite that was in the car and took a swallow. It exploded in my mouth because suddenly, all the carbon dioxide was released. I thought I was going to choke. When I got back to Voi, we left the car at a service station and called Bill Curp to meet us at the Nairobi bus station at midnight. The next day, he and John Taylor went to Voi and brought the car to the mission garage at Brackenhurst for repairs.

The summer of 1979-80 (December to March) was very dry and the major rivers had very little water flowing in them. The result was very low power generation in the country and Uganda where some power could be purchased. Nairobi and surrounding areas had rationing and most days, power outages lasted for six hours, creating a lifestyle change.

My work with the twelve churches in Muranga District was blessing me. The first Sunday in March, the Tigoni church choir went with Nancy and me to a special celebration in the association. It was a fund-raising event to collect donations to expand their Bible School facilities. I was excited to see the people of the churches donate $10,000 that day. Another blessing was the three-hour rain which began the long rain season.

During RVA long weekend in February, we went to Malindi and drove up to the space center on the coast a few miles north on Saturday morning. What a blessing as we saw a total solar eclipse including a beautiful corona. Even though it was a quick trip, God blessed us by the beauty of this phenomenon making it well worth the seven-hundred-mile trip. The next weekend was the junior senior banquet. Andy and Becky Boyd enjoyed it together.

Since Nancy was the chairman of the MK committee, we went with other missionaries and journeymen plus all the juniors and seniors to Lake Baringo for their retreat. The camp where we stayed was about one hundred fifty miles north of Nakuru over a very rocky road, making it a long trip. The Island Camp, owned by Jonathan Leakey, required a boat trip; thus, we left our car on the shore. He had a farm on the mainland and we bought some delicious cantaloupe, the first we had eaten in Kenya. His parents were the famous anthropologists. The kids seemed to enjoy the retreat.

The convention meeting was at the Mombasa Baptist High School. We went a couple of days early to relax before the meeting and Clay Coursey asked me to teach bookkeeping to Malindi pastors. The convention met at the high school in Mombasa. Nancy went every morning to have a clinic for the sick ones. The Tigoni Church choir attended to sing, and they had Baridi ask Nancy to bring them some ice water because Mombasa was so hot. Most Kenyana do not like cold drinks.

During this term, many new missionaries were arriving, and many churches were being started. A major portion of my time was spent going to various places to help local missionaries in their search for land for mission houses and church plots. Nancy could travel with me on most trips because Andy was living at RVA during school terms. I was very thankful for many close friendships which developed as we stayed in their homes. Missionaries truly became the brothers and sisters I never had as an only child.

Andy was in a play his senior year and we were proud of his performance. He also prepared our newsletter in his graphic arts class and enjoyed his senior year. Andy was looking forward to graduation in July, but he got into trouble at school about a month before graduation. His siblings always said they did as many "bad" things as Andy but he was always the one to get caught. RVA had two forms of discipline, detention hall lovingly called "D" hall, and demerits. Demerits were serious since six or more in one term meant expulsion and twelve in a year also meant expulsion. That June day, Andy received five demerits bringing his total for the year to eleven. Andy had a couple of Baptist classmates who also seemed to live on the edge of violating the rules. One evening, he and Doug Blakely were horsing around. Doug was standing on the porch of Kiambogo and Andy was watching him from near the flagpole. It was dark, and all the lights were off in the building when Doug "mooned" Andy. Naturally, Andy returned the favor. His white skin glistened in the moonlight and unfortunately for him, a single lady teacher was "hiding" inside the dark building looking out the window. Nancy and I prayed Andy through the remaining weeks of his senior year. Graduation day arrived, and we began to relax before the ceremony until I saw Andy standing with his friends. Several were hiding cigars in their suit coat pockets. "Andy, put that away if you want to graduate today!' I said. Graduation was completed, Andy got his diploma, and we breathed a prayer of thanksgiving.

At mission meeting, a decision was made to move the treasurer's office to the large farm house at Thika Road which had been designated for the mission offices. The mission voted to add a fulltime business administrator position who would also work out of those offices.

Mission meeting was very special to us because our guest was Ken Medema. He thrilled all of us with his music and I was amazed to see him compose songs "on the fly." My favorite of his compositions has always been "Moses" and especially when Glenn Boyd sang it. Andy joined other MKs in operating the canteen and other tasks to add to the Lottie Moon Offering.

We had a frightening experience one night at the end of August. We were awakened at midnight with a knock on our door by Rosslyn's Principal. He and his family had been visiting some friends and were driving home on a lonely road near Nairobi. The road was blocked, and his family was attacked by a gang of thieves. After being beaten and robbed, they were taken to a tea estate near us and dumped out of the car. A helpful African found them and brought them to our house which was not very far away. I carried them home to put their two children to bed and carried them to the hospital to be checked by a doctor. The wife had a cut, and both were severely bruised, but the children were not harmed. The children did not seem to be emotionally upset. After I took them home and got back to Brackenhurst, it was 3:00 am.

Since I needed to go to Zambia in September, we also planned a trip for the four of us to visit South Africa. Tom's round trip ticket from the FMB was issued to Johannesburg and our furlough tickets could begin there. We had to buy two one-way tickets from Nairobi to Johannesburg since Zambia was paying for my ticket. We had a wonderful time in South Africa. One day we drove to Pretoria and visited a huge memorial. The urban areas were impressive, but the most surprising store was their Wal-Mart type one. When we finished looking and shopping, we went to checkout. I was not sure which of the eighty-four lines to enter. I had never seen more than eight lines in the US. On Sunday, we went with Clarence Allison to Soweto for church and had a good worship experience.

We flew to Victoria Falls on the Zimbabwe side and had a very charming hotel. We walked over to the Falls and enjoyed the view the next day. When we checked out of the hotel, we took a taxi to the border, cleared customs, and walked across the bridge over the Zambezi River to Livingston, Zambia, where we went to the airport to fly to Lusaka. After I finished the audit, we flew back home.

We lived at Brackenhurst until October when we moved our office and home and were functioning by November. The apartment building behind the guest house in Westlands was two stories with a two bedroom and a three-bedroom apartment on each floor. Our apartment was the three-bedroom one upstairs and the Jay Stewarts lived across the hall. The two-bedroom apartment downstairs was assigned to Mildred Cagle and the Amis Daniels, current pastor of Parklands Baptist Church, lived in the three-bedroom one.

Because the Vacation Bible School program included me as one of the missionaries, I received more than 250 letters from the kids. Nancy helped with the response to each one, but she wrote most of them. Hearing from so many encouraged me, but quite a few did not have a return address.

I finished my office work at the beginning of December, so that I would have a couple of weeks to pack and store our personal effects before our year's furlough in Lithonia Georgia. We were looking forward to a restful year in the U.S. and visiting all three kids who lived there.

Chapter Eleven
Training and New Challenges

After we visited our families upon arrival in Georgia, we began to get settled in our missionary house connected to First Baptist Church in Lithonia, Georgia. Lithonia was a suburb of metro Atlanta on the east side and the church was located on a hillside overlooking the interstate highway, I-20. Pastor Jim Martin, his wife Bonnie, and the members made us feel very welcome as we learned about the church ministries and met many members. This furlough was the first we had experienced that was connected to a church new to us. One of the new experiences they gave us was participation in a youth "lock in" where we stayed at the church from Friday evening until Saturday evening. We enjoyed the fellowship and worship when we were not on the road speaking at other churches.

During the spring, my most enjoyable speaking opportunities were in many parts of Georgia at associational WMU spring meetings. Nancy travelled with one of the Georgia WMU staff, Evelyn Blount, whom we had known at seminary, and I accompanied Rachel Howard, the Georgia WMU President. For a few weeks, we spoke at several associations each week. WMUs were very active in those days and the women seemed very interested in learning about our ministry in Kenya. Over the years, we frequently heard from ladies who had committed to pray for us.

For most of our missionary service years, we heard regularly from a group of men at First Baptist Church in Dalton, Georgia. One of their ministry commitments was regular prayer for missionaries whom they chose to be their prayer focus and I was very happy for the opportunity to speak at their church in February to thank these men. We know without any doubts that we were protected physically and saw ministry blessings because of our faithful prayer warriors. One good example came during our first term when our vehicle had been in the shop in Nairobi. Nancy was driving back to Brackenhurst up Banana Hill Road and as she neared Tigoni, she was driving through some sharp curves where there was a drop-off with no guard rail. She lost control when the steering wheel did not turn the car because a tie rod had become disconnected. Because she was driving slowly, she stopped before she left the road. This scary event happened on her birthday when it was early morning in the USA and people were praying for her. We can remember many other examples.

Tom and Andy moved from my mother's house to live with us. Since Andy was not ready to go back to school, he got a job at Kroger and worked a while for Will Stucky, a good friend of the Evanses. Will owned several apartment buildings and hired Andy to help with maintenance. As he tells it, Tom Jr. spent too much time at BSU and his grades suffered so he did not return to Georgia Tech. During the year, they both began taking courses at DeKalb Community College and because we lived in the county, school fees were quite low. When Sally finished the spring quarter at Georgia Southern, she came to live with us and take a course at Georgia State University because it was not offered during the summer or fall terms at Georgia Southern. While she was taking this course, she became convinced God really wanted her to be a nurse. She transferred to Georgia State to begin studies for a bachelor' degree in nursing which required three additional years of college work.

Because I still believed the mission would eventually use computers, I looked for opportunities to study computer science. I found a short course at Mercer University teaching basic programing using an early Apple computer. This course did not satisfy my needs. I found a course of study at DeKalb Community College and enrolled for the spring quarter to take Cobol programming, a business language. It was an interesting experience since the code we wrote was prepared to run on the huge IBM mainframe computer using IBM punch cards. In the fall, I took a second course in Cobol and one in data communications. This study prepared me for later computer work in the mission and my work during the 1990s.

In June, Nancy and I spent a week at Camp Pinnacle for GA camp. We had done another camp in South Carolina during a previous furlough and this one was enjoyable, too. One of the camp counselors was Judy Hayes who became a lifelong friend. Her mother was a nursing student at Georgia Baptist Hospital when Nancy studied there. Judy visited Kenya on a volunteer mission trip and has been a leader in the Baptist Nursing Fellowship, both in Georgia and nationally.

Mildred Cagle was covering my furlough as treasurer when she developed some severe health problems. She needed to travel to the USA for treatment and the FMB asked me to return to Kenya to bring the records up to date. Because my passport had expired, I flew to Washington, D.C., early one August morning to have it renewed at the passport office. While I was waiting for the new passport to be processed, I went to a nearby park to sit on a bench and read a book. An elderly African-American lady was walking by and stopped to speak to me. She told me she had some health problems because her "pituti" gland was not working. I was gracious and did not even smile although I wanted to laugh out loud. When my passport was ready, I flew to New York to continue my journey that evening.

While I was in Nairobi, I learned about events which had taken place during my furlough. Roy Brent had been asked to become the second fulltime administrator, the Business Administrator. A job description was prepared which transferred the portfolios of housing and transportation and outlined other responsibilities. I welcomed the addition and looked forward to working with Roy. I also heard Elma Morgan, a retired Army Sargenat, would be coming as a long-term volunteer to cover Mildred's time in the U.S. As I later got acquainted with her, I saw that she was a go-getter, full of energy. At that time, the FMB policy was that no one could serve, either missionary or volunteer, after their seventieth birthday. One year at mission meeting, Davis Saunders told us he was supposed to tell Elma she had to return to the U.S. because she was seventy, but he could never catch up with her to tell her. While I was living in the U.S. in the 1990s, Elma went as a volunteer to witness with some young men to the Maasai between Athi River and Kajiado. She said they walked many miles each day. The first day, the young men asked her if she would like to stop and rest and she said she was fine. The third day when she said no again, they told her to please rest because they were tired. She was in her eighties.

The mission heard a report from the Long-Range Planning Committee concerning the development of a "Primary Documents Manual" and held lengthy discussions. Because action was postponed, the edited version was not approved until 1983.

After a month, I returned to Lithonia in time to return to my computer studies. I sat at the kitchen table many late evenings working on my programs and correcting errors. These studies were always enjoyable because they complemented my engineering background, and I will always be proud of my 4.0 grade point average at DeKalb College. Of the five colleges or the seminary where I studied, DeKalb and Marietta Colleges were my only 4.0 averages.

In November, Nancy and I were invited to speak at the New York convention meeting in Albany. We left Lithonia late one afternoon to drive. When we made a rest stop near Spartanburg, South Carolina, I discovered I had left all my suits hanging in the closet. We called the boys and back-tracked to Commerce, Georgia, to meet them bringing my suits. We continued our trip and arrived just in time for the meeting. The period for the Lottie Moon Offering emphasis was an active time when we spoke in many churches. One I remember was a trip to Columbia, South Carolina. A friend from Georgia Tech was on a church staff and he and his wife plus a couple from their church carried us to a very fancy restaurant for dinner. It was the first time I had ever been served sorbet to "clean my palate" after one of the many courses. My friend told me later the bill was about $100.00 each. I could never afford to eat at a place so expensive when I was paying, even if it were a special event only for Nancy and me. As soon as we finished our speaking circuit, we began to get ready for our return trip to Nairobi where we would live for the first time except for a few weeks before furlough.

Back to Kenya

We left Atlanta and flew directly to Brussels where we had a long layover during the day on the first Sunday in January. This flight was very full, and the only available seats were in the smoking section, much to our chagrin. I managed to sleep a few hours in the day room at a local hotel before we returned to the airport for a second consecutive overnight flight to Nairobi, which would arrive Monday morning. When we had cleared customs, we found that no one had come to meet us. I called Dale Hooper and he came and took us to his house for a good bath and lunch. We learned our telex with the arrival time had not been received. After a tasty meal, we went to our apartment behind the guesthouse in Westlands. Joe Powell, who was a volunteer working in the Treasurer's Office while we were on furlough, had been living in our apartment and moved to a guest house down the road when we arrived. We slept in our own beds the night of our arrival, a rare experience.

The next day, I went to the office on Thika Road to see how things were and make plans to begin learning the tasks in my near future. For several days missionary friends invited us for meals which were always appreciated. After a few days, we enjoyed having our meals and afternoon teatime on our veranda. It was very pleasant there and we could see and hear many species of birds singing. The flowers were colorful and in full bloom which added to the restful environment. Our dog, Acha, was very glad to see us and we really enjoyed having her again. Nancy began to love on her flowers which quickly returned to good health.

In mid-January, Atlanta had a major snow storm. Tom and Andy talked for years about the fun they had sledding. Amsterdam Avenue, parallel to Bellevue Drive, was much longer with a level section at the bottom of the first hill and then a short steeper section we called Devil's Dive when I was a kid. The level section crossed a divided parkway street. They had a three-wheeler which they used to pull the sled back to the top of the long hill and the one riding the three-wheeler would post himself as a guard to make sure cars did not pass when the sled was crossing. They spent at least two days sledding.

At the Muranga pastor's meeting in March, I began teaching the principles of church planting and encouraged the pastors to find a community which their church could adopt for a new church location. One Sunday, Nancy and I went to a church new to us and I preached to a crowd of about three hundred. Another Sunday, I visited a church for mediating a possible split in the congregation, my first experience in this type of ministry challenge. Some Sundays, church services lasted five hours and I was glad we did not have to drive the same distance as when I ministered with the churches in Nakuru.

When we moved to Nairobi, we had an abundance of furniture because we had filled the huge Brackenhurst house. We put a couch and some chairs in my office but still needed to downsize more. We began having yard sales and advertising but were still in this process when our crates arrived from the U.S. Our house was very cluttered for a while. Before we left the US, Sally got a job as a live-in child care provider.

Four-year-old Trevor's single mother was a flight attendant with Delta Airlines; thus, Sally carried him with her sometimes when she visited her grandmothers. Tom and Andy also had jobs. Tom worked for a boy's club in a needy section of Atlanta. Andy had a job in a warehouse facility. All three continued their college studies, Sally at Georgia State and the boys at Dekalb Community College. Andy came to Kenya in June on his FMB paid trip and Tom and Sally went with the youth choir at Second-Ponce de Leon Baptist Church for their mission tour.

The mission experienced a tragedy in June. Sheri Richardson, a nine-year-old MK in Nairobi, rode the school bus home to Shauri Moyo on the last day of school because she wanted to be with her friends. When she got off the bus, the driver closed the door, catching her dress. Without the driver's knowing it, the bus dragged little Sheri, knocking her off her feet. Her Daddy, Jim, was following the bus and when he could get it stopped, he rushed her to Nairobi Hospital where she was admitted to the ICU unit. Nancy, Andy, and I were with Jim and Marsha a couple of hours later when Sheri's Jesus wrapped His loving arms around her and took her home to heaven.

Chuck and Betty Evans were leaving for furlough on Saturday night July 31, 1982. As usual, they were behind schedule getting ready and we rushed them to get to the airport just before midnight. They made their flight and we went home to Westlands to rest before church Sunday morning. Early Sunday morning, we were awakened by what we thought were bombs exploding and the sound seemed to be coming from the area where the Kenya State House, the residence of the president, was located. We soon learned a coup attempt was in progress.

I was pleasantly surprised when the phone rang in the office Monday morning to hear Tom's voice. He had been trying to call every few minutes and we wondered how we could let the family and FMB know that all missionaries were safe to our knowledge. For several days, we watched people walking on the streets with both hands held high in the air, holding their identity card in one hand. We learned after things settled down that our journeymen, whose apartment was near the radio studio, had hidden under their beds for several hours while the shooting was very near.

The following is what I wrote to Sally and Tom later in the week about the events:

> I am writing you together because so much has happened this week and I want to try to tell you a lot about the events. Please share this together. We carried the Evans to the airport on Saturday night and left the airport a little before midnight when they went back. Everything was normal, and we came home to bed. About 7:15 I was awakened by what sounded like bombs or heavy explosions coming from the direction of State House. Then we began to hear small arms fire.
>
> About then the Stewarts rang the doorbell and said the radio was announcing a coup. We got up and began listening to the radio. The announcements were that the military was in charge of the country and for everybody to remain calm. They were critical of Moi's government but did not say much else. Our thoughts were that the Communists were in charge because there has been a lot of unrest at the University and some student leaders have been making Marxist statements and have been quoted in the newspapers. At any rate, in the early morning we had a lot of uncertainty. All the folks here got together at our house- Elma, Tope, Stewarts, and Stickneys. The radio went off the air at mid-morning and when it came back on just before noon, the announcement was that certain officers-Major General Mohhamed and others were in the studio and that things were in control-Nyayo Juu. We all cheered because this meant that they were loyal to Moi and democracy.

We had been hearing gunfire all morning which sounded from Westlands. The Africans said there were problems at Westlands. About noon, Andy, Tope, Stickney, and I decided to try to go get Shane at the Wallaces since Alice was worried about him and the phones were not working. When we got to Church Road, we met two Asians who were very afraid and said they had been mobbed at Westlands, bottles thrown at the car, etc. We decided to go the back way.

On our way back, we saw lots of people with loot from Westlands, office chairs, food, clothing, loaded tea trollies, and even one guy with the big scales from the butchery. At mid-afternoon, we heard on BBC that the loyal forces had retaken the Post Office.

About five PM Rhoda, Mom's friend from Emory, walked in and said her matatu dumped her at Westlands and she couldn't get to the hospital and couldn't get a matatu back home at Kikuyu.

Andy and I carried her and her sister back to Kikuyu. The road was very quiet and there was no evidence of a problem except one police road check. Her brother told us Moi had just passed by. This was the first word we had he was still alive.

He had been in Nyeri for the Show and went to his farm at Kabarak in the middle of the night and then returned to Nairobi late afternoon after things appeared to be in control. He made a brief statement on the radio and announced the curfew. By then the word was filtering out that it was the air force and students which were involved. A few planes had been flying over during the day and about 4:30 we had heard another bombing which we later learned was the GSU head quarters on Thika Road.

On Monday Elma and I went to the office and it was good to talk to you. The phones were still not working, and no external calls were going out. There were a few local calls, but we didn't know how we would get word to you. Lavern Tope was expected to call in but had not. After talking to you I went to find Mom at SDA where the OCEAN meeting was being held. On my way back to the office, I drove through town to observe the situation. There were very few autos on the road-perhaps fifty in all the town. I found empty shell casings on the street near the Post Office and there were cars with bullet holes in them in many parts of town.

One in front of the Kenya Cinema had about fifty holes in the side and blood all over the hood. There has been sporadic shooting every day as they have been looking for the rebels. On Wednesday Eastleigh was completely sealed off as they were conducting a house to house search for the rebels. Since the air base is near there, there were rumors that rebels were hiding in some of the houses. Wednesday night, a half dozen rebels attacked the Central Police Station where some of their buddies were being held.

Looting has been wide spread. Every shop in Westlands was broken into and as I drove around on Monday I noticed that all Ngara, River Road, much of Tom Mboya and Moi Avenues and the Hilton area as well as Biashara were damaged. It appeared to me that it was mostly Asian dukas which were hit. They tied the iron security bars to vehicles and tore them off and then broke the glass out. Besides looting there was a lot of vandalism where perfume bottles would be smashed on the floor or stuff just tossed around. A lot of businesses will go bankrupt because most goods were on consignment and the shops will still have to pay for them.

By Tuesday there were a lot of people in town in the morning but by 3:30 pm town was dead with everybody rushing home to beat the curfew. Few busses were operating, and town was completely shutdown. The last couple of days it has been more normal. Yesterday the curfew was relaxed to 9:00 pm to 5:00 am so I feel businesses will begin to function normally again. You still must hunt for some foods like milk, but I don't think many have been hungry for very long.

The papers indicate that around 125 have been killed but I think it is a lot more, probably 500-1,000. The morgue is supposedly full, and it holds 500. Some bodies have lain on the streets for days and I doubt if we will ever know the total. There were 2,500 air force troops and we hear 2,000 are in custody. I don't know if the rest are dead or if some have been released after questioning. The University was closed, and reports are that many students were killed during the rebellion. Apparently, the air force went to the campus and aroused the students who took to the streets. Several hundred were involved in the looting.

Bilhah, our receptionist, had her house searched on Wednesday by the police. They went through her area house to house looking for loot. They have done this in many areas and have recovered a lot.

Wednesday 327 people were in court for looting, so they have moved quickly. Most of the week on Jogoo Road there have been all kinds of furniture along the side of the road where people have gotten frightened and put things out of their houses.

I have enclosed articles from the papers this week. Please save them so we will have them later. Andy has most of the papers from this intact which he will bring with him later.

I hope you are fine. Please thank the people for all their prayers We are safe and thankful. We hope that it will not take too long to have a complete recovery. I hope Kenya has learned a lot from this experience.

After the addition of Roy Brent as a second fulltime administrator, the mission began to discuss the advisability of adding a third one to handle personnel matters. This concept met with more resistance than adding the business administrator because some missionaries thought it would interfere with the ministry freedom they preferred. Over a period, missionaries began to again recognize the voluminous time spent on meetings requiring time away from their ministries. At mission meeting in 1982, it was approved to create the position of Mission Administrator which would oversee the work of the other two administrators and personnel matters. A plan to define the position, prepare the job description, and necessary changes to policy was approved. MSC was instructed to propose a person for this assignment.

In the fall, Tom Jr. went to investigate a transfer to Southern Tech to study Mechanical Engineering. When Andy came to Kenya for his visit during the summer, the warehouse management told him that when he returned, he would be promoted to a supervisor's job in the warehouse. However, when he returned to work, he learned not only was he not promoted but he did not have a job. He was very disappointed. Sally learned she was not chosen to sing with Revelation, the youth ensemble at Second-Ponce de Leon Baptist. She was very hurt and disappointed. Tom was the "sound man" again for the next school year.

My mother's oldest sister, Winnie Mary Dean, never married. When my grandmother had serious heart problems and my granddaddy was aging, she left her job with the Clinchfield Railroad to live with them in Martin and care for them. During several summers when I was in primary school, I spent two to three weeks with them after my grandmother died in 1941. Aunt Mae was a very caring woman which made it easy to love her. Like many people who were young adults during the depression, she was very thrifty. When I wanted to buy a couple of vacant lots in Baton Rouge, she graciously loaned me the funds and I made a small profit two years later when I sold them. After Granddaddy died in 1947, she returned to Tennessee to work for the Clinchfield again. When she retired in 1971 and returned to Georgia, she restored the original home place where her grandparents lived after they married in 1850. This is the house where I now live.

On the Sunday morning before Thanksgiving in 1982, her sister Ruth went to her house to help her dress for church. Aunt Ruth found her in the bathtub where she had laid all night without being able to get up. Uncle Richard came and the two of them helped Aunt Mae get into bed to get warm under the electric blanket. Her doctor and his nurse wife came in the afternoon and had an ambulance take her to the hospital. She fought a good fight but finally succumbed to pneumonia on December 22nd. Tom and Andy were pall bearers and Sally attended the memorial service at Martin Baptist Church. All three had a tough time dealing with her death. Nancy and I were thankful they could represent us. Close family deaths are always hard for missionaries and we missed many over the years.

During 1982, Morris Wanje, Moderator of the Baptist Convention, approached me to work with a few Convention leaders to develop a Primary Documents Manual for the Convention. He had learned about the proposal of the mission's Long-Range Planning Committee to develop this process for the mission and thought it was a promising idea for the Convention to follow. He suggested the documents should include doctrinal, philosophical, and policy statements, objectives, and goals related to the convention's ministry. We met many times to discuss the content which would include the constitution, by-laws, and job descriptions for elected leaders, employees, committees, and boards. I served as secretary of the group and after many hours of discussion and review of draft proposals, the group finalized a book including the legal documents and thirty-two job descriptions. The group had Baptist Publications print the book with facing pages in English and Swahili. When it was presented to the Convention's Executive Committee meeting before the AGM in 1983, it was rejected. I was disappointed because I perceived the plan would yield a more cohesive operation for the convention's growth. On reflection, I understood it was an action before its time. Members of the Executive Committee were primarily pastors with little education except Bible School or local seminary training and did not have the training or experience to see its value. Many commented it was not African but a white man's document.

In January 1983, Tom Jr. enrolled at Southern Tech to continue his college work. Andy was still looking for a job, but we were thankful when he got one in mid-January. His job was answering the phone and monitoring the security cameras at Campbellstone, a retirement community in Buckhead. Sally decided she would continue her position taking care of Trevor to make sure he had Christian influence. She was happy to have returned to nursing studies. She said her clinical studies in the hospital at Crawford Long were much better than the previous term at Grady Hospital. Georgia had another snow storm in January while Mom Jones was in Toccoa with Aunt Ruth to probate Aunt Mae's will. She and Aunt Ruth received all the personal effects and Uncle Robert got the house. Since He wanted to rent it, they had to move everything out.

Because God always blessed us with the excellent support system Southern Baptist missionaries received, Nancy and I saved enough money to purchase tickets for all three children to come to Kenya in June for a few weeks. It was a rewarding visit for us because they helped make our twenty-fifth anniversary very special.

Since the mission did not have a doctor assigned to the Matheri Valley clinic, Nancy began to seek governmental permission to reopen the clinic with her in charge. She finally found a Kenyan doctor who agreed to supervise her work and she got permission. The doctor made very infrequent visits and loosely supervised her work. Nancy was very happy to have this ministry again.

When the mission acquired the Thika Road property, we created plans for the use of the property. It would include the publications and communications building and, because of the missionary staff whose ministries would be based there, it would include six housing units. A design for a two-story apartment building with two bedrooms in each unit was designed and built. Joan Carter and Mildred Cagle were assigned these apartments. Two buildings, each containing two town houses with three bedrooms, were built. The Brents and Joneses, administrators, and Stewarts and Cooks at publications were assigned to these units. Nancy and I moved from Westlands to Thika Road in 1983.

The mission held a called meeting on June 4th to consider recommendations concerning the Mission Administrator position. After discussions, the mission approved the job description and changes to the constitution, by-laws, policies, and procedures. Jack Conley was recommended for the position and elected by secret ballot.

From the time the Kenya Development Council was organized in 1973, the work of this joint group of missionaries and Kenya Convention Baptists seemed to be functioning well. We had discussed our work strategies, new work locations, and missionary assignments. I felt our relationships were developing well. We had a scheduled meeting in September of 1983, and

I felt truly blindsided when we were told the Executive Committee of the Baptist Convention had instructed their members to no longer attend these meetings. This development prompted a crisis for planning and implementing ministry objectives. As a mission officer, I along with the other officers and the officers of the convention held a meeting to discuss this crisis. We missionaries met and listened to the issues as described by the Kenyan leaders and reported to the MSC that the relationship was broken. Church Developers requested a meeting with the Mission Administrator Jack Conley, which resulted in a proposal that the Mission choose six members and ask every association chairman and the convention moderator meet to seek a resolution and options to find a working solution to the issue of relationships. I was one of the missionaries elected for this task. It was necessary for the mission to assume responsibility for decisions which had been made by the KDC.

At Christmas, my mother came to spend a month with us, but we truly missed being with our children. I wrote them a long letter; some parts are reproduced below.

> This year has been one of many joys as well as some deep disappointments and hurts. Mom and I thoroughly enjoyed the time when we were all together. We treasure the memories of having the whole family together. It was especially meaningful to us to celebrate our 25 years together with all of you.
>
> As you know, this year has been one of some stress in our work. Mom has finally gotten approval for Mathari Clinic after a long frustrating time of chasing the government offices. I have struggled with how to try to respond to and relate to the Convention leaders who seemed to be bringing division to the work rather than advancement. We both have determined to leave these matters in the hands of the Lord since we have no power to change them. We have every confidence that He will complete His work in His time as He sees fit. Thank you for your prayers on our behalf.

In January 1984, the special mission committee met to seek ways for the mission and convention to find reconciliation. There were chairmen from nineteen associations, the moderator and three officers from the convention who met with the six missionaries. I thought it was a good meeting because the Kenyans felt freedom to openly express their concerns and attitudes. They made an extensive list of observations about missionaries and I saw some common threads in the observations shared:

1. Many misunderstandings are the result of missionaries not understanding the language or culture of the Kenyans they work with.
2. Many specialist missionaries are not actively involved in a church or witnessing.
3. Missionaries make changes too rapidly for Kenyans to understand.
4. Many times, the wrong Kenyans are chosen for a position by missionaries. Often, they chose a person based only on English skills.

Mission officers met with convention officers in May and again in September to seek enough agreement to establish a working relationship again. Both meetings were positive. A major issue was the lack of understanding by Kenyan Baptists of polity in Baptist Churches. They asked Sam Turner to write a book which resulting in the publishing of Baptist Beliefs and Customs.

The mission sent a request for a U.S. state convention to partner with Kenya Baptists. The Kentucky Baptist Convention agreed to a three-year partnership beginning in 1985. Ten people from Kentucky were in Kenya two weeks in May to assess ways Kentucky Baptists could help Kenya Baptists. This partnership was instrumental in restoring relationships between missionaries and Kenyans.

Nancy received permission to reopen Mathari Clinic in January 1984. The patient load quickly increased, and she was seeing over 150 patients a week very quickly; the highest single day was 110 patients. Sally came for six weeks after she graduated from Georgia State with a Bachelor in Nursing and helped Nancy in the clinic. When she returned to Atlanta, she began working at Crawford Long Hospital.

Andy came to Kenya in 1983 for our anniversary and, because he was not sure about his future, he stayed for a year helping us in many ways and returned to the U.S. in July 1984. Tom Jr. continued his study at Southern Tech and had a job with an audio-visual services company based in a hotel in Marietta.

I continued to work with the churches in Muranga District. There were seventeen churches and one was brand new at Gachathiini. This church grew quickly and over eighty people were baptized in the first few months. In July, the pastors and I began to plan to plant a church in Saba Saba. It is one of the three major towns in the district with a population of oer one million people. Other churches were experiencing renewal and the work was encouraging.

I cannot say this ministry was always a blissful experience. Sometimes, I was frustrated by the response of the pastors. An example had occurred in a pastor's meeting one month. It was during the time the mission was reducing subsidy to associations at the request of convention leaders. The plan was to reduce the subsidy 20% per year which would eliminate any subsidy in five years. After about three years, I began encouraging the pastors to begin to consider their church becoming the sponsor of a new church. They seemed reluctant and I realized they were dividing the subsidy among themselves and another church would reduce their income.

At one meeting, the pastors spent nearly two hours debating how to spend ten shillings, about $1.50. I became so frustrated I stood and said, "You have used the last two hours talking about something that is not important in the Lord's work. When you want to discuss how to draw people to salvation or how to start a new congregation in a village where there is no church, I will be back." This attitude made the results I saw in 1984 a true blessing to me.

There was a huge drought in Africa in 1984. Nairobi had the lowest rainfall since 1933 and we fed 47 jobless, destitute families in Mathari Valley where there had been nine recent deaths from starvation. Several other missionaries were distributing food in many parts of Kenya. The local purchase of corn and beans became very difficult and we began to search for other food options to feed the hungry people. We were very thankful Southern Baptists provided funds to help feed the starving Kenyans.

In late August, we left Kenya for a six-month furlough and had arranged to live in the mission house provided by Second-Ponce de Leon Baptist Church in Atlanta. We needed a restful time because, in recent months, Roy Brent had been on furlough, adding to my work load. Our dogs had puppies recently, and Andy and Sally each wanted one. Thus, being "good" parents, we arranged to take two pups (Blitz and Raha) as carry-on luggage and were given bulkhead seats on our KLM flights. What an adventure!

Chapter Twelve
A New Church, A Wedding, and A New Partnership

The mission house in Buckhead was very nice and well furnished. The kids lived with us and we became quickly known as Sally and Tom's parents, the missionaries. Sally and Tom Jr. had joined Second-Ponce de Leon Baptist after they returned for college in Atlanta. In 1982, they went on the youth choir tour where they gave twelve concerts. Sally sang a solo and Tom Jr. had a monologue and was the sound technician. Andy went to SPDL some but did not make friends; therefore, he joined Wieuca Road Baptist and really enjoyed his time there. We joined the church and adult Sunday School classes and thoroughly enjoyed the fellowship. We also joined the adult choir to get to know some people in a different generation. The WMU invited us to share and this group became a real support. I already knew some of the senior adults who were friends of my parents and others I knew growing up in First Baptist. I quickly made friends with the pastor, Bob Marsh, who had led this strong church for many years. Later, Bob and Myra made a couple of trips to Kenya for ministry projects.

We had a good Christmas visiting family and the following week all five of us went to Nashville, Tennessee, for a conference. Every five years, Southern Baptist had a meeting primarily for college students and the FMB asked Nancy and me to be on the program. The meetings were held in the Opryland Hotel and I especially remember the huge Christmas tree in the lobby. We enjoyed the week very much and saw many friends. John Cheyne stopped us in the hall one day and wanted to talk with Sally. He told us he had just received an urgent request from Ethiopia concerning the African famine and desperately needed a nurse to join Mary Saunders to go to a remote area to help set up a feeding station/clinic. He knew Sally had just gotten her RN and that she knew Aunt Mary. He asked if she could go for six months to "buy time" to mobilize a group of people for a longer term of service. Sally agreed, and we began to make plans for her to go to Nairobi with us and wait there for her resident permit. Mary laughingly said they were the "Alpha and Omega" team because she had worked with two generations of nurses.

The first week in January was extremely cold. One morning Andy got up very early to go to work and called me about 6:00 am. His car had quit, and he walked a long way when the temperature was ten degrees below zero to get to an open fast food place. I did get my car started and went to collect him since he was very chilled. We found out later there was some condensate in his fuel and the fuel line had frozen. I had a chance to share the mission story in a few places in January and February before we returned to Kenya. In mid-January, I spoke at a church in a ski resort in north Georgia, Sky Valley, and was very glad it was not snowing, or we would have never arrived. The most meaningful one was to speak to my Dad's Sunday School Class at First Baptist Atlanta.

We had a chance to rest some but needed to begin the preparations after Christmas to acquire goods to ship to Kenya. I remembered the enjoyment in a previous furlough attending WMU associational meetings with Rachel Howard. Since her husband owned a grocery store, I asked if he could get some cases of food for me to ship in our crates. He was gracious and only charged me his actual cost. One day I went to his store in Tom Jr's truck and loaded it. When I went around a curve on East Wesley returning to the house, a case piled on top slid off the truck, spilling cans of soup all over the street. I spent some time chasing a few down the hill. I had failed to secure the load and paid a price for this omission. One crate was completely full of three-ply computer paper for the treasurer's office. I built the crates in the back yard and when the truck came to get them, it was too big to pass the house, making them difficult to load. We finished our packing, said goodbye again, and flew to Nairobi in early March 1985.

When we left with Sally for her to go to Ethiopia, Tom Jr. and Andy moved to live with my mother again. This trip was blessed because Nancy and I were upgraded to business class and were seated upstairs on the 747 flight to Amsterdam. We had day rooms in a nice local hotel where we got a relaxing bath and a good nap before our night flight to Nairobi. A large crowd had met to welcome us at the airport and we went to a tea at Joan Carter's house next door to ours on Thika Road. Our dogs, Acha and Heidi, were very glad to see us. Since our house was set up, we were very glad to collapse in bed because we were very tired when we left Atlanta.

Mary Saunders flew to Nairobi with Sally's work permit and they travelled together to Addis Ababa in mid-March. The first letter we received from her was full of information about the ministry and living conditions in Rabel, Ethiopia. She described it to us:

> I am here in Addis for the weekend and decided to write a collective letter so that I could get everyone written. When looking on the map, the town of Rabel looks quite close to Addis Ababa,

but they were years apart. The ride in the car took us 11 hours, and I came to Addis in the helicopter this time and I was on the mission compound in three hours. We've decided that the helicopter is a way to go.

Rabel is a town of approximately 500 people. Most of the housing is rock with grass roofing. They have a Red Square for the military marching. On the edge of town is the site of our feeding center. We can see the government clinic from our on-site feeding shelter, but the care is free. Each day we register a different farmer's association which is the way the sections of land are divided since they have no town as such. The people go through a process of giving their names, and if the babies have no names, we give them one. There are several little girls named Sarah now! After their names are given, the children are weighed and measured for height. This is to find the percentage of ideal body weight of the child. The children measured must be under five years of age, or they move into the destitute category. Those who are destitute must share their monthly ration with five other people considered to be destitute. They are counted last. Rather than wait and share, many times mothers will bring in eight-year-old children or above saying that they are almost five.

If those weighed are less than 85% ideal body weight, they're given a month's ration of grain, milk, and oil, all given by people of the United States of America. It is touching to see them handshaking one another with those words on the side of a grain bag. If they are less than 70%, we allow them to stay in the on-sight feeding program which allows them two blankets each, and four meals a day. We also make rounds twice a day to give out vitamins and other needed medicines. Yesterday was bath day. In Rabel, eucalyptus trees grow, so we made bath shelters covered with leaves. It smelled very good to go back there to check on the people. We had no running water so ladies each morning bring big pots on their backs from the stream at the bottom of the hill and pour it into barrels. We bathed the people sparingly, needless to say.

We nurses live in the mud house with wooden doors and windows, but we have the privilege of having a tin roof. The only problem is that we have several pigeons who love to crawl all over the roof and make lot of noise. In each room, we have a sheet of corrugated plastic to serve as a skylight. It is very nice during the day and provides great light. I was surprised how dark the houses in Addis Ababa are during the day. We have a very big room which serves as our kitchen, dining room, living room, and storeroom for some of our drugs etc.

We've made the most of this room I think. As soon as the folks left us alone, we reorganized the kitchen area, put down grass mats, and made it quite homey. Originally, we had an old camping stove with two burners to cook with. On one of the trips, we were provided with a four-burner stove with a small oven and a refrigerator. I was thrilled because we had ice. The only problem was that the refrigerator only worked for one day. We tried everything, but not being a mechanic, I couldn't get the thing to work. It is more frustrating to have the thing in sight every day, than to just do without cold things. We had just been sent several pounds of ground beef and veal roast, so we had to cook it right away, and share with our staff. It actually worked fine because we had a good-bye dinner for one of our volunteers. Aunt Mary and I each have a bedroom with two homemade beds and we use empty biscuit tins as bedside tables and shelf space. It is really quite nice but we can hear everything that the other does even with the doors closed. I think that is from the roof being corrugated and there are holes between the rooms. But we love each other, so all is fine.

Right now, we're feeding over 100 people in our shelter. Some of these children literally were on the verge of death from starvation.

The first day I arrived, I was overwhelmed by the people bowing to kiss our feet in appreciation of the food and blankets given to them.

We of course told him to thank God because it was because of His love that they were there. We have seen some real miracles in that shelter.

The children would come in lethargic with no extra tissue on them, just skin and bones. After a few days, their eyes would become bright and a little smile with appear on their faces and we could see actual weight gain in a matter of three days. Each of these is reward enough for being here.

I have included this section of our letter because I believe it describes the living conditions of many missionaries serving in the Third World. An understanding of the lifestyle of those missionaries enables prayer warriors to know how to pray more effectively. Nancy and I never had to live under these conditions except for the many trips of few days we made to remote areas.

Soon after Sally and Mary were established, the FMB and the SBC sent a team to videotape and photograph the ministry for publication and presentation at the SBC convention in June. A news anchor from a Richmond TV station also came. We saw a clip of Sally taken during a prayer time which gave comfort and encouragement about God's protection and blessings. We felt joy and were proud of the way God was using our daughter. Nancy reopened the Mathari Valley Clinic on March 18 and the film crew also went to Mathari Valley to capture footage about this clinic to help Americans visualize the living conditions in an African slum. As the word spread that the clinic was open again, the patient load quickly increased to more than 100 patients per day. Nancy was very thankful for all the volunteer help, especially Betty Evans whose Swahili was the best of the volunteers. Her friend, Margaret McDonald, the wife of the manager of the largest Standard Bank in Kenya, also volunteered as did many journeymen and MKs. Sally helped the two weeks of her visit when she came from Ethiopia to celebrate her birthday with us. Angus McDonald, a Scotsman with a brogue, teased Nancy about her Kirk maiden name. He told her people named Kirk instead of Kirkpatrick or Kirkland, probably dropped the last part because they were brought to Georgia from a debtor's prison in England.

My reentry into the treasurer's work went slowly at first because Mildred Cagle was in the hospital when we arrived. She had an undiagnosed fever troubling her, an eye problem, and back pain so by the end of the month was still not working in the office. Nancy helped me in the office during this time. In addition to the Mathari Clinic, Nancy had a ministry helping missionaries with medical questions and visiting them when they were hospitalized. We were pleased to have a new Peugeot 504 assigned to us as our mission vehicle this term. Very quickly, I discovered I needed to start with the records when I left for furlough, so that the books would balance properly. It took several months to get completely caught up.

Andy had gotten a job with a roofing company and was working on large projects. When we learned he was working on the roof of the 34 story King and Queen Buildings in the Perimeter Center, we were a little nervous. Later, another project was the massive distribution center for United Parcel Service.

During Easter weekend the Kenya Safari Rally was scheduled to pass by the mission property on Thika Road. On Monday morning, several of us carried a picnic lunch to the road side to watch the cars on their final stage returning to Nairobi. We enjoyed the fellowship and the view of the rally cars speeding by our entrance. It was a tough rally; seventy-two cars started but only twenty finished. On Easter Sunday, the Stewarts went with us to the church at Marumi, one of the larger churches in Muranga Association. It was an appropriate time to encourage the people and celebrate the Resurrection.

The Baptist Convention held their annual meeting in mid-April preceded by an Executive Committee meeting which I had to attend as a member. The day this meeting finished, Sarah arrived to spend two weeks with us and celebrate her birthday.

Harold and Betty Cummins moved into the mission house at Thika and were assigned the church ministry in Muranga. I went with them to attend an associational EC meeting, to introduce them and share my appreciation with the leaders for the opportunity of ministering together with them for several years. Mike and Charlotte Livingston were new missionaries assigned to minister with churches in the Kitui section of the Kamba people. I was asked to minister with those churches until they finished language school and moved to the area.

In the middle of 1985, the Kenya government began a major highway expansion of Thika Road in front of our property, making it difficult for us to leave and impossible when the rains came because of the severe mud. Missionaries visiting the office had to park their vehicles across the highway and walk to our offices. Nancy and I missed many times of fellowship with people and meeting some of the Kentucky volunteers who were coming to do volunteer ministry. One day when they were grading, they broke a major water line, but we were thankful we had a supply in the overhead tanks in our house. With conservation, no baths and infrequent flushing, we survived the three days required to repair the line.

Naturally, this complication occurred the week our crates from the US were scheduled to be delivered. Roy Brent and I spent two whole days at the clearinghouse to have two container shipments cleared by customs. Besides our crates, the shipments for three other families were in these containers. In May, the CID (Criminal Investigation Division, Kenya Police) discovered and investigated a major fraud by the bursar of Mombasa Baptist High School. I obtained the records for an audit which showed that many students had not paid school fees and the audit confirmed missing funds of approximately Ksh 240,000. The mission had funds which would cover the deficit with a loan. However, they denied a request to add a third stream of students. The mission instructed the school administration to follow government guidelines; they would give a grace period of two weeks for fee payment at the beginning of any term. If fees were not completely paid by then, the school would send the student home and he or she could not attend any class until the fees were completely paid. I knew a young man from Muranga, a pastor's son, who had just finished his studies and I recommended him to become the new bursar. At my last knowledge, he was still the bursar, the school was financially viable, and he was a deacon in his church.

On the first Sunday in June, I was scheduled to preach at a church in Muranga. The Courseys were staying with us and Clay went with me to this church. His going with me was a real blessing from God because as I was walking toward the church building talking with someone, I was not paying attention and walked directly into a tree branch. The impact split my forehead and I was bleeding severely. We told the congregation we were disappointed, but I needed to go see about the injury. Clay drove, and we stopped by our house to get bandages before we went to Parklands Baptist Church where Nancy and Pat were worshiping. A missionary doctor from Uganda was there, he examined it with Nancy, and they concluded that I did not need stitches. We went to lunch with my bandaged head and I went home with a bad headache. This incident provided another proof God meets our needs before we know we have one.

One June Saturday night we had a "kwaheri (goodbye) party" at our house for all the journeymen who had served in Nairobi and on Sunday night we did the same for three journeymen from Georgia who had spent two years in Uganda. These young people made a great contribution to the ministry as did many others we had over the years.

At the end of June, my Mom fell in her driveway and broke her hip. Tom Jr. was there, heard her call, and took her to the hospital. Nancy's brother Frank had a heart attack prompting Nancy to leave for Georgia to help with their medical needs. Briarcliff Baptist Church in Atlanta was building a retirement complex and Mom had decided she would move there someday. Her fall accelerated her decision. Sally left Ethiopia in July, spent a few days with me, and went to the U.S. to prepare to move to Fort Worth to attend seminary in the fall.

Tom Jr. graduated from Southern Tech with a Bachelors Degree in mechanical engineering. He returned to Kenya with us for a while before he started working. He was a huge help for moving all the furniture. Sally's brothers and some friends helped her move to Fort Worth in August before I arrived in the U.S. She began using her birth name Sarah in college. We recognized when she first met a person by the name they called her.

I worked hard unpacking the shipped items we had not unpacked before Nancy left. One of the things we brought was a small metal storage building to store the lawnmower and tools instead of the storeroom where we put the cases of groceries and other things. I am a chemical engineer, not a mechanical one; thus, I found the assembly instructions to be poorly written for "dummies." Several times, I put a part in backwards or in the wrong place and had to change it. As a result, it took me two full days to complete the task.

Mildred Cagle was on furlough and a volunteer from Kentucky, Edith Killip, was helping me in the treasurer's office. She was very good, and I began to use a dictation machine. She had drafts on my desk quickly, accelerating our productivity. Many people were on furlough including Jack Conley. I spent many extra hours in the office keeping up and preparing for the Convention EC, MSC, and Mission Meetings which overlapped at the beginning of August. Mission Meeting was a good one, passing the budget and all financial matters presented in one hour. MSC did have some items agreed in their meeting which were approved quickly. The Bible study on Colossians was special. A few of us met with the Uganda missionaries and some were considering the possibility of returning to Uganda. George Berry, their treasurer, could stay in Kenya to cover my assignment while I went to the U.S. to move my mother.

The mission strived to reestablish working relations with the Baptist Convention which were necessary because of the partnership with Kentucky Baptists. James and Wilma Whaley had arrived in January 1985, to become the Kentucky field coordinators for the project. The mission established a long-range planning committee, and we held our first meeting which was a very good one in August. The partnership began a healthy process in our working relationship but a few bumps dotted the road. Arthur Kinyanjui and Sampson Kisia helped us make progress.

We were seeing significant response by the Maasai to the Gospel and many were being saved. Baptism was an issue for many because of their culture. At mission meeting, several missionaries wanted to make all requests for assignments as new church developer type missionaries to work with the Maasai. I believed with the significant current response in other people groups, we needed a more balanced approach, touching all responsive people groups. When I made this comment, attendees made a significant negative response to the idea. I kept quiet. Harold Cummins, who worked in a responsive Maasai area near the Kamba people, had seen several saved and planned a baptism service. When several Maasai were very reluctant to join him in the local pond, he asked why? Their response was, "Bwana, there is a python who lives in this pond."

With the rebel war in Uganda, many Ugandans fled to Kenya and were living in refugee camps near the border. We had a significant ministry to those people which reminded me of the urgency to share the Gospel with these Ugandans because, when people are displaced or under other stresses, they are seeking an anchor and will be more responsive to the love of Jesus.

Nancy and the kids started helping Mom pack before I arrived in September for her move. We filled her apartment at Kingsbridge with her furniture, got a contract to sell her house, and bought one for Tom Jr. and Andy to live in while we were overseas. We moved more of her furniture into our house. Mom and Nancy's mother were packrats, and I got very frustrated going through all the stuff Mom kept. This year, I'm thankful because I found over 500 letters plus newspaper clippings they kept for us to have. My memory has been brought to life as I have read and reread this information during the writing of this memoir.

I flew to Atlanta in early September to help Mom move to Kingsbridge and get all the business affairs settled for her and our kids. We visited Sarah in Fort Worth before beginning our return trip to Kenya with Tom Jr. where we spent Thanksgiving Day in Amsterdam. Somehow trout was not an adequate substitute for turkey and dressing for the three of us.

With the current mission structure, I was on several committees because of my assignment. I represented the mission on the convention Executive Committee and the special committee to reestablish good relationships with it. I was on three school boards, the two high schools and the Arusha seminary. I was also on the Long-Range Planning Committee and the MSC. Preparation and attendance at these meetings plus audits for other missions required significant travel.

The mission held a prayer retreat in April 1986, which was very refreshing, and Keith Parks, President of the FMB, visited Kenya for a few days. I also spent four days at convention meetings. We enjoyed the time Tom Jr. spent with us until April and he was involved in ministry. We visited several game parks while he was in Kenya. The most memorable one was our trip to Amboselli where we stayed in the self-help bandas. It was nice, right on the edge of the plain looking directly at Mt. Kilimanjaro. As we sat on the porch after supper, an elephant came toward us, used her trunk to grab some of the trash can lid from the can that sat just in front of the bandas, and tried to shake open the trash can. A security guard threw rocks at the elephant making her leave. We watched the moon as it rose over the horizon and then went to bed. Sometime after midnight, an extremely loud roar from a male lion woke us. We got up, peeked out our window, and saw him pass within ten feet of our banda. We heard his roar until he was probably close to two miles away, walking toward Kilimanjaro. It was exciting, but we went back to sleep.

James Whaley used Tom as a driver, taking some of the Kentucky volunteers to various places for their ministry. One trip, Tom Jr. took a couple with their 16-year-old daughter to minister in Kakamega. The father was a dentist and he expected to work in a dental clinic to help patients with problems in their teeth. When they arrived in Kakamega, they stopped by the Horton's house and found the big steel security gate padlocked. Tom called Ed who came and unlocked the gate for them to visit. Then he took them to the local hotel to spend the night before they started ministry the next day. The next morning when he went to collect the dentist for his ministry, he was told that they had made reservations to fly back to the U.S. that night from Nairobi. Tom drove them back and carried them to the Whaley's house in Nairobi. As we learned the story, the teenage daughter was very upset for two reasons. Her parents had just given her a new BMW car as a present on her 16th birthday and she had just broken up with her boyfriend. She was very upset and did not want to be there. The father paid about $3,000 extra for the tickets to go back to the U.S. early. They became very frightened with both the Whaleys and Hortons having strong security gates at their houses. Also, at the hotel they had heard drums and loud music most of the night. This event was very unusual because most volunteers adjusted very well and had a wonderful experience ministering with local pastors. We had many volunteers who spent one to two weeks tent camping in Kenyan villages.

We began to hear from Sarah about her seminary studies and people she met. She mentioned one man, John Davenport, and as we learned the story, we realized how God can orchestrate our lives. John's best friend at seminary was Kim Johnson who had been a journeyman living at Brackenhurst. When a video about the famine in Ethiopia was shown at chapel one day, the clip of Sarah praying was shown. John commented to Kim that he liked the way the girl prayed and would like to meet her someday. Kim's response was that he knew her, and he could introduce them at the seminary. So, they met, quickly became interested in one another and in early 1986, Sarah called us to say that she and John were engaged and planned to be married in May. This created an interesting challenge for the logistics of their wedding. Sarah and John lived in Fort Worth, the wedding would be at Second- Ponce de Leon Baptist Church in Atlanta, John's parents were on the field as missionaries in Argentina, and Nancy and I were on the field in Kenya. So, we began to plan the wedding from afar but most of the planning was done by the bride and groom to be.

We requested a month's leave of absence without pay so we could fly to Atlanta for the wedding in May. A leave of absence was required since we had already used up all our stateside time helping Mom the previous year. When we arrived in Atlanta, Nancy begin preparing for all the food which we would self-cater since the wedding with our tickets was going to cost so much money that we didn't have at present time. She made the wedding cake and the groom's cake and some friends helped with the preparation of the other food.

The husband of one of Sarah's good friends was a chef and made a beautiful ice carving to be used at the reception. The rehearsal dinner was catered in Chastain Park and the food was tasty. It was a wonderful celebration on a warm sunny evening. Afterwards, we went to the church for the actual rehearsal. When I stopped by the church to let my Mom out of the car, she fell and broke her ankle, so I had to take her to the emergency room, get it x-rayed and casted. After the rehearsal, some of the groomsmen and others came to our house in Norcross. We worked half the night polishing my Mom's and our silver, and cleaning other things that we would use for the reception. Kim Johnson ironed the tablecloths. The wedding the next day was a beautiful occasion. Everything was just outstanding; John's Dad did the ceremony and I assisted which was my first attempt to be in a wedding besides my own or being a groomsman in other weddings of friends or family. Our good friends, Glenn and Jeanine Boyd drove from Oklahoma to sing. The wedding was made special when good friends made the effort to make the wedding extra special. The reception was enjoyable and after the wedding couple was on their way for their honeymoon, we went back into the church kitchen and begin cleaning up. Several church friends that we met during our furlough in 1984 came and assisted us. I was especially intrigued when a board member of a local bank was in the middle of cleaning the pots and pans. All in all, the day was extra special when Nancy and I went home, happy and very tired.

Andy was very active in Wieuca Road Baptist Church and had some responsibilities with the singles group. He was also a Royal Ambassadors (RA) leader and sang in the choir. He wrote to us and commented he was unsure of the Baptist church. This "crisis of faith" was a surprise and concerned us; therefore, we asked him to write and share what the issues were. In his August 1986 letter, he wrote the following:

> About Baptist, I don't really have anything against the basic beliefs: the priesthood of the believer, the virgin birth of Jesus,

> autonomy of the local church, etc. I guess it is more to do with the emphasis that they have. It might be Wieuca but other people that I have talked to see the same in their churches
>
> At Wieuca, the emphasis seems to be on numbers, dollars, and people. Money doesn't bother me because it is needed. Dr. Self has been gone for a month and will be back next Sunday. On the past Monday, the church had an outreach and inreach drive. I didn't go but I talked to someone who did. She said she was uncomfortable about the emphasis. The mail outs and phone calls were to the effect of "come to Sunday school and church and make Dr. Self proud." That is wrong. It should be "come and worship God." We have people joining every week but there's nothing there to keep them if they are looking and desire spiritual growth. The things are there but they are not talked about enough. There is a lot more, but I want to sit down and talk with you face-to-face. It seems that the church has their eyes off Jesus Christ.

At the end of his letter, he referred us to Philippians 1:6: "For I am confident of this very thing, that He who began a good work in you will perfect it until the day of Christ Jesus" and 1 Corinthians 16:13, 14: "Be on the alert, stand firm in the faith, act like men, be strong. Let all that you do be done in love."

I was proud of my son for recognizing there are churches and church leaders who lose sight of the big picture, who get caught in the syndrome of letting the vision stagnate or permit their focus to be drawn away from making Jesus priority. Satan always attacks Christians or churches where the Holy Spirit indwells the congregation. Baptists have been accused of giving priority to the three 'B's: Budgets, Buildings, and Baptisms. I believe we often lose sight of balancing the instructions of the Great Commission. When Jesus said, "make disciples," His command was to share the Gospel message which draws a person to confession, asking forgiveness, and inviting Jesus to give them eternal salvation. Baptism was the instruction to immerse saved people as a testimony of their surrender to the Lordship of Jesus Christ. The teaching command is the lifelong commitment of ministers and congregations to continually encourage Christians toward real mature faith which never falters, and their life exhibits the fruit of the Spirit. When this balance is maintained, the church, as Paul wrote in Ephesians, "causes the growth of the body for the building up of itself in love."

After we returned to Kenya, Nancy was busy with her cake ministry. Arthur Kenyanjui's son got married in September and he asked Nancy to decorate the cake. She started at home, but we went to Al and Peggy Cummin's house in Nakuru for her to finish it. She still had to repair it at the venue and was very nervous when she heard President Moi was attending the wedding. Then at the end of November Nyeri Baptist High School had a "Harambee" fund raiser and she and Patsy Dison made a huge cake.

I had another difficult week in early September when errors were discovered in the finances of Nyeri Baptist High School. As mission treasurer and a Board member of NBHS, I was heavily involved in determining the facts and the Board's discussions about actions to take. The Board decided to suspend the Headmaster Michael Maragu until we could satisfy the correctness of our research. This decision was difficult because Michael was a respected leader in Nyeri Baptist life. I was very thankful for Jack Conley, Arthur Kinyanjui, and Samson Kisia, also Board members.

Sarah and John called us on Nancy's birthday, September 10th, to tell us she was pregnant with our first grandchild. What a great gift for her birthday and Sarah wanted Nancy's mother to come to Fort Worth to help her when the baby was born. We greatly anticipated seeing the baby when we went for our furlough on October 15, 1987. We planned a trip to Mombasa for some rest at the Plaza Hotel, but it gave me an opportunity to work with the bursar at the high school.

I had several visitors from the treasurer's office in Richmond to do audits and train me for some new procedures they were implementing. The changes were challenging but we had a good administrative conference in Harare in October. Jack Conley, Roy Brent, and I attended this conference and enjoyed meeting administrative people from other countries in Africa.

Charles and DeeDee Evans arrived at the end of September as volunteers to assist me with computer work. I wanted to develop a sharable relational database for mission information to reduce the volume of data storage. Charles had been a co-op student at Southern Tech working with IBM and had done the evaluations of the first version of the word processing program. Charles was like another child of ours because of our close friendship with his parents. Part of the closeness was our Georgia heritage. Our mission was overwhelmed with Texans.

We were guardians for several MKs from other countries over the years. RVA required someone in country to be a pseudo parent for students whose parents lived outside Kenya. One of the MKs from Yemen, Mark Pirtle, broke his leg playing rugby so Nancy went to RVA to check on him. He was doing fine and would go home to Yemen in a week, so that his doctor father and nurse mother could take care of him.

The year 1986 was an exciting year because of the Kentucky partnership. Jack Conley and I discovered early in the year a major issue which we needed to resolve with the convention leadership. Reportedly many pastors were asking volunteers for a lot of money for diverse types of things, both family needs and materials needed to erect church buildings. This constant asking was not in keeping with the understanding we had in the partnership agreement, both with the Kentucky Baptist Convention and the Baptist Convention of Kenya. Jack and I met with convention leaders and we were very forthright by saying if they couldn't put a stop to all this begging, we would cancel the project. They were very understanding and agreed to take up this matter with all the pastors. We found that the environment changed dramatically as we began to see very superior results from the partnership. I wrote a letter at Thanksgiving 1986 to share with our family and the people who pray for us. I reported an exciting time and the following is what I wrote.

> These past few months have been exciting times for us. We're seeing a significant outpouring of the Holy Spirit among Baptist in Kenya. We had just finished compiling our statistics for the 1986 FMB report and it shows a 40% increase in the number of churches and preaching points. The 1986 congregation total is 956. Our membership has increased about 50% to 47,000. Some of this may be due to better data gathering but most of it is real growth. For example, in Mombasa, a city of 500,000, we have counted nearly 15,000 decisions for Christ in the past four months. One new church has over 1,000 people attending regularly. We are being granted government land for Mombasa church sites for the first time in 15 years. A pastor of the area told me last month that his church baptized more people in the past three months than for the previous two years together. Other parts of Kenya are also having significant growth in the churches.
>
> We have planned an evangelistic project in Maasai land to begin in about two months. A few years ago, we did not have a single Maasai Baptist church member. Today we have over 20 Maasai congregations. In August, we went to a youth and choir festal for an association of 17 Maasai churches. There were 800 attending and we enjoyed the fellowship and music. After that trip, Nancy and I decided we might be getting too old to sleep in a pup tent. This very noble looking tribe is turning rapidly to the Gospel because their culture is in a state of change. It is our mission's goal to share

the gospel in every Maasai village during the next two years. The mission family has set aside the first Monday of every month for prayer and fasting for the evangelization of the Maasai and the urban people of Kenya. Please join with us in this commitment.

I observed another event recently which I consider a miracle. It is normal for six months to ten years to lapse between the time funds are approved to purchase land and the completion of the property transfer. One Monday, I received a request for approval to purchase a church plot for a large village near Nairobi. That day, I obtained approval from the committee and signed the purchase agreement on Wednesday. It had a bank lien and I thought it would take the usual time to complete the transaction. On Friday morning, an area pastor came with the owner and papers to take to the government land office. I gave him the funds for the transfer taxes and at 3:00 PM he returned with the title deed in the name of the Baptist Convention. I'm still amazed at what God does when it pleases him.

Andy came to Kenya in mid-December to spend Christmas with us and we had a special time with him. I had a church developer's meeting following Christmas. On New Year's Day, we went to President Moi's house in Kabarak for a special day for all the Baptists in Kenya. There were probably one thousand Baptists present and it was an exciting time. We spent two nights at Amboselli National Park the first week in January before Andy's return scheduled on January 13th.

We got a phone call January 9, 1987 saying Sarah was in labor because her water broke. Joel Stephen Davenport was born two months early and weighed three pounds. I got Nancy on the first plane to Atlanta where she met her mother and the two of them flew to Fort Worth. We spread the word about needed prayer and many people in Africa began to pray. We heard later there was a little conflict at the FMB prayer time because both the South America office and the Africa office thought Joel was their new MK. Nancy stayed in the U.S. visiting with John and Sarah and other family until she returned to Kenya February 20th. Joel was in NICU for a while with lots of tubes until he gained enough weight to go home.

John and Sarah quickly realized they could not continue seminary studies and John needed to work to pay hospital bills and extra expenses with their new baby. When he had been in college at Furman University in Greenville, South Carolina, he had worked as a counselor at a residential facility attached to a hospital in Greenville. This facility met the needs of emotionally challenged boys and when he contacted them, they immediately offered him a position. They were also blessed because an elderly church friend of John owned a house which had been her fathers. She offered this house to John and Sarah rent free. They made plans to move in February and in early March, Tom Jr. and other friends went with John to Fort Worth to move all their possessions to Greenville. Sarah and Joel stayed in Atlanta with my Mom while the guys went to Fort Worth. Both great-grandmothers were very pleased to see Joel and help with his care. They both wrote about how happy Tom Jr. and Andy were to be able to hold Joel and play with him.

Mom spent Easter and a couple of weeks with my Aunt Louise in North Carolina. She was my Dad's baby sister and my favorite of his siblings. She was the only aunt or uncle of Nancy or me who visited us in Kenya. Andy was in Kenya when she came. Our trip to Amboselli included getting stuck in a huge mud puddle. Andy and I pushed the Peugeot 504 while Nancy drove so that we could get out of this trouble. It was also the trip I almost ran over a twenty-foot python sunning across the dirt road.

Since Nancy's favorite exercise was swimming, she got an annual membership at the Safari Park Hotel across Thika Road from us. She, Beth Butler, and Joan Carter went swimming there often until the weather was getting cold.

The first week of April, Nancy and I went to Samson Kisia's house in Kakamega. It had been several years since we were there and were pleased with the development Samson had made on his stone house. Because there still was no electricity or running water in the area, Nancy said we camped out. Samson and Jerida made us feel very welcome. We visited two new preaching points and I preached Saturday and Sunday morning. After the Sunday service, we walked a long way to a creek where church members had built a dam for the baptism of sixteen people. Because of my bald head, I had adopted the practice of wearing a baseball cap when I was outside. The water was about waist deep, but the bottom of the creek was "V" shaped and very slick. The tenth person to be baptized was a very large lady and, when I lowered her into the water, my feet slipped and we both submerged under the water. When I regained my feet, I saw my cap floating down the creek past the dam. Thankfully, someone rescued it for me. One of the preaching points gave Nancy a live duck. I thought it would be nice to take a picture but when she held it, she said, "The duck did its business all over my dress." She was not very thrilled and as she wrote her mother: "Needless to say, we left that darling duck with Samson's mother."

Over the years in Africa, I baptized people in many different settings. I have baptized inside and outside church buildings. I have baptized in creeks, ponds, the Indian Ocean, and a cattle dip. I began to report three types of baptisms in Kenya. Water baptism was the type Americans see in their churches and we had that plus in the creeks and ocean. "Wallow" baptism happened when there was very little water in the creek. To immerse the people you had to press them down in the mud and wallow them around to immerse them. We also had "coffin" baptism. In many areas, there is no water source near the church. Clay Coursey and others had welders fabricate a sheet metal box and carried this "coffin" and containers of water to the church in Landrovers for the baptism service. The people were always glad to keep the water for their use at home. Usually, it was still more pure than what was available to them.

I became the treasurer for Uganda while their treasurer was on furlough. This job required a couple of trips to Uganda. I especially remember one trip when I flew into the Entebbe airport. I hired a local taxi for the ride into Kampala to the mission office. On the twenty-mile trip, we were stopped at more than ten police checkpoints. At each one, there were at least two soldiers with AK-47 guns. Most of them were not more than fifteen years old. I arrived safely but this experience made me sensitive to the way our missionaries in Uganda and some other countries lived every day. We planned for our furlough from October to January 1988. Roy Brent would be treasurer assisted by Charles and DeeDee Evans.

Our dog Heidi was pregnant, and I built a doghouse to allow the puppies to be trained outside. She had seven pups in May, two females and five males. They were all red short hair Dachshunds like her. We hoped Tom Jr. did not want a female because there would be problems with Blitz and his sister in the same household.

At the end of May, some of us had a nighttime adventure. James Whaley had taken someone to the airport and on the way home he decided to drive through the Nairobi Game Park in the late afternoon. We got word about midnight he had not returned home. We organized a search party. Roy Brent, Bill Curp, and I met at the gate of the park, told the ranger on duty our problem, and received permission to enter the park to search for James and the others. We agreed on where we would meet to consult as we drove on all the roads in the park. We finally located their van about 3:00 a.m. The road he was driving on had some deep ruts from the heavy rain and he had slipped into the ruts. The van's frame was on solid ground and the wheels had no traction. We got out to push the van to get back on solid ground. Suddenly, I saw the eyes of an animal a few feet from the van. We got into the van quickly with Bill Curp diving into the back and over the seat. We waited until the female lion left the area before continuing our efforts and finally got home before daylight the next morning.

Two Kentucky volunteers were assigned to witness in Mathari Valley in June. It was a valuable time and we enjoyed hearing their stories in the evenings after supper. We were very happy they stayed with us. Nancy carried them to the church every day where a church member met each of them and translated as they witnessed. One day I went and after getting them started, I walked through the valley. As I was walking along the path between houses, a man ran up to me and said "I need Jesus." While I was sharing the Gospel with him, I realized he was quite drunk. He wanted to introduce me to some friends, so that I could tell them about Jesus. I entered the house and found several men who were obviously having a drinking party. I shared a short while and left because I knew they were drinking "changaa," the local white lightening brewed along the banks of the Mathare River. This experience was certainly new for me, but one never knows how God might use a faithful witness.

Andy had quit his roofing job when he visited us at Christmas time. When he returned in January, he became a salesman at a car dealership. He spent many hours there but did not sell many vehicles. In July, he moved to Greenville and began working at the children's program where John worked. He lived in the hospital where the boys were housed and was the person responsible for the boys at night. I think he had a valuable experience and enjoyed helping the boys and encouraging them.

The Kenya Mission dealt with a lot of issues in 1987. It was the last year of the Kentucky partnership and God blessed the efforts. When we summarized the year's results, we discovered we had enough new church starts to say a new church was started every day of the year. A lot of discipleship investment was also made. Jack Conley said it was truly Harvest Time.

The FMB made a major change in regional leadership. Davis Saunders was elected to be a Regional Vice-president for Eastern and Southern Africa. James Hampton moved to Richmond to become an Administrative Associate for Cooperative Services International, a group to develop ways Baptists could work in countries that would not approve resident permits for missionaries. John Faulkner from Zimbabwe was named Area Director and moved to Nairobi as the location for his office.

With the creation of several International Ministries based in Kenya, the Kenya Mission was confused about the interpretation of a FMB poiicy defining the relationship of missionaries assigned to those institutions and the Kenya Mission. The mission had no control over the number of missionaries in this category, but was expected to provide support for housing, transportation, MK schooling, and other financial matters in our budget. The policy stated we were to provide among other things "moderate mission activity and responsibility." The mission appointed a committee to meet with the Area Director and the Regional Vice President to seek a resolution to the developing friction.

The plan for the Maasai Project had been patterned after the Giriama Project and it would not transfer to another people group easily. Maasai elders would not give permission for the teams to enter bomas; thus, the plan was modified in keeping with Maasai cultural practice.

Jack Conley was nearing his time of retirement and discussions began on the procedure for the selection of a new Mission Administrator. This selection was to become difficult to resolve before Jack Conley retired.

Ancestors

Grandparents
A.M. & Orrie Jones

Grandparents
R. A. & Lucy Dean

Parents
J. D. & Sarah Jones

Tom & Nancy Jones

Our Kids

Andy Makes Three

Rugby Player, Tom Jr.

Easter Finery

Sarah's RVA Graduation Day

Happy Kids in Kenya

College

Grandkids and Great Grandkids

Joel, Amanda and Wyatt

Wyatt

Aaron, Jess, Ruth and Titus

Marisa and Ruth

Marisa

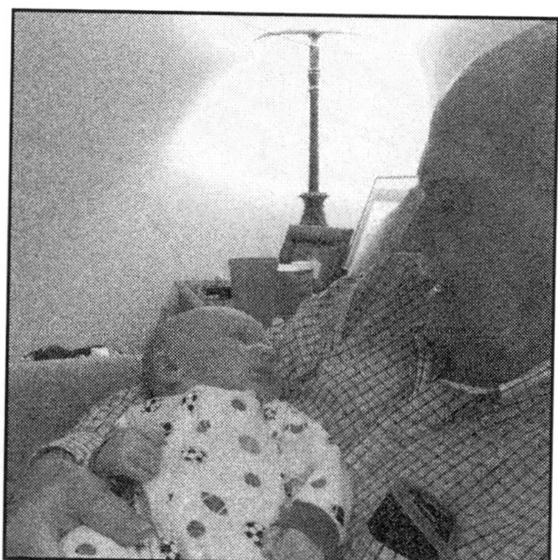
Babu and Titus

Professional Offices

My Marbon Research Team

Kenya Mission Administrator's Office

Marbon Research Lab

Administrative Assistant Nancy

Kenya Treasurer's Office

Seminary Business and Finance Office

Clinics

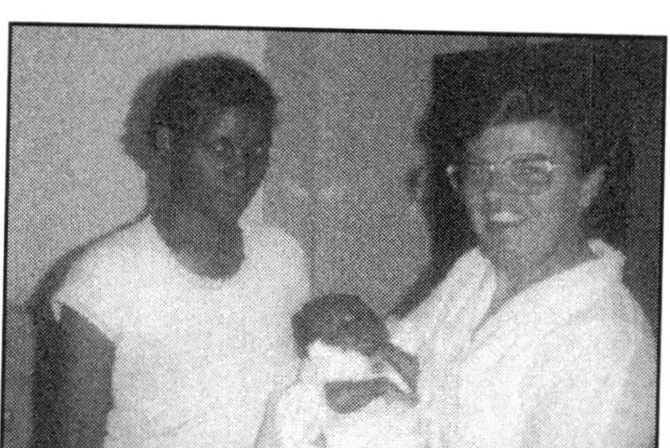
Nancy at Mathare Valley Clinic

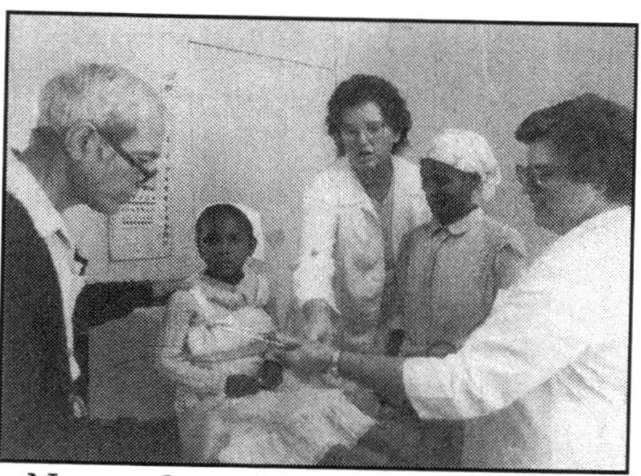
Nancy, Sam Cannata, and Betty Evans at Mathare Valley

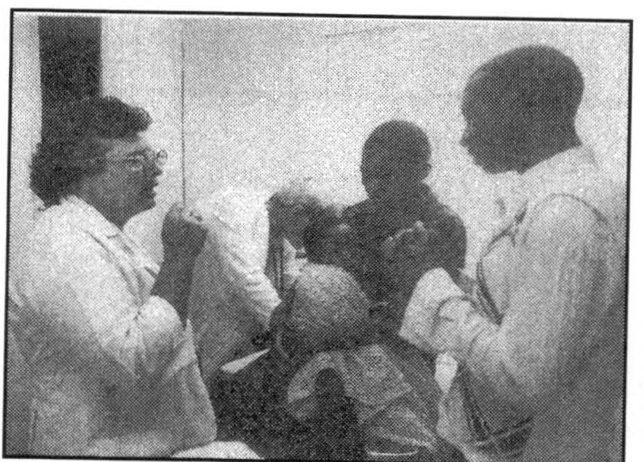
Translator Helping Nancy

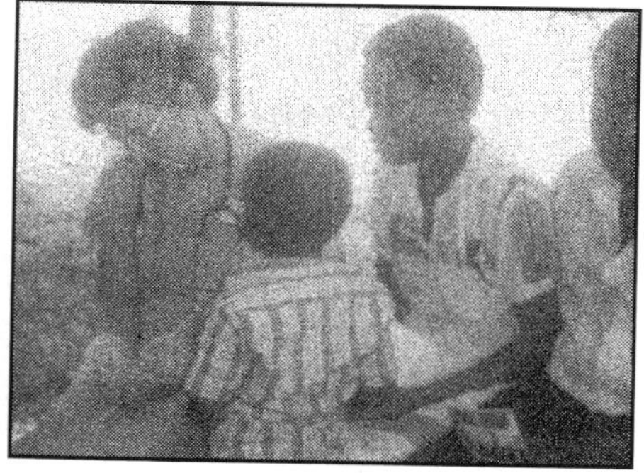
Nancy at Rural Church Clinic

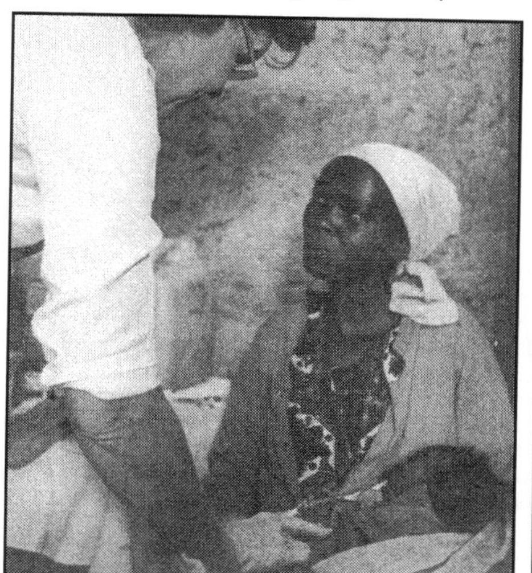
Sick Child at Mathare Valley

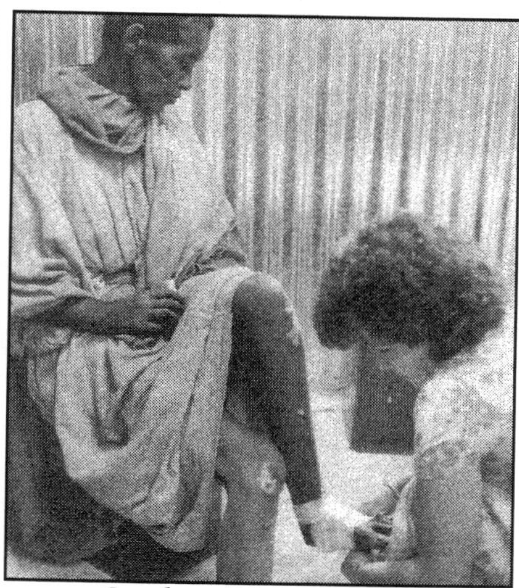
Sarah at Ethiopia Clinic

Church Ministry

Banana Hill Church Beginnings

Teso Church

Daniel Kinuthia Ordination

Ridgeways Baptis Church 2004

Samson Kisia's Village

Ridgeways Baptist Church 2011

Baptism

Tom's First in Kenya

Tom in Mombasa Channel

Tom on a Slippery Slope

Mombasa Channel Fence Keeping Sharks away

Eliud Mungai in a Pond

Maasai on a Mountain

Human Needs Ministry

Food Distribution During Drought

Ten Days to Build and Dedicate

Picking Up Spilled Beans

Baptist Member of Parliament Dedicating

Mathare Valley Food Distribution

School Cistern Dedication

Arusha

Mount Kilimanjaro

Seminary Class

Downtown Arusha

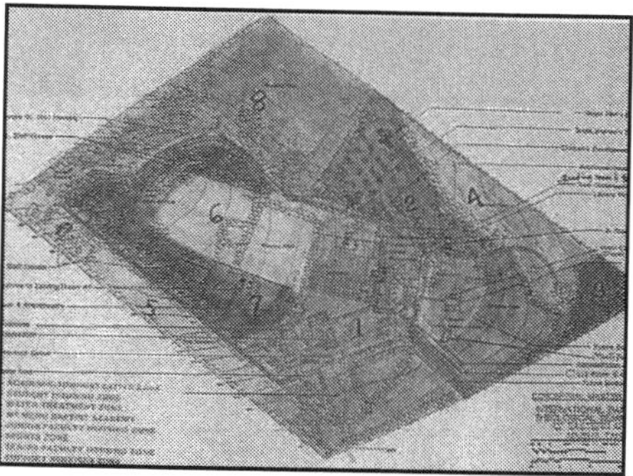

Mount Meru University Plan

Our Seminary House in Arusha

Seminary Maasai Gate Guard

ESL and Homes

Instructions to All Classes

Senior Class Graduation Certificates

Baton Rouge, LA 1957-1959

Belpre, OH 1959-1968

Duluth, GA 1997-2012

Hartwell Lake 1988-

Refugee Sewing Society

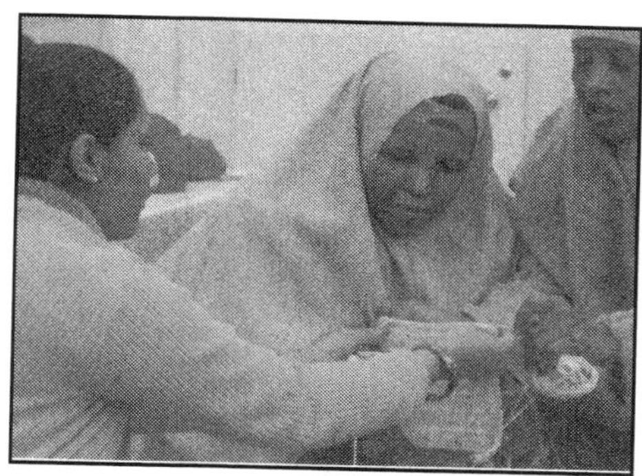

A Buddhist Helping a Muslim

Planning Session with Cathy

Cathy Teaching Sewing Class

A Friendly Muslim

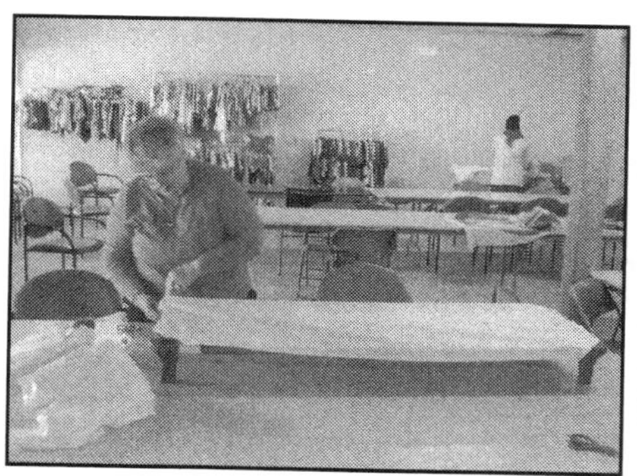

Nancy's Quality Control Test

Our Goodbye Party

Good News Center

Church Planting

Discipleship Training

Bible Distribution

Medical Unit Donated by the Georgia Baptist Medical Foundation

Jesus Film Showing

Childrens Home for Orphans

Baptist Retirement Communities Hiawassee Park

Spring Has Come

Frozen Lake Chatuge

Christmas at the Joneses

Baby Blue Bird
Ready to Fly

Flag Pole Dedicaation

SAR

Induction of Three Jones Men

Chapter Officer Swearing in

Supplemental Certificate

Andy's Grave Marking Ceremony

Certificate to Deputy Sheriff

Towns County Commisssioner Certificate

Chapter Thirteen
A Major Project and a Difficult Decision

Nancy and I left Kenya on October 17th for our furlough with a stop in Amsterdam. On this visit, we went to the tulip market and saw hundreds of thousands of flowers being prepared for international shipment. With all the conveyor belts and action, it was an impressive sight. A tour bus carried us to view a dike which reclaimed many acres of land for cultivation. We enjoyed the visit and rest before continuing our plane trip to Atlanta and arriving in the evening of October 21st. After two days resting, visiting Tom Jr. and my Mom, we went to Greenville, so that I could see and hold Joel for the first time. We left there and went to a conference in Richmond. After the conference, we were invited to visit Grace Baptist in Parkersburg where I preached.

We had one day at home in Norcross before we went to Nashville for the annual meeting of the Baptist Medical Dental Fellowship. Nancy always enjoyed these meetings where she saw many nurse friends and many medical missionaries. Before or after every meeting we visited with some we knew. The two weeks beginning the Sunday after Thanksgiving until mid-December were filled with speaking engagements. I spoke ten times in two states those two weeks. The next week I had another trip to Richmond for a meeting.

We began to be concerned about my mother's health after she broke her hip in 1985. Some of her letters said she sometimes took a longer route home after church or other outings. She said she was not steady, walked with her African cane, and seemed to be having some confusion. She was also having problems with her eyes, had gall stones, and had a hiatal hernia causing distress when she ate.

During the first week in 1988, I spent three days in computer classes which would help me on the field. A memorable event occurred on January 12th when we spent the evening with a Sunday School class from First Baptist Norcross at the home of Jim Ellis. Jim owned several automobile dealerships and was a committed teacher of his class. The fellowship was inspiring, and the Ellis home was very impressive with its lofty ceilings and awesome decor. We enjoyed the Christmas and New Year's holidays with family and friends and left for Kenya for our new term on January 15,

1988.

As usual after a furlough, getting updated on the status of the treasurer's work and the situation within the country and mission ministry consumed my focus for many days. I made a quick trip to Mombasa to check on the financial situation at the High School.

Our development work on the relational database had been finished. Charles, DeeDee, and I had spent many hours testing it on Kenya records and made corrections for the bugs we found in the program. We named the program Baptist Information Management System (BMAS). It was designed with four modules which were linked together in a way to minimize any data duplication. These modules contained data for finance, personnel, business, and churches. It was networked together to allow many users to simultaneously access data within their specific permissions. The most difficult challenge was in the financial module. Missions used national currencies. but all reporting to Richmond had to use the equivalent value in U.S. Dollars. Since exchange rates changed every day, a method to adjust bank balances to reflect current values of each bank or cash balance was required. After much thought and experimentation, the team concluded the best method was to calculate the bank balance value using a "rolling average" by adjusting the current value with each deposit to any bank account. Charles and DeeDee wrote a huge manual for users of the software. This quote from the BMAS Manual about history and acknowledgements shows the manpower investment and history of this project:

> The initial plans and many of the concepts of the BMAS were developed by Tom Jones, financial administrator of the Kenya Baptist Mission. Over the years as a mission treasurer and through some additional study in computer science, he formulated an overall plan for a mission's management system.
>
> In 1986, he requested that Charles Evans, a software analyst with IBM Corporation at the time, come to Kenya to help in the development. This plan was supported by Carl Johnson, John Moyer, and John Faulkner at the board. In consultation with John Moyer, the overall design of the system was formulated. This plan was presented at an administrator's conference in Harare composed of the administrators, treasures, and business managers from Eastern and Southern Africa. A training conference for treasures was held in Nairobi to introduce the concepts of BMAS and to begin training them on the system. Many other improvements were made due

to suggestions by Bob Hunter, Tom Jones, Roy Brent, Mary Ann Chandler, John Farris, Roger and Beverly Swan, Larry Dreman, and John Moore.

In order to develop the multi-mission concepts, Charles spent several weeks with Cliff and Philecta Staton at BIMS discussing and planning the multi-mission and multi-user adaptation of BMAS. Charles & DeeDee Evans traveled to the various missions in the area to install the system and train the beta testers of BMAS. The system's versatility and adaptability was improved due to each country's needs and unique methods of management.

Once the team thought our beta testing was adequate, Charles and DeeDee went to other missions in the region to install the software and train the mission leaders to learn to use it. This system was used in the region's countries in Africa for more than seventeen years until Richmond required adoption of a new accounting system used worldwide.

Nancy and I began our individual ministries quickly and during the first weekend in February, she attended the Kenya Baptist Women's meeting while I spent Saturday at Rosslyn. Rift Valley Academy had advised us they had no plans to increase their student body and could no longer guarantee Baptist MKs a place in the school. The MSC considered a desire of other mission groups to start a new school for MKs, but decided to pursue an expansion of Rosslyn Academy to include twelve grades. Herb Cady, the principal, asked for another assignment and the mission agreed to second Jim Richardson, a Rosslyn Board member, to become Principal of Rosslyn and to develop plans to add the grades required for a high school.

At the February meeting, a discussion included Mike McGlocklin representing the Assemblies of God who wanted to join the partnership with Baptists and Mennonites. The mission worked out details with them for developing the three-way partnership and the Area Office agreed to the proposal. In June, Jim Richardson reported the school had been offered an additional twenty acres of land and requested a loan to be repaid within three years. The mission placed this item at the top of the capital priority request list.

February and March were busy with meetings. I was involved at a church for a deacon's ordination and Mathari Valley Church had a week's revival. A theological education conference during the first week in March included me because I was the chairman of the Arusha seminary board. My roommate for the week was Dave Parker, the Principal of the Zambia Seminary. When we were on stateside assignment in 2004, Dave was the pastor of

First Baptist Duluth located a mile from our house. We had gotten tired of the twenty-eight-mile trip to Second-Ponce de Leon Baptist and had moved our membership.

April included a prayer retreat in Mombasa and the Kenya Convention AGM with Adrian Rogers as the guest preacher. Rogers was the current president of the SBC and missionaries wanted to get acquainted with him. At the end of the month, there was an Arusha seminary board meeting. Nancy also went with me to visit missionaries in a couple of towns. With the restructuring of the administration, it seemed there was a lot of travel instead of committee meetings.

May was a busy month because Wayne Dehoney brought a group of about eighty volunteers to hold an evangelistic crusade in Mombasa. Nancy and I traveled with the group to help because Nancy's mother and Judy Hayes were part of the group. Judy was a nurse and had been a friend since we met her when she was a counselor at G.A. camp one furlough. Roy Brent was going on furlough, so Jack Conley and I began getting up to speed on his assignment, so we could cover it for six months. Budget discussions were on the agenda for the June MSC meeting, so I had to prepare for that meeting. Ralph Bethea Sr. had been helping at Mathari Valley Clinic for a period before his furlough giving Nancy some relief.

Another tragedy hit the missionaries when Carl Hall had a sudden heart attack in Kisumu and died instantly. There was a memorial service at Brackenhurst in early July before Gerry and Duane took Carl's body to Arkansas for burial. Byron was already in the U.S.

A volunteer group from Second-Ponce de Leon Baptist Church arrived in July including Tom Jr., Pastor Bob Marsh, and his wife Myra. They ministered at our Mission meeting, our VBS for MKs, to youth, and to the mission with Bob as the speaker. A visit to the Ark before the meeting and Maasai Mara after the meeting was included in their schedule before they left on August 6th. Tom Jr. and I each drove a mission van for the safaris. I have one vivid memory of the trip to the Mara. One day, we had seen a lot of animals and in the afternoon, we found a large pride of lions, about twenty-five. I pulled my van above the right side of the pride which were lying in the grass and stopped for all to get an unobstructed view. With the engine turned off, it was very quiet as we watched the dozing lions. I happened to glance in the wing mirror and saw a camera peeping over the top of the van. Very nervously, I saw Carl Bedingfield lying on top of the van taking pictures. Quietly, I told him to get back inside. Carl, a choir member with a deep low bass voice and who was about six and a half feet tall, had climbed out the window to lie on top. If the lions were disturbed, it would have taken less than five seconds for one or more lions to jump onto the top of the van. Relieved, we returned to Brackenhurst safely the next day.

On August 10, 1988, we received a phone call saying Aaron Thomas Davenport had been born, our second grandson. We rejoiced because his birth had been normal. Years later, I thought about never seeing my daughter when she was pregnant, a blessing I missed.

The rest of the year was filled with many meetings: MSC, the called Mission Meeting, Boards, and committees. In September we celebrated the 25th anniversary of Mombasa Baptist High School and Nancy had a WMU Leadership Training meeting in November. Samson Kisia's daughter was married in December and Nancy provided the wedding cake.

As the mission approached the selection of an Administrator to replace Jack Conley, I had some concerns about the selection. Jack and I had become very good friends, especially while he was Administrator and had a good working relationship with each other and with Roy Brent. I felt our administrative team was working very well together and wondered what the future held. MSC had developed a questionnaire to send to missionaries about characteristics desired in an administrator. At the March MSC meeting, the presider submitted a summary of the results and listed the five names of missionaries suggested most often. MSC asked for comments for three men because two had requested their names be removed from the list. At a called May MSC meeting, another man on the list asked for his name to also be removed. At that meeting since neither of the two remaining men had a consensus, MSC decided to add my name to the list and sent the information to the mission.

While I considered this nomination to be a compliment, I had a concern for two reasons. First, Nancy did not want me to be in the position. Secondly, I had the perception Kenya missionaries were seeking a spiritual leader and did not believe I had the necessary spiritual gifts. I had always believed if God opened a ministry door, I should not close the door myself. I thought this action was divisive and it was. An ad-hoc committee recommended an interim administrator be chosen and the mission waited for a clear direction from God.

On November 14th, a called mission meeting was held at Brackenhurst to approve a job description for the Mission Administrator, defining the procedure to follow in choosing one and changes required in the Constitution by these actions.

After questions and amendments to the job description were approved, the committee recommendations were superseded by an approved substitute motion for the following steps for selecting the new Administrator.

1. Missionaries would establish prayer groups by area.
2. Each area group would be given a list of missionaries who qualify for the position.
3. Each area would select a leader who would represent them in a later meeting of group leaders.
4. Each group would select a prioritized list of five persons.
5. Leaders would meet with the presider to review the lists and select one name to present to the mission for a vote which requires a 2/3 vote.

This motion was approved unanimously, 68-0. The presider instructed the groups to gather to pray and after supper, group leaders would meet with the presider to propose an administrator to the mission for election when the groups reconvened after supper.

When the time came for the prayer groups, Nancy and I went to our room to pray. We knew missionaries needed the freedom to openly discuss the choices and suspected I would be on the list. We spent our time in the room quietly praying and asking God to choose His person. I can honestly say I was surprised when there was a knock on our door and we were told I had been chosen to be the new Administrator. When we entered the room, the missionaries applauded, and my heart was touched. I made a commitment to seek God's leadership for every decision. The transition was to occur in 1989 when Jack Conley retired.

Nancy and I made plans to take our vacation in the U.S. from mid-December to mid-January 1989, before I began my term as Mission Administrator. While we were there, we observed my Mom and talked with some of her friends. We had become concerned during 1988 by her letters which signaled some confusion and a lack of being steady on her feet. We knew it was not good for her to live alone, even in the retirement center while she still tried to drive. We asked her if she would like to go to Kenya with us for a visit. She agreed and, thus, began a long-term arrangement with her in our Kenya home.

When we arrived in Nairobi, we settled into our routine and tried to help my Mom get settled. We noticed things which renewed our fear she would not be able to live alone again. Nancy and I started discussing the probability that she needed to stay with us while her physical health was good and hoped she would agree to continue to live with us. It was very stressful for us with the constant care and Nancy took the brunt of the 24/7 lifestyle of care.

Bob and Myra Marsh came back to Kenya in February at the invitation of Ralph Bethea Jr. to preach and teach the pastors at Mombasa. Nancy commented Bob would have enough "Bethea" stories to fill his sermons for a long time. We went to Mombasa with Mom and rode back with the Betheas and Marshes to Nairobi. We had planned an overnight stay at Ngulia Lodge and rode through Tsavo East the first day. A tour guide told us about a pride of lions and we found all eight lions in the pride. As we headed toward Voi, a fork in the road said one road was nearer to Voi than the other one; therefore, we went the short route, a big mistake. After we travelled half the distance, the road disappeared, and the vehicle quit running in the middle of nowhere -- near an elephant. After we discussed options for a while, Ralph crawled under the car and found a leaking fuel line. Ralph cut away the bad section and reconnected the fuel line. The engine started. We missed lunch but had plenty of ice water and bushes to meet our needs.

We arrived at Ngulia just before dark and discovered the spare tire had been "lost" at the service station where we stopped in Voi. After a good hot shower, we went to supper and saw three leopards that came to the water hole where a tree had been baited. Those leopards came and went all evening before bedtime. As we left Sunday morning, we had a beautiful clear view of Mt Kilimanjaro many times as we travelled to Nairobi.

We shared many funny stories, but Mom Jones gave Bob Marsh his biggest and longest chuckle. We had started sharing funeral stories when Mom piped up saying, "They put one of my relatives in the coffin upside down." When they opened the coffin of her Aunt Sally to "view" her, they saw her feet. Much later in the evening when there was a lull in the conversation, Mom said, "They did change it and put her in right." Bob said he kept laughing and laughing off and on all night.

The day after I became administrator and Ed Horton became Treasurer, the MSC met. Nancy, Ed, and I were somewhat apprehensive in our "new" positions. I think we all survived. Nancy felt like she had a lot to learn about being my secretary. I did have Cecilia as an assistant, but I felt there were some confidential items and correspondence which I preferred Nancy to handle. She also took on the task of producing our monthly newsletter, News and Views. Nancy said the first day she had to learn the elements of being a good secretary—always proof-read documents before you pass them to the "boss." She was under pressure to get ready for the MSC meeting and gave me an outline to present which was missing several items.

By March, Mom felt comfortable enough to walk from our house to the office building. I knew Nancy was feeling pressure for me to discuss a long-term solution for Mom to live with us but with the work pressure of getting ready to become Mission Administrator on March 15th, I was procrastinating. I was also concerned about how to approach the subject with her, and I admit that I "drug my feet." When I did talk with her, she did not make any comment.

Our phone rang in the middle of the night in March when my Uncle Richard called and wanted to speak with Mom. I told him she was asleep and asked him to tell me what was going on because I could tell he was quite upset. He explained events which had taken place concerning the family. When Aunt Mae died, in her will she had deeded the nine-acre tract where the "home place" was located to Uncle Robert and his daughter Mary. After Uncle Robert died, Mary sold this tract and some other parts of Granddaddy's farm without consulting any family member. All of us understood a general agreement in the family that no one would sell any part of the farm without giving all members of the family opportunity to buy the land. Mary did not follow this understanding. Uncle Richard was so upset when he found out about the sale the week after closing, that he offered the developer buyer 15% more than he paid to purchase it from him. This offer was rejected. I told Uncle Richard I would explain it to Mom and she would write to him. She seemed to accept the matter gracefully and I think she thought this might occur when Aunt Mae's will was read.

The mission experienced another tragedy when Stan Cannata, Sam and Ginny's son was killed in a road accident in Ethiopia. Stan had been in Tom Jr's RVA class and was serving as a volunteer in Ethiopia. He was driving on a mountain road with an Ethiopian when they got stuck in the mud. The Ethiopian was scared; therefore, Stan told him to get out, gunned the vehicle, and lost control. He failed to regain control and the vehicle rolled down a 3,000-foot cliff with Stan still inside. It was believed Stan died during the descent. A Baptist nurse arrived on the scene via helicopter within an hour. Stan was engaged, and they were to marry in May. Bill Curp led a Memorial Service in Nairobi for Stan because he and Beverly had served with the Cannatas in Ethiopia.

I planned a short seminar for first term church developers at Brackenhurst. The Kirkpatricks, Hesses, and Harold Cummins helped Nancy and me lead the sessions. The new missionaries felt it helped to talk about problems and joys and about how "veteran" missionaries have coped with experiences, succeeding or failing. They asked for additional dialogue at the next church developer's meeting.

We invited Jack and Sally Conley to dinner before they vacated their house in Westlands so that the Housers could get settled. The Area Office had requested the mission give the house where the Aministrator lived in exchange for funds to build a house for the Kenya Administrator at Thika Road. This house was under construction when I began the position. I believe Jack felt he vacated the Administrator's position too soon. He commented he was a lame duck when I was elected, but his furlough time did not begin until six weeks after I assumed the position.

The second week in April was our Spiritual Retreat at the Two Fishes Hotel on the beach south of Mombasa. The guest speaker was O.S. Hawkins and it was a very valuable time of reflection and prayer. They asked Nancy to bake a cake for a celebration to say goodbye to the Conleys. Nancy agreed and suddenly realized she needed enough cake to feed everybody at the retreat. She was sorry she had said "yes" because she was still struggling to prepare the News and Views. She worked long hours as she learned the use of newspaper columns in Word Perfect. Her reward was the praise she got from missionaries about the content of every issue.

She wrote the following to our kids on April 5th about our new assignments: "Ed and Mary Horton feel about like I do, only worse, about their new work load. Ed has apologized to Tom several times already for EVER criticizing him in the treasurer's job. Ed has spent long hours and every weekend in the office since taking over March 15th. But, he's about to get ahold of it. Mary is helping him a lot with the books, computer, etc. Poor Tom—all the years he hasn't had me to help. But, it has taken 20 years for the treasurer job's present state."

In my opinion, Nancy missed the point about helping me with my work. She had her ministry with the clinics, women's work, being a hostess, and taking care of the kid's needs. I had plenty of help with all the journeymen, Elisha Chagusia and Joseph Okulo, Mildred Cagle and the volunteers. It was not until I became Administrator that I really needed her help in the office.

An event which I considered as my first major crisis occurred soon after I assumed the Administrator's position. The MK Committee had planned a retreat for the high school kids and we had received permission from RVA for our students to spend the weekend in a lodge at Lake Naivasha. The committee asked two new missionary couples to lead this retreat. They left the RVA campus Friday afternoon and would return Sunday afternoon. Early Saturday morning, I received a phone call from one of the missionaries saying there was a problem and he needed me to come and help him. I immediately drove to the lodge and heard about his problem. During the night, one MK had climbed into the bar area and selected something to drink. Another boy had been found in one of the girl's rooms. I listened to the stories and as I remember, I met with the MKs and told them it was necessary for me to meet with the Principal at RVA and explain. If we tried to hide it, the consequences would be more severe. I explained I was very disappointed in them because we expected a Christian behavior from them. I knew there would probably be a serious backlash from parents, but I was confident I was making the right decision. I left and went to RVA to meet with Roy Entwistle, the Principal. I told him I hoped he could make it a teachable moment when the kids returned to campus. Sunday afternoon, Roy Entwistle called me and said they had interviewed the students who had given honest replies and they were suspending a few who had made mistakes. There were two parent couples who were out of the country and I needed to collect those two students. I brought them to our house to stay until their parents returned. I was pleased because those two-showed respect to me and were contrite. The criticism I expected from parents did not happen openly. My relationship with several of these MKs became very warm and friendly.

Joseph Maisha, pastor of Ushindi Baptist Church in Mombasa, invited Samson Kisia and me to assist in their baptism service Easter Sunday. Joseph was a very charismatic person with some Pentecostal tendencies, but his church was growing rapidly. They had obtained a plot and were meeting outside for worship. He asked me to preach and he followed with another sermon. After the service, we walked to the Indian Ocean channel that surrounds Mombasa Island. On the way, Joseph informed Samson and me that the three of us would baptize since he expected eight hundred to be baptized that day. When we arrived at the channel shore and saw the ships anchored at the port farther away from the ocean, I noticed several men unrolling a chain link fence and walking into the water, so the fence formed a semi-circle around us. I had a helper for the baptism as did the other two men. After about three hours when we had baptized the last person, I asked my helper why they had made the fence around us. His reply: "Bwana Tom, last week, an underwater welder was welding on a ship anchored just there and he was eaten by a shark." I said a prayer of thanksgiving for chain link fences. I was very tired as we made our way walking back to the church site. But, it was a blessed day.

One Sunday evening Lena Crabtree, a journeyman who worked in the Area Office, knocked on our door. She led a Bible study at Kariobangi Baptist Church and when she was on her way there with Elle and Emma Sweatman, a drunken man walked into the side of her car. He got up and walked across the road almost getting hit again and fell into the ditch at the roadside. Lena came to ask me what she should do. I carried her to the police station to give a report. She gave the information to an officer and was told if anything else was reported, they would contact her.

While we were gone, Elle and Emma Sweatman stayed with Nancy and Mom. While Elle was looking at our photo albums, she saw a picture of Joel just after he was born and asked if he was premature. This gave Nancy an opportunity to tell Joel's story including his cerebral palsy. Since Emme also has CP, she openly talked with Nancy about her premature birth, her challenges with CP, and her physical therapy. Nancy described Emme as a cute, very intelligent teenager. This conversation was very encouraging to Nancy and she was deeply touched by Emme's openness. Again, God brought a special blessing during a demanding situation.

Lena's event was not significant as compared to the experiences of several missionaries. The Africans were not careful when walking or riding bicycles and several were killed by vehicles driven by missionaries. Most of the accidents were investigated and no charge filed against the missionary. There was one where I was deeply involved as the legal representative for the mission. John Saunders, Davis and Mary's son, was working in the student ministry in Nairobi. One evening, he was riding his motorcycle along Haile Salassie Avenue in downtown Nairobi. A man stepped in front of him and was killed when the motorcycle hit him. John was charged and given a summons to appear in court. I contacted our Advocates (legal firm) and confirmed Amos Wako would act for John and the mission. Amos Wako became the Attorney General for Kenya in 1991 and had a strong legal mind as our trial attorney.

On the first court date, the police had not completed the investigation; therefore, another court date was set. The three of us appeared at court twenty-six times and there was always a postponement due to non-appearance of the prosecution or other excuses. When we went the twenty-seventh time, the Judge had had enough, chastised the deputy prosecutor because the prosecutor had not attended court as directed and dismissed the case.

On June 14th, Sarah called to tell us Aaron had emergency surgery for cancer. I immediately made plans for Nancy to fly to Atlanta while Mom Jones and I would keep our plans to fly to the states in mid-July. We were in the office when Sarah called. The staff gathered around us to pray for Aaron and all the family. Mary Horton called all the missionaries to ask them to also pray. When Nancy arrived in Atlanta, Tom Jr. met her at the airport and carried her directly to Greenville. Besides Sarah, John, and Joel, Andy, Nancy's mother and two of her aunts were also there. On June 21st, the oncology doctor called with the good news that Aaron would not require any chemo therapy, but they would check his blood every two weeks for a period.

There was a Long-Range Planning Committee meeting where a long discussion was held concerning the configuration of church developer (further referred to as CD) missionaries in western Kenya. Several CD positions were approved by the committee for several areas in Kenya.

The June MSC meeting had several interesting discussions. I had sent a questionnaire to MSC members asking for comments about my function as mission administrator (later referred to as MA) and my weaknesses. There was generally good support except for one member who will forever remain unknown. These results confirmed my perception that I had turned a corner and was developing trust and a real support base in the mission. The other major discussion revolved around a letter received from the Area Director concerning the relationship between the MA and the Area Office. John Faulkner told me most Area Directors had given the authority which the Associate previously had to the MAs and he felt like a lone wolf. John wanted to take this step and create a staff position in the area office for a counselor for missionaries. I had lobbied for such a position while I was treasurer because I perceived missionaries were unwilling to share personal stress issues with any peer missionary in their mission who made any decision related to their work. Several MSC members were not ready for the MA to be given this authority and requested John Faulkner discuss this issue openly at our mission meeting.

The first week in July before I left for vacation, I had accepted an invitation from Samson Kisia to preach at the Ruiru church when they would have a baptism service. Bill Curp was supposed to help with the baptism but he sent word he would not return home in time for the service. Samson wanted me to do the baptism, but I convinced him he should do it as pastor. I missed the dedication service for the new church building two weeks later when Samson had asked me to preach again.

Mom and I flew to Atlanta four weeks after Nancy because we had planned a vacation trip, so that she could see her friends and talk to Uncle Richard about the sale of the family land. Her confusion seemed to be getting worse and we knew the three-week visit would be therapeutic for her. On the Saturday, a week before our return trip to Nairobi, we were visiting Uncle Richard and Aunt Joan. While we were talking about the nine-acre home place tract, Uncle Richard told us that the developer had agreed to sell any two of the twelve tracts to a family member who was interested. Uncle Richard looked at me and said: "Everyone in the family has a house on the lake but you so you need to buy the tract with the home place."

I replied: "I do not have money to buy it even if the price is good."

My Mom said, "I received 10% of Mae's estate and you are welcome to it if you want to buy the house tract."

The developer had divided the tract into twelve building plots with an arcing road between the eleven building plots and the original house which had a two-acre plot. All the others were about 0.6 acres. While I was thinking, Nancy and I were looking at each other, Uncle Richard left the room to return in a couple of minutes and he said, "There is someone on the phone who wants to talk to you." When I answered the phone, the developer told me he would make me a decent price if I wanted to buy the home place. He offered the house with the two acres at $130,000 which was only twice the asking price of a 0.6-acre lot. I countered with $117,500 and he immediately accepted which made me wonder how low he would have gone because Uncle Richard had hassled him so much. I told him I was flying to Nairobi in six days and would try to arrange a loan and close before I left the country. I knew this happening would be a miracle from God.

The next day we attended Second-Ponce de Leon Baptist Sunday School and worship. The Director of our adult Sunday School department was Denton Harris and I knew he was a Board member of a local bank. I asked him if he thought my need was possible and he said he would call the bank president the next day. When the bank president called me Monday to seek information, I told him the amount I had for a down payment and that I only had a picture of the house. I carried the picture to the bank and he called the developer to get a faxed copy of a sales agreement for me to sign and the legal description. He approved the necessary loan and scheduled a closing for Thursday. So, we made an offer, got a loan, and closed the purchase in less than one week. If that was not a miracle, I cannot recognize one. The house was rented to two single engineers who worked at the Milligan plant in the area.

When we returned to Kenya after our short vacation, there was a large group of volunteers and Nancy had to spend a lot of time with them in the clinics. My Mom had a "meltdown" when she learned Nancy and I would be out of country for a conference for a week and she received a bulletin from her Atlanta church saying she had moved to Kenya to live with us permanently. She had not realized this was our plan for her even though I had discussed it with her. Nancy and I went to the conference in Harare for a week. Howard Foshee led it. Being away was therapeutic for us. Patsy Dison stayed with Mom but, when we returned, we learned Mom had one very dreadful day. She had refused to take her medicine, told Patsy we did not love her because we really did not have a meeting and her grandkids did not love her either because she never heard from them. She told people if she could get back to Kingsbridge, she would never return to Kenya.

Her dementia was getting worse and she acquired some unpleasant habits which caused us to laugh so that we would not cry. She became a kleptomaniac with bath soap. She had to share the bathroom with our house guests and would take the soap and clean bath cloths we put there for the guests and hide them in her suitcase. If we carried her when we visited missionaries, we would find she took their soap when we left. It was a constant vigil for us and a lot of apologies.

To help her adjust, we planned a short furlough from mid-December to mid-March. The mission house being built for the administrator was nearing completion and we needed to move before this furlough allowing the Hortons to move to our house at Thika Road.

Howard Foshee and his wife Zola stayed with us in early October. Zola was an immense help for Nancy because she and Howard had kept her mother in their house for ten years. She listened to Nancy and shared that her mother was very much like Mom Jones. They thought Mom's issue was senility, not Alzheimers. Howard led discussions at the MSC meeting on management and organization principles. He had recently retired from the Sunday School Board. The same week was my Mom's birthday. Nancy baked a cake and we celebrated with the office staff and MSC members during morning tea time. Molly Houser also took her to lunch for her birthday.

Since Mom knew we would be taking furlough in December, she seemed more satisfied and we did not feel as much stress in November. The new house still had no electricity at the beginning of the month, but we began slowly moving our furniture there.

Ralph Harrell asked me to preach the first Sunday night in November at Brackenhurst for the English service. Nancy wrote our kids, "Tom did well with his sermon although he was a bit apprehensive because of all the preacher types and one visiting seminary professor who attended."

MSC had a difficult decision in the November meeting. Ralph Bethea Jr. had received a proposal from Texas Baptist Men to purchase an airplane and eighteen-wheeler medical/dental unit with a trailer. After a long discussion, we declined the offer because it did not fit our strategy, budget, or government restrictions. MSC did approve assigning senior church developers to mentor new missionaries, and Mary Horton and I organized a prayer chain for urgent requests.

Chapter 14
Challenges and Transition

The night before we left for our furlough during Christmas week, I had a horrible gall stone attack, the worst I ever had. I was nauseated, had severe pain, and could not get comfortable. I took four hot baths to try to relieve the pain and the only way I could get relief was to lie with my stomach over the hassock with my head down. The next day, the pain was diminished, and we made the flight to Atlanta without a further incident. We got Mom settled at Kingsbridge and went to our house in Norcross to crash. I did not have another attack and we enjoyed celebrating Christmas with all our family.

After Christmas, I called Dr. John Atwater's office to get an appointment. Dr. Atwater, an internist, was the doctor in Atlanta the FMB used for furloughing missionaries and referrals to specialists. He arranged a visit with a surgeon and on January 23rd, I had my gall bladder removed. When I had my pre-op visit, the surgeon told me he was learning the laparoscopic procedure but because I had so many small stones, he was not comfortable using laparoscopy to remove my gall bladder. The surgery went well, and I recovered quickly. When Nancy saw Dr. Atwater, he referred her to my surgeon to also have gall bladder surgery. The surgeon decided to remove hers by laparoscopic surgery. Her recovery from the surgery was not as rapid as mine and I think she never forgave me for my quick recovery. We had planned to return to Kenya in March but because of our surgeries, we did not get medical release to return until early May and arrived with my mother on May 10th. Four days after arriving in Kenya, I began a five-day week of three board meetings. The next week, I spent four days at the coast visiting with missionaries. While in the U.S., I thought and prayed about my ministry goals as administrator for 1990. One goal with highest priority was to visit with all Kenya missionaries during the year to hear firsthand their view about their ministry successes, disappointments, and failures. These visits would give me an opportunity to encourage them and help them reflect on their ministry opportunities and goals. I also wanted to get a feel for their attitude about the Kenya mission strategy and focus. The next week I spent two days in Kisumu.

My June began with a four-day church developer's meeting and a Mombasa High School Board meeting while there was an evangelistic crusade in Nairobi led by Larry Jones. The following week was a four-day MSC meeting and a Coastal Crusade Steering Committee meeting.

After I became Administrator, I began to receive many more invitations to preach or teach in locations all over Kenya. I happily accepted as many as I could, keeping in mind the opportunity to build relationships with many more Kenyan pastors and congregations. It was a joy and the preparation kept my spiritual life more focused than previously. I always tried to preach encouraging messages, focusing on sharing the Gospel and planting churches in opportune places. This part of the office was the most enjoyable. I always thanked God for giving me a gift in Swahili, something I had not had in other languages.

MSC had dealt with several critical issues while I was in the U.S. Vance Kirkpatrick had requested to change the name of the theological studies at Tigoni to Baptist Theological College, paving the way for the future expansion to degree level studies. The request and a new constitution were approved in January. In March, MSC approved developing strategies to evangelize specific people groups. When I became Mission Administrator, this was one proposal I made. I had been looking at unreached people groups in Kenya and found twenty-five specific ones which had been identified by Christian researchers.

A crisis had developed between Parklands Baptist Church and the Kenya Convention. Arthur Kinyanjui, who had been Moderator of the Convention for six years, was now serving as the chairman of the convention's trustees. Arthur was well known by President Moi and had asked Mzee to grant an eight-acre tract in a strategic part of Westlands for a church plot. After a lot of political wrangling, the President had instructed the Commissioner of Lands to grant the plot to Baptists. Parklands had been registered as a Society and when the title deed was issued, it was issued to Parklands Baptist Church, not the convention.

When Arthur discovered this action, he wrote a letter to Jim Houser, the Field Representative, asking for the work permit for the pastor, Charles Tope, to be surrendered so that he could be deported. Arthur was probably distressed for two primary reasons. First, he along with many Baptist leaders, had belonged to other denominations before they became Baptists. These groups, such as the Anglican Church, had a hierarchical church government and some who had become Baptists had not completely understood the local church autonomy of Baptists. Secondly, Nairobi Baptist Church had been begun in the home of Davis Saunders when he and Mary arrived in Nairobi. The church had been constituted and registered but did not cooperate with other Baptist churches in Nairobi affiliated with the convention. Arthur feared the same thing would happen to Parklands. The issue eventually died without a real resolution.

A Coastal Crusade began in late June and continued a few weeks. Ralph Bethea Jr. had become acquainted with Jimmy Draper, pastor of First Baptist, Euless, Texas. Draper was later the President of the SBC and Lifeway. Draper chartered an airplane and brought a full plane load to Mombasa. He returned a few days later to collect the group, bringing another full load to minister. A total of 540 volunteers plus many missionaries were involved with local churches and pastors. Nancy, Mom, and I spent sixteen days in a Mombasa hotel working with them.

In Jo Scales's book, From Strength to Strength, "Clay Coursey reported that 56,332 decisions had been made . . . and eighty-three new churches started." Over three thousand of those deciding to follow Jesus came from a Muslim background but most were forced to return to Islam by families. Jim Slack reported the best follow-up happened in Malindi and Kwale, led by the Courseys and Musens.

July and August were filled with hellos and goodbyes as many missionaries returned or went on furlough. Many parents went to the U.S. with their graduating high school seniors to get them settled in college. I also had many committee meetings in preparation of our annual mission meeting in August. A new concept for church planter/developers was considered as we contemplated sending missionaries to more remote locations to minister with new people groups. Minutes from the meeting said,

> . . . there was much discussion about the need and desire of the mission to move into new areas looking at possibilities of living situations much different from what we have previously been accustomed to as a mission. It was brought out that other missions have sent people into primitive conditions, and they have been able to stay and begin work.

During the year, we began to have most committee meetings in the conference room at the Thika Road office enabling the administrative team to be available for consultations and for meeting any missionary needs for those who came to the office. School board meetings were still held at the school campuses. We had another 1st term church developer's conference in October to encourage those missionaries and for mentoring. Nancy continued to be asked to make special cakes and in November she made a wedding cake for Daniel Munyao's daughter. Daniel was the pastor at

Kariobangi. We spent a few days in December at the Aberdare Country Club for rest, to give me some time to reflect on the year, and to consider plans for my ministry in 1991.

The New Year began with several missionaries returning after furlough or vacation. My schedule was filled with the normal meetings and visits with missionaries. Nancy and I planned to take our vacation in the U.S. in May to give my Mom a chance to see her family and friends since we knew it would help her attitude. The date was accelerated to mid-March to mid-April because Nancy's mother had a health issue and Nancy needed to be there to help her. Vance Kirpatrick became acting administrator while I was away.

I had been advising missionaries not to travel on rural roads at night because there had been a lot of robberies and car thefts in remote places. Ralph Bethea Jr. had been robbed on the Mombasa Highway one night and I had emphasized to him to not drive at night again. While we were in the U.S., on the night of March 27th, Ralph and Lynda Bethea were driving just before midnight into the Rift Valley Academy campus from the upper road. Shortly before the railroad underpass, a man was lying in the road and Ralph stopped to help him. As he leaned over to ask him his problem, the man raised his gun and demanded money. Ralph gave him what he had and heard a tire being slashed by a panga. Ralph yelled, and the robbers ran away. Ralph drove to a place to change the tire and, when he stopped, they were attacked by others. Ralph was badly hurt, but Lynda sustained two major blows to her head and died.

Missionaries held a memorial service for Lynda on Good Friday at Brackenhurst. The Presider of the Mission, Vance Kirpatrick, led and Janie Basham, a missionary friend who also lived in Mombasa, shared memories. Arthur Kinyanjui, Moderator of the Convention, brought a message of condolence from the Kenya President, Daniel arap Moi. There were some delays in getting the body released by the police, but Ralph and their five children could accompany Lynda's body to the U.S. for burial in early April.

When we returned to Kenya in mid-April, I sensed the grief missionaries were feeling and tried to give words of encouragement about God's peace which Christians can have. As I listened to missionaries and nationals, I heard some missionaries express a sense of responsibility toward Ralph Jr. because he was driving so late at night. I also heard some Kenyans talk about relationship issues between Ralph and people in Mombasa. As I was struggling with ways to restore unity and ministry focus, God blessed me with a visit by a FMB Trustee who was a friend of Ralph's. We went to Mombasa together and visited with several Kenyans and missionaries.

As we were reflecting on what we heard and the rumors that the police wanted to interview Ralph again because they were suspicious of his statements about the incident, we decided I should call Ralph and advise him to not return to Kenya now. I also believed his kids needed time with the extended family to help in their grieving process. When the trustee returned to the U.S., he met with Ralph and Ralph decided to resign from the FMB. Missionaries at Mombasa, primarily the Bashams, assumed the responsibility of selling and shipping the personal effects of the Betheas. As administrator, I hurt over the circumstances but had peace, believing the correct final decision was made.

Nancy and I took Mom on a two-day rest trip to Maasai Mara in mid-May. We found many animals to watch which always thrilled me: a big Lion pride, several cheetahs, and many elephants, buffalo, and huge groups of plains animals. We were still trying to recover from colds and flu we had caught in the U.S.

Several personnel assignments and changes occurred during 1991. I have used Jo Scales' book to refresh my memory and supplement my records. Ron Ragan was the director of Baptist Communications. He and Lynda began a church planting ministry in Ngong town, a suburb of Nairobi. Soon after this project began, they faced serious illness of their parents and requested a leave of absence. Like many missionaries, the illness became more long term and they resigned from missionary service. Beth Butler became acting Director of Baptist Communications when they left Kenya.

Ed and Mary Horton continued to feel stress in the treasurer's assignment and requested to be relieved of the position at least by their furlough in 1992. The mission was blessed when Ron Hartell, assigned to the area office, was assigned as treasurer in September 1991. Ed was given a temporary assignment as pastor of Parklands Baptist Church until furlough. After their furlough, they transferred to Belgium to pastor at an English speaking international church.

Jon and Priscilla Sapp transferred from Zambia when Jon became the Associate to John Faulkner in the Area Office. Jon was administrator of the Zambia mission and I had met him at a regional administrator's meetings. I had high regard for Jon and expected him to make a strong contribution in this new assignment. Jim Houser moved to Richmond to become the Associate in the home office.

We also had additional transfers from other missions in 1991. Mary Jo Stewart transferred from the Publishing House in El Paso, Texas, to replace Joan Carter as women's work leader since Joan was retiring. Phil and Lotela Cole came from Liberia to teach at Mombasa Baptist High School. Howard and Belinda Rhodes were to come at the end of the year from Ethiopia. Betty Evans returned to Kenya as a volunteer to assist the administrators by organizing the archives, a much-needed task.

The mission dealt with an issue for the location of the Ruaraka Baptist Church. When the original development plan was made for the Thika Road property, we assigned a plot adjacent to the highway as a church location. The congregation requested that this plot be changed to the rear of the property near a housing area. After a lot of discussion, their request was honored and today, a strong church with an elementary school is located on the tract ultimately assigned to them.

Texas Baptist Men offered to provide well drilling equipment. Two Texas men arrived in June to investigate the possibility of working with the mission. Even though they did not represent Texas Baptist Men, rather Living Water International, the mission through the Human Needs Committee approved establishing a working relationship with them.

The four missionaries assigned to evangelism among the Maasai brought a two-year project proposal to visit bomas to share the Gospel in all areas where the Maasai lived. The mission approved this proposal and requested funds for the project from the FMB.

Nancy made another hurried trip to the U.S. in late October because her mother was in the hospital. She stayed in her mother's hospital room until she was discharged a few days later. She needed to stay in Toccoa until her mother regained some strength. Nancy's mother always hosted Thanksgiving dinner which was a special family event. Her sister, Aunt Frances, always came and brought a caramel cake. The nieces and nephews whispered they were getting tired of those cakes. Nancy's mother always made several cakes for Thanksgiving. I could always count on having fresh coconut cake, lemon cheese cake, and Japanese fruit cake.

Tom Jr. and Andy were staying with their grandmother for the holidays and Nancy knew she needed to help her mother get through the holidays. They made reservations at a mountain hotel for Thanksgiving dinner. Nancy and our sons and her brother Frank and his family joined her mother and Aunt Frances for this unique event of going out to eat on Thanksgiving. I was very happy to see Nancy when she got off the plane in Nairobi just a few days later.

Soon after she left, our crate from the U.S. arrived. I opened it and took everything into the house one afternoon, but it was a few days before I could unclutter the house. Mom and I travelled a lot while Nancy was away. I had to attend a conference at Brackenhurst and we were both tired from our travels and meetings. She seemed a little confused during our trip to Kisumu. When I told her Sam and Bonnie Turner would stay with her while Samson Kisia, Vance Kirkpatrick, and I made a train trip to Mombasa, she smiled and was very pleased.

Samson Kisia was in good spirits because a real spirit of unity was emerging in the churches. Patrick Kimani, pastor of the Mathare Valley church, met with the local chief and got permission for us to move all the medicines out of the clinic building. There were relationship problems between the church and neighbors, prompting me to close the clinic down. We had had problems staffing this ministry.

Mission and Convention leaders had been meeting for some time discussing ways we could reestablish a working relationship together since the Kenya Development Council had failed. The idea of creating a Baraza surfaced. Baraza is a Swahili word meaning "a meeting, reception, public audience, court of law, or council." It also means "members of the council, cabinet, committee, or elders of the tribe." I believe the idea was a meeting where we could brain storm, discuss issues, explore ideas, and follow the African concept of decision making, consensus. The Convention EC approved this idea in 1992 and it was a new beginning in relationships.

In January, Samson Kisia, Moderator of the Convention, and I flew by helicopter to visit the area where the Pokot live. It was an amazing trip. We drove to Kitale where the Swiss Helimission helicopter was based and flew to a remote area where we met about fifty Pokot Christians and the Zehnders. Some of the Pokot had walked three days to arrive at the site. Women walked nearly ten miles and back every day to bring water from the nearest seasonal river. The Zehnders brought some building supplies to build a shelter for worship. It was an interesting challenge to teach a few Pokot men to climb a ladder and hammer nails into wood. We spent three blessed days building and teaching.

Because of the success of the partnership with Kentucky Baptists in 1985-87, we began dialogue with the FMB about another partnership. South Carolina Baptists agreed to explore the possibility and in January 1992, a survey team came to investigate and develop a strategic plan.

The six-member survey team included Carlisle Driggers (Executive Director), Debbie McDowell (SCBC Partnership Coordinator) and three other leaders of the South Carolina Baptist Convention, SBC plus Dr. Ed Johnson, President of the Baptist Education and Missionary Convention of South Carolina, a National Baptist Convention representing African-American churches. Thus, a four-way partnership was established between Kenya Baptists and South Carolina Baptists. This last week of January saw my last official acts as Mission Administrator.

I submitted my resignation as Administrator in a letter written to all Kenya missionaries on January 17, 1992. The text of the letter is transcribed below.

> Nancy and I have reached a very difficult decision this week. I am resigning the position of Mission Administrator effective February 1, 1992. We plan to go on furlough when possible after our eligibility on March 10 and are requesting a leave of absence from the Foreign Mission Board when our furlough finishes. Until our departure, we will be available to help in the transition of administration. This decision has come because of our current family situation.
>
> It has become increasingly more difficult for Mama Tom to live in Kenya because there are no activities to occupy her time. With her current level of health and functionality, we believe that her life will be more joyful and fulfilled to be near friends of her age group and activities of her interest again. Additionally, Nancy's mother had a stroke this week.
>
> While her condition is not currently critical, we do not feel that we can continue to live in Kenya now with the uncertainty of her health condition. We believe that it is the responsibility of children to care personally for the needs of their aging parents and we plan to try to care for their needs in the best way possible. When their needs are met satisfactorily, we will consider returning to an overseas ministry.
>
> I want to also thank you for the opportunity to minister to you as Administrator. God has brought blessings to his church in Kenya. I am very thankful to have been a part for these nearly twenty-three years.
>
> Thank you for sharing your lives with us.

As we officially finished our ministries at the end of January, I wrote the following article in the *News and Views* to express my feeling about leaving Kenya.

> *Kwaheri ya kuonana* are words that have taken on new meaning in the past three weeks. They have frequently come to mind as has the hymn, "God Be With You Till We Meet Again." The decision to leave Kenya because of our family situation was not an easy one but one made with the real sense of rightness. Paul's letter to the church at Philippi confirms my feelings as I can find contentment in

any circumstances because the Lord is with me. There can be peace of heart when a correct decision is made. There can be a confident assurance that God will take care of you, even when there is no known employment for the near future. We can trust God to provide for every eventuality. Therefore, we leave with an optimistic hope for the future because our God is in control and He will reveal our future to us when we need to know.

This does not mean that we will leave without a sense of loss. We will miss the comfort of knowing that you have prayed for us daily because you have told us about your prayers for us. We will miss the frequent phone calls, even those when Louis Scales said this is "Trouble" calling again. We will miss the opportunity to minister when someone called and said I need some counsel. We will miss being in the middle of the "prayer chain" for the mission family. We will miss the warm prayer fellowship on Monday afternoons with the office staff. We will miss the joy of singing and clapping to the Swahili beat in worship services. We will miss Chai and chevda, curry and roasted goat, honey with bee legs still included, ugali and githiri, the Hong Kong, and other things that have become so much a part of our lifestyle. We will miss the warm smile of our African friends, the handshake which seems to go on forever, the touching of the village children who never had seen a "Mzungu" up close. We will miss the temperature being stuck on "perfect" in Nairobi, the visits to National Parks, and the beauty of all the perpetual flowering trees.

If I have any regrets about leaving, it is that we will no longer be a part of the emerging history of the church in Africa. There are too many signs that God is up to something great for Christianity in Africa. Kenyan people are so open to the gospel, so willing to share a good word about the Lord. It is challenging when we realize that you can start a church just about anywhere. When I think about my recent trip to Pokot, I remember the joy found in the group of Christians who have nothing by the world's standards. I think about the response of the Maasai during the first visits to every boma as planned for the next eight years. I think about all the dreams we have written as our plans for the rest of the century, and I believe that God will fulfill those plans. Reflecting on these things and what I believe will happen during the next 10 years shows me that I will truly miss out on some fantastic opportunities. I challenge you to keep your minds on these things, those which are from above.

> Do not let your focus shift to the many things which could occupy your mind; the political scene, the problems of human needs, conflicts between church leaders, etc. Rather, let your mind focus on what God wants to do through you. God's Spirit is at work in you and, as Ken Medema's Moses says; "He uses availability rather than ability". Make yourself available. This is my viewpoint.

Vance Kirkpatrick became acting administrator and the mission quickly chose Sam Turner as the new administrator effective March 1st. I believed Sam was an outstanding choice and was glad the mission could agree quickly without the controversies when I was finally chosen. He could move into our house in late March after we left for our few days of furlough, arriving in Georgia on March 14th. Our leave of absence began April 1st. We had a whirlwind five weeks of sorting, selling, and packing our personal effects to ship to Norcross.

Chapter 15
Adjusting to USA Life in Norcross

When we realized in early 1992 we could no longer care for my mother in Nairobi and our ministry properly, we requested a leave of absence from the Foreign Mission Board effective April 1st and arrived in Atlanta March 14th for our seventeen days of furlough. Since we were in our late 50's and not able to retire, we began looking for work because we had no income beginning in April.

Carlisle Driggers invited me to attend the annual meeting of the National Baptist Convention in May at Gaffney. Samson Kisia and Elijah Wanje were visiting South Carolina and were also at this meeting, a special time for me. Ed Johnson gave me a warm welcome.

George Bullard, one of the South Carolina Baptist leaders on the partnership survey team, asked me to help develop a training manual for their volunteers. I made several trips to Columbia as we developed the handbook. He also invited me to attend training sessions the SC convention was giving to select people. These sessions prepared advisory teams to work with associations and churches to guide them in the development of vision and strategic plans. It was an enjoyable time for me and the convention paid my expenses to travel to Columbia for these activities. I was assigned to work with a team of facilitators assisting the Greer Baptist Association in the development of their strategic plans. We finished our work and submitted the plan in May 1993. The committee was divided into two sub-committees to gather, analyze, summarize, and present the data analysis. My assignment was the committee investigating current church involvement in meeting community needs. At the same time, the South Carolina Convention was developing a strategic plan for their vision focus: Empowering Kingdom Growth.

I knew it would be difficult for me to find work in engineering since it had been 25 years since I had worked in the field. I did expect Nancy to find a nursing job quickly. I explored opportunities in ministry as a church administrator or director of missions. Dr. Griffith, Executive of the Georgia Baptist Convention, arranged an interview with the Georgia Baptist Hospital IT department since I had set up a computer network in our Nairobi office. I quickly discovered I was not qualified for any opportunity they had with mainframe computer networks. The Beaverdam Association in South Carolina, located near our lake house, considered me for their Director of Missions (DOM) but decided to select a pastor in the association. I interviewed for a position as the Baptist ministry coordinator for the 1996 Olympics to be held in Atlanta and again was not chosen.

Nancy checked with hospitals and discovered she needed a refresher course since she had not worked in a hospital since 1959; she had only done "bush nursing." She enrolled at Piedmont Hospital in Atlanta for a refresher course and completed the six weeks of training. Available nursing positions at Piedmont Hospital were night shift jobs and neither of us wanted her to work that shift.

We immediately became involved at Second-Ponce de Leon Baptist and thoroughly enjoyed Bob Marsh's preaching and the worship. I returned to George Ray's Sunday School class and Nancy was in a women's class. We joined the adult choir led by John Condra.

As we resettled Mom at Kingsbridge, we moved her apartment to the floor dedicated to residents needing personal care. It was a secure floor with their own private dining area. We felt comfortable with this location and visited her as much as we could. The manager, Gayle Shaw, was my childhood friend at First Baptist Church. I knew Mom would be looked after very well. My Aunt Lucille, Uncle Yow's widow, and her sister Agnes were also residents in the complex.

In the meantime, Tom Jr. had been talking with his boss Earl Poythress, President of Diversified Energy Services, Inc. Earl wanted someone to upgrade computers by replacing motherboards and other parts.

Tom said, "My dad can do that."

Earl said, "Sure."

I worked a few hours on their computers. One day in August when we had had no fixed income since April 1st, I was working on computers and Earl was complaining because they did not have enough staff to check the engineering drawings before the deadline to give them to clients.

I said, "Earl, I can do that."

He got a strange look on his face and said, "You sure can. Come to work Monday."

The same day, Nancy had an interview at Georgia Baptist Hospital to be a floor nurse. As she and the interviewer were walking down the corridor to the office, they met Dr. Charles Hancock, Chief of Surgery. Charles said: "Hello Nancy" and they continued for the interview. Charles was a friend from the Tech BSU who studied mechanical engineering and became an orthopedic surgeon. His wife was in nursing school with Nancy.

It was an awesome day of blessings because we were both employed again beginning August 17th. Nancy received another blessing because when they set her wage, they gave her credit for all the years of experience in Africa where she was a nurse. She was assigned to the orthopedic/neurological floor and worked three twelve-hour days every week.

When we carried my Mom to Kenya to live, we gave her car to John and Sarah in exchange for a small red Subaru they owned. In her confused state, Mom said, "That man took my car." We celebrated our new jobs by buying a new 1992 green Honda Accord since we needed two cars.

DESI was a small civil engineering consulting company whose clients were primarily utility companies. The main contracts were with pipeline companies although there was some work with electric and communication companies. The work for clients included selection of pipeline routes, obtaining right of way agreements, pipeline location surveying, engineering drawings, permission from government agencies as required, and liaison with construction contractors. Thus, my process of learning civil engineering began. Earl told me the first day the work would be very easy to learn as it was not complicated.

In the beginning, my assignments were checking the engineering drawings and route maps, and having the draftsmen make necessary corrections. As Earl mentored me and I learned the engineering principles, he began to send me to Court Houses to do title searches on property where we needed easements. We had a major contract for a petroleum products pipeline from Tampa to the Orlando Airport in Florida and I did office work on this project. One task was to determine the value of orange trees in a grove we were crossing.

We began hearing about the concern of FMB missionaries about the organization created in 1991 called Cooperative Baptist Fellowship. There was uncertainty about how this grouping would affect both the FMB mission program and its financial support. For several years, I had jokingly said, "If the SBC ever splits, I want to be on the side of the WMU and the Annuity Board." Some fear about how the long-term impact of this new organization would affect us evolved. In March, John Faulkner, Area Director for Eastern and Southern Africa, sent a letter addressing these concerns. It basically said only God could control what would happen and our action should be to pray for revival in the SBC and renewed support for missions.

In March 1993, Atlanta had the "Blizzard of 1993." It was called the "Storm of the Century" and Atlanta shut down. There was nearly a foot of snow in the metro area and North Georgia had three feet. The interstate highways were clogged with stranded or abandoned vehicles.

Some reports said the perimeter highway around Atlanta, I-285, had nearly one hundred thousand abandoned vehicles on it. Over one million customers were without power for several days. Nancy spoke at a Georgia Baptist Nursing Fellowship meeting in Smyrna the day before the blizzard. Nancy's mother, who lived with Aunt Frances, fried eggs on a candle several days for their food.

In early 1993, our renters at the lake house moved and we began making many weekend trips to maintain the grounds and to make needed house repairs. Nancy began volunteering at the church's Family Life Center, taking blood pressures and counselling members about the results. She was active in WMU and I received several invitations to speak at churches. The American rat race almost overwhelmed us after a slower pace of life in Kenya. The twelve-hour shifts fatigued Nancy. With the extra time to share patient information at the beginning and end of the day, she left home at 6:00 am and most nights did not get home until after 8:00 pm. Her commute was over twenty-five miles one way. Part of the year, Tom Jr. and I rode together to our office in Dunwoody, but he was assigned to fill a contract position at Plantation Pipeline at their office and we had to commute separately.

Sarah, John and the grandkids lived in Arlington, Texas, where they had returned for John to finish his Masters degree at Southwestern Baptist Theological Seminary, graduating in 1991 with a Masters Degree in Marriage and Family Counseling. In May, he was promoted to therapy supervisor at St. Theresa Children's Home. Andy continued his construction job in Greenville, South Carolina. The boys had a boat at the lake and during the summer, many of their friends came on the weekends. They were some help with the maintenance but disappeared in the fall.

My Mom's dementia was diagnosed as Alzheimers. I got her into an experimental drug program at the Mercer University School of Pharmacy. It was a blind test and she did not make any improvement. I was never told but I have always believed she was given a placebo, not the real drug. Nancy's mother was 89 and her health seemed to be good. She had been a walker and many days after she retired, she walked two to three miles, mostly on the hilly streets of Toccoa.

We did have some contact with missionaries in 1993. The Disons and Courseys visited us and we went to a Recognition Service for Joan Carter in Madison, Georgia. The Courseys had been at a mission conference in Spartanburg, South Carolina.

New Church and Job Responsibilities

Bob Marsh resigned as pastor in late April to study and reflect on his ministry. Later he spent some years at European Baptist Churches through the Foreign Mission Board. In the fall, Second-Ponce de Leon elected me a deacon and member of the mission committee. Nancy and I sang in the Christmas Pageant and the final song reminded us of our missionary colleagues in Kenya as we sang "Go Change the World." They were literally changing Kenya as they shared the Gospel message of Jesus Christ.

In 1994, DESI acquired contracts for natural gas pipelines in western North Carolina and we had several projects with the Public Service Company based in Gastonia. The longest was from Black Mountain to Marion. Earl and I made several trips together researching a route, and by 1995, I was making most of the trips by myself.

DESI's owner, Charles Moore, sent me confidential correspondence in June in which he referred to comments I had made in a conversation about the need for a comprehensive computer strategy. He asked me to prepare an initial plan outline which we could review together privately. If he were satisfied, he would ask Earl Poythress, President, to procede with authority to begin implementation of the plan. During this time computer hardware and software technology was developing rapidly. It was the beginning of a transformation of our computerized work procedures, improving our productivity and effectiveness in customer service.

Nancy was having a problem with high calcium in early 1994 and had parathyroid surgery. The surgeon removed two glands, but it did not clear her problem. Our lives were concentrated on work and church for most of the year. That routine changed dramatically in July when Nancy's mother was hospitalized because of severe dehydration. She got a staph infection, her kidneys failed, and she died on July 20th. We celebrated her life on Friday, two days later, and she was buried in the Toccoa Cemetery next to her husband Frank. Because Nancy's brother had had heart problems, Nancy, Frank's wife - Faye, and I spent hours at Juddie's house going through all the things she had saved, decided what each family wanted, and moved everything out to prepare for the sale of her house. It was a stressful time.

My mother had increasing problems due to her Alzheimers. At first, I was hurt when she introduced me as her brother one time. I began to feel she really thought I was my Dad when we were together, especially when she tried to kiss me on my lips. In late August, Kingsbridge told me they could no longer care for her and I needed to arrange her move to a nursing home. We found one in DeKalb County and moved her there in

September. It was a very emotional experience for me to go see her. She would keep asking, "Why am I here? I want to go home." When Nancy and I would leave, she always tried to sneak out the door with us. On her eighty-eighth birthday, October 2nd, she had a small stroke, fell and broke her hip. She was transported to Georgia Baptist Hospital to repair her hip. She had other episodes and died in the hospital October 11th. I was at work when Nancy called me to come quickly, but she died before I arrived. We held her memorial service at Patterson's Funeral Home at 14th Street and a graveside service in Martin Baptist Cemetery. She had purchased eight burial plots when the church opened a new section. Her parents and Aunt Mae were buried in the old section. Henry Fields, Pastor of First Baptist Toccoa, led the graveside service. He was my friend from GA Tech BSU. Later, I arranged moving my Dad's remains from the cemetery in Northwest Atlanta to the Martin Cemetery.

In the middle of these three months, our lake house was burglarized, and I had to deal with insurance, police, replacing the riding lawn mower, and other stolen items. I was cutting two acres of grass, so a good lawn mower was necessary. This job was a challenge for me since we always had a Kenyan to work in our yard and garden. I never really enjoyed doing yard work and still do not like it. Nancy and I thought about all our years in Kenya without a break-in only to have it happen in Georgia. It was the same as driving twenty-three years in Africa without hitting a wild animal but hitting a deer in West Virginia a few years earlier. The police caught the burglar and I was summoned to attend court. When his case was called, it was announced he had pled guilty and there would be no trial. We never recovered anything.

Jim Dennison came from Midland, Texas, to pastor Second-Ponce in June 1994. Jim had taught at Southwestern Seminary and was very innovative. He led the church to begin a contemporary worship service, hoping to draw the younger generation professionals living in Buckhead to the church. Tom Jr. was employed by the church to operate the sound system for this worship service. I was always amused when Jim talked about all the trees in his yard in North Atlanta. He said, "There was only one tree in Midland, Texas."

In late 1994, I was with the survey party chief climbing the mountain behind Old Fort looking for a good pipeline route. There right in front of us was an adult black bear. We did not tarry, and I think Stan was more alarmed than I was because I had wandered in wild animal territory in Kenya while hunting. The only difference with this incident was I had no rifle. This pipeline route went from a station in Black Mountain, under Interstate-40 in front of a Ridgecrest parking lot, across a small section of Ridgecrest property, followed the old US-70 highway through the national forest, across a hill behind Old Fort, and followed a power line to Marion. Later during construction, several black bears were seen jumping across the ditch for the pipeline before the pipe was welded together and lowered into the ditch.

At Christmas time, Nancy and I sang in the pageant again and Tom Jr. was the lighting director. The program was excellent and we both thought it was the best pageant yet. We were particularly touched by a song new to us — "Mary, Did You Know?'

In January 1995, we were surveying the crossing under I-40 at Ridgecrest with about four inches of snow on the ground and it was very cold. In our route selection, I needed to convince several land owners that the best pipeline route was across their property and there would be a minimal impact on their land. Earl and I were successful in all but one case where the banker land owner did not want a "scar" on his mountain and we found a better route.

I had conferences with many political leaders in the several counties where we had construction. I found most to be very pleasant and supportive because of the positive economic impact the project would have on their communities. I thought the biggest challenge would be permission to cross the national forest between Ridgecrest and Old Fort. I had very good meetings with the Chief Forest Ranger and because we had chosen to co-locate the pipeline in the old US-70 highway corridor, permission was easily obtained.

Nancy and I wrestled with a lot of change and potential additional changes during the year. We were still trying to sort through both our mothers' possessions when Nancy's Aunt Frances died on Mother's Day. We were both in the hospital room when she finished her earthly life. She was like a second mother to Nancy, causing Nancy to feel much more grief about her death. We had to deal with family issues over Aunt Frances's will. Her will explicitly mentioned a few items which certain nieces and nephews would receive, and the rest was to be divided by each selecting a remaining item in a specified "pecking order." We were dealing with more furniture than would fit in two houses, especially since the Norcross house was not very big.

New Missionary Generation and New Calling

Sarah and John began the appointment process with the Foreign Mission Board in 1994 and were appointed in February 1995 at Southeastern Baptist Theological Seminary. We attended the service, and Joel and Aaron sat with us. We were amused by six-year-old Aaron's comment at the end. He said, "Cucu, did you know it lasted ninety minutes?" They expected some complications in the appointment process because of Joel's cerebral palsy but the medical staff at Richmond were more concerned about Aaron's cancer. They were assigned to South Asia before their training at the Learning Center in Richmond. Just as they finished this program, they learned Joel needed surgery on both hips. They did not leave the U.S. until September and lived with us most of this time. They had a rental house in the region of their people group in South Asia. Sarah home schooled the boys and they studied the local language. We could communicate by email, something we were never able to do while we were in Kenya.

When we were at their appointment service, we visited with James Hampton, a leader in the Cooperative Services International Department. He was a good missionary friend from our years together in East Africa. He asked if we were willing to consider reappointment to serve overseas in his department. I joked that I would if it was an English language assignment and said, "I am too old to try to learn another language." He replied there were no opportunities in English and we went back to our work. A while later, he called and told me Mike Stroup, the CSI leader, was based in London and needed a finance person there. We began the process and a while later, Mike called and told me he was moving to Hong Kong and wanted me to serve in the office in Singapore. We began to pray about this change. It was attractive because the location was near Sarah and John. We met with our personnel associate Danny Broski on September 25th in Augusta, GA. The candidate conference in Richmond was just a few days away and we were invited. We talked the entire trip home and prayed a lot for an answer from God. I never had peace in my heart about Singapore because my heart was still in Africa. We called and withdrew from the process for Singapore because we did not want travel expenses paid for us if we would not be appointed. We had many confirmations as time passed that this decision was correct.

Before our potential return to the mission field began, I traded the Subaru for a used Jeep SUV. I dealt with a cousin who was a salesman at the Toccoa Chevrolet dealership. It turned out to be a lemon, and after a few months, the dealership gave fair value in exchange for a new 1995 Chevrolet Blazer SUV. Since I was travelling a lot on my job, I knew I needed a good reliable vehicle and one I could use "off road."

When Earl found out I was considering missionary service again, DESI made me a project manager and gave me a significant raise. I became responsible for the projects in North Carolina. With other projects around Lake Norman and east of Gastonia, we opened a field office in Hickory to be a base for our right-of-way agents and survey crews. This assignment gave me an opportunity to visit with my first cousin, Betty Gayle, and my uncle Jim Jones who lived in Hickory. I often spent two to four days per week in North Carolina.

The most interesting thing to me on these projects was watching a horizontal drilling operation which went under Lake Norman. The gas pipeline went under a large cove about two thousand feet long. I had read about this process and the installation of the huge pipelines under the Mississippi River, some exceeding seven thousand feet. After these projects were complete, I was assigned a few projects with The Atlanta Gas Company in metro Atlanta.

Tom Jr. had been employed by Welker & Associates in late 1994 and was still enjoying his work in 1995. He was in contact with managers of local municipality gas operations, selecting their employees for drug testing. He continued living with us in Norcross. Andy had been promoted to Site Superintendent by York Construction Company in Greenville. His first project was an office complex and when it was finished, he was transferred as superintendent at the Cryovac plant at Simpsonville where he had worked before he was promoted to foreman. He knew many of their managers and workers.

Nancy's brother, Frank, had a good friend in Toccoa who owned a printing business and had a contract with the athletic department at Georgia Tech to print the football programs. With this connection, he had four season tickets located on the fifty-yard line about three rows from the top of the west stands and a box. For a few years, he agreed with Frank to sell the tickets to me and we enjoyed most of the home games. When he lost the contract, we began to buy our own tickets as an alumnus, but they were on about the 10-yard line in the lower rows of the upper section. When Tech started adding a surcharge, I quit buying tickets.

A friend of Tom Jr.'s bought two season tickets for the Atlanta Braves and wanted to share. We bought one third of the 81 games and went to those twenty-seven games travelling on MARTA. During this period, the Braves had a good team; therefore, we bought the tickets for three seasons.

When church leaders for the new year were chosen, I was made

Vice-Chairman of the Mission Committee and Chairman Elect for 1996. The new pastor, Jim Denison, had led in establishing a Strategic Action Task Force to develop plans for a contemporary style worship service and needs based ministry to enable the church to fulfill our stated mission purpose: "To take Christ to our community and beyond." I was chosen to be the chairman of the sub-committee to develop the needs based ministry program, including the demographic study of the community and to define our focus community.

Aaron Brent graduated from Georgia Tech in June 1996, and Roy and Dena spent an enjoyable week with us. Nancy and I were both summoned for jury duty in the spring, during two different weeks. Nancy served on a case where there was video evidence of a theft in a store which the woman denied. A guilty decision was easy to make. On the day I was questioned for a case, I was discharged immediately when the attorney's questions confirmed I was an ordained Baptist minister.

Second-Ponce started a 1st Place program which Nancy attended. It was a program to help people develop good eating habits and Nancy attended every week for a few months. Dr. Russell Dilday, a former pastor, came to preach a week's revival in April. We were involved in as many activities at the church as we could.

Nancy's New Ministry

In July, Georgia Baptist Medical Center started a new, innovative program to bring health care to the local church. John D. Pierce, Managing Editor of the Christian Index, wrote the following in an article published in the January 2, 1997 issue.

> Registered Nurse Nancy Jones became the first Georgia Baptist congregational nurse when she joined the staff of Peachtree Baptist Church this summer. To kick off the new program, and demonstrate the effectiveness in outreach as well as pastoral care, the church sponsored a free health fair which drew neighbors who otherwise had no relationship to the church.
>
> Peachtree pastor Perry Ginn sees the addition of a congregational nurse to their ministerial staff as a perfect fit. He describes Peachtree as "a church in transition with a diverse congregation." The addition of a nurse along with health and wellness programs communicates to the community "that we care," he added. Already, the church is making good contacts through the Congregational Nurse Program.

He also sees the benefit of having a staff nurse to serve as a resource to the church's preschool program.

Jones was working at Georgia Baptist Medical Center when she saw a posted notice about the program. "I thought, 'Lord, I guess this is the next door,'" she recalled from her initial impression. As a former missionary in Kenya for 20 years, Jones was attracted to a medical ministry with direct ties to a local congregation. She began the 24 hours per week assignment at Peachtree on July 15th.

The program reminds Jones more of her overseas ministry, in terms of function, than hospital nursing, she said. The similarities include working out of a church setting, teaching preventative health and talking with people about spiritual needs. More pointedly, it is in the ministry of "interruptions, people coming and going" that Jones finds her work to be rewarding.

Nancy attended her first church staff meeting on July 10th and had orientation at GBMC the following week as she began her ministry. She met Dr. Perry Ginn, pastor, and Harriett Watkins, associate pastor, and other church staff. When Nancy began this assignment, she needed to become a member of Peachtree Baptist. I did not feel comfortable leaving my ministries at Second-Ponce as deacon and missions committee member. As a result, we agreed to be in separate churches, the only time in our marriage. We each attended activities in both churches.

The first Saturday in October, Peachtree Baptist had a health fair which Nancy organized. Georgia Baptists had a mobile dental unit and it was a part of the fair where people from the community could get free service. It was an effective day of ministry to about 200 people.

As she began her ministry, she and Harriett became close friends, visiting together and becoming prayer partners. Harriet was an interesting African-American lady. She was from New York and before she became a minister, she was an attorney certified to practice before the Supreme Court. Her husband Hank was also an attorney and at that time, he was the Chief Judge for the Social Security Administration based in Atlanta. They were both very articulate, dynamic people and I enjoyed being with them.

The Olympics came to Atlanta in July, the bicycle race passed in front of Second-Ponce and we went there to watch. The course passed the church a few times and members of the church passed water to the riders. Tom Jr. and I went to the Braves stadium for the championship baseball game. We took MARTA (Metro Atlanta Rapid Transport Authority) but instead of taking the north-south route close to our house, we drove to the east line near I-285 because the passenger volume was much lower. This was an exciting time for Atlanta.

Second-Ponce de Leon Baptist chose me as chairman of the mission committee for 1996-1997 composed of twenty-three members. Recognizing this sized committee could not effectively function without some organization, we developed four sub-committees, each with five to six members.

Second-Ponce had a long history of partnering with groups planting new churches in the northern suburbs of Atlanta. The Church Planting sub-committee was expected to seek opportunities to continue this heritage.

There were two language groups meeting in our facilities, Spanish and Vietnamese. It was a challenge because people speaking these languages did not live near the church location. The growth of the Spanish speaking group was hampered because of the wide variety of nationalities and the pastor only related well with people whose roots were found in his country. The Vietnamese group was started by a missionary couple in the church who had served in Vietnam and had good leadership. As the group strengthened, our church assisted them in the purchase of a church building in an area of the city where many Vietnamese speakers lived.

The Outreach sub-committee was challenged to seek ways of ministry to the young professional community and college students. The chairman was a Baptist campus minister. Also, our pastor, Jim Dennison, was leading the church to target this generation.

The other sub-committee was focused on social ministries. Atlanta Baptists supported two community centers; Techwood and Grant Park. This committee enlisted volunteers for these ministries and sought other places of need. Churches located in the Buckhead area had a partnership for referral of persons seeking financial assistance.

Our monthly meetings gave opportunity for the sub-committees to meet and bring recommendations to the full committee for approval. All decisions were prayerfully made.

In mid October, a reunion for East Africa missionaries was held at the Gulf Shores Baptist Conference Center in Mississippi to celebrate our 40th anniversary of ministry in Africa. I was on the committee to plan the meeting and when most of the committee members "bailed out," I had more work than I had accepted. Despite this complication, the celebration was wonderful. I still have my T-shirt made for the occasion by Betty Ann Whitson. The program was full of opportunities for sharing memories of God's blessings, funny stories, and prayer needs. After the meeting, the Conleys and Mildred Cagle came to our house in Georgia for a visit.

The following weekend Nancy and I went with Bill and Margaret Ann McCurry to Ridgecrest for a couple's weekend where Henry Blackerby led a conference on Experiencing God. It refreshed our spirits and we came home with new energy for our ministries. In early December, Nancy and I sang in the Christmas Musical entitled Living Pictures at Second-Ponce.

Nancy began a 1st Place group at Peachtree in January 1997, and a few from other churches joined the group. It became a very tight group and began to meet for fellowship after we retired. Because Nancy quit driving in Tanzania, I was included as the "token" man. She had some classes in Word Perfect software to improve her computer skills. Brenda Gunter became a congregational nurse and Nancy had training sessions with Brenda for her assignment.

Early in the year, I received a proposal for managing the tree farm near Hartwell Lake. We clear cut all the sections which had not been planted by my Mom in the late 1970's. The cutting was finished in May and the plan called for replanting the cleared area after chemical treatment. We completed the replanting in the fall of 1999 as a drought began.

In February, my boss, Earl Poythress and I flew to Houston to attend the annual meeting of the Petroleum Users Group sponsored by ESRI, Inc., the developer of the Geographical Information Software being used. It was an opportunity for us to learn about the implementation of this software being adopted by the industry. We also had an opportunity to visit with several of approximately fifty vendors with displays. It was an interesting experience. We ate very outstanding food at a Papacita Mexican restaurant.

After this meeting, we located a local start-up GIS company named Geofields, Inc. We developed an alliance with them where we planned to teach them the pipeline industry and they would teach us the technology of GIS. In April, I contacted our client, Plantation Pipeline Company to propose the possibility of providing a migration plan from current data and engineering processes to a GIS system. Bill McCurry was an upper level manager at Plantation. Brad Schaaf, President of Geofields had met some Plantation staff at a meeting of the American Pipeline Institute. Brad, Earl, and I met with some upper management staff at Plantation. Unfortunately, they were not prepared to consider this transformation of data storage and usage at that time.

In May, we made plans to visit Sarah and John in Pakistan leaving Atlanta on the 23rd. Sarah called the day before departure and told us Joel had fallen out of bed and broken his hip. They were coming to Atlanta for him to have surgery on June 4th. We cancelled the trip and got a refund from Raptim for our tickets. Joel had his body cast removed in mid-July and they left for Pakistan October 6th.

Tom Jr. was given permanent employment with benefits by DESI on August 18th. From time to time, he was assigned to work in the offices of clients in their drafting departments. I was always amazed at his competence using AutoCad, the standard drafting software for many engineering and architecture companies. His drafting speed was amazing, and he made fewer errors than our other draftsmen. He understood the engineering concepts well and found many shortcuts in the use of computer software. It was always a pleasure to work in adjoining offices.

Our Norcross neighborhood began to transition, and Nancy was disturbed by the chalk profanity written on our driveway by teenage boys. I talked with some church friends working in real estate, both residential and commercial, and they advised it was good to sell and move before a downturn in prices. The wife of a staff minister at Second-Ponce was a real estate agent who helped us research good opportunities. I told Nancy I thought we should move to another location in Gwinnett County because of taxes and county government. She agreed. Our agent and I rode through about twenty sub-divisions and looked at many houses which were for sale. I chose a few I liked, and Nancy went with us to evaluate them. There were two houses in one community which were similar. We liked the area best because it was near I-85, a large mall, and several strip malls. The house we chose was four years old and new houses were still being built in the sub-division. It was near the cul-de-sac on a short street with about fifteen houses. The owner had built storage cabinets in the two-car garage and finished part of the full basement. We closed the purchase on August 14th with a major payment from the tree farm income and began moving three days later.

As the first congregational nurse, Nancy had the opportunity to assist in the orientation of other nurses as they joined the program. She helped some of them in events at their churches. She also received training at several conferences in Atlanta and one in Chicago in September. She also took the short course offered by GBH in clinical pastoral counseling.

Chapter Sixteen
A Multi-ethnic Neighborhood

Jim Dennison and John Condra planned a missionary educational trip titled IN THE FOOTSTEPS OF PAUL: A STUDY TOUR OF GREECE AND EPHESUS. Nancy and I decided to join it in October 1998 and the group flew to Athens, Greece, on October 20th where we visited places where Paul planted churches until October 29th when we flew to Istanbul, Turkey, for two additional days.

We rode a bus from Athens to Phillipi and Thessaloniki. In Acts 16, the Bible records the visionary call Paul received from the Holy Spirit to go to Macedonia instead of staying in Asia. His visit to Phillipi was the first time the Gospel was preached in Europe. Paul's call has always bothered me because of his immediate response: going straight away to Phillipi. I never had a vision of my call but for years heard the still small voice of God that I should be a missionary. I kept pushing this thought away because I did not feel qualified.

Paul found most people in Phillipi were very proud to be committed to the Roman Empire and there were very few Jewish people. When they did not find a synagogue in the city, they went outside the city to the river, seeking a place to pray on the Sabbath. They found a group of women there and began to share their faith in the Messiah. A woman named Lydia and members of her household believed and were baptized. For mature believers, this passage is a well-known.

As we arrived, we noticed a church building located near the river. Since one of our leaders was John Condra, the minister of music, it was natural for the group to go inside the church building there to sing. The acoustics were outstanding. The fact that the first believer in Europe was a woman has always intrigued me. My exposure to the culture in rural Africa leads me to believe the purpose of the women being at the river was to do their laundry but the Bible does not give a reason. Sitting by the river, I had one of the most worshipful experiences of the tour.

The Bible story continues with the story about the slave girl who was freed from her demon and started praising God. Her masters were very angry and had Paul and Silas thrown into jail. In the middle of the night, as the other prisoners were listening to Paul and Silas pray and sing praises, God caused a strong earthquake and all the doors inside the prison sprang open. The jailer started to kill himself because the law was if anyone escaped, he would be executed. Paul yelled, "Don't do it, we are all here." With a light, the jailer saw all the prisoners were still there and said, "Sirs, what must I do to be saved?" (Acts 16:30 is a favorite Bible verse of mine because I had been asked the same question.) The jailer and his household believed and were baptized. He took Paul and Silas to his home and fed them. The next day, Paul claimed his Roman citizenship for protection and they were released. Reflecting on this story while looking at the river, my mind led me to rejoice because I was seeing the presumed place where Lydia was saved.

Paul also visited Thessaloniki during his second missionary journey and Silas was with him during this part of the journey about AD 50. It was a key city located on the main route, Via Egnatia, going east from Rome and on the southern end of the route connecting Greece with the Balkans. Acts 17:1-9 describes Paul's visit when he held discussions in the synagogue during three Sabbaths. Luke wrote that some of the Jews, a multitude of God-fearing Greeks and some women, were persuaded to believe in Jesus.

The fundamental Jews became angry, created a mob to find Paul and Silas, and when they did not find them, they dragged Jason, their host in this city, and told the political leaders he was harboring those traitors. After paying a fine, Jason was released and assisted Paul and Silas to leave for Berea as he had agreed with the politicians.

Every time I read Paul's letters to the Thessalonians, I am reminded about my belief the people in this church held a special place in Paul's heart. His salutation and prayer at the beginning of the first letter were complimentary but I also believe he truly respected them for the way they stood against persecution. I respect some friends because I have seen the way they have overcome persecution and remained faithful to Jesus.

On this trip, we also visited Delphi which is not mentioned in the Bible. It was an important ancient Greek religious sanctuary sacred to the god Apollo near the Gulf of Corinth. It was first settled during the Bronze Age about 1,500 BC. Delphi, as with the other major religious sites of Olympia, Nemea, and Isthmia, held games to honour various gods of the Greek religion. The Pythian Games of Delphi began sometime between 591 and 585 BC. One of the sites we visited was the stadium ruins. It was originally built in the 5th century BC but was altered in later centuries. The last major remodeling took place in the 2nd century AD under the patronage of Herodes Atticus when the stone seating was built and the arched entrance. It could seat 6,500 spectators and the track was 177 meters long and 25.5

meters wide.

We also visited an ancient theater nestled in the hills. Early games were singing competitions and athletics were added later. The ancient theatre at Delphi was built further up the hill from the Temple of Apollo giving spectators a view of the entire sanctuary and the valley below. The theatre was abandoned when the sanctuary declined in Late Antiquity. Jim Denison's notes gave us a brief history of Greek civilization which began twenty-five centuries ago when the belief in individual freedom was born. They also believed in obeying the law and were committed to self-control and moderation.

We returned to Athens on the 23rd and visited the Parthenon. The Parthenon is a Doric temple with Ionic architectural features. It stands on a platform of three steps. In common with other Greek temples, it is of post and lintel construction and is surrounded by columns. There are eight columns at either end and seventeen on the sides and it is regarded as the finest example of Greek architecture. The temple was dedicated to Athena at that time, though construction continued until almost the beginning of the Peloponnesian War in 432 AD.

A key point in Paul's ministry was his visit to Athens. He left Silas and Timothy in Thessaloniki and other brothers in the faith accompanied him. I have always been intrigued by his sermon on Mars Hill and was excited to see this prominent place in scripture. To say I was disappointed was a vast understatement. It was a 'mole hill' compared to the hills of north Georgia or the hilly areas of West Virginia where I had traveled extensively. But, as I climbed to the top of the small granite hill, my mind turned to the importance of the message Paul delivered on this Areopagus.

As Paul waited for Silas and Timothy to join him in Athens, he went to the synagogue and talked with the Jews and God-fearing Gentiles. He also went to the markets and had discussions with philosophers and others who heard him talking about a "strange God" as he proclaimed the Gospel found in Jesus Christ. They took him to Mars Hill and asked him to explain this new teaching. They recognized Paul as a highly-educated man because they had listened to his teachings. On the top of Mars Hill, Paul complimented them as very religious people and commented about their altar dedicated to an unknown god. Then, he proceeded to explain that the god unknown to them, was the one and only God whose Son, Jesus, was the Messiah. Some refused to listen further when he spoke of the resurrection, but others wanted to hear more as he left this crowd. Those who believed followed him (Acts 17:22-32). To me, this message has always been powerful.

We boarded a cruise ship, MTS Odysseus, to visit some islands in the Mediterranean Sea and Ephesus in Turkey. I was excited to be going to Ephesus because Paul's letter to the church there has always been my favorite Pauline letter. In Chapter 4, Paul exhorted the believers to unity in the fellowship and outlined the purpose of spiritual gifts. Both are powerful for the believer's belief system and for church fellowship. I have always preferred the Swahili translation of Ephesians 5:14 over English translations. "Wake up sleeper and Christ will cause you to shine" instead of "Awake sleeper . . . and Christ will shine on you." Christians who have experienced spiritual warfare absolutely find much encouragement in Chapter 6 where Paul outlines the armor of God.

Founded by Athens as a colony in the 10th century BC, it was established as a city dedicated to the Goddess Artemis known as the maiden huntress goddess of Greek culture. It was one of the twelve Ionian cities of the Classical Greek era and was given to the Romans by the Greek King in 133 B.C. Ephesus became a large, important city of the ancient world while a part of the Roman Empire. Trade was very strong because of its strategic port in the Mediterranean Sea. The Ephesians built a giant temple dedicated to Artemis which was the focus of pagan beliefs in the area.

Its strategic location made it a gateway between Asia and Europe giving opportunity for the advance of Christianity during Paul's missionary period. It survived many years as a Christian city.

Our ship anchored off shore and we were taken to the mainland by small craft. The Asia Minor ancient Greek city Ephesus is located near the mouth of the Menderes River in what is today West Turkey. Three major roads led from the seaport. One road went east towards Babylon via Laodicea, another northward via Smyrna, and a third south to the Meander Valley. South of Smyrna, it was a great Ionian city known for its wealth and became the leading seaport of the region.

The first-time Paul visited Ephesus was during his second missionary journey estimated to have been A.D. 49 to 52. He had been in Corinth where he met and worked with Aquila and Priscilla who were tent makers as was Paul. After some problems with the Jews there, Paul with Aquila and Priscilla set sail for Caesarea in Syria. They stopped in Ephesus where Paul taught briefly in the synagogue. Although he was asked to stay longer, he left Aquila and Priscilla there, continued his journey to Caesarea, and went to visit the church at Antioch.

On his third missionary journey, estimated to have occurred A.D. 53 to 57, Paul left Antioch in Syria and visited Derbe, Lystra, and Iconium before arriving in Ephesus. When he arrived, he met some believers who had been baptized for repentance as John the Baptist taught. Paul baptized about twelve men in the name of Jesus and they received the Holy Spirit's Power. He taught in the synagogue about three months. Some became disobedient; therefore, he took the believers to Tyrannus's School where he taught for about two years. Many Jews and Greeks believed as they were taught there. God did many miracles in Ephesus during this time.

As the number of believers increased, Demetrus, a silversmith who made shrines of Artemis, gathered others in this trade together and they created an uproar because their businesses were threatened. The town clerk quelled the crowd and when this uproar died down, Paul encouraged the believers and left for Macedonia.

Later in this journey, Paul stopped at Miletus and sent word for the elders in Ephesus to join him. He gave instructions to them (Acts 20:18-36). Because Paul's team had spent so much time in Ephesus, they had deep love for the believers there and Paul wanted to leave a final word because he did not expect to see them again in this life.

As we began our visit in Ephesus, we found the ancient theater nestled in the hilly area. The acoustics were outstanding as some in our group stood on the stage and spoke. I was impressed at the clarity and volume of the sound.

When we walked on the marble road, I saw many inscriptions and wondered what the text meant. I did not know Greek script and still do not. (Because of my limited linguistic abilities, I was thankful when I went to seminary that I did not need to learn either Greek or Hebrew.) But, engineering training made me consider the techniques and manpower used to place all the massive stones we observed. We paused to reflect on what we were seeing as we strolled along the marble road. The marble slabs were no longer a smooth road, requiring that we be careful not to trip because of the unevenness. I tried to imagine how the people of Ephesus lived two thousand years ago. I gave up because my mind could not really perceive it.

The library was a very large facility which could be seen as we walked down the hill on the marble road and where we stopped often to take a close look at the ruins on either side. There was another facility which we saw in the ruins of more than one city of antiquity, the public toilet. In America, our restrooms have cubicles for privacy. I had seen unisex restrooms in Europe as we travelled there but the openness of the ones we saw on this tour were surprising with their stone seats side by side. When I have spoken about what I saw, the question has always been if men and women had certain times of the day to use the facility. My honest answer has always been, "I have no idea" because as I have searched online, I have never found information about this aspect of their culture.

At the end of the day, we boarded our ship for an overnight cruise to Patmos to see the place where John wrote Revelation. It is a small, rocky island in the Aegean Sea about thirteen square miles. The capital is Chora and we sailed into the port at Skala. The churches on the island today are Greek Orthodox.

Little is known about the early Greek period. During the Hellenistic period about the third century B.C., fortifications and towers were built. John wrote in Revelation he was on the island because of the word of God and the testimony of Jesus (1:9). Some Biblical scholars believe this statement is an indication that the time was during the persecution in Nero's period about A.D. 64 after the burning of Rome. Other scholars believe John moved from Jerusalem to Ephesus about A.D. 67 before the destruction of Jerusalem which does not give time to establish a growing ministry in Asia. Therefore, they believe John's vision occurred about A.D. 95 to 96 when he wrote Revelation. After this period, Christians on the island, built basilicas about 300-350 A.D. Christianity barely survived Muslim raids in the seventh to ninth centuries. A monastery was built in the twelfth century. The Ottoman Empire controlled the island for many years. In the twentieth century, Italy gained control during the war with Turkey and later the Nazis received control during WWII. At the end of the war, Patmos became autonomous but joined independent Greece in 1948.

Revelation can be outlined in three sections: Events which had been observed (Chapter 1), current events (Chapters 2-3), and events of the future (Chapters 4-22). The second section is messages to the seven churches in Asia and beginning with Ephesus, they are listed in a clockwise order. The Holy Spirit gave John a message for each church which outlined the spiritual health of the congregation. I have preached many times from these scriptures but must confess only recently have I seen something which I consider significant. The Holy Spirit told five of the churches their spiritual health was poor. The Holy Spirit criticized those five churches for not holding to their faith beginning with Ephesus where they lost their first love, Pergamum where some followed the teachings of Balaam instead of Jesus, Thyatira where Jezebel was tolerated when she proclaimed false teachings, Sardis where faithful examples had died, and Laodicea where rich people declared they had everything and needed nothing, so God wanted to spit them out of His mouth. Contrast this with the encouragement for Philadelphia because they had persevered during persecution and God would protect them or Smyrna who would face persecution and prison, but God would give them the crown of life if they overcame. With all the world learning about the persecuted church and Christians today, I believe the Holy Spirit is protecting and rewarding those who hold onto their anchor of faith.

As we walked on Patmos, we saw the monasteries and walked to the church located at the cave where tradition says John lived and wrote Revelation during his exile on the island. I was surprised how small the cave was and had a challenging time imagining how John could write in the darkness. We were there on Sunday and there were people worshipping. I had some guilt feelings as we viewed the cave because we were disturbing their worship. As I thought about this situation, I realized visitors were probably a regular Sunday activity.

After visiting the cave, we returned to the ship to sail to Rhodes. The only place Rhodes is mentioned in the Bible is Acts 21:1 where Paul and his companions were sailing from Miletus via Cos, Rhodes, and Patara where they changed ships to sail to Tyre. Luke does not say how long they might have stayed in Rhodes, an important port, but it was brief since there is no reference to any witnessing. The island is located about twelve miles off the coast of Turkey.

After we landed in the afternoon, we spent our time wandering the streets in the village near the port. The streets were interesting, narrow with shops on each side. To our great surprise about the time darkness fell, we spotted an internet café. Nancy and I decided to enter and send an email to our sons in the U.S.

After a very enjoyable afternoon seeing the sites of Rhodes, we returned to the ship for our overnight trip back to the port near Athens. Like any cruise ship, the food was plenteous and delicious. Therefore, our eating discipline disappeared those three days. The Mediterranean Sea was smooth, unlike our Atlantic crossings, so Nancy and I slept like babies the three nights we sailed on the cruise ship. When we arrived in Athens the next morning, we had a relaxing day to see more sites before members of the group returning to the U.S. would get their flight. Part of the group, including Nancy and I, would extend our trip by flying to Istanbul, Turkey, for a two-day visit.

I was interested in seeing Istanbul because of the little bit of world history I had been required to study in high school. It had been called Constantinople when I read the stories. I had learned it was the gateway between Europe and Asia, the two continents being separated by the Bosporus straight. On our bus ride one day, we rode across the bridge separating the two continents. It was my first time to visit Asia even though I did not set foot on the ground. It was a cool rainy day as we viewed the sights during our ride.

The first day we were in Istanbul we visited the Hagia Sophia. It has an interesting but turbulent history. It was originally built as a cathedral in the sixth century A.D. It is huge, 270 feet long and 240 feet wide with a dome that is 118 feet high inside the building. In 1453 A.D. the Byzantine Empire was defeated by the Ottoman Empire and the Sophia was converted to a mosque. In 1934, the Turkish government converted the Sophia to a museum and when we were visiting, renovations were in progress. It was a very impressive site.

The famous Blue Mosque is very near the Hagia Sophia and we went there to see this well-known Mosque. It was built on the site of the Byzantine temple and opened in 1617. Built facing the Hagia Sophia, the twenty thousand beautiful blue tiles inside the mosque have caused people to call it the Blue Mosque. There are six minarets and cascading domes making it an impressive feature of the Istanbul skyline. Six minarets make it unique since most mosques have one, two or four. Many in rural Kenya had only one. The six minarets caused a major controversy since the famous Haram Mosque in the religious city of Mecca also had six. The issue was resolved when the sultan in Instanbul sent his architect to Mecca to add a seventh minaret to the Haran Mosque. The many domes are cascaded to focus on the main dome providing beauty by the symmetry.

The west entrance is very ornate, but the sanctity is preserved by requiring non-worshippers to enter through the north entrance. As we entered there, we followed the Muslim custom of removing our shoes at the entrance where shelves were provided to store them. We were not able to take photographs to show the beauty of the magnificent tiles but there are amazing pictures on the internet.

After visiting the mosques, we went shopping at the mall which was more like an arcade named Bazaar54. We were interested in a Persian carpet and we found a beautiful one which was eight and a half feet wide and ten feet long. It was expensive and is now located in the master bedroom at the foot of the bed in the lake house where I live. We also stopped by a jeweler and found a very unusual ring. This "harem" ring was made with 14 carat gold. It has four bands, each with four stones of a distinct color, and the bands are connected opposite the stones. The four stones were sapphire, ruby, emerald, and zircon. Nancy proudly wore it as we returned to Duluth on November 1st.

Work

After we returned home, we picked up our busy schedule. Nancy attended additional training for "parish nursing" mid-month and we had all the Brooks family at our house for Thanksgiving. It was quite a crowd. I sang in the Christmas Pageant at Second Ponce and we both had speaking opportunities about missions during December.

Earlier in the year, upgrading the DESI computer network was approved. We hired an Internet Technologist to assist me with the technical details. We decided to install a Dell RAID server (Redundant Array Inexpensive Disks). This server was somewhat more expensive but offered the highest level of data security. We used a star protocol cable system and connected nine work stations for the engineering department. Other departments operated on a different system. After installation and the operation was working smoothly, I prepared an agreement with the IT consultant company for ongoing technical support beginning July 1, 1998. Much of this work could be done remotely from his office.

As we continued our GIS conversion project in 1998 for Colonial Pipeline Company in cooperation with Geofields, Tom Jr. and other draftsmen began modifying the AutoCad alignment sheets for Texas, Louisiana and Mississippi to standardize pipeline data text and format along the routes. It was important to move this data to separate drawing layers to allow easy conversion to ArcInfo software. Since we were developing the conversion methodology, there were many GIS design issues to be resolved while we converted the data on this segment. These changes were a part of the learning curve as we developed the techniques for conversion.

In March, I had been assigned a project with Atlanta Gas Light Company in Smyrna. Georgia. It was a short natural gas pipeline just over a mile long along Atlanta Road. The scope of our contract was to acquire the right of way on thirty-eight tracts of land adjacent to the road easement. This section was in a lower economic section of the city. I hired two right of way agents who negotiated an agreement with property owners for an easement for the pipeline and temporary work space during construction. Our drafting department also created individual plats showing the easement on the tract. The project was completed in mid 1999.

The year was filled with normal activities except for two things. As mission committee chairman at Second-Ponce, I guided the church to resolve a developing issue about mission offerings. In its history, the church had always given generously to the Lottie Moon Christmas offering for international missions. With the development of the Cooperative Baptist Fellowship and its location in Atlanta, some leaders and employees of the organization had begun fellowshipping at Second-Ponce. The question of giving to their offering was complicated by the Executive Director's joining the church. After much prayer and extended discussions, we recommended that the pledge cards and offering envelopes be modified so each church member could specify which organization would receive their mission offerings, SBC or CBF.

The other major responsibility I had was to plan and guide a volunteer team to go to Kenya in May to assist the annual meeting by providing ministry for all the Mission Kids. We solicited volunteers for the project and had a large group committed to join Nancy and me on the trip. We held our training sessions. Then I collected all 22 passports and sent them to the Kenya Embassy in Washington, D.C. about three weeks before our departure. When we had not received our passports with the Kenya visas the week before our flight, I called the Kenya Embassy in Washington and was told they had no record of receiving our passports. Naturally I panicked and called Jane Clifford, one of the volunteer team who was a flight attendant with Delta Airlines. I asked if she could get a buddy pass and fly with me to Washington to talk to the passport office and the Kenya Embassy. The passport office told us if everyone completed a new application and brought them back on Thursday, they could process the applications for us that day. I called Jeff Byrd, mission minister at Second-Ponce, and asked him to have everyone go to the Post Office, get applications and have them ready that evening. Jane and I went to the Kenya Embassy to see if they could trace any records. I was very nice, spoke to them in Swahili, and they were very cooperative. They searched and found nothing. Disappointed, Jane and I returned to the airport to fly back to Atlanta, but we did have a promise the Embassy would process the visas while we waited the next day. When we got off the plane in Atlanta, my brick cell phone rang, and it was Tom Jr. He was very happy to tell me the box with passports had been delivered at the DESI office while we were in the air. Jane and I spoke a very happy prayer of thanksgiving, knowing we could fly on schedule in two days.

We had a pleasant flight to Nairobi where Sarah, John, Joel, and Aaron joined us, flying in from Pakistan. The meeting was both fun-filled and challenging. Nancy and I were assigned to take care of the two-year-old children which challenged me since it had been so long since our kids were that age. Part of the meeting was challenging as the missionaries were introduced to the latest paradigm shift in strategy called New Directions. There were many questions as missionaries tried to merge this new strategy with their existing ministry plans and strategies. One evening, the Mission Administrator, Glenn Boyd, led a fun/game time where everyone relaxed and enjoyed the fun. I was especially amused as Joel rolled his wheel chair to the front, turned to face the crowd and said, "I am Joel, your sit-down comedian," then proceeded to tell some jokes.

Just before we left the U.S., I had agreed with our realtor that our Norcross house was ready to list for sale. We had made some repairs and a few upgrades after we moved to Duluth the previous year. The day after our arrival at Brackenhurst, I received a telegram saying she had an offer for the list price and asked if I wanted to accept it. I replied yes, I would accept it and sign the documents as soon as I returned. Nancy and I said a prayer of thanksgiving.

After the meeting, our group went to Maasai land to do ministry. Nancy and Sarah, with help from others, held clinics where the most prevalent disease treated was trachoma, an eye disease caused by flies. Because of the herds of cattle and goats, there are millions of flies in the Maasai bomas (family villages). Bomas are usually surrounded by thorn fences to keep wild animals away from their homes and livestock. We also had a dentist with us who examined teeth and treated as best he could under the circumstances. Many Maasai were intrigued by Joel's wheel chair. Joel used this interest and opportunity to tell the ones who gathered around him about Jesus. After these clinics and witnessing, the group went to the Ark, a lodge in the Aberdare Mountains. We had a nice overnight stay, viewing many animals. At the Ark, when a special animal comes in the middle of the night, a buzzer is rung in the rooms to alert the residents.

With a plan to visit Amboseli National Park the next day, we left Nyeri mid-morning to drive to Namanga at the Tanzania border on pavement and take the dirt road into the park. We made a brief rest stop at Namanga as darkness arrived. A very heavy rain storm occurred as we began our safari to the game park along what was becoming a slippery muddy road. When one of the vans began having trouble climbing a steep hill, the driver was unable to go any further. Jeff Byrd, the mission minister from Second-Ponce, a couple of other guys, and I got out to push the vehicle. As we started pushing, my feet slipped, and I fell face down in the mud. Just then, a Landrover approached from the park's direction and told us the road was washed out and we could not get to the lodge until perhaps the next day. The driver recommended we spend the night at the local "hotel" in Namanga. Since I had stayed in this hotel a few times, I knew the accommodations and the mosquitos would give our volunteers a miserable night. I told the group we would return to Brackenhurst for the night and go to Lake Nakuru National Park the next day and spend the night there instead.

As we were turning the vans around to return to Namanga, the headlights on the van illuminated a five-foot puff adder in the middle of the road. We arrived at Brackenhurst about midnight, a very muddy and fatigued group. The pavement between Namanga and Nairobi was full of potholes which made this leg very slow. Sections of Lake Nakuru National Park were covered with flamingos and we saw wildlife near this alkaline lake in the Rift Valley. It was a nice respite after the adventures of the previous day.

We had a few more days at Brackenhurst with Sarah and her family before they returned to Pakistan and we returned to Duluth. When the group had a fellowship back in Atlanta, Susan Seaman, a graphic artist and wife of the dentist, gave every one of us a t-shirt with a logo and title "KENYA POTHOLE TOUR ~1998."

Marissa Joins the Family

Sarah and John had told us they hoped to adopt a little girl. When they returned to Pakistan, they heard in early June about a newborn baby girl who had been abandoned in the Gujarati region of Pakistan. The baby had been rescued by a Christian family who had heard Sarah and John were looking for a baby girl to adopt. They made a three-day journey to the area using multiple modes of transport with the last one being a horse drawn cart. As soon as they held her in their arms, they knew she was God's precious gift to them. They took the premature baby home with them and she weighed three pounds. Because she was premature, the whole family pitched in to feed her with a medicine dropper. John began the process to get custody from the government. The Pakistani Government only gives custody to males. Marisa grew quickly, and we were so thrilled to have a granddaughter. Nancy and I looked forward to the day when we would be able to hold her in our arms.

In June, a weekly management staff meeting was begun at DESI. The team included the owner, the president, the CFO, the drafting supervisor, and me, the project manager. The minutes reflected the item's description, origin date, due date, and assigned team member. This record gave us a checklist for non-routine pending items.

In January 1999, DESI was approached by Dixie Pipeline Company to do a conversion of their system to GIS. By the end of March, I had collected data necessary to prepare a bid package for the one-year project costing over $400,000. A sizeable portion of the cost was due to data history. Alignment maps last updates were five years old and land ownership had not been updated requiring significant courthouse work. My memory is that Dixie chose not to proceed. Unfortunately, not all bids are approved.

South Asia Travels

Early in 1999, the Second-Ponce mission committee began to investigate another mission trip, this time to prayer walk in Pakistan. John and Sarah lived in the northern area in a town named Gilgit. There were two main people groups in this region, Shina and Balti. The predominate branch of Islam in the region was Ismaili, followers of the Aga Khan. We asked the church members to pray for the Shina, a people group of five hundred thousand with ten known Christians. As the team with a variety of skills formed, we studied and prayed together. Paul McNeal and Dan Hayes were ministers at Second-Ponce. The dentist, Brad Seaman, and his wife Susan plus Jane Clifford were on the Kenya team and joined Nancy and me. Cleo Mansour, wife of an Egyptian surgeon at Emory Hospital, brought the unusual gift of speaking ten languages, including Farsi. Pakistan's Urdu speakers can understand Farsi. Allan McArthur and one other church member were also on this prayer team.

We flew from Atlanta to Islamabad in the middle of May where John and Sarah met us. Nancy and I were thrilled to see our family but the special thing for us was to see and hold Marisa for the first time. After getting acquainted with Pakistani food and seeing sites in the city, we boarded a DC-3 airplane to fly to Gilgit the next day. We were not certain which day we would fly because cloudy days cancelled flights since the flight path was between two high mountain ranges.

A long section of the Karakoram Highway between Islamabad and Gilgil is greater than thirteen thousand feet elevation. The highway connects the Pakistani provinces of Punjab, Khyber Pakhtunkhwa and Gilgit-Baltistan with China's Xinjiang Uyghur Autonomous Region. The highway is a popular tourist attraction, one of the highest paved roads in the world. The pass in the Karakoram mountain range has an elevation of 15,397 ft. A section of this highway used the Silk Road from ancient times. I did not see any guardrails as we travelled the road and some edges of the road were sheer drops of two thousand feet. Part of the highway parallels the Indus River and there is a bridge across the Indus in Gilgit. Development of the Silk Road began in ancient times as a trade route for the transport of silk from China to the west, as far as the Mediterranean Sea. There were three routes of the Silk Road: northern, southern, and southwestern. The southern route left China, passed through northeastern Pakistan, Afghanistan, Iran and arrived at the coast of Syria. It included part of the Karakoram Highway.

On arrival, we checked into our hotel, got settled, and visited the town. We walked the main street and saw the stadium. The various shops advertised their products in many ways. There was a tea shop where Allan McArthur and I stopped to order a drink. I was especially interested in comparing the chai in Pakistan to Kenyan chai and the Indian chai I drank in Nairobi. It was similar but did not have the smoky flavor of chai brewed in a Maasai hut. The ladies on the team visited the tailor shops because they wanted to purchase local clothing so that they could open relationships by wearing culturally appropriate attire. Many Pakistani women wear a shalwar kameez. They can be a range of styles, designs, and colors. Often, they are decorated, especially with embroidery.

We visited a Christian eye hospital, another organization operating in Gilgit, located near the Indus River. Part of the team visited with patients as they waited to see the doctor. Susan Seaman worked with staff to develop brochures for the hospital to distribute and I worked with the accountant to set up a good accounting system for the hospital.

We spent two days visiting a local private school located just across the Indus River bridge in another section of Gilgit. John and Sarah had developed friendships with the teachers and students. With some human needs funds given by U.S. churches, they had provided a freezer. The owners of the school worked hard to provide good facilities and a good education for the kids. The buildings were adequate with crowded dormitory rooms having several bunk beds.

We thoroughly enjoyed our visits with the friendly students who were well dressed. Sign language was the method of communication since most did not know English. As I looked at the community, I could not help but compare the school facilities with the schools in rural villages in Kenya. This school's facilities were much better than many in Kenya where classrooms did not have windows, students shared rough wooden desks, and many rooms had dirt floors.

One day, the group travelled to see the Baltit Fort in the Hunza valley. The original fort dates to the 1st century AD but the current fort's foundation dates to the thirteenth century. In the seventeenth century, a local prince married a princess from Baltistan who used her dowry to bring Balti craftsmen to renovate the fort. This fort was abandoned by the Hunza Mirs in 1945 when they moved to a palace down the hill. The old fort began to decay, and the Aga Khan funded restoration completed in 1996. The fort is currently a museum.

On another day, Dan Hayes, Allan McArthur, Jane Clifford and I rented a World War II type jeep with a driver to travel into the Naltar valley to see a mountain area near a military training base. It was a twenty-five-mile trip which took two hours to reach a "local hotel" where we had lunch at the Pasban Inn. The road was very narrow, one lane most of the way. We crossed one river on a narrow wooden bridge. I rode in the back on the very narrow wheel well without padding so my one hip was very sore on arrival. We did not see the ski resort which has a ski lift built over ten years later and has become an area tourist attraction.

Sarah took Nancy and other women to the Kohistan region to hold clinics for the women there. This district borders Gilgit and Kashmir on its eastern side. Nancy told me these women are very conservative Muslims and their burkas completely cover every inch of their bodies. The women portrayed the typical symptoms of sunlight deprivation. Their culture prevents any treatment by a male doctor. As a result, the clinics were important for their health. This region is located at the junction of three magnificent mountain ranges. The southern end of the Himalayas is east of the Indus river, the Karakoram range ends northeast of the Gilgit River, and the Hindukash range ends west of the Gilgit/Indus River. The women expressed thanksgiving for the opportunity to minister to these women who live in a demanding situation.

Part of the group went to Gich, the home village of a friend of John and Sarah. It was a developed village with stone houses and we had an opportunity to visit in the friend's home to share a cup of tea. The drive was pleasant, and we had a glorious view of the mountain range during our drive.

While we were in Gilgit, there was another skirmish in the disputed territory of Kasmir between the soldiers of Pakistan and India. We heard about it on the news and later learned some Indian soldiers had been captured and brought to the Pakistani Army base in Gilgit located near our hotel.

One of the impressive sights to me was the river cascading down from a mountain with rocks breaking up the flow. It reminded me of the scripture verse found in Psalms 78:16 which says, "He made streams come out of the rock and caused waters to flow down like rivers." (HCSB)

One of the events which bothered me during our visit was the evening John asked me to go with a secret believer to help carry some literature to his house to share. We walked there. I visited briefly and walked back to the place I was staying. The next morning, we learned the police had gone to his home after I left, carried him to the police station, and beat him in the jail for having Christian literature. Americans still do not understand the price some believers pay as they live with persecution.

We boarded our bus to return to Islamabad one morning. We had shared stories and observations in the evenings and discovered we had many things to praise God for but needed to mobilize our church for more intense prayer when we arrived home. We took two days for the drive and spent a night at a hotel in Basham. The next day, we continued our safari and as we neared Islamabad, we passed through Abbottabad, the place where Seal Team 6 located and killed Osama bin Laden.

The next day, we said goodbye to the group as they returned to Atlanta, and Nancy and I remained at the guest house where John and Sarah stay during their visits to Islamabad. We were joined by John's parents and celebrated Marisa's first birthday on June 4th. Too soon, the time for us to return home to our work and responsibilities arrived.

On July 18th eight of our team gave reflections during a report to the church. We shared nine prayer requests and asked the church to commit to regularly lift these petitions to God.

New Project

DESI acquired another project with Atlanta Gas Light in Marietta for a 24-inch gas pipeline from Canton Highway to Johnson Ferry Road. We negotiated easements on ninty-four tracts with thirty-two road crossings. It was an expensive project due to the high land value where one-third of the tracts were over $100,000 per acre and the highest over one million. We had two survey crews and five right-of-way agents on the project.

We negotiated an agreement with Georgia Transmission Corporation to co-locate the pipeline in their right-of-way for a 115-kV power line. I spent two days with two construction contractors reviewing the route concerning difficult areas for the construction. I had interesting negotions with one land owner along Roswell Road who was the aunt of Travis Tritt, the musican. We held several discussions and reached an agreement acceptable to both parties. It reminded me of the tract in North Carolina where the pipeline crossed land owned by a leading NASCAR driver.

Geofields received a contract in September from TRANSCO, a natural gas transmission company, to convert their lines in South and North Carolina to GIS. We were sub-contracted to convert the pipe data to a database format. I developed a project management schedule to begin September 1st and be completed by the end of January 2000.

God Calls Again

The other major event in our lives occurred in November. I received an email from Vance Kirkpatrick inquiring if we would consider an assignment to serve at the seminary in Arusha, Tanzania as the business/financial officer. We consulted Vance further and contacted Larry Pumpelly in the Richmond Office. They both emphasized the match between the field's needs and our skills and experience. Nancy and I discovered during our volunteer trip to Kenya in 1998 that we still had our fluency in Swahili and our heart had been left in Africa. Nancy's immediate response was "when can we go?" We concluded God was opening a door for us to return to our ministry calling in East Africa.

Vance had told us we could be "fast-tracked" through the reappointment process since the need was critical but this idea proved to be untrue. I asked if we could be reappointed as career missionaries and this request was agreed, allowing us the opportunity to achieve Emeritus classification.

We began the paperwork, including a life sketch, an update to our life history, and answers in a doctrinal questionnaire. We completed all this paperwork by the end of the year and looked forward to our return to East Africa.

In 2000, the contract between the Georgia Baptist Health Care System with Peachtree Baptist Church ended. Nancy said goodbye to her friends there and accepted a new assignment on the staff of the Atlanta Baptist Association. She and Joel Harrison, the Lead Missionary, began to develop the plans for the position.

She wrote a letter to all the pastors in the association to share information about her ministry and to encourage them to seek ways this ministry could help their church. A portion of the letter follows:

> Let me introduce myself. I am Nancy Jones, the new Congregational Health Ministry Coordinator for the Atlanta Baptist Association. The Georgia Baptist Health Care System Congregational Health Program is working with the Atlanta Baptist Association to provide this service. The goal of these two groups is to assist the churches to fulfill their spiritual commitment to the physical, emotional, social and spiritual aspects of health care. I will be working out of the Atlanta Baptist Association office 24 hours per week. I want the opportunity to help you provide a health ministry for your congregation and community.
>
> Some of the ways I, as your Congregational Health Ministry Coordinator, can promote a health ministry in your church are as follows:

1. To assist your church to provide a health ministry in needed areas through your church members and local resources. If your church is a large one, with a health ministry already in place, volunteers from your church could partner with a smaller, more needy church to provide a health ministry in its congregation and community.
2. To provide education and training to enable your Christian health care workers (interested volunteers chosen from your church to provide whole person health ministry in your church and community within the Atlanta Baptist Association.
3. To be available to consult with you and your congregation as you desire to provide screening, educational and/or healthy living events in your church and community.

After Nancy began working for the Atlanta Baptist Association, I became acquainted with the staff, especially the lead missionary, Joel Harrison. During our discussions, we talked about the strength of the Association and the ministry to the legacy churches for strengthening and to consider starting new churches. One day, Joel asked me if I would consider flying to California with three other men in the Association to evaluate a ministry he had learned about. This ministry was targeting people with issues such as drug abuse and alcoholism where they had the opportunity to hear the gospel. Joel wanted to know if this type ministry would be reproducible in Metro Atlanta areas where these social issues were rampant. We flew in to the Ontario airport in California with a stop in Phoenix. We stayed in a medium-priced motel which was adequate. As we visited the ministry, we learned they had a "ranch" where the addicts were taken when they agreed to receive help. This remote location was too far to walk away, and each could "dry out" from their addictive alcohol or drugs. Every day, they were required to attend a Bible study. When they completed this phase, they were brought to town, introduced to those who had recovered, and given work to do. When I was there, I met two men who were renovating an old movie theater the ministry had purchased to become a new church. On Sunday, we visited the "mother church" for worship and learned the practice was to baptize once a month those new believers. That Sunday, they baptized forty-three people and I learned this was a normal number. After we returned to Atlanta, the ministry location of one of our team who went to California was designated as a trial site. It had a good opportunity to reproduce the ministry in Atlanta, but I do not believe it happened. I believe the reason was a remote location to allow recovery was never located.

In July, Swain Guzzardi, one of our right of way agents, and I met with representatives of Bechtel Corporation to discuss the possibility of acquiring sites for the location of cellular towers. They had a contract with AT & T. We were assigned four sites immediately, but further contracts were not obtained.

DESI continued to support the data conversion for the Colonial pipeline system. Automatic importing line location data points from the AutoCad drawings had a prominent level of errors. As a result, Tom Jr. and I spend a few weeks at Geofield's office manually creating a database for this information.

After finishing all the International Mission Board (IMB) interviews, medical tests, and approval by the Personnel Department, Medical Department, and Trustee Committee, we were reappointed in July 2000 at Ridgecrest during Mission Week subject to further studies on Nancy's parathyroid problem. A fifth parathyroid was found behind her esophagus. It was the bad one and was removed.

But, we were required to be "retreaded" by attending a training session at the International Learning Center near Richmond, Virginia for six weeks. This retraining was justified to us based on the paradigm shift called "New Directions" which had been implemented while we were working in the U.S.

As soon as we were appointed, I wrote a resignation letter on July 15th to Earl Poythress, my supervisor at DESI which is copied here:

> When Nancy and I returned from Africa eight years ago, you were kind enough to give me a job, even as an older adult. I deeply appreciate your trust in me and the way that you have taught me and supported me during my learning process of the civil engineering industry. It was my goal to become a valuable and trustworthy employee and I hope that I have succeeded in this effort. I know that I have acquired significant knowledge and skills and have many more skills than the first day I arrived for work. It has been a very pleasant experience working for you and the Company.
>
> As you are aware, I was approached by representatives of the International Mission Board and asked to consider returning to Africa to meet a critical personnel need at the Theological Seminary at Arusha, Tanzania. After a lot of soul searching, Nancy and I felt that we should consider this change, even though we are

old enough to retire. The personnel selection staff recommended us and last Thursday, we were approved by the Board of Trustees and re-appointed as career missionaries. After four years of additional service, we will be eligible for full retirement benefits including full medical insurance for life.

My one regret is that I cannot continue to work with DESI. Therefore, I am offering my resignation effective July 31, 2000. I need the month of August to prepare our shipment to Africa and we are required to be at the Missionary Learning Center on August 30th. We plan to leave for Tanzania about October 20th. If there are some urgent items requiring my help during August, I can be available a few days.

Nancy has an appointment with a surgeon on Monday about her parathyroid problem and if for some unknown reason, this prevents us from going to Africa, I would like to continue working at DESI.

Thank you for your consideration and for your support these eight years.

Nancy also submitted her resignations to the Georgia Baptist Health Care System and the Atlanta Baptist Association.

Chapter Seventeen
Retread Training and a New Country

We arrived at the International Learning Center near Richmond for our training. The living area in each quad consisted of four sleeping areas, each with a bathroom. They opened into a shared area. As we moved into our rooms, we met our quad mates: one couple had a baby, four journeymen, and another young couple with a five-year-old son who was not well behaved. Our meals were in the dining hall and we had several classes each day. We were encouraged to have Bible study and prayer time in our quads. There was also exercise time and a part was running around a home-made track. My distance running was never very good, even during the track course required at Georgia Tech. I tended to vomit after a longer distance.

A couple of MKs had been appointed as career missionaries, but Nancy and I found ourselves serving as mentors for many of these new missionaries. They bombarded us with questions and wanted to learn what issues we had faced and how we dealt with them. We received this ministry as a compliment and enjoyed these discussion times very much. This service made the times when the teaching covered things we had learned and experienced during our twenty-three years of prior service less stressful. Because I had attended the sessions about New Directions at the Kenya Mission Meeting in 1998, I had previously heard about the current missiology strategies. When this training was completed, we returned to Duluth to pack and crate our shipment. We finished our packing, planned our travel itinerary, and scheduled our departure to Nairobi for October 20th. We were excited to be returning to our adopted home and to see many friends there.

When we arrived in Nairobi, we stayed at the Guest House a few days to rest and get acquainted with current circumstances in the mission and places to shop. We looked for items we needed to take to Arusha including furniture which was not in our crates. We heard a missionary from another mission group was leaving Kenya and selling furniture. Nancy and I planned to meet the Steve Box family to see what they were selling which met our needs. We hit a jackpot when they had a coffee table, dining table and chairs plus two china cabinets made from Meru Oak. They also had two single beds, everyday dishes serving twelve, and a woven river grass sofa and two arm chairs plus hassocks. On November 2nd, we finalized an agreement and arranged to store these items until they could be shipped to Arusha. The Boxes had two dogs and one was a miniature red Dachshund. Since we loved Doxies, we asked if they planned to take Shelly with them to the U.S. They answered they had not decided and we told them if they did not take her, we wanted her as our dog and would love her. At Christmas time, we learned they left Shelly with a Nairobi Baptist missionary for us to collect.

The Tanzania Mission had left a Toyota Land Cruiser in Nairobi which would be our assigned vehicle to use. It was a huge vehicle and I was a little nervous driving it with the steering wheel on the right side for the first time in over eight years. After a few days in Nairobi, we drove to Arusha to meet our missionary colleagues and get settled in our house at the seminary. The house we were assigned had been built while we lived in the U.S. and was conveniently located near the top of the hill. It was furnished with volunteer furniture for us to use until we could get our things from Nairobi and our shipment from Duluth.

We were welcomed by Bob and Cheryl Headrick, Doug and Laura Lee, and Barbara Brown. Bob and Doug were on the faculty and Barbara was the librarian. She had been the interim treasurer until I assumed the office on January 1, 2001. The Headricks and Lees were the same age as our children, a combination which created a different dynamic in colleague relationships. The only African faculty member I knew was Joseph Kahindi who was a Kenya pastor when I left in 1992. The missionary team leader was Bob Headrick and we began to learn about the current strategy and operation at the seminary. Since I had previously been the chairman of the seminary board, I was curious to learn changes in the functioning of the school in recent years. Harrison Olang was the principal and the other key faculty member was Ezekiel Kipimo. I was introduced to the student body during the first chapel meeting I attended.

Nancy wanted to refresh her Swahili since the quality of the language spoken in Tanzania was much better than the "kitchen Swahili" spoken in the Kikuyu community in Kenya. There was a language school in Usa, a town on the Moshi highway east of Arusha, a one-way trip of about thirty miles. The highway passed the edge of Arusha and was filled with bicycles and carts pulled by men or donkeys. Driving alone on these trips made her very nervous and, when she finished her study, she gave me the keys to the Land Cruiser and said, "I am not driving anymore." She never drove in Tanzania again.

In November, the missionary team at the seminary had some brainstorming sessions to define the mission/vision for the seminary because of the Tanzanian Government's recent decision about accreditation. We produced a report to the faculty detailing questions to answer in five areas of our ministry. We identified eight training levels beginning with TEE and ending with Masters degrees. The second issue was the curricula needed for each level, and thirdly, how we coordinated all levels of training at all Tanzanian locations. The fourth issue was how to determine locations for programs and the last issue was the development of a long term financial plan.

We learned the places to shop in Arusha which was like shopping in the early days in Nairobi. John Wayne's movie Hatari was filmed in the area. One section was filmed in town where the baby elephants roamed, entered a grocery store, and knocked over stacks of groceries. We bought a lot of items in that store. Arusha is halfway between Capetown and Cairo, 2,500 miles each way.

In early December, we went to Arusha to find a Christmas tree. We searched and finally found a man selling trees on the road. He had three left and we chose the best one which was still very puny by U.S. standards. We found a few ornaments but no lights in a store in town. We decorated it and prepared for Sarah and family to arrive from Pakistan to spend Christmas with us. We drove to Nairobi to collect them at the airport and bring them to our house at the seminary. It was a blessed season. Marisa had grown into a sweet, beautiful girl who was very proud of her American Passport. She loved for her mother to read books to her. All our family recognized what a special gift of God she was because of the way her life began.

One of the events we enjoyed was a visit to Tarangire National Park. It was an interesting park with a tent camp operated by a RVA graduate and his family. The tents were typical game park structures with a shower and toilet in a concrete building connected to the tent and we enjoyed the food very much. We found elephant and giraffe, and we enjoyed standing by a huge baobab tree.

When it was time for Sarah and her family to return to Pakistan, we returned to Nairobi Airport to say goodbye. We collected Shelly and returned to Arusha, praying there would be no problem getting our dog through the border at Namanga. The immigration and customs agents on both sides of the border did not check our vehicle and we breathed thanks for answered prayer as we drove to the seminary.

The telephone service was almost non-existent. The phone number 2412 had been assigned in 1962 and was still the only one available on campus in 2000. Most of the time, it was out of service because the wires were strung on poles. The Waarush people group (cousins to Maasai) cut the wires and used the copper wire to make jewelry. Since cellular service existed in Arusha, we bought a cell phone. We were dismayed to learn it was necessary to drive to Arusha before we could get a signal to use the cell phone. Thankfully, the cellular system was under development and after a reasonable time, a tower was built nearer the seminary and we began to have usage at home.

The furniture we purchased in Nairobi arrived before the Davenports. We discovered the people who loaded the truck put the dining room table in the truck standing on its legs. On the rough road, the vibrations broke two legs away from the table top. One of the students who was a carpenter repaired the table for us. During this process, Joseph Kariuki and I became friends when I realized I knew his pastor father in Kenya.

My assistant in the Finance Office was a fine Christian gentleman, Israel Olkiarishoi. He was a Waarush who was short compared to his very tall Maasai cousins. His father had been the first convert when our missionaries moved to Arusha and began the seminary in 1962. He had been a committed layman since then. Israel was very proud of his father who taught him about their culture but also the priority of his Christian heritage.

Israel lived near the campus and walked to work every morning six days a week. His house had mud walls, a dirt floor, and a metal roof. Israel had a dream to build a larger stone house and began construction before we left our seminary ministry in early 2004.

As Israel and I began working together, we spent many hours discussing the recent history of the seminary, information about the students, and policies needed to guide our decisions for managing resources. I made him responsible for the petty cash box, so that he could handle certain payments, especially during my absence. He related to the students well and explained our policies much better than I did. His one weakness was that he could not say no to faculty requests if they violated our policies. Constantly honoring requests when he should not have ultimately caused a critical issue with cash flow, but I never criticized him because it was a cultural issue.

The seminary had received a request from the IMB Regional Office through the Board to develop strategic plans for pastoral training in Tanzania. A faculty sub-committee was chosen to address the issues and report to the January faculty meeting. Bob Headrick and I met with the Tawi regional training center directors and prepared a list of eighteen issues which should be considered by the faculty. The faculty met at the end of January and delineated five issues needing attention in a meeting with Vance Kirkpatrick and Bill Eardensohn from the Regional Office and Tanzania Bible Schools. Pastor training to meet the ministry needs were the issues: be culturally sensitive, specific for Tanzania, follow Baptist strategy, and develop program coordination.

Nancy and I looked for a church where we could invest the spiritual gifts God had given us. In April one of the students invited us to go with him to an established church up on the side of Mt. Meru. It was an interesting drive and we had a beautiful view.

International Baptist Theological Seminary of East Africa (IBTSEA) had developed a partnership with Southeastern Baptist Theological Seminary (SEBTS) in Wake Forest North Carolina for Master - in - Theological-Studies degree. The first two faculty and their families from SEBTS spent four weeks on campus in July and August 2001, teaching the beginning courses.

One Sunday, Doug Lee invited me to go with him to a Maasai church north of the seminary where there would be a baptism. I agreed because I had never attended a baptism of Maasai people. We drove north on the Nairobi highway a few miles and turned onto a very dusty road of lava ash. The windshield wipers were going full blast on the two-inches of dust and still did not clear the windshield for good vision. We drove to the end of the road and got out to walk to the church. It was a significant hike as we climbed over a thousand feet to the top of a ridge and then down to a valley and up another ridge. Near the top of this ridge, we passed a small spring emerging from the ground. When we got to the top of the ridge, we saw where the Maasai had dug a pit and lined it with plastic sheeting. There were several fifty-five-gallon steel drums which were filled with water the women had brought from the spring in small containers. I praised God as the people were baptized because I realized the extreme effort required to build and fill the temporary baptistry. After I hiked back to the Land Cruiser and rode home, I was exhausted.

A Kenya student was getting married in August and knew Nancy baked cakes. Daniel Joseph asked if she would prepare a cake for his wedding at the seminary. It was a grand celebration and everyone in the wedding party was beautifully dressed. I was impressed with the cake Nancy decorated and was always amazed by her skill.

Nancy's first birthday in Tanzania was on September 10th and I wanted to do something special for her. I learned satellite TV was available and arranged for service to be installed at our house on this birthday. The men came on the 10th to attach the receiving dish on the side of our house. In the afternoon, they told me they did not have all the tools needed to complete the installation and would return the next day to finish their job. We were disappointed, but complications like this one were normal in Africa. True to their word, they arrived with the necessary tools and completed the installation in the late afternoon September 11th. I was very happy Nancy's birthday gift was operating, turned the TV on, and set the channel to CNN. The first image was the second airplane hitting the Twin Tower. We were stunned and notified our missionary neighbors who came to watch this tragedy with us. It was a day etched in our memories just like the day President John Kennedy was assassinated and the day President Kenyatta died.

Tom Jr. and Andy were scheduled to fly to Tanzania on Friday, three days later. There was uncertainty if air service would be reestablished that quickly. We were thankful they came as planned and they said security was good. I asked Dan Rorabaugh if he would take Tom, Andy, and me hunting while they were in Arusha. He agreed, and we had an enjoyable safari to an area south of Arusha where Tom killed a wildebeest. We planned a safari to Ngorongoro Crater while the boys were with us to coincide with Tom's birthday, October 3rd. On the way, we stopped at Gibb's Farm which began in the 1920's as a coffee farm. They built one of the earliest guest houses in northern Tanzania. Stopping there was a nice respite. We had lunch, bought some coffee beans, and hiked to a lookout point overlooking the valley. We continued to the crater and stayed at a very nice lodge on the rim.

The next morning, we drove down into the crater and had a wonderful day of seeing the wildlife. It was a sunny day and we saw a variety of animals, a view we never got tired of seeing. The most interesting was a group of hyena cubs, lying in the shade of a rock pile. In the evening, we returned to the lodge for the night and returned to the seminary the next day. It was a wonderful trip.

As Tom and Andy prepared to fly back to the U.S., we loaded the vehicle for the trip to Nairobi Airport. All the flights to Europe from Nairobi departed at night; therefore, we planned to stay at the guesthouse in Westlands. Those few days were a blessing since we had not seen our sons in a year.

In the fall term, I taught my first course at the seminary, a bookkeeping course for church/association treasurers. I included some principles of planning, setting goals, and other tools for church leaders to use to develop a vision.

In late October, a theological conference was held at the seminary in Arusha with national and missionary representatives from Kenya, Uganda, and Tanzania. This meeting was planned because the Tanzanian Government had passed an education regulation requiring all colleges and universities offering bachelor or higher degrees to be accredited by the Tanzanian Ministry of Education. Since this edict would dramatically impact the Baptist Seminary at Arusha, the faculty had employed a consultant to guide the development of a ten-year master plan. Other documents were required for accreditation so that the bachelor degrees currently being offered would be legitimate. Another objective was to clarify the future relationships with the theological schools in Kenya and Uganda.

The faculty recognized that many Tanzanians had low level ability in English which would preclude them from more advanced studies. It was recommended that a six-month curriculum be developed for a Certificate of English Proficiency

Because all our children and grandchildren would be in Georgia for Christmas, Nancy and I made plans to take our vacation, so that we could spend the holiday season with them. Celebrating the Birth of our Savior together has always been a special time for us. Nancy was always successful in decorating a beautiful tree except for the puny Tanzania trees we had in Arusha. Beginning with a Christmas gift from her brother's family of a Snow Village house, our family had gifted her with many additions to this village and she spent hours arranging huge displays every Christmas in the U.S. until 2014 when she was dealing with chemo therapy.

In early January 2002, the Principal's Advisory Committee (PAC) met with a Higher Education Accreditation Council (HEAC) inspection team concerning our application for the first stage in the process. The inspection team chairman told us the team's purpose was to verify the correctness of the details in our proposal. He defined seven issues they had evaluated: available land, buildings, library, organization structure, governance, long range plan, and academic programs. They gave recommendations for specific corrections or additions to our documents and advised they would give a one-year approval for a stage one accreditation granting time for amending our proposal to achieve stage two status.

Since Harrison Olang was granted a sabbatical to pursue his Doctorate, Joseph Kahindi was acting principal when the final report was received in September. I carefully read the document and found three significant issues and eight minor issues requiring improvement. I recommended to Joseph that PAC should make assignments to various staff to make recommendations for each item. Furthermore, each faculty member should carefully proof read all the documents and report their findings.

Nancy and I talked with Joseph Kariuki and Robert Okuna about beginning a new church in the Arusha area. We had visited the existing town church a few times and knew the Headricks and Olangs were committed to this church. Also, it was in a low-income area and I knew the hope for strong urban churches was a church located in a more affluent part of the city which would attract more educated people with leadership skills. Robert was headed toward becoming a member of the faculty teaching diploma courses and Joseph was a gifted musician who played a guitar. We recruited a few students to help deliver invitations for neighbors to come to a commercial building we rented in the Njiro community.

There was a group of people at Second-Ponce de Leon Baptist who wanted to come on a mission trip and do a project with us. They arrived in March and stayed in the guest houses on campus. We also kept four at our house and enjoyed fellowship with all of them. We spent time visiting in the Njiro community and Earl Poythress, my former boss, and I looked for land we might buy for the church. The team also did a variety of other projects.

I had a very good relationship with one team member and teased him incessantly since he could be gullible. One day, he came to my house and asked if he could bathe at our house because he thought the water would be cleaner than the guest house water. I explained the water came from the same well and storage tank. On our trip to Tarangiri, when we arrived at the gate to enter the park, I asked him if he brought OFF to kill the mosquitoes. He said yes, and I told him it was a problem because it was illegal to take it into the park. After he stuttered a little bit, I told him I was teasing.

We had a favorite Indian restaurant where we frequently ate. The owners were Muslims and the wife was very friendly with us, always coming to our table to talk. As our friendship developed, she began asking me to pray for her and her family. I always stopped when she asked for prayer and prayed with her. When we went there with the team, our routine of prayer occurred. I believe this example spoke a message to the team about opportunities to witness.

I was proud of my driving history because I had only had two accidents in my life before I moved to Arusha. I was rear-ended in Smyrna, Georgia, leaving a dentist's office during the 1990's with no damage to my car but considerable damage to the other car because of my trailer hitch. The other time was hitting the deer in West Virginia during a furlough. We were assigned a Toyota RAV4 by Sonny Sledge, Tanzania Logistics Coordinator, several months after arrival. I was upset when I came around a sharp curve and hit a Maasai donkey in the herd standing on the road. The donkey did not seem to be injured but I left the scene because I did not want to see the Maasai owner. In June, I was driving a replacement RAV4 passing a heavy truck going up a hill. When I got even with the front of the truck, a donkey ran across the road in front of the truck and I hit it. Sonny named this vehicle Punda 2 (donkey 2). I delivered Punda 3 to Sonny in June 2003.

Doug and Mary Sue Brown joined the faculty in the summer and moved into their house in July. Because Doug was Barbara's son and Mary Sue, a librarian, they were a great asset to the faculty.

At the Tanzanian mission meeting in July, Frank Peavey presented twenty-five-year service pins to Nancy and me. It was hard to believe we had achieved this service record. God had blessed us in so many ways during our ministry in Africa. We had developed deep family ties with our missionary colleagues and several became the brothers and sisters I never had. We experienced the joy of loving relationships with a host of Africans from many cultures. We received a wide variety of blessings, some being true miracles.

Curtis and Linnie Porter came for two weeks in August for Curtis to teach the diploma upgrade class. It was great to see our pastor from Parkersburg in the early 1960's. We thoroughly enjoyed the fellowship, sharing many mission stories with them. The students related to Curt very well and were complimentary of his teaching. The time was too short and soon they returned to their ministry in the Kansas City area.

We had a number on our support staff. We also provided work scholarships for some of the students. There were five auxiliary operations on campus not related to academic programs: Chickens, Dairy, Domestic Science, Academy, and Garage. As I monitored the operating budget, it was obvious changes in these programs were necessary since all of them significantly overspent their income. The Domestic Science classes were for wives of students who were not enrolled as students in academic programs. The Academy was a school for children of students living on campus.

I lobbied to close the dairy and sell the cows. The herd of twenty-five cows produced about five liters per day per cow. At the sales price to students, we were losing about one million Tazanian shillings per year. We did agree to increase the sales price per liter to fifty shillings, but this change was not implemented for six months, continuing the operating loss. Since my cousin in Georgia operated a dairy farm, milking over three hundred cows every day, I knew his production was about eight gallons per cow per day. I interpreted our results to be hopeless because of the quality of the cows and feed.

Our support staff included the guards and we had a good group at night. Tim Tidenburg lived a few miles from the Kenya border on the highway between the seminary and Namanga. He was a Kenya MK who became a missionary working as church planter among the Maasai and recommended some men to us for our guard staff. The Maasai were considered by other people groups as very ferocious. When people learned our guards were Maasai, there were few security concerns.

There was a significant issue with one faculty member. He had taken sick leave for three months ending in June. When this leave was finished, he did not return to teaching, saying he was expecting a scholarship to study overseas. When he did not report to teach in August as requested, the matter was referred to the Board. The Board Secretary was instructed by the Board to write a letter notifying him that he had "self-terminated" per staff regulations and to vacate his residence within seven days of receipt of the letter. He also needed to pay several back months of electricity bills on the residence and clear his loan debt to the school of nearly three million Tanzanian shillings. The seminary never recovered those funds.

In October, I prepared a presentation to the PAC titled IBTSEA FINANCIAL PLANNING STRATEGIES. The purpose of this report was to facilitate our transformation to Mount Meru University. The first section in the paper covered the historical perspective of the seminary. The second section about financial strategies is copied below.

> From 1962 until 2001, the school received direct subsidy from Southern Baptists. This current administration changed this philosophy beginning in 2002 to become an institution dependent on fees rather than subsidy. Currently, about 50% of our income is derived from scholarships given by Southern Baptists through the International Mission Board. This is not inconsistent with the level of scholarship support Southern Baptists give their own seminary students in America.
>
> Beginning in 1997, a plan of reducing subsidy, now scholarship support, was begun by the Regional Office. In 2003, the ratio will be 4:1 where an approved scholarship for a Tanzanian student will be 80% of the fees. Scholarships for Kenya and Uganda students will be limited to the amount of scholarship available for that student if he/she attends the Baptist Seminaries located at Limuru and Jinja.
>
> The International Mission Board (IMB) has deemphasized financial support to leadership training and theological education in their latest changes in strategy. The Regional Office will continue to be under pressure from leadership in the SBC and IMB to re-

duce our scholarship assistance. Our current administration wants to prepare for this eventuality and assist our Regional Leadership Team by taking initiative to reduce the current cap in scholarship funds as the ratio continues to decline. This strategy presents a real challenge to Baptist leadership in East Africa, but we believe that our constituency is ready to stand in the gap if they are properly informed and motivated. Most theological schools started by Southern Baptist Missionaries are in countries where the per capita income is significantly higher than East Africa. For example, the per capita income in South Korea is more than fifty times greater than Tanzania according to Operation World, a publication of the IMB. In China, where there is a major focus on a church planting movement, per capita income is 15-20 times higher. It would be easy to continue to say we are so poor, we cannot do it. However, the Bible tells us that our God owns the cattle on a thousand hills, contrary to the Maasai culture that says they own them all. Our administration believes that with the right leadership from East African national Baptist leaders, Baptists will respond generously with their gifts.

People with relationship personalities generally make poor managers or administrators. Throughout this school's history, its leadership (both missionary and national) has not been effective in developing good management practices. This current administrative team intends to change this history by evaluating all our operations and making necessary changes to insure viable financial security for the school. We are intentionally studying each support operation and will implement a fee structure that covers all the costs of certain supporting operations such as student housing, child care and education, and auxiliary projects, such as the farm.

One of our long-term goals is to develop financial stability that will enable us to maintain and develop our facilities to meet the demand that transforming to Mt. Meru University will bring. The quickest way to achieve this goal is to significantly increase our student body. If we have 25-30 students in every class instead of the current 8-15, our cost will be significantly reduced because of the heavy fixed cost that we currently have. We need the support of Baptist leaders and missionaries to change the perception that many have of the school and to become active in our recruitment program. Accepting ownership of the school by conventions/unions will accelerate this change.

Our administration is proposing a challenge to East African convention/union leadership, our Regional leadership for the IMB, and our Seminary Board members. The challenge is this:

1. That we fix our student payment for fees at 20%, the rate to be in force for those receiving scholarships in 2003.
2. That as the ratio changes in 2004-2006, the conventions/unions raise scholarship assistance for our Baptist students so that by the end of 2006, the 80% scholarship will be equally supported by the conventions/unions and the IMB.
3. That the conventions/unions continue to increase their scholarship fund so that by the end of 2010, all scholarship funding will come from our churches in East Africa.

In 2001, we had begun construction for a two-story multi-purpose building which would contain offices, classrooms, and a cafeteria. By graduation time in July, it was at a stage where we could hold graduation. We planned to use it since we were expecting to have about five hundred people attending the ceremonies. We had the ground slab, columns, second floor slab, and the roof in place.

This building was located near the original chapel building. We were following the African philosophy of building. You use available funds and construct as much as possible; then raise more funds to continue the project. While slower than American strategies of borrowing from a bank, this approach produces a debt free facility. In my opinion, this plan reduces emotional stress concerning loan payments, giving the organization a more positive attitude.

As we migrated to Mount Meru University (MMU) in 2003, a University Council was created to replace the faculty controlled management. In my first report to the Council, I stated there was an operating loss in 2002 exceeding thirty-five million Tanzanian shillings. This loss was caused by major expenses for the Higher Education Accreditation Council (HEAC) inspection team, major necessary repairs to student housing and classroom buildings, underestimated budget needs for the MTS and English programs, and a major generator repair.

We took steps to install a computer network for the campus. When I attended the annual meeting of the Arusha Node Marie (local internet service provider), I learned there were special rates for schools offering computer training for students. I made an application for this special rate. I performed an analysis of electricity costs and learned we could reduce our costs by splitting service for different campus areas, a separation which would involve installing several meters. They would facilitate the allocation of these costs to the newly established cost centers. We received approval from Tanzania Electric Supply Company Limited (TANESCO) and they installed additional electricity meters. The International Baptist Theological Seminary of Eastern Africa (IBTSEA) Board had instructed me to seek investments for accrual funds of staff retirement and other monies we needed to escrow. Because of my relationship with the Kentucky Convention, I received permission from the Kentucky Baptist Foundation to invest these funds with them and began to receive quarterly reports.

As we developed financial strategies for MMU, we investigated medical insurance for staff instead of refunding expenses with a cap reimbursement. We negotiated an attractive agreement with Arusha Medical Clinic, a major improvement in staff benefits.

I sought approval from the Principal's Advisory Council (PAC) to begin the use of zero based budget planning procedures for the 2003 budget. It was a learning process for the staff and we made many mid-year corrections because of incorrect analysis of expenses. It was also necessary to adjust the method used to spread overhead expenses to the various cost centers. One impact was changing the fee structure between tuition and room-and-board charges. The boarding portion would be implemented when the cafeteria began operation. This change was important as we began to enroll day students and open a branch campus in Arusha town and in other cities in Tanzania.

The ministry at Njiro continued to be blessed and we held the first baptism in March. Since our rental building did not have a baptistry nor did any church in Arusha, we used the huge molded plastic bin made to fit the roof rack on Land Cruisers to carry luggage. I carried it to the rented building along with a garden hose to fill it with water. We filled the bin and Robert Okuna baptized in the building. The church continued to be blessed, and Nancy and I enjoyed the fellowship. When Nancy Gidden's parents joined the faculty as short-term volunteers, they added their blessings to this church ministry.

Living on the campus had its blessings and challenges. We had the normal Africa seasons, wet and dry. I was always amazed when the Poinsettias turned red in July and we saw them along the roadside, sometimes five or more feet tall. We had one in front of our house over four feet tall. It was a thrill to see Mt. Meru with a snow-capped peak from our yard some mornings. The dry season was a challenge since the yard became very dusty and we were continually wiping dust off the furniture and window sills. We had a small vegetable garden that our outside caretaker planted, and he cut grass when we had some.

Missionaries learned quickly after the first few days' power outage that a generator was needed. We bought one producing enough electricity to operate our appliances and everything else except the hot water heater. We put it in the small storeroom behind the house and connected it to be an alternate power feed. We were thankful because there were three-week outages twice while we lived in Arusha.

Graduation was held in July again and each class had distinct color robes. They were excited, and I took many colorful pictures of the various classes. It was a wonderful day of celebration.

Faculty had to prepare a syllabus for each course to be offered for every degree offered at MMU. I prepared the two for the courses I had taught: Accounting for the Church and Stewardship and Church Finance. The accounting course covered all the aspects of accounting and each student had two projects, a ten-page paper about teaching tithing, and the development of a local church budget plan. The other course description was "An examination of the nature, principles, tools, and application of the planning process, basic accounting and Biblical teachings concerning stewardship of resources, time, and spiritual gifts."

I created a recommendation for the land use and prepared a map showing use for each purpose. We finished all the documents required for the second stage of the accreditation process in August and submitted them to HEAC. Finishing the plan was a great relief.

Tom Jr. came for a brief visit in late August and planned to return to Duluth with us when we went for my cataract surgery on September 16th. We had a good visit and he had an opportunity to go hunting with Doug Lee. He killed a Wart Hog and an Impala. We made sausage out of the entire Wart Hog and it was fabulous eating for a long time. Tom wanted head mounts for both animals and Doug introduced us to his friend who did the taxidermy for Tom.

The Masters of Theological Studies (MTS) class was on campus at Southeastern Seminary for their final course work, and Nancy and I planned a visit to see them the month we were in the U.S. Dr. Bush, the Academic Dean, gave us a personal tour of the new Missions Center which was impressive. He and his wife also hosted a dinner for all the MTS students and for us in their home one evening. We stayed in a seminary guest house and enjoyed seeing all the African students.

When we left to return to Duluth, we went by Little Washington, N.C., to visit Aunt Louise, my dad's "baby sister" and it was the last time I saw her.

She was my favorite and had the same birthday as Andy. She died three months after her one hundredth birthday in 2009.

My surgery on both eyes, done two weeks apart, went well. I was thankful for it as my vision had changed so rapidly the last several months. I had had my glasses changed and the TV screen was fuzzy within three months. My night vision was also significantly improved.

In December, I presented my last Treasurer's Report to the University Council. The criteria for accreditation required for the Bursar to be a Certified Public Accountant and I did not qualify. Additionally, my relationship with Harrison Olang had become stressed due to problems of communication. I tried my best to explain the financial matters, but I failed to make him understand. He and Joseph Kahindi did not seem to grasp the risk of unpaid student fees while permitting students to attend class against the school's policy. When we adhered to the policy preventing class attendance until all fees were paid, students cleared their debt immediately. Faculty were permitted to borrow large sums from the school and there was usually over five million shillings in accounts receivable for senior staff. Another issue involved the staff's checking to see if they still had funds in their expense budget before authorizing expenditures and their failing to consider the shortfall in revenue.

There had been operating losses in 2001 and 2002 totaling about Tsh 50,000,000. In 2003, the five auxiliary operations were projected to have an operating loss of 7.5 million shillings. Four maintenance accounts exceeded their budget by eleven million shillings and Margaret Burks, a regular volunteer, promised to pay for the new phone system. When we did not receive this gift, we charged 2.8 million to the operating budget.

We made significant changes to the 2004 budget proposal. We changed the financial plan to report net income/loss for each auxiliary department. We removed all auxiliary operations from the budget and expected departments to have their individual bank accounts and their financial records audited each year. We set a square-foot rental rate for use of MMU buildings for each non-academic function. Overhead expenses were to be allocated based on their share of the expense budget. Several new senior staff positions were budgeted for a total of eleven plus missionaries. The fee structure was changed to reflect the MMU organization. I proposed a direct deposit system for salaries of senior staff. I also recommended an aggressive student recruitment program since our student census proposal in the budgets had never been achieved. Physical assets were estimated at just less than 852 million shillings. The operating losses were primarily caused by the failure to adhere to established policies.

The Davenports came to Arusha to spend Christmas with us again. It was a wonderful time, but the Christmas tree was still anemic. They were three days late arriving because the planes were grounded for four days due to severe weather in the mountains and the roads were blocked by landslides. We carried them back to Nairobi in early January to return to Pakistan on January 10th.

A Ugandan woman was employed in January 2004 to become the Bursar for MMU and I worked with her that month. It appeared she had never used accounting software and I did not feel she acquired the necessary skills before my agreed departure date on January 31st. I had adopted the use of a strong Peachtree accounting program and had a good history in its effective use. I provided an extensive sixteen-page report to Harrison Olang. This report included a complete financial report for 2003. Some highlights were these:

- Revenues were fifty-eight million under budget
- Expenses were thirty-two million under budget yielding an operating loss of seventeen million
- Unpaid student fees in late January were six million
- Faculty debts were six million
- Accounts receivable were twenty-five million
- Current liabilities were forty-four million

The Region Office asked me to evaluate and develop a plan to sell the eight missionary houses in Mbeya which had been built for hospital staff. When the hospital was turned over to the Tanzanian Government, we kept those houses. In 2004, the need for those houses evaporated because the deployment of missionary staff did not include this level of staffing in Mbeya. I spent most of February on this project and gave a recommended plan to the Nairobi office.

The people at Njiro gave us gifts as they told us kwa heri (goodbye), and Harrison presented a gift from the seminary of a framed ancient map of Africa. When I was responsible for immigrations in Kenya and visited their office, stacks of files sat on office floors. I was amazed they ever found the right file and understood why it took so long to get approvals: they spent hours searching for the correct file. My valid work permit for Kenya was approved February 28th. I considered it a miracle because they used the same number from my original permit in 1969, R265163. After this approval, we arranged for a shipment of our personal effects to Nairobi where we would begin a new term of service after a short furlough. When we had finished getting the arrangements for our shipment to Nairobi, we traveled with the truck to assist at the border on March 5th.

We planned our furlough to begin April 1st and spent the time at the guest house in Westlands until then. Trip and Beth Godwin, Nancy's best friend's son, came as volunteers to the Kikuyu Eye Hospital complex. We visited with them, showed them Brackenhurst and ate at Java House. It was great to see them. We spent a couple of nights at the Ark, one of our favorite game lodges. I especially enjoyed sitting in front of the huge plate glass window near the water hole. Because an elephant had broken the glass, someone had piled huge rocks in front of the ground level window.

Chapter Eighteen
A New Church and A New Ministry

We were happy to arrive in Duluth April 1st and hoped to have some time to renew our strength and recover from the emotional stress during our time in Arusha. Tom Jr. was living in our house and took care of it while we were overseas. We went to Second-Ponce for church on Palm Sunday and Easter. It was great to see our friends there again and to reminisce about the team's visit to Arusha. We drove to Richmond for the conference of missionaries during their stateside assignment. We took a leisurely route by driving along the Blue Ridge Parkway and spent the night where it crossed I-77. The next morning, we continued the drive, connecting with the Skyline Drive and driving on it to the crossing with I-64. We drove east and exited at Short Pump to find our way to the International Learning Center near Rockville.

ILC was a wonderful facility on land donated by the Cochrane family. The conference lasted four days and Saturday night was special because Larry and Sharon Pumpelly invited all the Eastern and Southern Africa missionaries to their house in Richmond for supper.

Nancy and I began to discuss our church membership. While we loved the people at Second-Ponce, it was a twenty-eight-mile commute in heavy Metro Atlanta traffic. We began to research churches nearer to our Duluth home. We learned that First Baptist Duluth was a mile from our house and the pastor was Dave Parker, formerly Principal of the Baptist Seminary in Lusaka, Zambia. I knew Dave from my visits to Zambia to audit mission financial records and theological education conferences in Nairobi. We visited there in early May, were warmly welcomed, and joined the church. We attended the new member classes on three Wednesday nights in May and began to feel at home. We joined the large senior adult Sunday School class taught by the emeritus pastor, Dick Baker.

Toward the end of April, we began the battery of physical exams required for a medical release to return to Kenya. While we lived in the States, Dr. John Atwater had retired, and we began to see an internist, Dr. Teresa Clark. We established a warm relationship with her and she was very active in the Baptist Medical-Dental Fellowship. We saw her at annual joint meetings with the Baptist Nursing Fellowship which we attended because Nancy was very active in BNF. I was treated for some skin cancers and had the colonoscopy as required. During this exam, some polyps were removed, and one was malignant. I was required to have another exam six weeks later to prove there were no problems before we received medical clearance to return to Kenya. I was also advised to have an exam every three years instead of the normal five-year schedule. This issue extended our time in Duluth.

Several of our friends wanted to visit with us and we met many for meals, some in their homes. Iris Shadrick was the second congregational nurse and had become a close friend with Nancy. Jeff had retired from the telephone company and they moved to Jekyll Island on the Georgia coast. They invited us to come visit them in mid-July and speak at their church on the island. They had a swimming pool and a jacuzzi in their back yard which was enjoyable. The pool was the first one I had seen treated with salt instead of chlorine. We ate lots of seafood and went one day to the club where we played croquet. It was a very restful few days.

Sarah and Marisa arrived at the end of July, so she could attend a medical conference in Dallas. They left Atlanta to return overseas on August 19th. Nancy and I flew back to Kenya two days later. Our time in the US had been busy but very enjoyable.

We arrived in Nairobi at midnight Sunday August 22nd and stayed in the Nairobi guest house a few days while we unpacked and set up our house on Thika Road. We were assigned the small, original farm house which had major restorations before the Musens lived in it and was very nice, but quite small. We always joked that every time we changed houses after living in the clubhouse at Brackenhurst, the house was smaller. This house had a good-sized living-dining combination room and a large master bedroom, but the second bedroom was narrow. The space between the two single beds was less than the width of a dining-room chair. The kitchen was a challenge because the distance between the sink and cabinets along the outside wall and the stove, fridge, and chest freezer on the other wall was not wide enough for Nancy and me to pass each other without one of us standing in the doorway to the bedroom. The best part of the house was the screened-in patio where we sat on the river grass furniture we bought in Nairobi and had our morning coffee or afternoon tea. Five days after arrival, we had finished moving and setting up the house, so that we could sleep there. We celebrated the beginning of a new custom by joining Nairobi missionaries going to Diamond Plaza for supper.

Eating at Diamond Plaza was a cultural experience. The parking lot was surrounded by multi-storied buildings on all four sides except the entrance road. Shops on one internal side and end were all like a food court and in front of each were tables and chairs. Each one served distinct types of Indian food: various curries, vegetables like palak paneer, and plain and garlic naan. We had our favorite cooks, and African waiters would go to the various shops per our instructions to get various kinds of food we preferred. We quickly learned that many missionaries made this a weekly Friday evening event. On some Fridays, as many as twenty-five of us shared this fellowship.

The next weekend about twenty-five Baptist missionaries attended a men's retreat at Mountain Lodge near Mt. Kenya. It was a good opportunity for me to get acquainted with the Kenya missionaries I did not know.

We began to get acquainted with Clinton and Teresa Woolf, a young couple with five children. They had previously served in Albania, and Clinton was the team leader for the research team. While my project was independent, we collaborated on my research.

My research targeted four large people groups and the two major cities in Kenya. The Kikuyu were the largest people group in Kenya, living primarily in the central part of Kenya. The Kamba were also a large group living east of Nairobi and their traditional land area went almost halfway to the coast, joining the Tsavo National Park. The Luhya were in the northwest and this group had about twenty-three sub-groups and several languages. The Mijikenda, composed of nine sub-groups, lived along the coast on land going both directions from Mombasa. The two cities were Nairobi and Mombasa.

The project's purpose was to determine the health of Baptist churches within these people groups and cities. The strategic focus of the IMB was church planting movements and our region leadership wanted an evaluation of churches reaching these people. The question was if we no longer have missionaries assigned to focus on these people, do the churches have the strength and vision to reach their communities with the Gospel and plant new churches.

I wrote a paper titled Church Planting Research Kenya in English and Swahili for the regional coordinators to distribute before we visited the associations. This paper is copied below and was distributed September 28, 2004:

> Southern Baptist missionaries entered Kenya in 1956, almost 50 years ago. The earliest evangelistic and church planting efforts focused on the cities of Nairobi, Mombasa, Kisumu, and large tribal groups. The first Baptist church was organized in Kenya in

April 1959. Fifteen years later, in 1971, the Baptist Convention of Kenya (BCOK) was organized. As churches have strengthened and matured, responsibilities for programs in evangelism and church planting in more established areas have been transferred to Kenya Baptist churches and other Baptist organizations. The latest example is Kenya Baptist Media. Beginning in 1998, missionaries turned their focus to evangelism and church planting efforts with people groups who are still unreached by the Gospel message.

Previous research efforts have been primarily directed at these unreached people groups. It has become obvious that if Baptists are to be successful in carrying out the Great Commission in Kenya, we need to learn more about established churches that have effectively implemented ministries for maturing members, starting new churches, and are growing numerically.

As a missionary who has spent most of the past thirty-five years working with Baptist churches and Baptist leaders in Kenya, I have been asked to lead this research effort. Our focus will be directed at churches whose membership is primarily Kikuyu, Kamba, Luhya, and Mijikenda. According to the latest census, these four groups represent more than half of Kenya's current population. Indications are that more than half of Kenya Baptist churches are in the traditional land areas of these groups and the cities Nairobi and Mombasa.

The project strategy will be to collect specific, detailed information about these churches. We need to learn which churches Kenya Baptists consider successful and why and to measure the characteristics of these churches against the teachings of the New Testament. We need to understand if there are any common practices or programs that cause these churches to grow, mature members, and start new churches. Once common characteristics are identified, ways to transfer them to churches that are stagnant, declining, or dying can be found.

The purpose of the research is to help Kenya Baptist churches to become the Bride of Christ that Jesus expects. To achieve this goal will require openness, honesty, integrity, and good cooperation. Churches can become vibrant again when their vision is renewed, and God's purpose becomes the driving force of the church's activities and ministry. My prayer is that God will build our relationship as together we search for truth to accelerate the growth of God's Kingdom.

I began the learning curve of changes in the Baptist Convention of Kenya since we took our leave of absence twelve years earlier. I discovered the BCOK had organized into eleven regions, each one with a coordinator working with all the associations in their region. I began to compile a list of every association in each region, the name of the coordinator, and the contact information for each association leader. The final association tally was one hundred-eight. An easy decision was to develop a partnership with those coordinators of the associations to be targeted for my research project.

The next step was to determine what data should be collected which would define the health of a church. After a lot of prayer, consultations with other missionaries and Kenyan leaders, I developed two questionnaires which were printed in English and Swahili: one six pages of church data and the other belief data. There were six categories of information including the congregation, pastor, leadership, facilities, volunteers, and worship practice. The belief form had fifty questions to answer yes or no. I invited all the coordinators to meet with me for a training session.

In our training session, I explained the purpose of the research and the details of the questions in the forms. I challenged them to ask God to give them a new vision for their associations and churches. I asked them to dream about churches who depended on God's provisions rather than what the missionary or volunteers would give them. I asked them to consider where their churches or associations should plant new churches. I asked them to share their vision with me as we met and travelled together.

We decided to gather data in personal meetings for each association and invite the pastor and a key lay-person from every church. We discussed issues about the meetings and they were concerned about expenses. I told them I had a small budget, but I could help with food in the middle of the day. The pastors and lay people would have to travel to the central meeting place without expecting any help from me. We identified seventy-six associations where we needed to collect data about their churches. The coordinator nearest to my office was Pius Watene, the coordinator with Kikuyu churches east of the Aberdare Mountains and north past Mount Kenya. We met our first association in Nanyuki the last Saturday in October.

The last Sunday night in October, we began a new monthly tradition. We invited all the missionaries who lived on Thika Road and in Ridgeways to our house for a supper fellowship of waffles and sausage gravy. We still had a lot of Wart Hog sausage in our freezer and everyone enjoyed this fellowship. Our house was almost "standing room only."

In November, I met with two more Kikuyu associations in Thika and Nyeri. Nancy wanted to visit Zanzibar since she had never been there. I had told her about my daytime stop on my return flight from Dar in 1970 when Ralph Harrell and I flew there to fulfill all the Tanzania legal requirements with my FMB Power of Attorney. We planned to spend Thanksgiving weekend with Sonny and Sherry Sledge in Dar es Salaam and fly to Zanzibar for a two-day visit. It was a wonderful time made special when we went to see a shop keeper friend of Sonny's. We saw a two-piece cabinet, drawers in the bottom section and a door with shelves in the section which sat on top. The glass door had a printed section of the Koran which looked like it was well over fifty years old. We also bought a hand-crafted corner cabinet about eighteen-inches along each wall. It had old ceramic tiles inlaid which made it very attractive. The shopkeeper suggested we also visit his warehouse and we found a treasure there, an Arab door about one hundred years old which had been taken from a Zanzibar house in old town. Sonny promised to bring them to Nairobi on his next trip and the shop keeper sent them to Dar on a boat. We walked along the beach and had a wonderful visit. When we got the two-piece cabinet to Nairobi, we commissioned an artist to paint a coastal scene to replace the old Koran text in the door.

When we arrived in Nairobi Sunday night, we received news that Nancy's brother Frank was in the hospital in a serious condition. Roy Brent got Nancy a ticket to Atlanta for Monday night. Since Nancy was in the US on my seventieth birthday, Bert Yates blessed me with a party. When Frank's condition began to deteriorate, I flew to Atlanta two weeks after Nancy did. Frank died a week after I arrived. Faye asked for a graveside service and I led it. Frank was buried in the church cemetery near the house where Faye grew up in Batesville. We spent Christmas with our sons and arrived in Nairobi on January 6,2005.

My travel schedule to meet with pastors in the various associations began in earnest after we returned. During the year, I spent a full day in each of forty-seven associations collecting data and challenging those who came to catch a new vision for their church. I focused on equipping members to become mature believers who would give a faithful witness to people they met in their daily activities. Matthew 28:18 "As you are going . . ." was the primary challenge. I charged these men and women to ask God to show them neighboring villages or communities where a church was needed and lead their church to commit to plant a church there.

The questions challenged them to catch this new vision and I began to see new enthusiasm about spreading the Gospel. One of the first evidences was demonstrated as I drove to a meeting with Pius Watene. As we drove along the road passing through villages, Pius told me he had visited several villages via matatu and in them were places needing a church. I began to be encouraged.

In February, I went on a survey trip to the area where the Teso people lived in northwestern Kenya. Their traditional area also included land in eastern Uganda. Often when colonists created boundaries between nations, they divided people groups placing them in different countries and creating future problems for these families.

The Teso are a Nilotic people as are Turkana, Samburu, and Maasai. I met the regional coordinator, Robert Nabirandah, and two pastors from the Kitale area who had felt called to reach the Teso at Busia, the Kenya town on the border. As we met and visited while we drank tea, the pastors told me about the Teso. They had been there the previous month and talked to people they met on the dusty streets. One man they met had been drinking and was obviously drunk, but he invited them to his house to visit. They shared Jesus with him and he decided to follow Jesus on January 7th. Two weeks later, they visited him again and as they told the story, he was praising God for his salvation. He said he had been the town drunk and a witch doctor, was now sober, and had given up drinking and burned his charms used in witchcraft. He told them the towns people saw the change and wanted to know what happened. He invited them to come and, as they sat under the tree, these pastors preached Jesus and the First Baptist Church in Angurai was born. These pastors told the people they would return when I came to visit and when I arrived, they were gathered under the tree in the man's yard. I also had the chance to share an encouraging word with the twenty or so people attending. One man was painting a sign for the church but his spelling in English needed some improvement (Fist Baptist Church). I came away rejoicing.

The next day, we drove on almost every dirt road in the Teso area of Busia District north of the main highway. There were an estimated half million Teso in Kenya and we saw only one church in the nearly hundred and fifty miles we drove on dirt roads that day. The pastors had located fifteen villages where they wanted to start a church. I left the area determined to encourage Baptists to seek to reach this people group.

In mid-March, the annual nursing symposium was held at Brackenhurst and Nancy went to brush up on her nursing skills. While she was there, I spent five days in western Kenya with different associations. I came home for Sunday and to see Nancy. On Monday I went back to western Kenya for three more days collecting data.

The following weekend was Easter and we enjoyed the worship celebration at our church, Ridgeways Baptist. The church was growing and had doubled the size of the temporary worship area since worship attendance was about 400. The pastor, Elijah Wanje, preached on prayer and the Bible Study times were also about prayer. This seventeen-year-old church had already started twelve new churches and had plans to start five more in 2005. Nancy and I helped the Associate Pastor for the Tuesday night Bible Study of T.W. Hunt's book In God's Presence.

A building committee had been established and I was asked to serve on it as we planned to acquire more land and build a permanent building at an estimated cost of one million dollars. It was a huge vision and the fund-raising activities had begun. The church planned to completely pay for it with local funds.

During the second week of April, Nancy travelled with me, so that I could meet with twenty-one associations in western Kenya to get data from five hundred churches. We planned to stay at the Rondo Retreat Center in the Kakamega Forest. It was located a few miles from Kakamega and well known for the many species of birds seen in the forest. Since we were bird watching aficionados, it was an exciting place to stay. The flora and fauna in this rainforest were beautiful and the coolness made for an enjoyable visit. I met with associations in Kakamega and Busia Districts and usually returned to enjoy afternoon tea with Nancy and rest in the coolness of the early evening. The following week was the annual meeting of the Baptist Convention at Brackenhurst.

Jane Clifford and Liz Mann from Second-Ponce arrived to spend a few days with us. They had been on a volunteer mission trip in Uganda. We told stories about the two projects I led to Kenya and Pakistan which they joined and had a very good visit.

Rosslyn Academy's graduation was held at the end of May. Nancy and I attended because some close MKs were graduating. We had gone to several events during the year. Foree Sledge and one of Cynthia and P.J. Cooley's sons played rugby and we had attended a couple of matches. We went to the spring music program and were surprised to learn a lady sitting in front of us was the wife of Uhuru Kenyatta who later became the President of Kenya. Jessie Yates graduated, and she held a special memory for me. She will "die" when she reads this story, but when she was two weeks old, Nancy was in the U.S. and I visited the Yates in Nakuru. I asked Bert if I could hold her and because she had just finished eating, I held her on my shoulder to burp. She did more than burp and upchucked all over my shoulder. She turned into a beautiful young lady and is a challenging and effective high school teacher.

During the first weekend in June, we flew to Chaing Mai, Thailand. Joel was graduating from Grace Academy and we wanted to see the family and attend his graduation ceremony. We visited an orchid farm and a park where I had the opportunity to ride an elephant with Marisa and Sabra Jones. Sabra's family previously served in Tanzania before transferring to India. After all these activities, we flew to Puket to spend a few days at the beach. It was six months after the tsunami devastated much of the Asian coasts. I was impressed at how rapidly reconstruction was taking place. Our hotel was about two hundred yards from the beach but had not been damaged. The door to our room opened onto the patio at the swimming pool. I missed much of the fun because I was sick in bed two days while we were there. I did get my one and only massage since it was a free service of the hotel.

The Yates left for stateside assignment soon after the Rosslyn graduation and I was asked to add the liaison responsibilities with the Kenya Convention to my assignment while Jack was gone. This work was helpful for my relationship with BCOK leaders and the coordinators. This assignment meant I was included in the meetings and training conferences for Strategy Facilitators and included a trip to South Africa for Nancy and me. While there, I replaced the diamond in her engagement ring which had been lost while we stayed at the guesthouse in Nairobi.

In June, I began my research with associations of 336 Kamba churches. Daniel Kambuni and I became close friends over the next year. Before the World War II era, the land had been productive and included large forested areas. As the population grew, the Kamba continued cutting the trees for firewood and making charcoal for cooking. The lack of trees caused the area to be subject to drought. For many years, Baptists had been distributing food through these churches. I saw the need for food distribution and received funding from Baptist Global Relief. We bought beans and other items to distribute in Ukambani through the churches. The most heart-rending scene I saw was the people picking up each bean that had spilled from one of the sacks. As I became acquainted with Daniel, he talked about the hunger and lack of clean water sources in much of the Kamba territory. He and Jack had started some projects to address the water issue. In many villages, the women were walking five to ten miles one way every day to fill a container of water and the nearest stream was often polluted. We had learned from our experience over the years that deep wells requiring a pump and generator were not practical. They functioned for a while, but the people could not afford the diesel to operate the generators and there were no local funds to pay craftsmen to maintain the equipment.

Jack and Daniel developed a partnership with a few communities to build cisterns. These cisterns which held about six thousand gallons were built above ground. Southern Baptists provided money through Baptist Global Relief to buy cement, rebar, and a few plumbing supplies, and to pay a craftsman if there was not one in the village. The local community provided the labor and other needed supplies. The cisterns were built adjacent to a building with a metal roof and gutters were attached to capture rain water. During my year with Daniel, we built more than fifteen cisterns beside schools, churches, and clinics.

I spent several days in July with Daniel meeting with more of his associations and looking at potential locations for additional cisterns. The last week, we joined all the missionaries in our cluster at Brackenhurst for our annual spiritual and planning meeting.

Doug Lee and I spent a few days in the Kakamega area in August for a teaching/training meeting with pastors. The remaining time in the month I worked on developing a database for data analysis from my research. I also attended a couple of institution's board meetings.

Roy Brent had setup a computer network in the Thika Road office. Because the internet connection over phone lines was so slow, we investigated other options. We discovered that a satellite internet system was available and began discussing this option. It seemed feasible to connect the houses using fiber optic cables underground. We requested funds for this project and they were approved. Having access to the network at home meant we could respond to emails in the evenings if something was urgent. We had been going to the office on Saturdays to Skype with our sons in the U.S. but after this installation, we could connect at home. Since it was only audio at that time, we did not have to dress unless we wanted to be ready to go somewhere when we finished Skyping. Janet McDowell had been the Kenya Logistics Coordinator for a few years, but she went on stateside assignment and requested a leave of absence. Journeyman Jonathan Parsons had been assigned to follow Janet, but his term was expiring. Ron and Nancy Copeland were appointed to assume this role but would not complete language study until about three months after Jonathan left for the U.S. Mark Hatfield, who was the regional associate for logistics and finance, asked me to cover this gap which gave me three fulltime jobs for three months. I had not done any logistics work since Roy Brent became the Kenya Business Manager; therefore, I had a learning curve about current policies and procedures. At the end of my service, Mark presented a nice plaque expressing appreciation for this ministry.

During the first weekend in September, Samson Ojienda, a BCOK employee, asked me to travel with him to meet with a Kisii church having serious conflicts which appeared to be a power struggle in the leadership. We met for hours before it seemed there was a need to choose one side to be given the leadership. It was one of the most difficult meetings I ever experienced.

Nancy's 70th birthday was on September 10th and I was determined that she have a special surprise party. I asked Bert Yates and Laura Lee if they would plan something which could be held at the guest house. During our extended time in the U.S., the tract adjacent to the guest house had been acquired. Three mission houses were built at the rear of the property and the section between them, and the original house along the road was made into a playground, and a sheltered picnic area was developed. I told Nancy the afternoon of her birthday I wanted to take her out for High Tea and as we drove, I told her I needed to stop by the guesthouse and leave some papers at the Woolfs. When we arrived, she was surprised. It was the first time I had succeeding in surprising her in a long time. She was a good sport as the younger MKs watched her blow out all the candles. I was so thankful for all the mission family who made this day so special for her because she had said it was her hardest birthday since her thirtieth.

During the rest of the month, I had several institution board meetings, a BCOK EC meeting, and Nancy and I went to Mombasa where I met with the two coastal regional coordinators.

Daniel Theuri from Nyeri was the current Moderator of BCOK. He asked me if I would develop a seminar for the leaders of the Convention about strategic planning. He had observed how the missionaries were planning their work and setting goals. In October, I held the first of several meetings with convention officers and a few other selected opinion makers who were pastors. We had some intense discussions about criteria for developing vision and purpose statements, defining core values, setting objectives and goals, and action plans. I told them we should revise the constitution and by-laws of BCOK because many things had changed since they were written in 1971. We set a goal to complete our work and to make recommendations to the EC and convention meetings in 2006. I had used Power Point presentations for these strategy meetings and I prepared two for those meetings. I was apprehensive because of the rejection of the proposals Morris Wanje and I had made in earlier years.

The first week in November, Nancy and I made a trip to Nakuru where I had scheduled six days of meetings with associations to collect data. We were staying in the Stickney's house since they were in the U.S. Wednesday evening after supper, we were talking about the week when my cell phone rang. It was Tom Jr. telling us he was on the way to Piedmont Hospital in Atlanta to be admitted. He had seen Dr. Clark about a fever and when she listened to his chest, she detected a murmur in his heart. Of course, we panicked when we could not call the U.S. on our cell phones and the Nakuru house phone did not have international dialing. I sent a prayer request for Tom to our prayer network because we did have an internet connection at the house. I called Roy Brent and asked him to get Nancy on a flight Thursday evening and me one for the weekend. Then I called Samuel Kamotho, the regional coordinator for the Middle Rift Region, and asked him to cover our meeting scheduled with the Solai Association on Thursday. Roy got Nancy's ticket and scheduled me to leave on Saturday night. God performed a miracle because Earl Poythress got my email, went to the hospital to see Tom, and was waiting for Tom when he arrived to be admitted. I followed Nancy after finishing with the other scheduled meetings that week, cancelled my remaining schedule for the year and arrived in Atlanta November 7th.

The tests at the hospital determined Tom had a leaking mitral valve caused by an infection in his heart. Open heart surgery was postponed until antibiotics could clear up the infection. Tom was blessed during the surgery because the surgeon was able to trim the valve to function properly rather than replace it with a pig or mechanical valve. After discharge, Tom had to go to get a series of antibiotic infusions. Thankfully, he has had no further issues.

Nancy and I had planned to take our vacation in the U.S. beginning December 9th and returning to Kenya on January 3, 2006. We took advantage of this time while Tom Jr. continued to recover and filled several medical appointments. I had been having some skin cancers, Nancy had her mammogram, and we saw the dentist. The Davenports were in the U.S. for medical issues with Joel and spent a week with us in Duluth.

We returned to Kenya rejoicing because God had met Tom Jr's health needs in a wonderful way. We also thanked God because we had visits with all our other children and grandchildren. We started planning the date we would take our last stateside time before we would retire. As we looked at the calendar, we chose October 1st because by leaving on that date with our leave time, we would reach thirty years' service with the IMB April 1st. As I was looking at Nancy's 2006 calendar for details of activities to describe in this book, I suddenly noticed February 17th. On this date, she had written 225 which began a countdown to our planned departure date for retirement in 2007.

The term had been a refreshing ministry for me and I thought Nancy felt good about her prayer ministry. I knew she had been under a lot of pressure during our previous two terms, the one before our extended time in the U.S. and our first one after reappointment. The period my Mom lived with us had taken a huge emotional toll on Nancy, and I finally realized the depth of strain this period was for her. Several incidents had been very challenging for me as mission administrator. During our years in Arusha, she did not have the ministry she enjoyed most -- nursing. Cheryl Headrick was also a nurse and was operating the clinic at the seminary. Nancy did have one interesting opportunity when a student wife went into labor and we were asked to take her to the maternity hospital one night. Another student wife was a midwife and went with us in the Land Cruiser. When we arrived, the gate was locked, and no one was in sight. I climbed over the gate and went looking for someone to open it. When I finally returned with someone to open the gate, we heard a baby crying. Nancy and the midwife had delivered the baby in the back seat. Nancy commented to me, "I was the catcher." The hospital's supplies were very limited, but the baby was in appropriate shape and came home the next day.

In mid-January, we spent a week at the coast for my research in meetings with most of the ten associations of Mijikenda and at Mombasa and returned to Mombasa again the next month. During the last week in February, we went to Johannesburg for a region wide Strategy Facilitators conference which lasted until March 6th. We enjoyed seeing and visiting with people from the seventeen countries of Eastern and Southern Africa. Back home, I continued my research and continued with the development of strategic plans with the BCOK leadership. A couple of water cisterns in Ukambani were completed and we were invited to the dedication services. On March 29th, we saw another solar eclipse which was beautiful. Our Easter celebration was a memorable experience followed by an Easter Egg hunt for all the little Mks.

The convention leaders and I had finished our strategic plan to propose to the BCOK EC and if approved, to the annual meeting of the convention. I developed two Power Point presentations to use. One was the proposed operations manual which included the constitution, by-laws, policies, procedures, and job descriptions. The other presentation was the strategic plan. It covered vision and purpose statements, core values, nine objectives, and goals for each objective until the end of 2008. The EC had many questions which our team answered effectively, and the EC recommended it be presented to the AGM. I was very relieved when it was approved. I heard from some of the team later that the plan was working, and I thanked God for each man who had contributed.

On every furlough and in letters, I pled with extended family members to visit us and see what international missions was like. Besides our mothers and children and grandchildren, no one except our nephew, Greg Kirk, and my Dad's sister, Louise, had ever visited. When we saw my relatives on the Dean side at Christmas, I told them if they wanted us to give them a tour of Kenya, it was necessary to hurry because time was running out. Therefore, I was quite pleased when my cousins Brown, Jo Dean and his sister, Rebecca Kennemur, wrote they were coming on April 30th. Brown's Daddy, Uncle Richard, had begun a dairy farm and Brown joined him when he graduated from the University of Georgia. When Uncle Richard was older, Brown bought his share of the partnership and, when he sold the cows in 2005, the dairy was milking about 350 cows three times a day. Brown could not take any extended vacation time before then.

We planned a game park trip for them and I was very disappointed that the only available lodge was Mountain Lodge on the side of Mount Kenya because I preferred other lodges. We became tour guides visiting Brackenhurst, Nairobi, Karen Blitzen's house, Giraffe Manor, and the elephant orphanage near Nairobi National Park. I knew Brown would be interested in the cisterns so one day we went to Daniel's house, met his family, saw his citrus farm, and a cistern. We went to a village "restaurant" for lunch and they had a "real" cultural experience. It was an open-air shelter with a thatched roof but no written menu. The Kamba waiter told us they had chicken, so we ordered baked chicken with boiled potatoes and a vegetable. The waiter took our order, brought a hot soda to drink, and went to the cooking area. An hour and a half later, he brought our food and the chicken was very tough. I decided the chickens were range chickens which had to be caught and killed before cooking. We finally laughed about it and every time we talk about their visit, we tell the story and laugh again.

But the day was not over. The Kamba are the world-renowned wood carvers of African animals. Daniel told us about a village where there were several shops where carvers showed their products. When we arrived at the village, it was almost dark. The others walked up a grassy hill to the shops about forty feet above the dirt road. While they were shopping, night fell, and a light sprinkle of rain was falling. I put the Land Cruiser into four-wheel drive and crept up the hill to keep them from getting wet. As I was driving up the slope, the right rear wheel skidded into a deep hole which I could not see, and I was stuck. When we looked at the situation, the "hole" was about six feet deep and four feet wide. I needed help!! We finally found a man with a tractor and he managed to pull the vehicle up far enough for me to get to level ground. The ride home was very muddy, and we arrived very tired, wet, and muddy after our day-long adventure. Since Nancy had told them we do not drive at night, they were quite concerned until we arrived at home. Brown said it was very quiet in the back seat the whole way.

As our time to retire in 2006 approached, the Kamba invited Nancy and me to a dedication ceremony for another cistern. The local member of Parliament was a Baptist and he led the dedication. A lot of local people expressed thanks to Baptists for the help. The Regional Education Officer was present, and he told me the results he had observed. He said, "We expected the health of the students to improve because they had clean water all day long, but there was also an unexpected result. We have observed the students are making higher grades on our national exams. We believe this is due to clean water." I also learned that during the dry seasons, the Kenya Government was delivering water to fill the tanks. My heart was so blessed by God's provisions through Southern Baptists which resulted in improved health and a hope for the future for the Kamba young people.

For the rest on of the month, I spent most of my time analyzing church data except for a week in a Strategy Facilitators conference. We prepared to fly to Thailand for Aaron's graduation from Grace Academy on June 7th. We spent a week in Chaing Mai and went to all the events for the graduating class. Aaron looked very distinguished in his cap and gown. We ate Thai food several times and went to a mall for a celebration of Marisa's eighth birthday. It was a momentous week, but I was happy to see my bed when we arrived in Nairobi after a week. The schedule of activities kept us very busy. The last week of June was filled with Kenya Baptist Theological College and BCOK meetin gs.

Tom Jr. and Andy arrived on July 2nd for a final visit to Kenya before we moved back to the U.S. We spent two nights at the Ark before the alumni weekend. They spent time at RVA where Tom played rugby on the alumni team. Rich and Monica Dean (Brown and Jo's son) arrived on July 9th for a visit. The six of us made a trip to Maasai Mara game park and saw many animals. When we stopped at the hippo pools on the Mara River, we saw hundreds of hippos. After we returned to Nairobi, one afternoon we visited the Maasai sales area at Village Market near the United Nations Headquarters, the American Embassy, and Rosslyn Academy. Tom and Andy showed Rich and Monica around. They observed the bargaining methods the boys used. I always bargained anywhere I could and usually found I could negotiate a price about 50% of the initial price. To be effective at bargaining, you must be willing to walk away without a purchase. Nancy and I went to find a place to sit down and soon Rich found us and asked if I could ship a carved wooden giraffe he wanted to purchase. Since I was shipping a twenty-foot container, I said, "Yes, I can." What he did not tell me was the wooden giraffe was nine feet tall and he also bought a five foot "baby giraffe." We did manage to get them inside our vehicle to take to our house. When we packed the container, they were laid on top of the boxes and furniture. We rested the remainder of the week before our Cluster Meeting the last week in July.

When we arrived at Brackenhurst to check in for the meeting, we were told our assigned cottage was just outside the side door to the dining room building. When we entered, much to our surprise and great delight, we discovered this cottage had been "upgraded" for special guests and it had a jacuzzi. Do not tell anyone, but I got in the jacuzzi every chance I had that week. On Thursday afternoon, the group had a special "Tea Time" to help David and Darlene Sorley and Nancy and I celebrate our retirement and for good-byes since some of the people would not see us again before we left in September. It was a special time.

Nancy and I spent a lot of time the next two weeks deciding what items we wanted to ship to Duluth, what we wanted to sell, and what we would give away. We prepared an extensive list of sale items with prices to distribute. The list gave September 16th as the date for items we needed to use until we moved into the guest house. Other items were available on payment. Since Nancy and I never liked to have a yard sale, this activity was a real chore for us. We chose to donate a few items which we had bought especially for our house to the mission and only had a couple of items we did not sell and that would not fit into the container when it was packed.

Our official departure date was October 1st, but the region was having a Summit Meeting at Silverdale Baptist Church in Chattanooga, Tennessee, beginning September 27th. We asked our leader Jon Sapp if he would like for us to be involved in this meeting which would require our departure from Nairobi a week earlier. He approved for us to join the summit missionary team and our official departure date to be October 1st.

A couple about our age welcomed us into their home. They were very active at Silverdale and we had wonderful fellowship with them when we were free. Pastors and mission leaders from other churches came to learn and be challenged. The worship times were inspiring, but the Sunday service was exceptional. During the invitation, the pastor gave an invitation for salvation, then he asked all the church members to bring their mission offering to the table in front of the pulpit. A flood of members carried their offerings. After the crowd returned to their seats, he asked for anyone whom God had called to volunteer for missions to come forward and the entire front of the church was crowded with people, mostly adults. This church has continued to be a very strong supporter of missions by their money and volunteers. We returned to Duluth, excited to begin our final stateside assignment.

Chapter Nineteen
Retirement = Ministry without Salary

When we arrived home from the Summit, Nancy prepared to celebrate Tom Jr.'s forty-sixth birthday. It was a good feeling to be near all our children and grandchildren. Tom lived with us in Duluth and Andy was living in our lake house, enjoying a new job he had started in 2005. He was designing custom cabinets, mostly for large houses in upscale communities. Sarah and John were buying a house in Moore, South Carolina, while they were on a year's stateside assignment. Joel was in college at North Greenville, a South Carolina Baptist Institution. A former Kenya Missionary, Jill Branyon, was a mathematics professor there. Aaron chose to take a gap year at Pine Mountain, Georgia. Truett Cathy and Chick-fil-A had just begun a program to give recent high school graduates a variety of studies. The curriculum was broad, including some cultural study, team building, intense Bible study, and an international mission project when Aaron went to Maldova. Marisa attended public school near their home.

When we returned to Kenya in 2004, we joined Ridgeways Baptist Church. Therefore, we immediately joined First Baptist Church in Duluth (FBCD) again in the fall of 2006. We joined the choir because we wanted to get acquainted with other generations rather than just our senior adult Sunday School class. Both of us had always enjoyed singing in our church choirs.

We decided to join the Y.M.C.A. to get some much-needed exercise. Nancy really liked water aerobics and we both spent time on the exercise machines in the weight room. We had a training instructor for a few weeks to make sure we knew how to use the myriad of machines. I ultimately used only ten of those available.

During the last two weeks in October, we were the missionaries in residence for the Senior Baptist Retreats held at Shocco Springs, Alabama. It was a wonderful experience enjoying the fellowship with people our age and older. We chose the theme Fan the Flame for Missions which was taken from 2 Timothy 1:6: "For this reason I remind you to fan into flame the gift of God which is in you." We challenged them to fulfill this instruction through prayer, focusing on the lost, creating a mission vision in their church, and adopting an unreached people group. Several hundred senior adults attended each week.

In this presentation, we also shared some of the health characteristics of the Kenya Baptist Churches we had researched. We learned the following and asked Southern Baptists hearing this report to consider which of these characteristics applied to their church:

1. Doctrine of church members and leaders is filled with syncretism from other denominations and culture.
2. The vast majority of members are nominal Christians - their commitment is limited to Sunday worship attendance.
3. Many pastors are very controlling and autocratic in their leadership style.
4. The financial program of most churches is weak because of poor records, a low trust level of treasurers, and the pastor is not demonstrating a commitment to tithe and to give offerings.
5. There is a prominent level of disunity within churches and between pastors and church and denominational leaders.
6. There is an elevated level of dependency on external funding.
7. Churches have not been accountable to follow-up on converts from the ministry of volunteers resulting in a lot of church start deaths.
8. A considerable number of church leaders are bound by tradition and resistant to try new methodologies.
9. Politics and power seeking by pastors and leaders is preventing the Will of God from being achieved.

We outlined the indicators of a healthy church learned from the research of Southern Baptist Seminaries and other researchers.

1. People are regularly being saved and baptized.
2. Church membership increases at least 7% per year.
3. The church has an effective training program for all its members.
4. The church is having new children (starting new churches).
5. The church has a good vision and plans its work well.
6. The church listens to God and to each other.
7. The pastor exhibits a servant style of leadership.
8. The church knows its purpose and shares in doing its

purpose.

9. The members are committed to work on the church's goals.
10. There is unity among the members.
11. There are effective communications within the membership.
12. The church has discovered and is doing the Will of God.

In February 2007, we began to seek ways we could have some ministry in First Baptist Duluth. We met with the staff at their weekly meeting and Nancy chose to become one of the members who spent one hour per week in the prayer room, answering the phone and maintaining the prayer list with most of the hour spent in prayer. I agreed to begin some demographic studies on the community because it was undergoing a serious influx of international people. This transition from a small rural community to a major suburb of Atlanta was challenging. The church was about 99% Anglo, but the community was rapidly changing. What should the church do? A quick check on 2000 census data for our zip code showed twenty-five countries represented in our census. Two (India and South Korea) had a population exceeding one thousand and the Mexico count neared three thousand. Pastor Dave Parker encouraged me to continue researching data about our community. Over the next several months, I collected several reports from the North American Mission Board and the Georgia Baptist Convention research groups about our community. We focused our study on both a three-mile radius and a five-mile radius from the church site. I was astounded by one thing in the GBC report. The population in the five-mile radius was 21,465 in 1980 but projected to be over 193,000 in 2008. The three-mile radius went from 8,755 to over 72,000 in 2008. The forecast for white population was less than 40%. Population density was about 2,500 per square mile.

At this meeting, Nancy and I shared the ministry she had at Peachtree Baptist using the Georgia Baptist Mobile Dental Unit for a health fair. It was agreed for FBCD to schedule a Health Fair for the last weekend in August. We called the event Meet FBCD.

Nancy's class at Georgia Baptist Hospital School of Nursing celebrated their fiftieth anniversary at the Mercer University campus in Atlanta. This school had received supervision for the nursing program and upgraded it to a Bachelor of Nursing Degree. My class at Georgia Tech also celebrated our fiftieth anniversary the next week. We thought several of our classmates looked very old. On most Sundays in November, we spoke at two different churches and some Wednesday evenings. During the first weekend we spoke at a multi-day mission conference held at Briarlake Baptist Church in Atlanta.

When Tom and Andy made their last trip to Kenya, Tom told us about a trip he had made one weekend to Savannah with two young women from First Baptist Duluth. We met Laura Deaton in Duluth after we arrived from Kenya. She told us later she was very nervous about meeting us because of her concept about missionaries being very different from "normal people." We had all our family for Thanksgiving dinner and Laura was included. We thanked God for healing Tom's heart the year before by open-heart surgery. That night, Tom told us, "I...gave my heart to Laura this Thanksgiving" and that they planned to marry in March 2007. We were pleased since Al Cummins had always teased our boys saying they were "socially retarded" because they were still single.

While we lived overseas, Uncle Richard's family invited Andy to join them to celebrate Christmas. They also invited my oldest cousin, Marcille, a widow whose children lived far away. We were included that Christmas and enjoyed the fellowship very much. It was fun being with our extended family but as the years passed, the cousins had grandchildren and the crowd became enormous. It was decided the children's families of Uncle Richard would celebrate together and my family would have our own celebration.

Little did we know what our future would be in 2007 as we celebrated New Year's Day with all the Davenports except Joel who went on a retreat. Aaron left on his mission trip to Maldova on January 3rd and we began to pack up all the Christmas decorations and the snow village. We travelled to Jackson, Mississippi, to attend the annual meeting of the Baptist Medical Dental Fellowship and enjoyed seeing friends. The next week Nancy had a bone density test and her first appointment with Dr. Nugent about knee replacement surgery. After all the tests, she was scheduled to have her knee replaced at Piedmont Hospital in late June followed by physical therapy. After the home therapy finished, we went to a therapy center in Duluth. We were very pleased with the team there. Many of their clients were professional athletes with the Atlanta Braves and Falcons plus others who lived in Atlanta during the off season. We were still getting requests from churches to "tell our mission stories" and were thankful for each opportunity.

Tom Jr. and Laura began to discuss wedding plans with us and asked me to lead the ceremony. They wanted it to be a small affair and asked if the wedding could be at our house. We agreed and began to talk about plans. Nancy and I went to church for supper and choir practice on Wednesday night, February 14th, Valentine's Day. When we were driving home, my cell phone rang, Nancy answered, and Tom said they were at our house and had something to tell us. We walked in the front door wondering what we would hear from them. Tom said, "We got married today and wanted to tell you before you read about it in the Atlanta Journal tomorrow." Then, they told us the story.

They had gone to the Court House to get their marriage license and were dressed very causally in sweat clothes. As they passed through security, Laura had an attack of tachycardia and fortunately an EMT was there with a wheel chair quickly. When her heart rate slowed, they went to get the license. The license clerk told them they should just get married while they were there, the courtroom was decorated, the judge was available, and it was free on Valentines. They entered the courtroom and met a very nice female judge who performed the ceremony. When she asked for the rings, they said they did not have any. The judge went to her desk, got two paper clips, and fashioned rings for them to wear. As they left the courtroom, a reporter for the Atlanta Journal was there, took their picture, and interviewed them. Sure enough, the next day's paper had their picture on the front of one section with an article "Cupid at the Courthouse."

We both visited our dermatologist to have a routine check because of our exposure to the African sun. I had the routine freezing of several places on my bald scalp. Nancy was referred to Dr. Olansky's brother who did the MOHS surgery for a place on her nose. The excision on her nose was extensive and she had plastic surgery on the site, using skin from behind her ear.

In April 2007, I attended the celebration of our 55th high school graduation anniversary. We met at the Henry Grady High building, had a view of the campus, and learned of the changes in the student body since we were students. When I was a student, a major portion of the student body was Jewish. During this visit, I became aware that a major area where students lived had transitioned to an African-American community.

On Sunday May 27, 2007, Dave Parker announced that the Stewardship and Finance Committee was recommending a reduction in the percentage of undesignated offerings to the Cooperative Program be reduced. The following day, I wrote an open letter to the congregation, transcribed below:

> I listened with dismay and deep disappointment as Pastor Dave made the announcement yesterday morning about the decision of

the Stewardship and Finance Committee to defer our contributions to the Cooperative Program and Gwinnett Metro Baptist Association. Although I understand the rationale for the recommendation, in my heart of hearts, I am convinced that this is an erroneous path for our church. I want to encourage you to join me by taking actions that change the conditions leading to this decision.

I believe in tithing and have tithed since my first job delivering the Atlanta Journal as a nine-year-old boy more that sixty years ago. I must confess that working as an engineer in my early married life with small children, there were two times that I felt paying my bills was more important and that I "could catch my tithe up later." Both times, my family struggled financially until we began to give our tithe first. When God called us to become Baptist missionaries, we took an income hit of more than 50%, but I can truthfully say that our lifestyle was never better because of the support of Southern Baptists through the Cooperative Program and the Lottie Moon Christmas Offering.

In my lifetime, I have been a member of eight Baptist churches in the U.S. and several in Africa. I have served on the Executive Committee of a State Convention and counseled the leaders of the Kenya Baptist Convention. I have observed many churches and their financial priorities. I have watched God bless churches who focused on ministries outside the four walls of the church building. I have seen God withhold blessings when the congregation focused on its members' needs. A few years ago, one church that I know well, was giving half of its undesignated offerings to mission type ministries. Then, during a recession, it reduced its giving to the Cooperative Program. A significant portion of the members left the church and today, its budget is less than 40% of the budget ten years ago. My observation is that churches begin to plateau and decline leading to death when their focus becomes inward rather than outward. I do not want that to happen to my church.

In Malachi 3:10, God challenges us to test Him by bringing the whole tithe into the church, so He can bless us more abundantly. I urge you to join me by giving the whole tithe and more to First Baptist Duluth. If you are not a tither, test God by becoming one and see how He blesses you. Let us join and change this decision that I believe is bad for the future of our church. May God bless you as you pray over your decision.

We had two families in East Africa named Cummins. We lovingly called them the girl Cummins and the boy Cummins. Harold and Betty had two girls, Cathy and Libby. Al and Peggy had two boys, Tim and Jim. Cathy was a very gifted writer who married Tim Palmer, a small-town newspaper editor. Cathy became a well-known author of Christian fiction with over fifty books published under the name Catherine Palmer. When she came to Atlanta for a Christian booksellers' convention in 2006, she connected with Tim. During their visit, Tim carried Cathy to Clarkston, a nearby suburb which has become a melting pot of ethnic people because the government has resettled refugees there, usually a few hundred new families a year. As they walked the streets, she met a Somali woman and greeted her in Swahili. The woman was so happy to hear her language, she invited Cathy to her home for tea. That night in her hotel room, she called Tim and said, "Tim, I think God is calling me to move to Clarkston." Cathy told me later Tim said, "God has not called me." God worked on their hearts and by 2008, they had sold their beautiful house by a lake in Missouri, had been approved by the North American Mission Board as missionaries, and had moved into an apartment in Clarkston. Nancy and my story with Cathy's ministry began here.

Our sub-division, Hampton Place, was a covenant community and had a Board to oversee the shared areas, club house, and swimming pool and to ensure that home owners follow the rules in the covenants. A pediatrician who lived near me and was in our Sunday School class at church was a member of the Board. His term expired, he recommended me as his replacement and I was elected in 2007 and served several years. This experience was a different type for me.

Alumni of the Georgia Tech Baptist Student Union from 1950 to the 1970's had a retreat once every two years. The first one Nancy and I had attended was held at a hotel in the north Georgia mountains in late July. It was good to see many old friends and make new ones who followed me at Tech. Several I knew had also married Georgia Baptist Hospital nurses and Nancy had an enjoyable time catching up with those she knew.

In August, I was elected as a deacon at FBCD for a three-year term. The last week, we held the Meet FBCD event and had over two hundred come to the fair. We had recruited many church members to help with the ministry including several nurses. Dr. Clark, our internist, volunteered to help with medical issues. Our dentist, Dr. Campbell, recruited two dentist friends from Duluth to help and my current dentist, Dr. Twilley, from Toccoa also volunteered. The volunteer team for the medical events provided basic tests like blood pressure, hearing, eyes, and other simple tests. The WMU sponsored a yard sale and the church's children workers led games and provided child care for the very young in the nursery. We had translation services, food providers, and a Red Cross blood drive. We also showed the Jesus film in the fellowship hall. It was a momentous event and we tried to follow-up with those who came.

The deacons were organized into four teams and each week of the month, a different team was responsible to minister to the congregation. We visited those in the hospitals, visited shut-ins, prayed with a minister, and touched other spiritual needs. My week in November was a rewarding experience. Sunday evening, FBCD held an ordination service for new deacons and installed all of us chosen to serve in the coming year.

Dave and I continued our discussions as we looked at Jesus's teachings in John 17. The prayer of Jesus emphasized three requests: Himself (v 1-5), His disciples (v 6-19), and we who believe because of His Word (v 20-23). Throughout the chapter, Jesus instructed believers to have unity. We discussed the church in the New Testament focusing on the church at Antioch when Paul and Barnabas were commissioned as missionaries in Chapter 13. The pattern in the church at Antioch was multicultural because of the five leaders of this church, two were from Africa, one from the Mediterranean, one from the Middle East, and one from Asia. I described Ridgeways Baptist in Nairobi which was a truly multicultural congregation. Members represented many Kenyan people groups, other African nations, Asians, European nations, and some from North America. We worshiped, singing in multiple languages like English, Swahili, Kikuyu, and Zulu. This diversity of cultures worshipping together had led me to believe the current mission strategy of homogeneous congregations did not follow the teachings of the New Testament. Jesus and Paul taught about unity in the church and it was true the church at Jerusalem had conflict between the Hellenistic Jews and the Hebraic Jews over equality of support for their widows. The twelve solved the problem by recommending that a group we now call deacons be selected to supervise this ministry. The problem was solved when they chose the majority to be Greek speaking Jews for this ministry.

During the second weekend in September, we went to Ridgecrest for the Week of the Emeriti the IMB holds every five years. They had special sessions for those of us who were just retiring and recognized each of us in one service. Jerry and Bobbie Rankin, President of the IMB, presented us with a certificate for thirty years of service. Nancy went to a WMU prayer retreat at Camp Pinnacle the weekend after we returned home.

Tom and Laura rented a cabin in the mountains of north Georgia the last weekend in October and invited us to go with them. It was a fun trip and the colorful leaves were impressive. We laughed a lot as they described a previous visit when it snowed, and they had some excitement trying to drive on the mountainous roads. It was a time of strengthening our relationship with them.

We attended extra choir rehearsals during November to prepare for the 2007 presentation. I preached at three churches on the December Sunday mornings emphasizing missions. Each trip was more than one hundred miles each way, but I managed to get home on December 9th in time to dress for the Christmas choir presentation. It was a meaningful worship experience. Our married daughter, Sarah, divided her holiday time with both sets of grandparents. As a result, we celebrated our Christmas December 27th.

The IMB gave John and Sarah a three-year assignment in the U.S. challenging churches in South and North Carolina to increase their mission vision and consider adopting a people group. They would provide training for the churches, connect them with an IMB field team, and assist in other ways. Aaron graduated from the gap year program and his girl friend Jess Johnson graduated from Grace Academy in Thailand. They both enrolled at Union University, a Baptist college in Tennessee.

About 7:00 pm February 5, 2008, a massive tornado struck the campus of Union University where Aaron and Jess attended college. They were in the student center when it struck and were safe, but Jess's dorm building was destroyed. We were thankful because God had protected them. The campus sustained about forty-million-dollars in damage, but Baptists rallied. Classes quickly resumed, and the academic and dormitory buildings were restored in record time.

We learned Rodney Woo had started a multi ethnic Baptist congregation in Houston, Texas, and Dave invited him to lead a seminar for select members of the congregation on March 17th. It was a wonderful learning time for me and I found three other books written on the subject.

In early April, I wrote a "white paper" about the transition from a homogeneous congregation to a multicultural one. Some excerpts are transcribed below.

> As Rodney Woo has written and said, there will be strong resistance on the part of some members to make the transition and this may lead to some loss of members. However, I believe the Biblical mandate requires us to move forward to reach our changed community. People in transition or crisis are the most open to

hearing the Gospel but we must be able to meet real or felt needs as we build relationships. We have the nucleus inside our membership and attendees to develop good cross-cultural networks. All the successful multi-cultural churches have diversity in leadership, including ministerial staff. Since our student members already attend multi-cultural schools, it should be easier to gain acceptance for an ethnic youth minister. Moving slower in the music area is wise but the new minister should be willing to ultimately teach the congregation different music styles, including ethnic music.

From my experience and reading, I believe there are three initial steps that we should take:

1. Restart ESL. I have offered to help restart this ministry.
2. Build fellowship networks. We should "recruit" Anglo members to join hands with Chip and Jeannie Williams to build friendships with the members of their Sunday School class and with those who attend worship but not Sunday School.
3. Develop a cross-cultural training system. I believe that many of our folks have not had the opportunity or felt the need to learn how to relate to other cultures. We need to find ways to encourage and develop cross-cultural competence in our congregation.

Dr. Woo says that four aspects attract people to a diverse congregation: curiosity, consistency, acceptance, and a rise in status. He also says that people come to his diverse congregation for the same reasons people affiliate with any church: friends or family invite them, the location is convenient, the people are friendly, they appreciate or are moved by the worship, or they are attracted by the available programs. He says there are three models of multi-ethnic congregations: assimilated, pluralistic, and integrated. The assimilated model embraces a few ethnic people into the majority group which is the current situation at FBCD. The pluralistic model is where there are more than one ethnic group meeting and worshiping separately in the same facilities. The integrated model is when all ethnics are incorporated into one congregation where leadership and worship style is representative of all the many cultures. Dr Michael Emerson in his book, *People of the Dream,* concluded that "integration helped people grow more secure in and proud of their cultural identities."

Nancy faced a series of medical crises beginning April 13, 2008. The

FBCD choir had finished our warm-up rehearsal and were walking down the corridor to enter the choir loft for the morning service. Suddenly she tripped and fell face down with her arms full. She tried to break her fall with her left hand but by the time I reached her, I knew she was hurt. Fortunately, there was a physical therapist and nurse nearby who reached her by the time I did. She was in pain as they sat her up. I went to get the car while they put her in a wheel chair and rolled her to the outside door.

At the emergency room at Piedmont Hospital, x-ray technicians x-rayed her shoulder and found it was dislocated. A nurse injected pain medication. The attending physician put the joint back into place and after checking her more, she was discharged with a sling and prescription for pain medication. She made an appointment with Dr. Nugent and, when he examined and tested her, he learned there was a major tear in the rotator cuff. He scheduled surgery on June 10, 2008, to repair the damage. The surgery was successful and when she was preparing to be discharged, Dr. Clark came by to check on her. She asked Nancy why she was still on oxygen and Nancy told her her oxygen was still in the low 90's. Dr. Clark immediately ordered a CT scan which revealed blood clots in both lungs. Her hospital stay was extended until the clots dissolved. Two weeks after surgery, she started physical therapy which continued for three months.

As Cathy Palmer prayed about a ministry, God led her to begin a micro-enterprise refugee business. She received permission to use a small room in the Clarkston Community Center and in November of 2008, began the first sewing class with one student. Nancy and I visited the ministry for the first time the following spring when we joined a group of Women's Missionary Union (WMU) volunteers led by Barbara Curnutt, Gerorgia Baptist Convention (GBC) WMU Director. They brought donations of fabric and sewing notions. I remember helping carry the donations into the building and arranging tables for snacks. The volunteers were buying sewn items made by the refugee women and I visited with two husbands of the students. Cathy asked me to collect the money for the bought items. Nancy and I were hooked. Cathy had her sewing class three days a week. and Nancy and I volunteered one to two days a week. The room in the community center was very small and we had to pack all the sewing machines and supplies and put them in storage cabinets at the end of each day. Since there was one row of two tables for the students and very little space to pass behind the students, we began to pray about a larger space.

The Northlake Church of Christ had a large area on the ground floor beneath the sanctuary which was unfinished and not in use. They agreed for the Refugee Sewing Society to rent a portion at a reasonable price and we moved into the area. We needed cabinets to store supplies and products. A volunteer from First Baptist Duluth and First Baptist Covington assisted me in the construction.

A major event occurred in our lives on July 12, 2008, when Nancy and I celebrated our 50th wedding anniversary. Sarah and Andy planned a wonderful event for this special milestone. A large group of friends and family were invited to our lake house to honor us by their presence. Andy did his usual grand performance as a chef and we were stuffed with delicious bar-b-que ribs with his unique sauce and all the trimmings. It was a beautiful sunny day, not too hot as we gathered in the front yard. Nancy was recovering from her surgery on her shoulder and was wearing her sling, but she was beautiful and as usual smiling even though she had pain in her shoulder. Many people from distinct stages in our lives came to celebrate with us. Several who were in our wedding were there, Tech and GBH friends, and several from two churches, SPDL and FBCD.

When we acquired our lake house in 1989, it was leased to two single engineers. When they vacated the house after we started living in the U.S. in 1992, we began to spend some time there on weekends. The two-acre lawn needed attention and we built a small dock to use with the boat the boys had purchased. The house needed some maintenance and I hired a couple of local craftsmen. One promised to paint the outside, requiring the removal of the shutters. Another worked on replacing the roof over the carport and kitchen/dining area. The painter did not finish the work and stole the shutters. I had made an unwise decision when I advanced some money to him.

During visits with Andy who lived there, we observed that the kitchen ceiling drywall had some water damage. Quickly, it got water soaked and fell to the floor. Obviously, the flashing connecting this roof to the second story on the house was not properly installed. After our sad experience with local repairmen, I asked some people at church who did construction about the possibility of going the eighty miles to work on this very old house. Gary Lancaster, a Sunday School teacher at FBCD, was trying to start a house renovation business. He travelled with me to investigate and after inspections and consideration, he agreed to take two helpers and spend about three days a week until the project was complete. As some progress was made, we discovered the exterior wall between the kitchen and carport had serious water damage. Because this part of the house was an addition made in 1850, one end had sagged, and the elevation difference was eight inches over the forty-foot length. With these two key issues, we decided to tear down all this 1850 addition, redesign it so the carport was a one car garage and use the rest to expand the dining area into an L-shaped great room with the kitchen. What I thought was a minor repair turned into a very expensive renovation. As we tore off the drywall on the interior kitchen and dining room walls, the original logs were exposed. Nancy and I thought it would be a beautiful period addition to have the logs exposed in the dining room. We also owned a tree farm my mother inherited and there was a farm house there which had not been occupied for more than twenty years. Its interior walls were cedar bead board. We collected enough to use for wainscoting in the dining/den area. These renovations took thirteen months and we finished in September of 2008.

When we joined FBCD again in 2006, Steve Brown was the minister of music. He was called to serve on the Georgia Baptist Convention staff in the music department. The leader of the department, Jon Duncan, who came to the GBC from a similar position in Oklahoma, became our interim minister of music. He recommended Travis Boyd to be our new minister of music and FBCD called him in 2008. Travis was a very gifted composer and the choir sang many of the praise and worship anthems he composed.

Dave Parker and I discussed the church vision to reach the community. We agreed the ESL ministry which had been defunct for a few years should be reestablished and I volunteered to lead the effort. We planned an ESL teacher training conference for August plus an advertising campaign to start classes in September. We had about twenty who received a certificate of completion of the training offered through the Georgia Baptist Convention.

Later in the year, Nancy had an infection in her shoulder and was given a series of antibiotic infusions at the hospital for about ten days. When the infection was not eliminated, Dr. Nugent scheduled additional surgery and discovered the infection was at the bone. He cleaned out the infection surgically, but the infection had destroyed the rotator cuff repair. Nancy was left-handed and with the damage, she could not raise her left arm without help from her right arm for lift. By bending her elbow, she could brush her hair, but she lived with this disability the rest of her life.

In September 2008, I was summoned to serve on the Gwinnett Grand Jury along with about 200 others. Two Grand Juries were empaneled to serve for six months on alternating Wednesdays and I was chosen for one. It was an interesting but sometimes emotional day when we met. We heard about five-hundred cases over the six-month session and sent all but one to trial. I was amazed at how stupid most criminals are. The most difficult case involved a Cub Scout leader who sexually abused most of the young boys in his pack.

Cathy was very happy when Nancy and I started volunteering. There was a couple who had invested in the ministry, Todd and Carol Harrison. Todd owned a business in Gwinnett County suppling goods for nursery schools. Todd's attorney had done the legal work for Refugee Sewing Society (RSS) to obtain a 501c3 tax status and registration with the State of Georgia. Carol was keeping financial records. Todd had hired Cathy's husband, Tim, as a sales rep for his company since the mission Board did not provide financial support for the Cummins. They were very supportive, but their time was limited for RSS.

Cathy's comment to me the first day was "Uncle Tom, I am very artistic and creative, but I have no business sense. Please help me." Often, when the students left, we would sit down and discuss ways to improve the operation, products, sales promotion, data needs, product pricing, inventory, and a host of issues of business management. When I started, Cathy was paying each woman 70% of the sales price in cash. I told Cathy this method must change because of tax regulations; therefore, we set up a monthly payroll system. The issue as volume increased was a system to record which product item was made by each woman so that we could pay her when her products were sold, not when they were made. This system was improved when a product tag was created for each product with the refugee's picture and brief information about her. I designed a database system to track production, sales and inventory which was very helpful. Most of the problems arose because most of the volunteers were artistic like Cathy, but had a challenging time using the prepared product list they carried to an event to record sales. The incomplete record was frustrating for the lady selling and me when the information was returned.

Before we volunteered, it was suggested to sell products and promote Missions in a Box. This was very creative idea and various groups ordered a box containing a variety of items made by the sewing class, yarn class, and jewelry class. We included information about the ministry, program ideas for a meeting, and a list of the items for sale. We requested a donation of $20.00 when a box was ordered to cover Fed-Ex shipping. This was a consignment sales plan and unsold items were returned with money for items sold. The other marketing plan was to solicit an opportunity for a volunteer to visit church meetings and secular club meetings to make a presentation and have a display of products for sale. Several of us had many opportunities to share the story in this type venue. In October, we travelled to Texas for the annual reunion of missionaries and others who served in East Africa. It was a blessed time of reunion and as usual, funny storied were shared in small groups during our times of fellowship. In November, we were invited to speak at the West Virginia State Convention meeting and were blessed by seeing old friends and learning about God's blessings on the Baptist ministry there.

Dave Parker announced his resignation as pastor of FBCD after fifteen years of ministry. He and Yvonne had been approached by John Brady of the IMB and asked to consider reappointment for mission service as the member care persons for the North Africa and the Middle East region. God had led them to accept this call. The church held a Celebration Service on January 25, 2009, to thank the Parkers for their years of ministry with the church and to commission them to their new ministry with the International Mission Board. We presented a book containing letters of blessing written by church members.

We presented the following charge to the Parkers:

> Because God has called you to a new ministry, we, the members of First Baptist Church Duluth, challenge both of you to have confidence in the Call of God on your lives. There will be times that only this confidence and Call will be the anchor that holds you faithful to your ministry responsibilities. As you trust and obey God, we are confident that you can ultimately say with the Apostle Paul as he wrote to Timothy: "I have fought the good fight, I have finished my course, I have kept the faith."
>
> We challenge you to have the "Mind of Christ" as you learn a new language, remembering that love covers a multitude of grammatical errors and pronunciation mistakes. The ability to laugh at yourself will endear you to the people you meet every day. As you become pastors, mentors, and ministers to your targeted people group, we challenge you to be sensitive to everyone you meet, regardless of their people group. We encourage you to find creative ways to share the love of God with each person you meet because some will have never heard about Jesus Christ.
>
> Your vision should be that a multitude from every language, people, tribe and nation will know and worship our Lord Jesus Christ. Keep God's purpose as your priority as you live out your lives daily. Concentrate your daily Bible study and prayer times toward having the "Mind of Christ". We believe that God will bring into your lives each day people that need to experience your love and caring ministry of encouragement and mentoring.

As Paul wrote, we challenge you to walk worthy of your calling "with meekness, with longsuffering, forbearing one another in love; endeavoring to keep the unity of the Spirit in the bond of peace."

"Since you have so great a cloud of witnesses surrounding you, lay aside every encumbrance and the sin which so easily entangles you, and run with endurance the race that is set before you, fixing your eyes on Jesus, the author and perfecter of your faith."

Therefore, we, the members of First Baptist Church Duluth, send you forth with our blessings and prayers to follow God's call wherever He may lead you. We send you to testify to God's love and grace, to comfort the hurting, to disciple believers, and to encourage the family of God.

The deacons presented the following motion at the next church business meeting:

> The deacons move that the church establish a Transition Team to assure that the functional roles of the pastor are carried out by ministerial and lay leadership during the transition time in a coordinated and unified way that glorifies God and honors the work of the church within our governing documents. The members of the Transition Team shall be: The Chairman and Vice-chairman of the Deacons, the Chairman of the Personnel Committee, the Chairman of the Stewardship/Finance Committee, and the Chairman of the Pastor Search Committee or their designees. The leader of the Transition Team will be the Chairman of the Deacons.

The previous year, the deacons held a weekend retreat and we planned an overnight at the Georgia Baptist Conference Center in Toccoa for Friday and Saturday, February 27-28, 2009, before our called business meeting. I was responsible for the program and invited Jack Partain, former missionary teacher at the Arusha Seminary, to be our Bible teacher. The Partains left Tanzania after Ruth was seriously injured in a wreck which resulted in some disabilities. Jack was one of the best Bible scholars I knew and was on the faculty at Gardner Webb University in North Carolina. I also invited Tim Cummins, a MK from Kenya. Tim was a missionary with the North American Mission Board and had an apartment ministry in metro Atlanta called Whirlwind Missions. Tim's topic was "relating to other cultures" since many residents in the apartment complexes he served had many ethnic peoples as residents. We also watched two videos presented by Jim Henry. It was a good meeting and we were challenged.

The deacon officers for FBCD for 2008-2009 were Chairman Steve Agee, Vice Chairman Tom Jones Sr., and Secretary Tandy Brannan, brother of Yvonne Parker. FBCD ordained its first non-Anglo deacon in the fall when Sam Seaborn, an African-American, was elected. Sam had been a member many years and God gifted him with a beautiful tenor voice. We held a called deacon's meeting on March 15, 2009, to approve a recommendation for a pastor search committee. The deacon officers and team leaders recommended a five-member committee chaired by Charles Summerour. It was announced that the officers would recommend a transitional pastor at the regular deacon's meeting and these two recommendations would be made to the church at a called business meeting on March 29th.

The responsibility for pulpit supply in the absence of a pastor was the responsibility of deacon officers as was an interim pastor. We chose to use the term "Transition Pastor" which was being done in many churches. We believed this definition was appropriate in our situation because there were some issues needing resolution by the congregation and we as deacon officers believed they should be resolved before a new pastor began his ministry. I suggested we consider John Bryan who currently held a key position with the Georgia Baptist Convention. I first met John when he brought a volunteer group to Kenya from Curtis Baptist Church in Augusta where he pastored for seventeen years. Curtis Baptist was larger than FBCD and he had served several Georgia churches as interim or transitional pastor. He had participated in training offered by the North American Mission Board for this type of ministry. The GBC offices were located about two miles from the church building which was very convenient. We approached John and he agreed to serve with us after approval by the church. He told us the GBC had a policy of six months but the Executive Officer of the GBC, Dr. Robert White, could extend the time if needed. I believed Dr. White would approve a request. I had a couple of seminary classes with him and his father had been the Chairman of the Africa Committee of the FMB when we were approved for missionary service. Dr. White had also brought a volunteer team from his church in Paduka to Kenya during our Kentucky partnership. (I was always amused by a story from one of the lady volunteers from his church. She observed the offering time in the Kenya church and saw the offering consisted of several stalks of sugar cane, cabbages, potatoes, and eggs. One Sunday morning in her Paduka church, she placed an egg in the offering plate to the surprise of the congregation.) The two recommendations were approved at the called business meeting and we looked forward to God's blessings through John Bryan and God's choice for our new pastor.

John Bryan became our transitional pastor and, at the first deacon's meeting that he attended in April, he issued challenges to us. He emphasized strength in teamwork, that we should be available and accountable to each other, and we should build bridges. He told us to not be just praying men but men of prayer. When we had made the recommendation for the pastor search committee, we intentionally recommended two women and three men who represented different generations because we believed the opinions of all age groups would be valuable. At this deacon meeting, we assigned each member to a deacon team for specific prayer support. My team was assigned Dustin Purdue, a young dynamic deacon who was a key leader in Royal Ambassadors, the mission organization for young boys.

The deacons did a "church culture assessment" taken from *SHAPED BY God's Heart* by Milfred Minatrea. There were nine categories of several questions, and deacons answered on a scale with 1 being false and 7 being true. We tried to analyze the strengths and weaknesses of our church which impacted our future spiritual health for reaching the changing community. As I analyzed the responses, I noticed the average for all questions was 3.95, almost exactly in the middle between not true and true. It seemed there was a huge challenge in changing the church culture as we sought to reach our changing community.

A search committee looked for a youth minister for the church since the previous one had resigned. This committee approached deacon officers because they were giving strong consideration to Chris Bryan, one of John's sons. They were concerned some in the congregation might think calling him would be a conflict of interest since the church had called his father as transitional pastor. We responded that John's position was temporary, and Chris could be supervised by Keith Murdock, the senior permanent minister on the staff. We told them if they believed Chris was the person God was calling to the position, we would give staunch support. Chris responded to the call and was a valuable minister beginning in June of 2009 until God called him to become campus minister for the colleges in Augusta, Georgia.

My grandson Aaron and Jess planned to be married on August 1, 2009, in Thailand where she grew up and her parents still lived. Aaron asked his brother, Joel, to be his best man. Joel had been Skyping with Amanda whom he met online playing a video game. She invited Joel to visit her in Calgary, Canada, where she lived. Joel's choosing to visit Amanda instead of attending the wedding was a major disappointment to the whole family. On July 4th, Joel and Amanda were married in Calgary.

We travelled to Fort Worth in April 2010 to attend the Baptist Nursing

Fellowship annual meeting. This meeting was always a key opportunity for Nancy to see nurse friends, and often a missionary doctor we knew was also attending. After the meeting, we drove to the Keith Oliphint's house near Waco where Eucled and Jannelle Moore joined us. After a couple days of wonderful fellowship, we left with numerous iris bulbs to bring to Georgia and plant in our yards. The ones planted at the lake house continue producing beautiful purple and yellow flowers. As we left Waco, we stopped at Jack and Sally Conley's house at Hide-Away-Lake and had lunch before continuing our safari home.

The last weekend in September, we travelled to Parkersburg as invited guests at Grace Baptist Church to celebrate the fiftieth anniversary of the church. It was a wonderful weekend as we reminisced and told stories of the early days. A good group of members and former members attended, and it was exciting to see so many we knew again.

In the fall, a vision group was organized composed of three ministers and six lay people which included me. We met several times, focusing on the church's core values, purpose and vision. Our conclusions were these:

Core Values

1. Biblical Teaching – We are committed to the authority of the Bible.
2. Faith – We are committed to faith in Jesus Christ as the only way to salvation.
3. Prayer – We are committed to prayer.
4. Outreach – We are committed to sharing the Gospel of Jesus Christ with ALL people in the greater Duluth area and leading them to personal faith in Christ.
5. Missions – We are committed to be a missional church. Acts 1:8
6. Serving – We are committed to serving God and people inside and outside the church.
7. Stewardship – We are committed to sharing financial and spiritual God-given gifts of time, talents, and tithes.
8. Worship – We are committed to offering our personal and congregational worship before God.
9. Discipleship – We are committed to becoming devoted followers of Christ through life-changing small groups.

Purpose

Honor Jesus Christ by loving God and all people through selfless service and ministry.

Vision

To be a caring family of Christian believers who understand and meet the needs of our ever-changing community by providing effective ministries which reach out to each individual and prepare them to impact the world for Jesus Christ.

The ESL ministry began in September and finished in May each year. I was the director for three years beginning in 2008 and ending in 2011. After a learning year, in 2009-2010, there were seven classes at five fluency levels with fourteen teachers. The thirty-one other volunteers helped with child care, refreshments, devotions, and testing students who joined after the first week.

These tests assisted the class placement based on English fluency. During this academic year, we registered 124 students from twenty countries. There were students from South and Central America, Africa, Eastern Europe, the Middle East, and South and East Asia. During the last class session, we asked each student or volunteer to bring ethnic food we could share together. After eating, we recognized students who had completed the book for their class level. The following August, I sent a letter to each student inviting them to return for the 2010-2011 session.

We spent a week in October 2010 travelling to Shocco Springs, Alabama, for the reunion of missionaries who had served in East Africa. It was a wonderful time of fellowship, Bible study, and praise. Vance Kirkpatrick challenged us with the Bible study and our guest preacher, John West, encouraged us. His church, Lakeview Baptist in Auburn, Alabama, has an extensive mission ministry where many people groups are the focus of international ministry.

First Baptist in Covington had sent many volunteers to assist the Refugee Sewing Society. Nancy and I were invited to bring a display and sell products the refugee women had made. It was a mission focus weekend and we had an opportunity to share mission stories from Africa.

I became Chairman of Deacons in September 2009. Because the Constitution Revisions Committee had recommended a change in the church year to the calendar year, my term lasted sixteen months. The Pastor Search Committee had been working hard and Charles Summerour invited me to meet a prospect the committee was considering during an on-site visit. As I discussed him with Charles after the meeting, it was obvious that he had several issues which did not make him a good prospect. Later in the fall, I was also invited to meet Mark Hearn during his visit. The committee believed God led them to invite Mark to visit FBCD on January 10, 2010, to meet the congregation and preach in view of a call to become our new pastor. At the close of the service, the church held a called business meeting where I presided as Moderator per the church constitution in the absence of a pastor. Charles Summerour made a motion from the committee that FBCD call Mark Hearn to become our new pastor. Ballots were distributed and after a prayer asking for God's will to be done, Tandy Brannan, Deacon Vice-Chairman supervised the counting of the ballots. After I announced the vote was 99.25% to call Mark Hearn to be our pastor, he addressed the congregation. Charles Summerour announced his first Sunday would be March 7, 2010, following a mission trip to India. Because the regular church conference was scheduled for this date, Pastor Mark asked me to also moderate this meeting.

One of the processes I learned during the accreditation process at Mt. Meru University was a "SWOT" analysis. This process can guide strategy through the minefields by identifying strengths, weaknesses, opportunities, and threats for the success of a strategic plan. I asked the deacons to discuss this analysis in their team meetings at the January deacon meeting and we compiled a summary report during our meeting. The deacons identified a total of thirty-eight items for the four categories. By April, we had developed a twelve-page report defining and prioritizing the study observations with a series of action steps to address each priority issue.

We set ministry priorities for deacons which were compiled into five groups of ministries defined as partners in prayer, guest and prospects contacts, family ministry relationships, training opportunities, and service ministries. Since each deacon team had primary ministry responsibility one week a month, I found my week to be very rewarding. I was especially encouraged by my deacon prayer partner and praying with the staff minister for the month. We assigned each deacon a Sunday School class as a communication focus and to learn of church families with a special need. We asked each deacon to choose a mission project to support during the year and to encourage families to also choose a project to join its team.

The Mayor of Duluth, Nancy Harris, was a member of FBCD for many years. Pastor Mark was invited to attend the session where her address "State of the City" was presented. A few days later, signs began to appear around the church building with the message "57." Members were quite intrigued and began to ask questions. Since I had no idea what the meaning was, I asked Mark and he replied, "The meaning will be explained in an upcoming sermon." When the designated day arrived, the sermon shared that "57" was the number of different languages spoken in the homes of students at Duluth High School. My demographic analysis of the school population had shown a dramatic decrease in white student population with a steady growth in Latino and black students and a slower growth of Asian students. By 2010, there was almost an equal number of students representing each group. Many in the congregation were astounded at this information. They knew their community had seen some ethnic people move in but had no idea of the rapid change in the Duluth community. Mark issued the challenge: "If we are to be an Acts 1:8 church, we must learn how to reach everyone in our community. God has brought the world to our doorstep." Our church leaders knew the challenge was to lead the membership to build relationships with people different from them, to reach outside their comfort zone.

A WMU magazine published an article about RSS and we sent a marketing letter seeking an order for a Mission in a Box or invitation for a presentation.

> Dear WMU Leader:
>
> The Refugee Sewing Society (RSS) is very excited by the article featuring our ministry in the August 2010 issue of Missions Mosaic magazine. Our prayer is to use the article as a springboard for promoting "Missions in a Box" – the RSS's unique program for missions-minded churches. We pray you will find an opportunity in the near future to plan a meeting using this article, along with information in the attached booklet, as a focus for your mission emphasis and prayer time. In our booklet, tragic yet inspiring stories of refugee women from war-torn countries will tug at your heartstrings.
>
> The RSS has been honored by the support that National and Georgia WMU have provided us. Currently, Georgia WMU is work ing with the RSS to create beaded bracelets to encourage prayer support for Project HELP: Human Exploitation, which is WMU's2010-2012 national emphasis.
>
> The RSS gives volunteers an opportunity to encourage and love hurting refugee women, letting them experience the redeeming love found in a relationship with Jesus. As our women learn and enhance their skills in sewing, jewelry making, and knitting, the RSS provides them a small income by selling the products they make. Seventy percent of the sales price goes directly to the women. The remainder covers RSS expenses such as supplies, transportation of refugees, space rental and other costs.

We are developing a variety of ways to purchase our women's products, including an on-site store where visitors can see the refugees at work, meetings in nearby churches and an ETSY online site. The RSS is particularly excited about Missions in a Box, a vision of one of our volunteers. Please consider a Missions in a Box event for your church. For only $20 to cover shipping, we will send you a variety of products you can offer for sale. Plan a party or a meeting and enjoy fellowship as your group learns and buys.

Teen-aged volunteers who assisted the RSS on a recent mission trip were so excited about the "Refugee Bags" that almost every visitor bought one.

More information about the RSS can be found at the web site http://refugeesewingsociety.webs.com. If you are interested in a Missions in a Box event, please complete the attached application form. Thank you for your support, especially through prayer. And may God richly bless your missions commitment.

In Christ's love,
Cathy Palmer (NAMB/MSC missionary) and RSS volunteers

Sarah and John spent Thanksgiving weekend with us and we had a wonderful family time of celebration. Mark Hearn had invited them to speak at First Baptist Duluth on Sunday and we were very proud of their presentation.

The second weekend in December, we travelled to Jackson, Tennessee, to continue our tradition of attending graduations of our grandchildren. Aaron was very handsome as he received his Bachelor Degree from Union University.

In January 2011, Duluth had a snow storm which lasted a few days. It was beautiful, and we enjoyed looking out our windows to gaze on the peaceful scene. It was a scene we always missed during our years in Africa. We never saw snow there, but a few years after we retired, there was a snow storm which blanketed the entire golf course at the Limuru Country Club. God proved again He has a sense of humor.

In February, we were invited to be the speakers at the annual meeting of the WMU in Rabun County. Rocky Grove Baptist Church was a small church located on a very crooked road in the north Georgia mountains. The crowd was small but warm and friendly and listened intently as we shared briefly about Kenya but focused our message on the needed ministry assisting refugees in Clarkston, Georgia, through the Refugee Sewing Society.

The following weekend, we shared two days with the WMU at Flat Creek Baptist Church in Fayetteville, south of Atlanta. The hundred women who attended the Friday night banquet were dressed in their finery, and we sold many RSS items Saturday as we shared our ministry with the refugees.

There was an invitation from the campus ministry at Georgia Perimeter College east of Atlanta near Covington. The students were interested in the refugee ministry and asked many questions. Driving to Princeton, West Virginia, to share with the Baptist women in the southern part of the state was relaxing, and the fellowship with the southern Appalachian Baptist women was friendly. They asked penetrating questions about the refugee women as we shared their story.

All the volunteers were Christian, our specific requirement. Like any volunteer group, we had a high turnover for normal reasons: no child care, schedule conflict, or health issues. We also had some relationship issues, especially with those who did not agree with the ministry strategy and philosophy and some who tried to assume authority they did not have. All this drama was very stressful on Cathy because she was such a sweet person and misunderstandings and conflict put extra stress on her. I did my best to encourage and protect her as much as possible. Nancy was also an encourager. Nancy was a roving assignment worker, filling in where there was a need. One period, she was the beginning sewing class teacher for a few months. Nancy, like Cathy and others helping sewing students, were especially frustrated when the machines did not work properly. I thought her greatest contribution was in quality control. She checked the quality of sewing products and returned for repair if standards were not met. Since we produced sheets for the baby cribs Todd's company sold, it was critical to insure these sheets were of high quality. Nancy's testing practice was to put each sheet on the crib mattress to confirm a proper fit.

I was always intrigued by the dynamics in the student group. We targeted older women with little education, so that they could become successful contributors to family income. They were refugees from several nations. While I volunteered, we had women from Somalia, Sudan, Congo, Bhutan, and Iraq. They followed different world religions: Islam, Hinduism, Buddhism, and a couple of Christians. They never ceased to amaze me at how well they related to each other despite cultural and religious differences. At lunch time, they shared their different food. When one had a problem with a sewing machine, product, or finding the right thread or yarn, a classmate from another culture would help. Most of the time, I was the only male and, in the beginning, many were very shy about talking to me. As time passed, most began to greet me on arrival with a smile and finally shake my hand. Everyone wanted me to eat their food and I ate many things which were not American or African and acquired a taste for many different foods. In the Muslim culture, women are not permitted to look a man in the face if he is not a member of their immediate family. When Sarah went shopping in Pakistan, she carried Aaron with her when she left home if John was travelling. Therefore, one day I almost fainted when one of the friendliest Muslim ladies greeted me and hugged me. She wanted her picture with me that day

We drove to Albany in April to attend the Georgia Baptist WMU annual meeting and to represent the Refugee Sewing Society. Nancy was very happy to stay with Winston and Trisha at their house and to catch up on the news of her nursing school roommate. One morning, we left Trisha's house to drive to the church. I put the church address in my GPS unit and it led us on a wild goose chase as we wandered along country roads. After driving an extra fifteen miles, we finally found the church. We had been discussing the need to downsize and find a senior adult retirement community. Everything we found in Gwinnett County was more than $5,000 per month or a purchase for $250,000 plus -- neither affordable for us. As I was walking by displays after lunch, I saw a display by the Georgia Baptist Retirement Communities for a new location at Hiawassee in the Georgia mountains. I found Nancy and we looked at the design plan and talked to Peggy Beckett. Nancy knew Peggy from her time on staff at the hospital. We signed up for a cottage in Phase 2 which was forecast for 2012.

A few Saturdays later, Tom and Laura drove us to Hiawassee to view the location. When we arrived, we found part of the roads had been paved but there was no other construction. As we gazed at the horizon, we fell in love with the location because the cottages would be located on the side of a steep hill with a view overlooking Lake Chatuge, the highest of the Tennessee Valley Authority power lakes at 2,500 feet above sea level. We also saw a mountain range past the lake and realized the highest mountain in the range was Georgia's highest, Brasstown Bald. Nancy smiled as she looked at me with awe on her face and said, "I think I can live here."

Another startling fact was that in 2011, over half of the population within three miles of the FBCD church building were Asian, primarily Korean. This ethnic makeup was true of the eighteen houses on our cul de sac where nearly half were Asian. My neighbors on either side were Gujarati from India and the remainder were Korean. The Korean church on Highway GA-120 near the entrance to our sub-division was the largest Korean church in the metro area. It had eight fulltime ministers but only one spoke any English. No wonder the Korean youth wanted to go to another church.

Mark had a very rewarding mission trip to India just before he became our pastor. In 2011, he wanted to lead a group from FBCD to India. His 2010 trip was arranged by Lifeway and Mark was included because he was a Trustee. When he planned the 2011 trip, he used the same group who were not connected to the IMB. Since Sarah and John were living in Delhi, I arranged a meeting with them and the FBCD mission team. They introduced Mark to Daniel Kumar who began the Good News Center. This connection has led to a partnership between the church and the Good News Center. Daniel's brother Kadmiel and his family lived in Duluth and they joined FBCD. This partnership was a present-day example of Romans 8:28. Since Daniel had a few other people in the U.S. who supported his ministry, a USA Board for Good News Center was organized. Mark, Lindsay Lapole, and I were chosen as members of this Board. I have been very pleased as I have learned how God has been blessing this ministry.

From the time my deacon term was completed at the end of 2010 and my responsibilities with ESL finished in May 2011, I had no major responsibilities in the church. Nancy and I continued to sing with the choir and she continued her time in the Intercessory Prayer Room. I continued to meet with Pastor Mark and we had several opportunities to share a meal with Mark and Glenda. I was very thankful for this close friendship. I have kept in touch since we moved in 2012.

The rest of the year was filled with church activities and several RSS events in various locations in Georgia. We also attended the East Africa missionary reunion in Texas and the Georgia Tech BSU reunion in Hiawassee. Our FBCD choir sang at the Georgia Baptist Convention meeting in November.

On July 4, 2011, we were at my cousin Rebecca's house at the lake celebrating the holiday when the next generation male cousins shot fireworks as they did each year. That day, we met a young lady named Twila, a friend of Russ and Lynn.

Over the years, it was an exciting time to see the beauty of colorful star bursts and other displays shining over the lake. Of course, there was an occasional interesting event. One year early in this tradition, there were about five guys, mostly young men who were no longer thin, standing on a small dock. They placed the fireworks canisters at the lake edge of the small dock, lit them, and scurried to the shore side of the dock. The fireworks went off and promptly flew over the houses behind them instead of toward the lake. Their combined weight had tilted the dock nearly thirty degrees toward the shore. We all collapsed with laughter. Fortunately, no fires were started on the shore.

In 2011, the ministers at Northlake told us they needed to develop the area we used for their church ministry and asked us to relocate. Cathy and Tim were members of the Clarkston International Baptist Church. The church owned a small house near the church building which we could use but it would require major renovations. When we evaluated it, it was too small to meet our needs. We began to look for other possibilities and found a building owned by an engineering company which was not in use and for sale. One of the owners was a member of FBCD and while we were considering ways to raise funds for purchase, the pastor of the International church offered part of the vacant third floor of their education building for a reasonable fee. We immediately accepted this option and made plans to move there. We had lots of volunteer help, but it was a lot of work due to the expansion of the ministry with over fifty students and four classes. There were two very large rooms and five smaller ones for storage, a sales shop, office, and tea room. It was the best of times.

As 2012 began, Nancy and I began to define our plans to prepare to move to Hiawassee Park. We started a list of repairs and potential improvements to our Duluth house to enhance its saleability. The first item on our list was to repaint the deck on the backside of the house. It was a major chore balancing the needed repairs, improvements like kitchen countertops, and available funds.

Over the years, Nancy and I both had numerous skin cancers. In January, I had my first MOHS surgery. It took several hours as skin was sliced off, given a frozen pathology test, and another slice taken when cancer cells were still observed. This time, the third slice was the charm, free of cancer.

Andy called Nancy one day and asked her if she had gotten a diamond ring from Aunt Frances's estate. She said, "No, but I have my mother's ring. Do you need one?" He responded he had fallen in love with Twila and wanted to propose to her. We almost shouted with thanksgiving. Later, Andy put the ring on her finger and asked me to perform the ceremony. They wanted a garden wedding at the lake house.

In early 2012, I told Cathy I needed to stop our ministry at the end of February to give us time to get our house ready to sell and move later in the year. They planned a celebration to say goodbye on February 29th. The Bhutanese women did traditional dancing, and all enjoyed the refreshments. It was a bittersweet day as we said our last goodbye. I did have a few opportunities to visit later and several of the women I knew were still there. It was a blessing to meet many new ones.

Cathy shared her dream about developing a refuge doll similar in size to the American Dolls. Her vision was to write a story about a refugee girl, maybe several small books about refugee girls to go with refugee dolls from distinct parts of the world. This dream was fulfilled after Nancy and I left the ministry. In July 2015, RSS launched a product package including a refugee doll and a small book, Nomi's Hiding Place, telling the story of a twelve-year-old South Sudanese girl.

Shelly, our beautiful miniature Dachshund we had gotten in Nairobi had been healthy and the most loving dog we had ever had. She was most happy sitting beside me in my recliner when I read or watched TV. Tom and Laura were visiting us the evening of February 11th when Shelly wanted to go outside. She climbed down and started walking toward the front door when suddenly she stopped. I picked her up and immediately knew something was seriously wrong. We got into Tom's car and drove to the emergency animal hospital in Suwannee. The vet immediately took her, put her on oxygen, and began tests. In an hour, he returned to say she had congestive heart failure and, on oxygen, she might stabilize overnight. We returned home and called the hospital to check on her about 10:30 p.m. The vet reported she was about the same. About 2:00 a.m., he called to tell us Shelly was laboring and there was little hope for recovery. I told him to give her medicine to die peacefully. Nancy and I shed a few tears over this special pet and agreed we would not have any additional dogs since we would be moving to the retirement community soon. The next morning, we went to the animal hospital, collected Shelly's collar, paid the bill, and gave instructions to the vet to take care of her remains. We had had many dogs over the years, given some away, had two killed by other Baptist dogs in a fight while we were in the U.S., watched another die in Nancy's arms as we frantically drove to the vet's, but Shelly's loss was by far the most emotional.

The next weekend, Nancy went with Judy Hayes and her mother to Norman Park for a Georgia Baptist Nursing Fellowship meeting. It was a nice respite for her. Because she was the prayer coordinator for the Gwinnett Metro Baptist Association WMU, she regularly attended the meetings of their Executive Committee. She was diligent in passing on prayer requests to WMU leaders in every church.

On Wednesday evening March 21, 2012, Nancy and I attended an appointment service for new IMB missionaries at First Baptist, Taylors, South Carolina. We were staying with John and Sarah in Moore because part of the week we were missionaries in a conference at their church in

Spartanburg. We borrowed their GPS because we were not familiar with the roads in the area and we had not yet bought our own unit. When we turned it on, the voice spoke to us in Japanese which we did not understand and did not know how to change the language. Nancy called them, got instructions, and the voice changed to English. John said Marisa had been "playing" with the unit. Their church's conference was very enjoyable, and we were happy to continue having opportunities to share about missions.

The next weekend, we were invited to participate in South Carolina's annual WMU meeting. One item on the program was special because Wanda Lee, the National WMU Director, interviewed Steve and Bonnie Davenport, John and Sarah, and Nancy and me together. Her questions were about the two generation families' service internationally.

When I learned that Benjamin Brown, my fourth great-grandfather, fought in the Revolution, I began a new quest to learn about my heritage. I studied requirements for documenting relationships to support membership in the Sons of the American Revolution (SAR). Through the help of Gordon Woodard and Bruce Maney, I discovered many online web sites to use as references for data collection. My family tree began to expand rapidly. I had been using ancestry.com for a few years but began to search the Daughters of the American Revolution database of approved applications. Record copies of more recent approved applications provided good supporting documents. Fold3.com has significant data about military service for all U.S. wars. Many counties have genealogical data sites online.

Armed with knowledge of these new data sources, I began to work on an application for Benjamin Brown. After several weeks, I bogged down because I could not find data to support a couple of generations. I began to look at my family tree and identified several patriot ancestors: fifth great-grandfathers (Captain Edward Herndon, James Seaborn Dozier, Thomas Rawls Sr.), fourth great-grandfathers (John Greshham Sr., William Benjamin Brown, John Jones), and third-great-grandfathers (John Gresham Jr., Samuel Dean Sr., John Craig). I also searched for patriot ancestors for Nancy and found five, all fourth-great-grandfathers.

I searched message boards for my Dean family and talked to my cousin Rebecca who had done extensive research on our family. Rebecca had the Dean Family Bible. With copies of this Bible, a Record Copy from DAR, Beverly Dean Peoples's book about Samuel Dean's descendants, birth, death, and marriage records for Nancy and me plus my parents, I had enough documentation to make an application for membership in SAR for myself and my two sons, Tom Jr. and Andy.

I had been attending Button Gwinnet Chapter meetings for a few months and met many of their members. The chapter was named after Button Gwinnett, a signer of the Declaration of Independence. One was a cousin of Nancy and I learned he had been the first President of this chapter. When my application was ready in June 2011, I gave it to Harold Ford, chapter registrar, for processing. It was approved and on April 12, 2012, I was inducted into SAR along with Tom Jr. and Andy. It was a special time for me. I continued attending those meetings until we moved to Hiawassee later in the year.

Andy and Twila set the date of their wedding for Saturday, May 5th. I asked Andy if there was any significance to this date and he replied, "Dad, I wanted to get married before I was fifty years old." He would turn 50 on May 18th. I worked on the ceremony, trying to make it special. Nancy prepared the wedding cake, and Tom and Laura made a huge contribution preparing all the flowers and the beautiful setting looking toward the lake. It was a beautiful sunny day -- perfect weather. Andy's dog Bud decided he should be included in the wedding party; thus, he planted himself near Andy during the ceremony. We were thankful all our family except Joel and Amanda who were in Canada could be present. Finally, all our children were married.

Nancy and I had been making frequent trips to Hiawassee to watch the development of the Hiawassee Park complex. We learned Phase 2 would be delayed and if we wanted, we could consider changing to a cottage in the first Phase. Tom and Laura carried us to Hiawassee May 19th to evaluate cottage 16. When we arrived, we learned there were three choices and we got the keys to look at each of them. We chose one on the top row and when we went to the office to sign up, we learned someone had selected it earlier in the day. The leasing agent told us he would call them since they had to sell their house. He called us to say we could have Cottage #26. It was an answer to prayer because we thought this cottage had the best view of all.

When we learned Nancy's cousin Jerry Mason had been diagnosed with cancer, we made a few trips to visit Jerry and Sandra. I had the opportunity to talk with Jerry about his salvation and he confirmed it with me. Jerry was called to heaven on July 8th and I was asked to lead the Memorial Service on July 10th.

In August, we began to move things we could fit into our car and arranged for electricity and internet. The EMC provided this service and their internet servers were in their office complex at Young Harris about ten miles away.

Our good missionary friend, Betty Evans, had been in declining health for a while and God called her to her reward in August. Charles and Kathleen invited us to come and share memories of Betty in her Memorial Service on August 18th. We stayed at Charles and Dee Dee's house and had wonderful fellowship those few days.

We had Direct TV installed on September 6th, finishing all our utilities since we planned to only use cell phone service. We celebrated Nancy's birthday September 8th since we were driving to Ridgecrest on her birthday for the year of the Emeriti celebrations. A week later, we hired a moving truck to move the furniture we wanted to use at Hiawassee. Later, we would decide about the remaining furniture left to show our house for sale.

Chapter 20
A Retirement Community and A New Church

On Saturday September 8, 2012, we went out to eat with Tom Jr. and Laura to celebrate Nancy's seventy-seventh birthday. We celebrated early because on her birthday, we were driving to Hiawassee Park to collect Flo Love who rode with us to Ridgecrest for the Celebration of Emeriti missionaries who had served with the International Mission Board. Flo and Max Love served for many years in Japan and their son was ministering in Japan. We had met them during a furlough and Max was the third Georgia Tech Alumni that I knew who ministered under the IMB. Flo was a resident at Hiawassee Park and the activities director. After we returned to Duluth, we celebrated again with Andy, Twila, Tom Jr. and Laura who were helping us pack in preparation for the moving truck to arrive on September 21st. We went back to Duluth to do final cleaning on the house before it went on the real estate market on Laura's birthday, September 28th.

We began to get settled in our new home. The cottage was very roomy, 1,750 sq. ft. with a large attached two-car garage. It had a large master bedroom which included a very large walk-in closet and a bathroom with a very nice shower. The second bedroom was smaller but sufficient to include a double bed and our two L-shaped office desks. We put a pole for a blue bird house just outside the window which could be seen by both of us sitting at our desks. We had many good views of the birds as they came to the nest. The great room had a living area with a built-in entertainment center, a nice dining area, and a large kitchen. We put a moveable island between the stove and the granite countertop cabinets separating it from the dining area. Doors to a pantry and a laundry area opened along one wall. The front door opened into a sunroom in front of the kitchen area. A covered porch paralleled the sunroom where we often sat drinking our second cup of coffee in the mornings or high tea in the afternoons, our Kenya tradition. The view was spectacular. Our cottage was on the highest row, about 2,900 feet above sea level. Sitting on the porch, we could look down on Lake Chatuge. It was the highest Tennessee Valley Authority's power generating lake whose pool level was about 2,500 feet. Beyond the lake on the horizon was the Blue Ridge range of mountains featuring the highest mountain in Georgia, Brasstown Bald at 4,784 feet.

Hiawassee Park had a therapeutic swimming pool, different from anything I had ever seen, and I believe the first in Georgia. There were two main rules, never enter the pool without a buddy and you must have training lessons on its use before swimming. The pool was small with a treadmill in the bottom and jets on one end enabling you to swim in place. Nancy and I enjoyed the pool and walking on the treadmill several minutes, adjusting the speed as we desired.

There were many activities in the club house for the residents in the community. When we moved into our unit, the first phase had been completed including the club house and twenty-two cottages. During our first month, we attended two luncheons, one where we were asked to talk about our Kenya Ministry. Several residents enjoyed jig-saw puzzles and often when I went to get our mail, people were staring at the pieces. Most completed puzzles were framed and hung on the walls. While we lived there, they had a once a month pot-luck meal and good fellowship. A local chef began catering a meal once a month.

As October began, we found ourselves involved in several activities. On October 4th, we went to North Georgia Tech in Clarksville for the graduation ceremony for Twila. She had married early and never finished high school. We were so proud of her because she had completed her GED and received her certificate that evening. It was a time of celebration, but the evening was not over. Andy and Twila had borrowed the car of Twila's brother Kevin. When we went to the parking lot, Andy discovered he had locked the keys in the car. Since we had no tools, Nancy and I drove around campus looking for a security person to get help. We finally found one and he had tools in his vehicle where he could "break in" the car to get the keys. It was a late night getting back to Hiawassee.

When we began planning our move to Hiawassee, I asked my friend John Bryan who was my transitional pastor in Duluth if he could recommend a good church for us to attend after our move. He recommended two, McConnell Memorial in Hiawassee and First Baptist in Blairsville. I checked the web pages for both churches and found both as good possibilities. As Nancy and I talked and prayed, we concluded we did not want the half hour drive to Blairsville because of our experience in Atlanta. Sunday afternoon after we visited McConnell, Cliff and Shirley Hood knocked on our door to express thanks for visiting and to welcome us to the community. The worship service was meaningful and on October 7th, we joined the church. We found a good Sunday School class taught by Bill Earnest who was serving as a minister of education and administration. The class was a warm fellowship and we thoroughly enjoyed it our entire time in Hiawassee. It was a reasonably large group with many who were active in the church ministry. Most were couples and there were social events a few times a year.

The church facility was extensive and located in downtown Hiawassee on US Highway 76 near City Hall and the Towns County Library. There were three full time ministers on staff: Pastor Don Pickerill, Minister of Music Gary Reynolds, and Student and Family Pastor Josh Rouse.

Andy made a friendship with Chris Moffitt who was interested in cooking bar-b-que. They formed a partnership called Hill Rat Bar-b-Que. They entered many competitions and we went to one venue. It was interesting to see all the competitors, many coming from long distances in their RVs. Andy decided he wanted to become a judge for the Kansas City style competitions and after study and an exam, he was certified as a judge.

In November 2012, we spent two days with our sons and their wives, one day in Dahlonega checking out craft and antique stores and the other time Thanksgiving Day at Tom and Laura's house in Duluth. Nancy had her first cataract surgery at Gwinnett Medical Center a week later and the second one on my 78th birthday.

In December, we enjoyed several Christmas events. Our Jabez Sunday School class enjoyed an event at Wayne and Judy Naylor's house in the North Carolina mountains just across the state line. We had two special times at Hiawassee Park where we stuffed ourselves with all the goodies of Christmas. We also made our way to First Baptist Duluth for their Christmas music program. We decided against another trip to Duluth for the Symphony of Keyboards where as many as eight pianists played together on four grand pianos. This annual event was always impressive.

The real estate lady we hired in September with a three-month exclusive contract was a disaster. She did not seem to advertise or promote our house, so I did not believe even a single person viewed the house in 2012. In early 2013, we contracted with a well-known agency who began to get some interest. In March, we made a few trips to Duluth to oversee cleaning of the house. Several potential buyers saw the house and the inspection required a couple of minor repairs before we had an agreement and a closing date of May 20, 2013. It was a major relief to have this financial burden lifted.

As we planned our move to Hiawassee, I researched SAR chapters in the area. I found the Blue Ridge Mountains Chapter which met in Young Harris, a few miles from our cottage. I attended a meeting in November 2012 and found a very friendly group. This chapter was much smaller than the Button Gwinnett chapter where I was inducted. Very quickly, I discovered two members from Button Gwinnett were dual members in the Blue

Ridge chapter since they also owned houses in the mountains. I quickly became friends with David Cook, the chapter president who was also an engineer. In the March 2013 meeting, I was elected to serve as the chapter secretary, preparing minutes of the chapter meetings and the Board of Managers monthly meetings.

The Blue Ridge Mountain Chapter had members in four north Georgia counties and two in North Carolina. As I became involved in the Blue Ridge Mountain Chapter, I discovered it was a very active chapter for its size. While I was the secretary, we planned visits to nursing homes and recognized veterans who lived there. We looked for businesses who properly displayed the American flag and presented a certificate recognizing and thanking them. We put flags on the local graves of Patriots who fought in the Revolutionary War on July 4th and Flag Day, held ceremonies to burn damaged American Flags, joined county parades, and many other events. Each spring, we judged posters created by 4th grade students on a specified Revolutionary War subject. It was exciting when our student won the Georgia competition and received national recognition. A couple of years, I joined David Cook when he made a presentation to the 4th grade classes in Towns County. Even though we had about thirty members, we won state and national awards, especially the poster contest.

On the first weekend in February 2013, we celebrated when we saw our first snow fall in Hiawassee. The ground was covered for several days and we were thankful the yard maintenance crew cleared the roads, so that we could get down the side of our mountain. The snow was a beautiful sight as we looked toward the lake and the Blue Ridge mountain range. After so many years in Africa without snow in our yard, we just kept looking and admiring the beauty of God's creation. It was just as thrilling as the awesome sunsets we saw in the evenings.

The following Friday evening, a group from Hiawassee Park went to Young Harris College's Planetarium for a presentation about an asteroid which was inside the solar system. We also had a magnificent view of the stars and an explanation about various clusters.

Nancy continued her involvement in the Baptist Nursing Fellowship. In April, we attended the annual national meeting in Birmingham and saw many friends. Later in the month, she travelled with Judy Hayes to Callaway Gardens for the Georgia BNF meeting.

Very soon after we joined the church, Josh Rouse resigned to begin ministry at another location. A few weeks later, Gary Reynolds also resigned to move to Columbus to care for a father with poor health. When Don Pickerill resigned early in the new year, I immediately contacted the

Chairman of Deacons, Chip Shively, and recommended the church plan for a transitional pastor and consider John Bryan who had a very good ministry at First Baptist Duluth. Since John had recently moved to Cleveland, a town within an hour's drive, he could be more available. Pastor Don's last Sunday was April 7th. The church approved a recommendation for John to become our Transitional Pastor.

Recommendations were made to call interim ministers for the other two positions. The church voted to ask Ken Edwards, a church member who was passionate for student ministry, to fill that position. Keith Chandler, a staff member at the Georgia Baptist Mission Board worship and music department, became the interim minister of music. We had several extra choir rehearsals in March for the special music for Easter Sunday, March 31st. Nancy was very active in the church's WMU and presented the program in April about our ministry in Kenya.

Chip Shively, Chairman of Deacons, wrote a letter to the congregation on April 10, 2013, outlining expectations for members of a pastor search committee and included a form for each member to recommend five church members to serve on this strategic committee.

In May, we began two regular activities which we enjoyed. On the first Monday of each month, several couples from Nancy's high school class began meeting for lunch. We explored different eating places in Toccoa and later expanded to other towns within easy driving distance. It was a warm fellowship and I felt welcomed as a part of this exceptional group. Most months, there were about six couples who ate together. During the summer months, the Veterans of Foreign Wars chapter in Hiawassee prepared a fish fry for sale to the community twice a month. Nancy and I tried it for the first time in May and were hooked. The food was tasty and had large servings of fried fish, hush puppies, french fries, baked beans, cole slaw, and cocktail and tarter sauces. We always took it home because the rooms there were crowded and filled with smokers.

Nancy and I were invited to speak at the Hiawassee Baptist Association WMU's annual meeting at Lower Hightower Baptist Church on a Saturday in May. I was thankful it was only about three miles from our house because when we were setting up, I discovered I had forgotten a key part of our display information. I rushed home to get it and the meeting was a rewarding experience. God always blessed us as we shared the mission story of God's intervention in the lives of people. Over the years, we were blessed with many opportunities. We received many gifts from those who invited us, and we thanked God for those blessings, even the $5.00 we received once when we drove a hundred miles to speak. Therefore, we were surprised that two strong local churches did not give us anything while we lived in Hiawassee, the only time it happened. The most generous gifts always came from the smaller churches.

A resident's daughter had an Alpaca Farm in the area so several of us went to see and learn about Alpacas. The owners made several things out of the wool from the animals which was very soft and felt nice. They also made soap and other products. We had a very nice view of the animals up close and personal. I loved seeing their red barn and pasture. Our whole crowd of old folks really enjoyed this outing and there were many more over the years. I was especially intrigued by the visit to the Blue Ridge EMC facility. With my engineering and computer background, I was interested in the control room for the power grid and the extensive array of computer servers which operated the internet network that we connected to at our cottage.

June 14th,2013, was flag day and we held a special event at Hiawassee Park to celebrate the new flag poles and raise the three flags for the first time. The flag poles were a gift from Ken and Flo Gerrard who had served our country. Ken was a retired Naval Admiral. Peggy Becket, President of the Baptist Retirement Communities of Georgia, led the ceremony. Special guests included Barbara Mathis, Mayor of Hiawassee, and the North Georgia Honor Guard.

In July 2013, our SAR chapter had a joint picnic with DAR at a state park in Blairsville. Nancy made friends with some DAR ladies who invited her to attend their meetings and I started research for her application for membership. One lady invited her to attend the meetings of United Daughters of the Confederacy when she learned Nancy had been a member of the Children of the Confederacy because her Grandmother Brooks was a UDC member. We had a copy of Mama Brooks' approved application. The UDC chapter registrar checked the registry, found Nancy's childhood membership, and made an application. She was inducted almost immediately. I spent a lot of research hours on her DAR information but never connected all the generations to successfully develop an approved application. We attended one joint picnic of UDC with the local Sons of the Confederacy. While my great-grandfather was a Civil War veteran, I was not interested in pursuing membership. The guys were friendly with huge, very scruffy beards and were the epitome of mountain men. I knew I would not fit in. Until Nancy discovered her breast cancer, she attended meetings with me and local DAR meetings while I worked on a DAR application for her.

After my application for Samuel Dean was approved, I turned my attention to John Jones and Thomas Rawls. Using family trees and census data, I traced my lineage to Captain Roger Jones, an English seaman of the 1600s. One son, Justice Frederick Jones, was born in Virginia in 1670 and was chief justice for North Carolina between 1718 and 1721 and had extensive land holdings in North Carolina. A published family history book for Captain Roger Jones documented his sons and grandchildren including Thomas, father of my John Jones. I found a SAR Record Copy documenting John as father of Seaborn, but it was too old to be accepted as proper documentation. After a year of intense research to confirm the John-Seaborn link and failing, I asked Bruce Maney for ideas. Bruce is the Georgia SAR Genealogist and dual member of the two chapters where I have been a member. Bruce suggested I eliminate all other John Jones Patriots. I located sixty-four patriots with this name but only four served in South Carolina. I documented the other three could not be my patriot because of their service records and the DAR database had no Seaborn descendant for these three. My application was finally approved in October 2014, two years after my original submission.

Andy's company had closed its doors due to bankruptcy and he was without work for about two years. He had an episode with his heart and spent a week in Northeast Georgia Medical Center where he was diagnosed with congestive heart failure. He had several doctor's visits and a stress test.

Nancy had begun to face a series of health issues. She had a few episodes of atrial fibrillation and Dr. Berndt, our Hiawassee internist, had her wear a Holter monitor for two days. She was referred to the Heart Center in Gainesville where we met Dr. Medepalli, an Indian lady cardiologist. She was an outstanding doctor and we respected her skills. The one thing which frustrated Nancy was, because of her culture, when she explained test results or plans, she looked at me when talking instead of Nancy. Even with medication, Nancy had some problems with atrial fibrillation the rest of her life.

There were some questions from her blood work and she was referred to Dr. Sachdeva in Gainesville, a rheumatologist. He suspected she had beginning Lupus but after a series of follow-up visits and tests, he decided there was no Lupus.

For many years when Nancy had her mammogram, a second test was required due to a suspicious spot on the image. Dr. Clark and later Dr. Berndt concluded the spot was an aggregate of calcium, so no action was required.

We were blessed over the years to have very competent, Christian internists. Beginning with Dr. John Atwater who was the IMB choice, followed by Dr. Teresa Clark, and then Dr. Holly Berndt, all were caring physicians. When we moved to Hiawassee, I asked Pastor Don about local internists.

His doctor was Dr. Berndt, but he said she was not taking new patients. He told me to call her office and tell them he would recommend me as a Baptist missionary. When I called, her receptionist said she would ask the doctor and let me know. I was pleased when we were accepted.

Dr. Berndt was quite young, a good-looking blond who might have been 4'10" tall and had a three-year-old daughter. Her husband was a church planter working on the beginnings of an interdenominational church in Hiawassee. She regularly prayed with us and displayed excellent medical knowledge.

Over the years, Georgia Tech BSU members from the early 1950s to early 1970s got together occasionally at a hotel in Hiawassee for a couple of fellowship days. The large group in the Atlanta area met one evening every few months but Nancy and I never joined them regularly. Since a big segment of the guys married Georgia Baptist Hospital nurses, Nancy always enjoyed these times. In August 2013, we gathered at the Tech BSU Center on Techwood Drive to celebrate Sue Woolf's birthday. We all loved Sue and Warren, the director while we were students.

Every two years in September, all who graduated from Toccoa High School met for a reunion. On Friday nights, a dinner was held at the VFW complex and Saturday a catered bar-b-que gathering on Boyd Field near the old high school named for the legendary football coach. Toccoa High merged with Stephens County High in the early 1970s. Nancy enjoyed seeing classmates and others at these events.

In the fall of 2013, the church chose me to serve in two ministries, as a Deacon and a member of the Missions Committee. One of the annual mission projects was focused on the carnival workers at the Fairgrounds each July. Nancy and I volunteered for the first time in 2013. The church rallied behind this project and provided a medical clinic plus the mobile dental clinic of the Georgia Baptist Mission Board. The chairman of the missions committee was Mike Worthy, a local dentist. He and others offered free dental services to these workers. Church volunteers also prepared food, did the laundry of the carnival workers, gave clothing, and bought medicines for them. This multi-day ministry was very rewarding to us. I had the opportunity to encourage and witness to them and to listen to stories about the hard life they lived while Nancy did basic health checks for them. Most worked only a few months each year and living conditions on the road were challenging, sleeping in windowless trucks and bathing in the basic facilities of the fairground.

MMBC's deacon ministries included a Family Ministry. I was assigned twenty-one senior adults, mostly couples. Nancy and I tried to visit each one during the fall to get acquainted and encourage them. One of the single ladies was a pastor's widow who had some health issues. We had a wonderful time of fellowship but had a problem finding her house on top of a hill across the lake from Hiawassee Park. Since all but two had email, I sent regular email information and encouraging words to them.

The Georgia Baptist music department had two special choral groups, Sons of Jubal for the men and Jubalheirs for the women. When they did a combined program with the orchestra and bell choir, there were more than three hundred musicians. In 2013, we attended a program of the Jubalheirs at First Baptist, Cleveland, Georgia, and the Sons of Jubal at MMBC. Of all the music Sons of Jubal sing, my favorite music is Midnight Cry. The director, Jon Duncan, told me I would be welcome to join them, but I finally decided at my age and voice quality plus travel requirements, it was a wise decision to skip this opportunity.

We stayed active in all the normal activities of the church, committee meetings, regular times of worship, study, and prayer. We attended the local association meeting at a Hiawassee church and attended the Georgia Baptist Mission Board's annual meeting in Dacula. I was interviewed by Dr. White about living at Hiawassee Park during ministry reports. Our Jabez Sunday School Class had some fun times as well as participated in some service ministries of the church. We sang in the Christmas program and enjoyed this special event.

In 2012, I had been chosen to be the chairman of the planning committee for the 2013 reunion of East and Southern African missionaries at Shocco Springs Baptist Conference in Alabama. When we were at Emeritus Week at Ridgecrest in 2012, we decided to join forces of the two regions since many years we had been one region and knew many missionaries from the other region. Our planning committee membership represented both regions. Our committee was quite pleased when about 125 attended.

We planned a theme of Fan the Flame for Missions and were blessed by our program people including Gordon Fort, VP of the IMB after service in Southern Africa; D. Ray Davis who led our music; Alan Duncan, Kenya MK who served in South Africa, and others. I went early and stayed late to make sure details were ready and finished. I was very thankful it went well.

We held another event after flood lights were installed to illuminate the flags at night in keeping with the protocol for flying the American flag. Hiawassee Park recognized its residents who had served our country in military branches by presenting a SAR certificate of appreciation to the veterans. It was my privilege to present certificates to six who served in the

Army, two from the Air Force, three from the Navy, one from the Marine Corp, one from the Merchant Marine, and one from the Coast Guard. I also presented a Flag Certificate to Peggy Beckett from SAR recognizing the proper display of the American Flag.

We had a few opportunities to speak at churches promoting missions and the Lottie Moon Christmas Offering. We had discovered the longer we were away from the field, the fewer invitations we received. Tom Jr. and Laura invited Andy and Twila plus Nancy and me to spend Christmas with them. We went Christmas Eve and returned home Boxing Day. It was a great family time as we celebrated the birth of our Savior and ate lots of tasty food.

Nancy and I stayed busy in December with Christmas dinners and parties: SAR, DAR, Sunday School class, church choir, and the Hiawassee Park Community. After New Years, we desperately needed to go on a diet. Nancy began to have repetitive issues with atrial fibrillation in early January 2014 and we began a long series of visits with Dr. Medepalli at the Heart Center in Gainesville. In mid-January, she had an echo cardiogram and a Pet Scan. In February, she made two visits to the emergency room at Chatuge Hospital, once by ambulance, followed by an ultrasound in March. Dr. Medepalli continued to follow her regularly until mid-year. We both had basal skin cancers removed in January.

The eight-member pastor search committee was formed with Phil Heard as chairman. They reviewed about 200 resumes, visited several churches in 2013 and by February 2014 began to zoom in on one potential candidate. Steve Taylor was recommended to be the next pastor and came to preach on June 1st when he was called by the church.

Steve was an experienced pastor having served Antioch Baptist in Waynesville, North Carolina, for twenty years as Senior Pastor. He had also served as a minister of youth, recreation, and education prior to that pastorate. He was a proven leader having been captain of his high school and college football teams. After graduating from Western Carolina University, he was offered a contract with an NFL team but chose to pursue ministry and got his Masters at Gardner Webb University.

We were very excited to hear Ruth Abigail Davenport was born March 14th, weighed six pounds two ounces and was twenty-two inches long. It was exciting to have a great-granddaughter. Nancy's cousin, Jerry Mason, had cancer and we made several visits with Sandra and him. When he died in early July, the family asked me to lead the memorial and graveside services. As we were leaving the cemetery, we discovered our favorite Bar-b-Que place was just across the road (Zeb Deans). We strolled there to have a satisfying meal.

When Nancy had her mammogram in April, once again a second one was required. When Dr. Berndt reviewed the results, she was suspicious that a lump was cancer and referred Nancy to Dr. Steven Efird in Blairsville, a surgeon who specialized in breast surgery. She had a consultation with him on May 29th and we were both impressed because his office was filled with Christian literature and he prayed with us. He scheduled a needle biopsy for the following week. We received the biopsy report on June 10th and it confirmed she had breast cancer, a tough type called HER-2. Dr. Efird performed a lumpectomy on August 6th as outpatient surgery. After this surgery, when the nurse and I were wheeling her through the hospital lobby, I noticed bright red blood all over her blouse. She went back to surgery to repair the leaking veins. During our visits to Dr. Efird's office, I discovered his partner, Dr. Willis Moody, and they both had bachelor's degrees from Georgia Tech. This fact made me like them even more.

In June 2014, Hiawassee Park held a dedication of the Memorial Gardens located at the top of the hill and the end of our street where it joined the main road. It was a beautiful place where residents enjoyed activities and a place to relax or play shuffle board or horse shoes. There was a nice gazebo, swings, a grill, and picnic tables. We had many events there, especially the cookouts on special days like July 4th. The youth at McConnell Memorial Baptist came several Saturdays to wash cars for the residents. We made donations to help their camp expenses in the summer.

A widow on my deacon's list, Nell Taylor Eskew, died in August 2014 and the family asked me to lead the memorial service at the retirement community on the hill above the church which offered personal care services. It was a sweet time of celebrating her life.

MMBC was involved in many mission projects in addition to the promotion of the three SBC mission offerings. In 2014, we had about fifteen local projects. Two of the biggest were the ministry to the carnival workers at the Mountain Fair and a ministry to hikers on the Appalachian Trail where hikers were fed a meal and encouraged by church members. Church members travelled to five countries for international mission projects. We gave staunch support to the Appalachian Backpack Project of the SBC and Operation Christmas Child sponsored by Samaritan's Purse. We also gave some financial support to two single missionaries and two couples who went to the field from our church. In August, Mike Worthy's term ended, and I was chosen to be the new committee chairman.

In 2011, we had worked with a financial plan to develop revocable living trusts and other planning documents. We learned in 2014 the Southern

Baptist Foundation was offering estate planning for IMB personnel where the foundation would cover the expenses. With some changing circumstances, I contacted Jon Kea with the foundation to inquire about modifying our documents. We discovered he had served as a missionary with the IMB and was very helpful. We were referred to John C Leggett, an attorney in Calhoun who did work for the Georgia Baptist Foundation. We contacted John Leggett, visited his office a few times, and had an amended trust agreement before the end of 2014.

We were referred to an oncologist in Blairsville, Dr. John Manfredi. When we visited the treatment center, we were very disappointed. The reception staff were not pleasant, the treatment area was a large room with about fifteen reclining chairs for patients in a very tight circle. Dr. Manfredi was rushed and did not explain his recommendations very well. We left saying we needed a second opinion. We talked with a few medical professional people at church. One friend recommended the Longstreet Clinic in Gainesville near the Heart Clinic Nancy visited. I went to the Internet and searched details about the clinic and the staff oncologists. I selected Dr. Charles Nash and we visited him on September 22nd. Dr. Nash was a committed Christian and his explanations set us at ease. The treatment area contained individual patient areas with a half wall separating them around the huge area. Two nurse areas were in the middle of the room and snacks were readily available. While both oncologists recommended the same chemo protocol, patient care and support were vastly different.

Tom Jr. and Laura plus Andy and Twila visited us several times during the year. It was always an enjoyable time having our family together. Laura and Nancy enjoyed unique events and festivals which were abundant in North Georgia. Sometimes we would just enjoy walking around interesting towns like Helen and Dahlonega. Often Nancy would comment on something Laura selected by saying, "Oh, I really like that." Laura would usually give it to Nancy and it became a joke between us.

Tom Jr. had been assigned by DESI to work in Plantation Pipeline's drafting department a few years previously. As I mentioned, he was a highly skilled AutoCad draftsman and it was not long before Plantation employed him fulltime. He enjoyed the work and was chosen to be the supervisor of the drafting department before long. Plantation was owned by several petroleum companies and was acquired by Kinder Morgan, a large pipeline and storage facility organization. In his supervisory position, Tom Jr. had frequent contact with the head office in Houston. When Kinder Morgan began migrating to a GIS system, they chose Tom Jr. to be the manager of the GIS operation for the Southeast Division. With each of these progressions, I was very proud of him because he was beginning to reach the full potential I had observed over the years.

Sarah, John, and Marisa spent a couple of days with us before they flew to Calgary, Canada to visit with Joel and Amanda on July 3rd. They were looking forward to seeing Wyatt for the first time who was born September 18, 2013. It was an exciting visit for them. They came to Hiawassee to celebrate my 80th December 4th birthday on John's birthday, December 6th. We did get the bonfire put out before it melted all the icing on the cake.

When the pathology results were received from Nancy's lumpectomy, there was one margin which was not clear. Dr. Efird recommended an additional surgery on October 1st to remove more tissue and ensure that all margins were clear. Later in the month, we attended a Chemo 101 Class to learn more details about the treatment. Nancy had her first chemo treatment on October 28th.

The center had a specialist to help patients choose a wig since almost every patient lost their hair. Nancy chose one which was free because of a donation to help patients. Other volunteers made knitted caps which were given to the patients. Each of the six treatments took several hours. She received three different chemo drugs in sequence and it took one or more hours for each IV to drain into the port in her chest. Because these chemo drugs attacked her white blood cells, we went back to the clinic the next day after the chemo infusions for a shot of Neulasta to accelerate the regrowth of the white blood cells. The chemo infusions were scheduled three weeks apart. For a week to ten days after each treatment, Nancy's energy level was very low. With her compromised immune system, she hibernated at home to insure she was not exposed to any infection. When we went for her fourth treatment December 30th, they postponed her treatment because her white cell count was still too low.

Andy had a few issues with his heart during the year. He had an echocardiogram in April and was monitored by a cardiologist in Gainesville. He was unemployed until September when he was hired by Toyota Corporation at their preparation center in Commerce. He drove cars from the lot where they were offloaded from the train to the various shops for preparation to deliver them to the dealers via truck. The cardiologists had put Andy on a restricted liquid and salt diet and he was careful to obey the guidelines. During his two years without work, he had become somewhat depressed and had gained a lot of weight. With the diet for congestive heart failure, the restrictive diet, and his new job, he began to quickly lose weight. By Christmas, he had lost forty-five pounds. He was feeling better and had a positive attitude. We had high hopes for his future. Twila's work since they married was difficult for her because of serious back issues. They were hoping she could stop working soon.

On New Year's Eve, staff at Toyota were released at noon and Andy came home. He and Twila talked about what they would do to celebrate and see the fireworks displays. He told Twila he would go take a shower and get ready for the events of the evening.

Meanwhile, Nancy and I were relaxing in front of the television and deciding we would follow our pattern for the last few years: watch a little TV and go to sleep early. My cell phone rang, and it was Twila in a panic. She said Andy had fallen in the shower and he was not breathing. She had called 911 and they arrived as we talked. Nancy and I quickly got into our car and drove to the hospital in Toccoa. I chose to drive through Clayton instead of Helen because we could take the road from Hollywood which led straight to the hospital. When we arrived, Russell was waiting for us outside the emergency room and said, "He did not make it." Nancy and I did not talk during our trip, but I knew in my heart Andy had probably had a heart attack and we would learn on arrival that he had died. We went inside the ER and visited with Twila and others. We hugged and cried together. The ER doctor came to talk with us and said it was a heart attack and he thought Andy had died before he hit the floor. We had them notify Whitlock Mortuary and while we waited, Twila wanted to go see Andy. I went with her because I knew she needed support. She hugged Andy's body and cried a lot. I stood nearby and touched his head in love. The coldness gave me a shock I will never get over since I had never touched a dead person before. As I drove home that evening, I thanked God Nancy had not had her chemo treatment the day before because I knew with the infusion, she would not have had the physical strength to endure the activities ahead.

Tom Jr., Laura, Sarah and John came the next day and we met with Twila and part of her family at the funeral home to plan the service for Saturday, January 3rd. John helped all of us word the obituary and Benny Slate from Whitlock blessed us with guidance as we planned everything. Since Andy and Twila had been attending Mullins Ford Baptist, we asked their pastor, Joey Stewart to lead the service and our pastor, Steve Taylor, to assist. John led the music.

We went to Alexander's Florist and Laura guided us in the selection of flowers for the blanket on the casket and other arrangements. Tom Jr., John, and Aaron were pallbearers along with Bruce Carbonaro and Bob Doppelheuer, Andy's close friends from Greenville, and Chris Moffitt, his Bar-b-Que partner. Honorary pallbearers were Russ Kesler, Joel, and Brian

Panowich, Twila's son-in-law. After the funeral, we went to Martin Baptist Church Cemetery where Andy's body was buried in the family plot where my parents are buried.

The memorial service was a real blessing to all my family. There was an opportunity for people to share memories after the pastors shared scripture and thoughts. Sarah and Tom Jr. were the first to speak. Sarah talked about Andy's hatred of hypocrisy and being a champion for victims. She communicated how angry Andy was when their church in Greenville decided to demolish an education building for a parking lot rather than use it to reach the transitioning community around the church. She told how Andy was very upset when she and John walked in the woods during hunting season and left their "human scent." She also shared the thrill of observing Andy watching Twila walk down the aisle at their wedding and the huge smile on his face. Tom Jr. said he and Andy had taken trips together and it was the best of times when it was just the two of them. He told how they planned a trip to visit us in Tanzania the week of September 11, 2001. He said lots of people asked if they were still going and they replied,"If the plane goes, we will be on it."

Marisa and Aaron read notes sent by Joel, MKs and friends. Michael Henderson followed them, and I was very touched by his comments. Michael was an impressive African-American who retired as a Lieutenant Commander in the U.S. Navy and was past president of the Button Gwinnett Chapter of SAR. He talked about how moved he was to know a family who had ministered in Africa. He said it was an honor to be able to induct the three of us into the SAR. He was followed by Joel Bedenbaugh who was very emotional and spoke quietly. Joel was in Andy's RVA class. My cousin Rebecca came next and told how Andy was very smart when they played games. She said Andy always knew every answer to the questions.

I was not sure I could speak without becoming very emotional. But God met my needs and I spoke clearly. I began by saying how thankful we were for all the messages we received including two international phone calls. The first was from Tim Tidenburg, a MK and current mission leader in East Africa with the IMB. He told me he was with a group of MKs having a retreat in a rural area. He said he used Andy as an example of how important the mission family became to him. Daniel Kumar, a pastor friend in Delhi, called from India to express his love and prayers.

I told stories from Andy's life: his birth trauma, how he stretched the envelope, his trip to the grocery store, and the rescue of Jimmy Turner, a two-year-old MK who was lost in the tea fields. I related the favorite hymn of a girl MK just younger than he was, "In the Garden," because "Andy walks with me, Andy talks with me." Andy had three passions: Fantasy Football, Bar-b-Que, and SAR.

The morning of the memorial service God gave me a vision before I woke up at 4:00 am. In the vision, I saw Andy sitting beside my Dad whom he never met on earth. Andy was asking my Dad about his life as a teacher. The conversation turned to church and Andy said, "I hope they will ask this question in in the service, "If you die tonight, do you know where you will spend eternity? Will you see me in heaven?"

Pastor Joey closed the service quoting 2 Timothy 4:7. "I have fought the good fight, I have finished the course, I have kept the faith."

As 2015 began, Nancy and I began to discuss ways to help Twila with her grief and living conditions. We recognized health issues with her back and her financial status would make it impossible to care for the lake house and we could not give her the needed assistance while living in Hiawassee. As we dialogued with her, she agreed with our assessment. She and Andy had been very close to Russ, Rebecca's son, and to Lynn. Twila was told Lynn's son, Luke, owned a single-wide mobile home which was located on Dean Road on a tract Rebecca had given him. Luke was willing to sell the mobile home and charge land rent for its location. Twila and I investigated, saw needed repairs, estimated the cost, and concluded it would be a suitable location for her and the repairs were doable. Nancy and I told her when she was resettled, we would move to the lake house to ease our financial stress of two houses.

Over the next few months, the mission committee tried to define which projects we would support and name a coordinator for each. We also worked on the 2015 budget plan and offering goals. We also began the planning for a major mission conference to be held in May 2015. For several years, church members had been involved in a ministry in Peru. In January 2015 pastor Steve made a trip with a few regular volunteers to evaluate our ministry there.

In the February 2015 committee meeting, details and guests for the mission conference were described. Missionary guests included representatives from the IMB, NAMB, GBC, missionaries sponsored by our church, and other ministries like the Refuge Sewing Society and Habitat for Humanity. In the April meeting, I announced my resignation as Chairman because of a planned move to Toccoa in June. I also resigned as a deacon. The May celebration attendance on Saturday was disappointing. Adjustments in Saturday's activities were made, and the Sunday celebration was inspiring.

For many days after the service remembering Andy, I focused on being the caretaker for Nancy. I fixed breakfast every morning and helped her get settled in the sunroom, sitting in her chair she called "my nest." She rested, had a second cup of coffee, a glass of juice, and her usual abundance of water. As she rested there, her attention was on her Bible reading and prayer list. Later in the morning, she usually took her shower and got dressed. I helped her as needed, especially for protecting her port from the shower water. She had the chemo infusion which was delayed on January 6th. After every treatment, she had minimal energy for a week to ten days and did not leave our cottage except for doctor appointments. She had her final three infusions on January 27th, March 1st, and March 22nd. She did attend church on Easter Sunday, April 5th but I noticed she did not recover as rapidly after this final treatment.

When we discussed radiation treatment with Dr. Nash, he recommended we go to Blairsville instead of Gainesville. He told us it was very professional and a closer commute. We made a couple of visits in March where they took x-rays and other tests to determine the focus of the radiation. Nancy had indelible ink markings in a couple of places on her body to insure the machine was properly focused. She had five treatments in early April.

On Sunday afternoon April 12th, she had a temperature of over 103 degrees. I asked her if she wanted to go to the ER in Blairsville, but she said we should go to the Chatuge ER in Hiawassee. The doctor did tests and said he could admit her to the hospital, but she could go home with medicine. She wanted to go home.

Tuesday evening, we were watching TV when Nancy became very confused in her conversation and I panicked because I thought she might be having a stroke. I called 911 and the EMT team was there almost immediately since their station was at the bottom of our hill. They checked her vitals, determined her oxygen was very low and soon after starting oxygen, her speech became coherent again. They told me they would transport her to Blairsville ER since the hospital was much larger.

I jumped in my car and tried to keep up with the ambulance. We passed through Hiawassee and were going about 65-mph in a 45-mph zone when I looked in my rear-view mirror and saw flashing blue lights. When the sheriff deputy came to my window, I told him I was following the ambulance because my wife was in it. He very graciously said, "Turn your emergency blinkers on and drive carefully." When I was climbing the mountain past Young Harris, a major rain storm started, and I could hardly see the road. I drove very conservatively the rest of the trip.

About 3:00 a.m., they showed me x-rays of Nancy's lungs and both were completely white with infection. The doctor told me that the pulmonologists in Gainesville were outstanding and they would transport her there by ambulance when they could get the transfer organized. When the ambulance left about 5:30 a.m., I drove home, took a quick bath, packed some clothes and left for Gainesville. I drove across the mountain to Helen, stayed awake for all the sharp curves, and started driving south of Cleveland before I got very drowsy. I opened my window, turned the radio on, and successfully arrived at the hospital without an accident.

I had called Sarah and Tom Jr. before I left Hiawassee to give them the news. Tom and Laura arrived soon after I did, and Sarah arrived from North Carolina just after noon. The ICU room was huge, bigger than our master bedroom at Hiawassee Park. There was a sign outside the room saying only two visitors at a time. The whole time we were there, no one reminded us of this rule and we had eight people in the room several times.

They had Nancy on 100% oxygen through a cannula and connected to many monitoring devices. She received medications through her port. All the nurses in ICU were very skilled but what touched me was their caring love. I sensed God had given each one a special gift which helped families and patients to be peaceful during their crisis. One day, I learned one of Nancy's nurses was our niece, Amy Kirk Caplan's best childhood friend, Robin.

During the week Nancy was in ICU, I left the room once to go get food and visited the bathroom on the hall where I sponge bathed in the mornings. My family was kind and loving to bring meals to me, so that I could stay with Nancy. Her condition remained about the same until April 21st, Tuesday afternoon. The doctor who visited her said he wanted to try steroids as "a last-ditch effort" for her improvement. She seemed to improve a little and the nurses began to wean her off the oxygen. When I went to sleep that night, her oxygen level was 50% and I was encouraged.

I woke up at four am to see nurses in the room and observed Nancy was having a significant episode of atrial fibrillation. Her oxygen had been returned to 100% and I realized she was not doing well. I called Tom Jr. and Sarah and told them to come. About six a.m., I called our pastor, Steve Taylor, to give him an update. By eight a.m., we were all gathered in the ICU room. Sarah had called John and told him to come.

About 8:30 a.m., Nancy was suddenly alert and coherent. God blessed us with more than three hours where we could talk with her, express our love for her, thank her for being a blessing to us, and say our good-byes.

She knew God was coming to get her that day because the first thing she said to me was "I love you, Tom. I am going to see my Jesus and Andy today." We asked her what she wanted in her memorial service: music, scripture, etc. I asked her which dress she wanted to wear, and she said, "The dress I wore to Andy's wedding." She also said, "Do not let them do anything until John gets here, Sarah needs him." A couple of missionaries had joined us, and pastor Steve prayed for all of us as she drifted to sleep. They gave her morphine to ease any pain and we began to wait. After John arrived, they reduced her oxygen to 50% and she peacefully slipped away until she received her angel's wings at 9:15 p.m. Many will not understand when I say God blessed me tremendously that day. I got to say good-bye until we meet again in heaven. That was a blessing I never had with my son, Andy, or either one of my parents.

When we met with Benny Slate the next day, John helped again with the wording of the obituary. I believe he really captured her personality and the essence of her love for others.

The following is a portion.

> After graduating from Toccoa High School and Georgia Baptist School of Nursing, she and Tom married and lived some years in Louisiana and Ohio until called by the Lord to East Africa. All together they served 30 years with the International Mission Board, SBC in Kenya and Tanzania. She showed her passionate for Africans in women's ministry and health care.
>
> Nancy was an active member of Second Ponce de Leon Baptist Church in Atlanta, Georgia., First Baptist Church in Duluth, Georgia, and more recently McConnell Memorial Baptist Church in Hiawassee, Georgia. Prayer and service marked her life, and she was the prayer coordinator for the Greater Gwinnett Baptist Association and Hiawassee Baptist Association. She enjoyed being a part of Baptist Nursing Fellowship of Ga., and worked as a nurse for Camp Pinnacle, Georgia Baptist Hospital, and as a congregational nurse for Peachtree Baptist Church in Atlanta. She also loved her Friends, and actively participated in missionary reunions, gatherings with classmates, and church events.
>
> Her mission family knew her as "Aunt Nancy" and her African friends called her "Mama Tom." She was cherished for her love, her hospitality, and her laughter, and Nancy was well known for her cake decorating, bird watching, and nurture of flowers. Nancy's kindness, generosity, and sacrifice were an inspiration, and she will be missed by so many!

When we began the discussion about pallbearers I was surprised and immensely pleased when Tom Jr. wanted to honor his mother by being a pallbearer. We added our two grandsons, Joel and Aaron Davenport; our nephew, Greg Kirk; P.J. Caplan, husband of our niece Amy, and Brown Dean, my cousin. We named Alan and Ken Duncan who were MK neighbors in Kenya and close friends of our sons as honorary pallbearers.

As we met with Benny to set the date and time of the memorial service, it was suggested we hold it on Saturday, April 25th. I immediately asked, "Sarah, that is your birthday. Should we find another day?"

She responded, "It is ok. It would have bothered me if she had died on my birthday." We asked Steve Taylor and John to lead the service, and Travis Boyd and Karen Johnson from First Baptist Duluth to lead the music, sing, and play the piano.

My pastor began the service by welcoming everyone and read scripture from 2 Corinthians 4:7-18. After explaining the text focusing on "we do not lose heart," he began to relate his conversation with Nancy in the ICU room. He asked her for suggestions and she said, "Make it short."

He replied, "Nancy, you are asking a preacher to make a promise he cannot keep!" After Steve's comments, the congregation of over 200 sang "Because He Lives."

John began by sharing the comments the family shared when one said, "Today is a blessed day because it is raining." This was a common African belief. He continued describing the strong family relationships inside the mission family. John said missionaries work on these relationships. For missionaries like me who have no siblings, missionaries became my siblings. He talked about Nancy's ability to welcome anyone into our home, her clinic ministry in Mathare Valley, Nairobi's largest slum. John said Nancy's final Wednesday was a gift of God, an example of His grace.

Travis Boyd sang "The Love of God" in his rich baritone voice as many gasps were heard in appreciation of the message. Steve described looking at Nancy's Bible to see what scripture she had highlighted and underlined. In the front of her Bible, she had recently written two references, Romans 15:13 and 2 Thessalonians 3:16. Steve made some statements which had an impact. "Christians can shed tears and still have joy. Death is a transition, not our final destination. If God is for us, who can be against us. Faith is confidence in which we hoped for and do not see." A reading of Hebrews 11:6 followed and Travis sang "It is Well with My Soul."

My Dean relatives had prepared a meal at Martin Baptist Church for anyone who wanted to fellowship after the brief service at the grave site in

Martin Baptist Cemetery. I was disappointed at the small crowd.

The next afternoon, the women in my family blessed me in a distinct way. Sarah, Laura, Marisa, Amanda, and Jess gathered in our bedroom. While I watched, they took all Nancy's clothes out of the closet and dresser drawers. Since Laura was the only one Nancy's clothes would fit, she made some selections and they boxed the rest to give away. They also followed this procedure in choosing her jewelry for each, selecting some for Twila since she was not in Hiawassee. This help was such a blessing because it took this stress off my shoulders.

Marisa returned to Wake Forest and school with her brothers while John and Sarah stayed a few days to help with the task of packing to move to Hartwell Lake. I began packing and moved in mid-June. It was hard to leave our beautiful view of the mountains but moving was a necessary choice. I still visit friends in Hiawassee occasionally. Friends began helping with the packing and one day, my sister-in-law and her husband came to help. I bought a 2010 Ford F-150 pickup and made a few trips to the lake moving boxes. On June 22nd, "Men on the Move" came to move the furniture. Leaving Hiawassee Park was bittersweet.

Chapter 21
Transition to Lake Hartwell

As I moved to the lake house, it was necessary to shuffle some furniture. Tom Jr. wanted the bedroom suite my Dad had found in an old barn in the 1950s. Dad restored and refinished it and it was a beautiful antique. We removed it from the downstairs bedroom to make that room available for the bedroom suite we had in Hiawassee. Sarah wanted my Mother's dining room furniture which made a place for the one we had in Hiawassee which had belonged to Nancy's mother. We put the African river grass furniture from our sun room and the Zanzibar cabinet in the great room with the dining room furniture. Later, Tom Jr. wanted to return the Kenya dining room furniture to me, and Sarah wanted her grandmother Kirk's dining room table and chairs.

The Sunday after I moved to the lake house, Sarah and John were still with me and we decided to visit First Baptist Church in Toccoa. We had been members during our first two stateside assignment periods. Henry Fields had retired after many years as pastor. The service was very traditional with hymns. After all my years in Africa, it did not meet my worship needs. Sarah and John came to the same conclusion. I had made the decision to visit several churches before deciding on a church home. I felt I should also visit Martin Baptist because my cousins Rebecca and Vickie were members there. It was more appealing, but I still did not feel I had a true worship experience. Nancy and I had spoken at Popular Springs Baptist on Gum Log Road toward Lavonia. It had been an enjoyable experience with their interim pastor who was a retired IMB missionary. They had a new young pastor and we were warmly welcomed. The message was good, but I was distracted by the music. We sang a few hymns which was fine, but the woman music leader stood in the pulpit but never gave any direction about singing. The pianist never missed a beat between verses, all of which did not make it worshipful. I did visit again when Sarah and John came to visit. I knew I wanted to visit Ebenezer, but I visited with the Director of Missions for the Tugalo Baptist Association to ask about good churches. He mentioned two additional churches which he considered to be strong churches. The next Sunday I visited Ebenezer and I was hooked.

During the following week, Jerry Stowe, Senior Adult Minister, called me to thank me for my visit. I asked about the Bible study groups called small groups. He told me each small group decided their study plan. Some used literature while others chose a Bible study plan. He mentioned the class taught by Larry Carter who chose specific books in the Bible to study. I decided to visit this group first and when I did, I received a warm welcome. Larry obviously did a lot of study preparation because he brought in related passages, history and culture of the period. I did not visit any other group. When I joined, the focus book was Revelation. The group had twenty-seven members with ages from thirty-seven to eighty-two (me).

Andy Childs had been pastor for about thirteen years. His preaching is very creative and solidly Biblical. When I first joined, I told a friend I had to pay close attention because of the speed of his speech. After two years in the church, I have learned he is also a gifted pastor, a knowledgeable administrator, a visionary, and an outstanding leader who develops plans with other ministers on staff and gives them freedom to do their assignment. His skills have been recognized by Baptists because he is a Trustee of the North American Mission Board and has been Vice-Chairman of the Executive Committee of the Georgia Baptist Mission Board for the past two years. He became Chairman in 2018.

As I adjusted to life at the lake, I began cutting the two acres of grass. Since we had groundskeepers in Kenya, Tanzania, Duluth and Hiawassee for the past forty years, it was a change in lifestyle. I quickly learned that cooking, laundry, and cleaning house was time consuming. I was happy with the only ministry I had, the prayer network for former missionaries and others who had served in East Africa, about 250 contacts on my email list. My other project was the genealogy research.

Genealogy

Gordon Woodard gave me a reference to a newer approved application for Benjamin Brown. This record copy filled in the missing documentation and I applied in 2015. It was approved in January 2016. Gordon and I attended the 235th annual celebration for the Battle of Kings Mountain where Benjamin fought in October 1780. It was an exciting celebration with the Color Guard dressed in Colonial uniform, a musket salute, and many wreaths presented from SAR and DAR chapters from several states.

Over the years, several friends had commented I should write a book. I never gave it much thought because of my English skills and my only writing experience was business letters and technical reports. When we emptied our mothers' houses, we packed several boxes of memorabilia and put them in the storerooms with other stuff. I consolidated everything into one storeroom and brought boxes of historic papers to the lake house. With encouragement from writer classmates at Hiawassee Park about my short stories, I began examining those boxes. What a treasure trove they were. I found letters Nancy had written to our mothers almost every week while we were in Africa, newspaper clippings, photos, calendars, and notebooks. Armed with this information, I talked with two MKs who were outstanding writers, Catherine Palmer and Deanna Moore Brown. Cathy had published over fifty Christian novels and Deanna had a high-quality blog. Deanna wrote a blog about Andy after his death which was not only a tribute because our families were close, but explained the special relationships MKs have with one another. I began to develop an outline for this book.

As I opened box after box labeled historic papers, I put letters to our mothers in yearly files, later organized chronologically. I created files of letters between Nancy and me, our children, and missionary colleagues. I created files for individuals and organizations where newspaper clippings, report cards, and other items were placed. By the time the organization was completed, I had four full file drawers and three remaining boxes of calendars and other items.

To help people who read the book understand why I am the way I am, I decided it was important to begin with my birth and give some information about my parents and grandparents. Those stories illuminated my lack of self-confidence in my childhood and youth. I now realize I compensated for those feelings in adulthood many times by appearing unbending in certain situations. I assume this memoir will explain why the personality traits in the Myers-Brigs evaluations all flipped after twenty years when I did the evaluation a second time. I still do not believe I am an extrovert as the second test indicated.

While this book may never get published, it has been a very rewarding experience and therapeutic for facing the grief associated with the deaths of Andy and Nancy. My faith has kept me strong and the major issue in my future is the loneliness of living alone.

The Blue Ridge Mountain Chapter had members in four north Georgia counties and two in North Carolina. There were many activities such as giving certificates for the proper display of the American Flag, putting flags on graves of Patriots on July 4th, ceremonies to burn damaged American Flags, presentations to fourth grade school classes about the Revolution, poster competitions about the Revolution, county parades, and many others. Even though we had about thirty members, we won state and national awards, especially the poster contest.

On November 7, 2015, the Button Gwinnett Chapter assisted by the Blue Ridge Mountain Chapter held a Grave Marking Ceremony for my son Andy at the Martin Baptist Church Cemetery. About fifty attended this ceremony which was very special to my family. Several cousins attended. SAR members placed a SAR Medallion on his gravestone.

After I moved to Hartwell Lake in 2015, Peggy Beckett, President of the Baptist Retirement Communities, asked me if I would consider becoming a Trustee on the organization's Board. She thought it would be helpful to have a member who had lived in a community. At the annual meeting of the Georgia Baptist Mission Board in November 2015, I was elected to a five-year term. In 2016, the Trustees also asked me to serve on the Executive Committee of the Board.

Sarah and John invited me to spend Christmas with them in Wake Forest, North Carolina. As we were finalizing the date for me to drive to their house, they called to tell me the mother of a very good friend had died, and the funeral would be in South Georgia near Metter. They planned to spend a night with me, take me with them to the funeral since I knew their friends, spend a night at my cousin's motel in Metter, and drive to North Carolina after the funeral. The trip to their house was difficult because of Christmas traffic on I-95 and it rained the entire nine-hour trip. After Christmas, I flew back to Atlanta where my cousins, Brown and Jo Dean, met me at the Doraville MARTA station.

There were several medical and dental issues during 2016. For several months after I moved to the lake house, I had more serious issues with sinus drainage, a life-long problem. I made a couple of visits to an allergist in Gainesville who prescribed a couple of nasal sprays. Neither helped so I decided to "just live with it." Since then, drainage has been sporadic depending on what is blooming and grass cutting. When I saw Dr. Reynolds for a regular dermatology appointment, he froze the normal places for pre-cancers and biopsied a couple. One was the normal Basel Cell but the other one was a Melanoma, a type I had never had before. This made the third skin cancer type I had. He referred me to his partner, Dr. Smith, who performed all the MOHS surgeries. It was removed without complications. The major medical issue of the year was dental. I had a three-tooth bridge and several cavities treated. It was a major expensive medical year.

When Sarah and John lived in Malaysia, John made a trip to Nepal to visit with friends. Their full-blooded German Shepherd had puppies and John got a female to take home. When they were given an assignment as personnel associates in 2014, they brought Bella to North Carolina. In

2016, they bred Bella to a registered male. Just before Bella delivered her puppies, John was keeping Ruth, one of the grandchildren one morning. He left the house to take her home and forgot to turn the stove off where he was cooking chicken. When he returned home, the house was full of smoke and he could not get inside. When the firemen came and went into the house, they found Bella hiding in the bathtub upstairs and carried her outside. Thankfully, she had no ill effects. They asked me if I wanted a puppy and I thought a long time before finally agreeing. They brought the male to me in July and I named him Moshi which is Swahili for smoke.

Our boat had not been used since before Andy died, but I had it serviced and cleaned in May 2016. Brown and I used it some until October when I put it in storage for the winter. It was a 1997 model, a twenty-foot combination fish-ski boat with an outboard motor.

I continued working on genealogy and scanned some of my slides on the flatbed scanner I have in my office. This process was very slow, over one minute per slide. I saw an advertisement for iMemories, a commercial company who converted slides, photos, film and movies to a digital format. They had a special price for first time customers, so I sent about 300 slides. I was impressed with the quality and have sent a few hundred more for conversion and some 4x6" photos. Some of the pictures in this book were digitized using this service.

About four years ago, there was a roof leak over the dining room which caused some water damage to the ceiling and wall. I found a painter who was painting across the street and he repaired the damage and painted the area. He also painted the front porch and back steps and handicap ramp. In August, I employed a housekeeper and Kim has done a respectable job for me. She is an active Christian and we share prayer requests every two weeks when she comes.

On August 30th, I met Mark Hearn for dinner at a mall in Duluth. First Baptist Duluth had purchased fifty tickets for the launch of the *Insanity of God* movie which I was anxious to see. Reading the book had a major impact on me since I knew the author.

On September 8th, I drove to Belmont, North Carolina, to meet John who was taking Moshi home for them to keep while I drove to Falls Creek Conference Center in Oklahoma for the annual missionary reunion. I left very early Monday morning, so that I could hopefully pass through Atlanta before the morning commute on I-85. I had made a reservation for a motel room in Jackson, Mississippi, for that night. I made timely progress and when I arrived in Jackson at noon, I decided I was not ready to stop. Since I had planned to spend Tuesday night with Jack and Sally Conley, I called to see if it was possible to come a day early. Sally answered the phone and said she was very sick and I should not come. Since I knew Peggy Oliphint was living in the house with her daughter, Cynthia, and P.J. in Longview, Texas, I called to see if I could stay two nights with them. We had a wonderful visit. I went with Peggy to lunch Tuesday to meet with a church group who met for lunch and played games. The next day I drove to Falls Creek.

Falls Creek had extensive development since I had visited in 1973. We stayed in a new building and everything including our rooms, dining hall, and meeting rooms were in the same building. There were 107 registered and I was very happy to see Scott Whitson who brought his parents, David and Betty Ann, plus Boyd and Syd Pearce for a few hours one day. David's health was not good, and he met Jesus in heaven on January 2, 2017.

The program theme was "Faith in our Day" and we were blessed by Tom Eliff who preached and led Bible study. Anthony Jordan, Director of Falls Creek, gave an interesting history and update about the conference center. Tim Tidenberg shared current field information and the viewpoint of a MK who became a career missionary. It was a blessed time.

After breakfast Saturday morning, I drove to Oklahoma City and spent that night with Glenn and Jeanine Boyd. Our families have been close friends ever since the Boyds arrived at Brackenhurst. The morning after their arrival, I saw Glenn sitting on the steps of his apartment and I sensed culture shock had hit him. We sat there together for a long while. I shared some of my experiences and we bonded there. Every time Glenn sang Ken Medema's "Moses" or Jeanine sang "Worthy is the Lamb," I had to control myself or I would have shouted praises to God. Glenn has experienced serious nerve pain for several years and the medical community has not found any relief for him.

The next afternoon I drove to Lubbock to spend two nights with Clay and Pat Coursey. Our friendship went back to January 1969 when we arrived at Ridgecrest for our missionary training. I always enjoyed our visits when we went to Malindi or they came to Nairobi. Nancy and Pat enjoyed snorkeling in the Indian Ocean. Clay was a mango lover and Nancy was always thrilled to taste the ones fresh off the trees in his yard. I did not like mango and Nancy was always thankful to get my share. We had a good visit catching up and reminiscing. We went to Mike and Annette's goat farm one day and had a nice visit. I do not think I had seen Mike since he graduated from RVA. It was a blessing to see him again. One night, Scott and Rhonda came for supper and it was great to see Scott and meet Rhonda.

On Wednesday, I drove to Georgetown and checked into a motel because Al Cummins was in a rehab facility. I visited him there and had a wonderful visit with Peggy and him. We had great conversations that evening and again the next morning. We told stories of our African adventures together as I tried to encourage him. Peggy and I met Jim, his daughter and son-in-law, for lunch. After saying goodbye, I drove to New Braunfels to spend two nights with the Eucled Moores. He had had a difficult, progressive case of Parkinson's for a few years. We shared some stories from West Virginia and Tanzania, and I helped him transfer from his power recliner to his power scooter to relieve Janelle and Cindy while Jim was at work. Jim and Cindy had added onto the Moore's house in 2012 to help care for Eucled before Cindy was diagnosed with a rare form of cancer. She was between treatments and felt reasonably well while I was there. Cindy was a gifted artist and we have proudly displayed the original of an elephant that she used for printed reproduction. The elephant being one of four African animals, she had lovingly put charcoal on the paper and erased it to show the animals. Cindy gave me three color prints of some of her new art: a 10x13" Greater Kudu, a young African girl and an old man, both 8x10". They are on display in my living room.

After two nights of visiting, I left and drove to Baton Rouge, Louisiana, because I wanted to see the house where we lived and hoped to see some devastation of the recent flooding. I also wanted to eat some good Cajun food. As I approached the Mississippi River bridge, traffic on I-12 was stop and go the last five miles. I exited onto the river road to make a rest stop. When I got back onto the ramp to the bridge, traffic was still very slow as I made my way to 2139 Hollydale Avenue, not very far from the LSU campus. I did not recognize the house since new owners had created a beautiful façade across the front. I had three wonderful years there including our first married year. I left to find my motel and it was a disaster; in many ways like an African hotel. Major renovations were currently being made; the elevator, Wi-Fi and TV did not work. After getting the Wi-Fi and TV fixed, I left to find food. I went to the only nearby Cajun restaurant. It was closing and the food was not good. I was very disappointed. I went back to my room and crashed in bed.

The next morning, I woke up about 4:00 a.m., got dressed, and left. I never did see any flood damage and decided it must have been north in the city where I worked in the plants. I stopped at a Cracker Barrel in Mississippi to get a good breakfast and arrived home in the late afternoon, tired but happy after the day's six hundred miles.

The trip was long, over 3,000 miles, but I am very thankful I made it because of the serious health condition of some of my close friends. I talked on the phone with Al Cummins again after I returned, the last time we conversed before God needed him in heaven on Jesus's birthday, December 25, 2016. I am sure the heavens reverberated with his booming voice when he arrived. The heavenly choir was excited when Eucled Moore showed up on January 13, 2017 to add his beautiful tenor voice, singing praise to our God. Another friend of many years showed up on January 4, 2017, Dr. Sam Cannata. Heaven was enriched by these four saintly friends.

Moshi was very friendly, but he was a puppy and chewed on everything. I kept him in his crate but sometimes I put him in the bathroom where he chewed on the baseboards. At the end of September, I went to Wake Forest to visit a few days with Sarah and John and to bring Moshi home after my trip. Moshi and his mother, Bella, were very active in the yard, chasing each other all over the place. A week after we arrived at the lake house, I paid for obedience school where he stayed for three weeks at Alto. I had an hour's training each day for three days about the commands he learned. I know I was not disciplined enough to keep up the training properly. As he grew and I walked with him, he became very strong when he weighed more than sixty pounds. By early 2017, I was getting concerned because twice, he almost pulled me off the porch as we were beginning our walk. I thought he might succeed and I would fall, breaking something.

One of the girls I dated in Baton Rouge in the spring of 1956 was Margaret Ann Stacy. Bill McCurry always said when he showed up, he took her away from me and married her. I was glad he did. Margaret Ann began to have some dementia in 2015 and God called her in November. I went to Tucker for the memorial service on November 27th and Bill asked me to sit with the family. Bill and I have always enjoyed visiting and we still do.

Tom Jr. was an active athlete in high school playing four sports. In his early youth, he played softball several seasons and was an active golfer. As he aged into his fifties, he began having serious knee problems. As they got worse, he became bow-legged and had a high level of pain. Tom kept delaying doing anything because he had seen his mother's slow recovery, even though she was dedicated to her therapy and exercised. When he consulted a surgeon about knee replacement surgery, the surgeon told him his knees were some of the worst he had seen. The surgeon told Tom Jr. he rarely did bilateral knee replacements but because Tom's were so bad, he wanted to do both in one surgery. The surgery was scheduled for November 16th.

Tom and Laura asked me to come stay at their house to care for China, their blind white French bulldog. I went to the hospital, waited with Laura until he was in his room post-op and left to care for China. The next day, Tom was discharged, and he rode home with me because their SUV was too difficult for him to get into the seat. We got him settled on the sofa in the great room where he spent the night. I tried to settle in a nearby chair. He needed help several times during the night and I never got settled in the chair. With very little sleep, I was very tired the next morning. That afternoon, the physical therapist came, and we moved Tom upstairs to his bed with the flex and cooling machines for both legs. As night approached, I told them he seemed to be doing well since he was settled, I was very tired and thought I would go home. In retrospect, I should have stayed with them longer.

In November 2016, Pastor Andy announced in a worship service that the church had a surplus in the operating budget of $100,000 which would be given to missions. He always focuses on the generosity of the congregation, not legalistic tithing or pledge cards. These funds were in addition to about 20% of the budget which goes to mission programs. But his next statement astounded me beyond measure, one I had never heard another pastor make. He said that we have two worship services now and have sufficient buildings. As we grow, we will not build more buildings at the expense of missions but rather continue to be even more generous in missions giving.

Ebenezer has a strong mission program locally and several encouraging events for the congregation. We give dedicated support for a church plant in Nicaragua and some financial aid to former church members who raise their own funds for their overseas ministry. We partner with several new churches in the USA. One couple was commissioned by the IMB last year and another one is currently in the process.

Being new in the church, I have had the opportunity to absorb spiritual food from the preaching and Bible teaching which has blessed me. Having significant leadership responsibilities in my past three USA churches and overseas, it has been a blessing to get my batteries recharged. The deacons minister in what we call the Encouragement Room after each service. It is a place where people can receive counsel about spiritual issues and information about Ebenezer if they are considering joining our church family. I was asked to give counsel twice a year. Our choir is small and does not sing regularly but practices simultaneously with Andy's Bible study Wednesday evenings. I chose attending the Bible studies. We did have a special Christmas 2016 program featuring a living tree and I joined the eighty plus singers. The program was outstanding, and we have some great musicians.

In the past three years, I have become involved in two ministries not related to a local church. I was asked to serve on a USA based Board for The Good News Center, a ministry based in India. This is the ministry led by

Daniel Kumar based in Delhi.

Daniel is a visionary leader. He and his team have identified twenty-five gateway cities where they are sending church planters. As of December 2016, church planters have been sent to eleven of these strategic cities. They chose an Indian language, Sambapuri, without scripture for the nineteen million speakers. Good News Center agreed to sponsor a translation of the New Testament. A translation of Matthew was completed and printed in June 2013. The goal with sufficient financing is to complete the translation and printing of the entire New Testament, hopefully in 2017.

Good News Center staff worked with the group producing The Jesus Film and it was translated into the Sambapuri language. Once completed, teams to visit villages for a showing were developed. During the first eleven months of 2016, the film was shown 1,436 times and viewed by more than 425,000 people. Over 720,000 copies of Matthew were distributed. A team of eight disciple makers trained 350 which has resulted in 19 new church plants in 2016. Beyond this, the Jesus Film has been shown on local television. Initially, Good News Center paid for four showings of broadcast at Christmas 2015. It was so well received the station management asked permission to rebroadcast it at no charge. A total of twenty-eight broadcasts occurred that season. It is being regularly broadcast on a multiplicity of stations.

There are many service ministries: eight children's homes with 113 children, eighty-five Kid's Clubs in Delhi reaching nearly six thousand kids weekly, Slum Schools for kids living in slums (currently two schools for 116 kids), and ministries for women including sewing classes.

A major new health ministry was begun by a grant from the Georgia Baptist Health Care Foundation. This grant enabled a mobile health unit to be built in India. This ministry was begun in 2016 where the bus travels to eight villages twice a month to treat local people. This health ministry is opening doors for sharing Jesus with the people.

Moshi and I went to Wake Forest to spend several days during Christmas with John and Sarah, and to visit with the grandkids and great-grandkids. We had a wonderful time and I always felt the blessing of attending their church.

I had a few board meetings before I returned to Wake Forest the first week in February 2017 to celebrate Titus Davenport's first birthday. A year before, we had a serious prayer vigil because of the trauma of his birth. His mother Jess, a petite lady, and the obstetrician planned a natural birth. When she went into labor, her uterus ruptured, and an emergency Caesarean Section was required. When they got Titus, he was blue and was rushed to a neonatal ICU at another hospital. I prayed especially for Aaron because Jess was in one hospital, Titus was in another, and he had to take care of Ruth. After several days, all were at home and Titus's progress was monitored regularly. His first birthday was special because no ill-effects of his birth had been found.

March 14, 2017 is a date which will be etched in my mind forever, just like September 11, 2001, when we saw the plane hit the second tower, or collecting my Atlanta Journal papers to deliver on December 7, 1946 and reading the headline about the Winecoff Hotel fire killing 119 people. Others etched in my mind are July 12, 1958 when Nancy and I married and sitting by the radio December 7, 1941 listening to FDR describe the bombing of Pearl Harbor.

I had an appointment in the afternoon with Dr. Reynolds, my dermatologist. I decided I would go to my storeroom in Suwanee to get some boxes and continue to reduce the storage size needed. Boxes were piled high and I began to stand on some to reach the high ones. All went well, and I had about eight on the cart. I had been standing on boxes on a plastic footlocker and decided to put them on the cart. I was standing on the footlocker and reached up for another box above my head. I grabbed what I thought was a light box. It was not but a box filled with books. I lost my balance and watched as I fell to the concrete floor. When I regained consciousness, I realized my right arm was badly broken and I was lying on my left arm. My cell phone was on my right hip and I could not reach it. After a struggle, I freed my left arm and managed to stand up. My right hand was bleeding and my right arm was flopping. I slowly walked to the office, about one hundred yards.

When the office manager saw me through the glass door, she rushed to the door with a paper towel to stem the blood flow, got me to a chair to sit, and called 911. While we were waiting for the EMTs, I gave her my phone and she called Tom Jr. to tell him. She called Dr. Reynolds to cancel my appointment and after the EMTs arrived, she called Tom again to tell him they were taking me to Gwinnett Medical Center.

When we arrived at the hospital, there were no free beds in the emergency room, so I lay on the gurney in the corridor at least two hours. Thankfully, they gave me an injection for pain. I have no memory during the exams in the ER but was told there was no room on a floor when the x-rays were finished. They told me surgery would be the next morning. Tom called Sarah and she and John came the next day. He also called Twila to care for Moshi that night.

I know several people came to see me, but my memory is foggy. I know

Tom, Laura, Sarah, and John spent many hours in my room. I did not get out of bed until I was discharged Friday evening wearing a sling. I was not very impressed with the nursing care, the poor response to the call button, and the way they always seemed too busy to meet my needs.

Both families offered for me to stay with them during recovery. I chose Sarah and John because of the need for some nursing care. The bandages needed changing for several days until the surgical area was sealed without more drainage. Also, John did not have a distinct work schedule; therefore, he could help me during the day, getting dressed, checking my blood pressure, and meeting other needs.

I left the hospital with a prescription for Percocet for pain. We stopped at two chain pharmacies along the way and neither had any in stock. Getting desperate, I remembered David Steele with whom I had meetings about missionary service. He was a pharmacist in Toccoa and I had his cell number. I called; Maddox Drugs had the medicine, and David said he would wait at the store for us to arrive. What a blessing!

John slept on the sofa while I slept in my recliner, so that he could help me get up when I needed to get out of the recliner. The handle is always on the right side so when your right arm is in a sling, you are trapped in your chair. Tom and Laura came Saturday to visit, and several cousins and friends also came by to see me. I was very happy to see everyone and thanked them for all their prayers. Sunday morning, we left for Wake Forest and after arrival, John's friend brought a power recliner with the buttons on the left side. His company sells them, and I was very thankful to be slightly more independent.

Since I would be there several weeks, John contacted the Duke Orthopedic Trauma Clinic in Durham and Gwinnett Medical Center to have my records transferred for follow-up evaluation and treatment. After multiple calls and fighting the phone trees, he was finally able to get an appointment for March 31st. The traffic at the complex was heavy and the parking area was far away. John let me out at the door and I told him I would walk to the office and he could meet me there. Little did I know what was ahead of me. The building was beautiful but from the entrance to the check in desk for Dr. Della Rocca's office was over two hundred yards. Once I finished the paper work, I sat in a chair, quite tired. The nurse came quickly and took me straight to x-ray where the technician took several x-rays, putting me in several painful poses. When I got to the exam room and met John, the nurse took my blood pressure and got very nervous because it was 80/50, very low. I saw the Physician's Assistant and was very impressed with Jennifer Dye. She was very caring, explained the follow-up plan and showed me the x-rays. There was a major concern because one of the screws passed through the metal plate and the bone very near the shoulder ball joint. Dr. Della Rocca consulted with a shoulder surgeon colleague and they concluded that removing the screw surgically would be a high-risk due to the break near the ball. I was told it would be monitored and if I had significant pain after the bones healed and fused, surgery for replacing the shoulder would be considered. Jennifer took my blood pressure again and it was 100/76 with a pulse of 76. She encouraged me to stop at an urgent care facility on our way to Wake Forest. I told John, "Let's go to your house and check my bp again. If I feel bad and it is low, we will consider going." When we checked it at his house, it was normal, and I just rested.

I needed a lot of help when my arm was in the sling. I could not put a shirt on, could not take my blood pressure, and had limited ability to sponge bathe. It was challenging for an active person and I was thankful for the varied help including several fresh dressings the first few days. Learning to eat with my left hand was difficult and the first weeks when my jaw was still dislocated, I could not open my mouth to get a spoon inside to eat. Chewing food was limited without pain but I was grateful for answered prayer when my jaw reseated itself and I could begin to chew food again. I had a follow-up visit on April 25th when I was released from the sling and approved to begin physical therapy. John brought me home on April 27th and I began living alone again.

I can never thank Tom Jr. and Laura enough for all the help they gave at the lake house while I was in North Carolina. They worked in the yard and bought beautiful new cushions for the wicker swivel recliners on the porch. They bought four beautiful ferns and put them in wooden half-barrels for the porch and three red Begonias. They also steam cleaned the carpet, spruced up the bathrooms with new towel sets, bath mats, beautiful liquid soap dispensers, and a gorgeous mermaid lamp for the downstairs bathroom. I found timers on two lamps downstairs where people would see the car and lights and think someone was home. The house looked very nice and I was so appreciative.

I began physical therapy in Toccoa the next week and was approved for thirty sessions. There was a follow-up visit at Duke on June 13th and another on September 26th. The therapists were very good and made sure I completed all the tasks assigned each one-hour session. The Duke surgeon was quite impressed with my range of motion progress. On the June 13th visit, he gave instructions to begin strength exercises in addition to my range of motion. He told me I could push, pull, or lift any weight if it did not hurt. This permission helped the dumping of the grass collection bags on my lawn mower which could weigh fifty pounds.

I have recently connected with several descendants of John Craig whose granddaughter Mary Melinda Craig married my great-grandfather Russell Dean in 1849 and they were the first family members to live in the house where I now live. They moved into the house in 1850. A preliminary review of documents received from the Craigs completed a SAR application for John Craig and it is at the national headquarters awaiting approval. I will continue an active membership in SAR while I am physically able. I have started research on another patriot ancestor and hope I can document the rest of my patriot ancestors.

In July, I had the opportunity to visit with Deanna Moore Brown, one of my favorite MKs. She had been such an encouragement to me as I read her blog posts on Facebook and about my writing. She was in Athens visiting her son's family and I drove there for a several hours visit. We had a nice lunch at a local restaurant.

Later in the month, Tara Bateman Ship and her daughter, Kristie, came from North Augusta for a nice visit. I was always excited to see my close MKs. Tara was my neighbor in Kenya until she graduated from RVA. We had an enjoyable conversation as they told me about the wedding plans for Kristie in December.

Twila's mother had been living with her over a year. She had been a heavy smoker since she was sixteen. She told me her story: Her dad had told her she could not drink coffee or smoke until she was sixteen. On her sixteenth birthday, when she went to breakfast, there was a cup of coffee and a cigarette and matches beside her plate. Her dad told her she could now do both.

I had a special relationship with her and she loved to tell me stories. Even though I was three years older, I called her "You Old Lady." She loved it. Twila had been concerned because her Mom would not go to the doctor. I told Twila to make an appointment and I would help her. On the appointed day, I went into her bedroom and said, "Old Lady, get out of that bed. I am taking you to the doctor." I helped her to the car and she always agreed to go as needed after that day.

Her Dad's blessing on smoking led her to heavy smoking until she was seventy-nine years old and was diagnosed with stage four lung cancer. She was hospitalized a few days, put in rehab a few days, and transferred to hospice care at Twila's brother Kevin's house in Hartwell. Twila stayed there until her Mom went to respite care to relieve Twila of the care duties. When Granny left that facility, Twila and she moved to Twila's house and two of Twila's daughters stayed with them until the angels came for her at midnight. I got the message about 5:00 a.m. the next morning when I was to visit with Deanna. When I left Athens, I met them at Whitlock Mortuary for the planning. They asked me to lead the memorial service on July 9th. They decided for a time in the service for family and friends to share memories and all four children told me they would be too emotional to say anything. When the time came, Twila's brother Bill, the oldest, was the first and all four shared with very few tears. Their tributes were special as I listened. Bill had not had contact with the family for several years. When Kevin called him to say their Mom did not have long to live, Kevin went to Columbia to get Bill who did not have a car. It was a wonderful reconciliation with all five of them for two weeks prior to the service. There was laughter, a few tears, and many stories. Their story telling continued nearly an hour and one half. The last one to speak was a grandson, Justin, Bill's son. He was a very articulate young man with some military service. He said he had never met his grandmother, but they had talked on the phone often. He gave a powerful testimony and quoted scripture. It was quite moving. When he finished, I made a few comments, led in prayer, and visited. I told Justin I was impressed with what he said, that he had a preacher's voice, and he needed to be prepared for God's ministry call.

The Good News Center developed a web site in 2017. Board members were given a link before publishing it on the web. We had the opportunity to tweak it and I believe it will help everyone understand how God is blessing this ministry. Please check it out at www.gncindia.org Daniel has started a weekly prayer request email where a specific ministry is the focus each day. If you are interested in joining the prayer team, sign up on the web page.

Ebenezer uses 21st century technology which is a blessing for reaching out to the community and communicating with the members. The 10:30 a.m. worship service is live streamed and there is an Ebenezer app for our smart phones. It links to information on the web page, the worship service, a Bible app, and gives opportunity to give online or register for church activities.

In August, I had lunch with Pastor Andy. We discussed a variety of issues and my appreciation for his insight was increased. One issue was ways churches can minister to churches needing revitalization. Since I am acquainted with a few churches who are Elder led, I asked what his information about this practice included. He referred me to the Georgia Baptist website where there is a sample constitution and by-laws for this structure. I scanned the 21-page document and quickly decided based on my experience, it was written by word-smith lawyers and would create more problems for churches needing revitalization.

I had taught a class at the seminary in Arusha and led strategic planning seminars for several organizations. I discussed the life cycle of a church or organization in general, taken from Dream Again by Dale. There are nine stages, five healthy and four unhealthy. Healthy stages begin with a dream, followed by beliefs, goals, structure, and ministry. When a church plateaus, it must recast the vision or will begin the downward spiral to death passing through nostalgia, questioning, and polarization. In my church health research, I learned churches which reach the polarization stage cannot be revitalized. Even churches stuck in a plateau struggle with change. It is easier to start a new church than revitalize a church resistant to change.

Churches needing revitalization should have a simple, flexible guideline for how to be the church. Their status is a result of being locked into tradition, refusing to change as their community transitions, ministering to themselves, and never doing ministry outside the four walls of the church building. There is no discipleship training, no vision, and no accountability. If God gives me an opportunity to engage in this ministry, I would be ready to offer my experience and training. The church is blessing me, and I expect to continue at Ebenezer the rest of my life.

John Mattison contacted me and we had lunch together. John was my neighbor in Atlanta and we helped each other with our paper deliveries for the Atlanta Journal. John played trumpet in the Grady and Georgia Tech bands and taught me how to be the Tech Band librarian. He had lived in Toccoa several years and found out I had moved to the lake. It had been more than forty years since I had seen him.

As we have celebrated the 50th anniversary of the Baptist Retirement Communities ministry in 2017, I have remembered the first location at the old Winecoff Hotel in downtown Atlanta on Peachtree Street a few blocks from Five Points. This premier hotel in its day caught fire on the morning of December 4, 1944 and 119 people perished, many jumping to their deaths to avoid being burned to death. I remember that day as I collected the Atlanta Journal to deliver to my customers when I saw the banner headlines. It was restored but never achieved success again. Fred Beazley decided in 1966 to donate the hotel to a worthy cause to obtain a tax write-off since it was not profitable, and he could not sell it for value. When he gave it to Georgia Baptists, he included a cash gift of $50,000 for necessary repairs. Beginning with that donation, Baptist Retirement Communities have gone through name changes and several locations to arrive at today's ministry. Currently, three locations are in operation with each operating at near capacity of residents. Two locations, Hiawassee Park where I lived and

Clairmont Crest in Decatur, have waiting lists. When there is a vacancy, it is filled immediately. In the February 2017 Trustee meeting, it was reported these two locations had eighty-five on the waiting lists and Palmetto Park was at 93% occupancy. Palmetto Park is the only one with meal service. When the next phase at Hiawassee Park is completed, it will also provide meal service.

Because I had experience in strategic planning, Peggy Beckett asked me in early 2017 to assist the four administrators in acquiring skills in these processes. It has been a joy and an honor to be involved in long range and vision planning.

I know first-hand the value of this ministry as Nancy and I lived at Hiawassee Park for almost three years. We learned of the Hiawassee location plans before they broke ground in 2010 when we sent our deposit. The activities keep senior citizens young in heart and mind. I was very honored to be the first Trustee who had lived in one of the communities when I was elected at the annual meeting of Georgia Baptists in 2015. In the first Trustee meeting in 2018, I was elected as Chairman. I know as the concept of age in place becomes more fully developed, many will be blessed abundantly. We are in the process for a major expansion at Hiawassee Park.

In November 2017, I was asked by Andy Childs to lead a new study group at Ebenezer. This study called *Deepen Discipleship* is being developed by the International Mission Board for churches who have members called to serve as missionaries and who are in the approval process by the Board. David and Sara Steele have been called by God to serve and expect to be sent to the Amazon Valley in Brazil next year. The study is intensive, reading the entire New Testament in six months, and sharing insights gained from the study. Ways to witness and share Biblical truth will be learned and practiced. We will also learn about unreached and unengaged people groups and pray for God to call someone to live among them to share Jesus with them. For me, this is priority because Jesus said in Matthew 24:14 that He will not return until ALL peoples have heard the Gospel. There are over 3,000 groups waiting to hear.

In February 2018, I was added to the Ebenezer Mission Team and Pastor Steve Payson asked me to assist in encouraging with some training for the independent overseas missionaries from Ebenezer. As I have settled into life at the lake, I look forward to my remaining days which God graciously gives me. I plan to stay involved in ministry if God gives me the mind and strength to fulfill opportunities.

Epilogue

God has blessed me in so many uncountable ways. I have been a member of several God blessed churches. Unfortunately, when Satan attacked some, they did as the church at Ephesus did, lost their first love. They plateaued and declined and are barely surviving. I was blessed and trained by God during my years in West Virginia, by God's grace given responsibilities I did not earn. I saw a harvest in Kenya, built on foundations crafted by early missionaries, and was excited to see harvesters reap from seed planted by others. God gave me quality mentors when most needed, men and women who became trusted friends. I was blessed by a wife and children who loved me unconditionally, a wife who counseled me with love. I was blessed to see my children grow into responsible adults and to enjoy grandchildren and great-grandchildren.

Matthew 10:30 says, "But the very hairs of your head are numbered." I have joked to say it did not take long for God to count mine since my creation included future baldness. But like every creation, I know I was lovingly and wonderfully made. My commitment to God is to love my Jesus during the additional years He gives me a clear mind, physical strength, and breath. I know heaven is my home, but until God moves me there, my plan is to serve Him in any ministry He brings my way.

My prayer is that you will make the same commitment.

Made in the USA
Middletown, DE
19 April 2019